Martin Wetzel Walbert

The Coming Battle

A Complete History of the National Banking Money Power in the United States

Martin Wetzel Walbert

The Coming Battle
A Complete History of the National Banking Money Power in the United States

ISBN/EAN: 9783744723626

Printed in Europe, USA, Canada, Australia, Japan

Cover: Foto ©ninafisch / pixelio.de

More available books at **www.hansebooks.com**

The Coming Battle

A COMPLETE HISTORY OF THE NATIONAL
BANKING MONEY POWER IN THE
UNITED STATES

By M. W. WALBERT

CHICAGO
W. B. CONKEY COMPANY
1899

INTRODUCTION.

In this volume the author endeavors to give an accurate history of the present National Bank System of currency, including an account of the first United States Bank,—both of which were borrowed from Great Britain by those statesmen who, like the father of Sir Robert Peel, believed that a national debt was the source of prosperity.

It is believed that the facts adduced in the following pages will be productive of some good, in pointing out the immense evils lurking in that system of banking, —a system which has produced panics at will, and which is the active abettor of the stock gamblers, railroad wreckers, and those industrial tyrants of modern times, the enormously overcapitalized and oppressive trusts.

It is sought to point out the great dangers of delegating purely government powers to these greedy monopolists, by which they are enabled to organize a money trust, far more tyrannical than all the other combinations now in existence; and by which they absolutely defy the authority that endowed them with corporate life.

The issue between these banks and the people will be joined in the near future, and the greatest struggle the world ever witnessed will take place between the usurping banks on the one hand and the people on the other.

In the nature of things, unjustly acquired power of man over man generally rises to such heights of arrogance as to eventually create a public opinion that will grind tyranny of every form to atoms, hence, The Coming Battle that will surely take place in the near future and the victory that will be won by justice will be the noblest events in American history.

THE AUTHOR.

TABLE OF CONTENTS.

CHAPTER.		PAGE.
I.	Origin of the Money Power in America	7
II.	Origin of the Present National Banking System	43
III.	National Banks and Silver	89
IV.	Conspiracy of New York and London Bankers and Bondholders to Demonetize Silver	109
V.	Efforts to Remonetize Silver and Preserve the Greenback	158
VI.	The National Banks Wage War Upon the Credit of the United States	203
VII.	National Banks Secure a Continuation of Their Existence	236
VIII.	The National Banking Money Power Secures Complete Control of the Treasury	270
IX.	Money Power of England and United States Combine to Annihilate Silver	304
X.	National Banking Money Power Brings on the Panic of 1893	325
XI.	Special Session of Congress Repeals the Sherman Law	362
XII.	Senate Votes for Repeal	384
XIII.	Efforts of Administration to force Carlisle Bill through Congress	407
XIV.	National Banks and the Administration Combine to Issue Bonds in Time of Peace	439
XV.	Campaigns of 1896	460

CHAPTER I.

ORIGIN OF THE MONEY POWER IN AMERICA.

"Justice, full and ample justice, to every portion of the United States, should be the ruling principle of every freeman, and should guide the deliberations of every public body, whether it be state or national."— Andrew Jackson.

During the existence of the human race, from the earliest dawn of civilization to the close of the present century, the power exercised over the industry, property and conscience of man by cunning and ambition, has assumed many forms.

The form of power which first appeared to oppress and plunder the race, was exemplified in those celebrated conquerors of antiquity, who traversed the earth in their bloody careers, transforming blooming fields and rich and populous cities into deserts, overthrowing whole nations, sacrificing on the battle fields countless myriads of their fellow men—merely to satisfy a species of madness dignified by the name of ambition.

Another and a more dangerous form of misapplied power resulted from the intellectual tyranny exercised by that shrewd class, the priest-hood, over the conscience and religious beliefs of the great mass of mankind.

From the days of the Pharaohs down to this period, man, from his instinctive veneration for a supreme being, has been so peculiarly susceptible to the arts, wiles, and cunning of priest-craft to such a degree as to excite universal surprise.

Those gross superstitions, engrafted on the inherent religious nature of man, by that wary intellectual superiority, which weighed down the noblest traits of the human mind; which bred bitter religious animosities; unheard of extortions by the corrupt and infamous priestly aristocracies of various so-called religions, were the well-matured and craftily-devised schemes for plunder by designing men.

It is almost inconceivable that the ancient Egyptians, that admirable race, whose noble genius and wonderful energy reared those stately temples, the magnificent cities, and the stupendous pyramids along the valley of the Nile, should worship the man-eating crocodile, the savage vulture, the grinning ape and the crawling lizard.

This race is an example of that soul-darkening superstition which hung like a pall over the intellect of man.

The countless wars which afflicted Europe, Asia, and Africa for nearly eighteen centuries; which drowned the finest aspirations of humanity in blood; which desolated the fairest parts of the earth; which stemmed the tide toward a higher and a grander civilization, sprang from the base superstitions originated by the grasping priesthood, who lived in sloth and luxury upon the labor of the deluded mass of mankind.

The celebrated Vattel, in the twelfth chapter of that noble work, The Law of Nations, affords us a faint idea of the enormities practiced upon the people of Europe by the clergy.

Taine, in his History of France, shows that the

ecclesiastics had seized upon the most valuable and fertile portion of the territory of that country, and that the oppression practiced by them upon the French people was one of the leading causes of the great revolution.

The third and most insidious and most dangerous form of power that has yet appeared to threaten the material well-being of the race; which now holds every civilized and semi-civilized people in its merciless grasp; which is appropriating to itself the productive energies of the world; which is subordinating the press, the pulpit, and the statesmen of the day to its ambitious ends; which openly boasts of its nefarious methods in the courts, legislatures, and other parliamentary bodies of nations, is the modern money power.

That there is a gigantic combination of the money dealers, a powerful international trust of usurers, asserting a superiority above all jurisdictions, and having for its servants the so-called statesmen and potentates of various nations, who willingly register the decrees of this money power upon the statute-books of the respective states, is a fact that can be sustained by irrebuttable evidence.

This great international monetary trust now menaces the very life of this nation, and the people must dethrone it and subordinate it to their will, or American liberty will vanish.

The Declaration of Independence, which announced the true principles of government, was a memorable protest against the rapacious money power composed of the landed aristocracy, the trading, commercial, and manufacturing interests of England, which, by a long series of vicious and unconstitutional acts of Parliament, sought to eat out the substance of the colonists.

The war of the Revolution which followed, set its seal of approval upon the patriotic efforts of the colonists against oppression, and freedom was achieved.

Upon the conclusion of that most righteous conflict, a more perfect union was formed to establish justice, insure domestic tranquillity, provide for the common defense, promote the general welfare, and secure the blessings of liberty for themselves and posterity by the adoption of the Federal constitution.

General Washington was chosen the first President by an unanimous vote.

For his constitutional advisers he appointed Thomas Jefferson for Secretary of State; Alexander Hamilton for Secretary of the Treasury; James Knox for Secretary of War; and Edmund Randolph for Attorney General.

Jefferson, who was the most accomplished scholar in America, the profoundest thinker upon the principles of Government of any age, the friend of humanity and a staunch believer in the capacity of the common people for self-government, was a representative of that industrial element which sustains society by its labors.

Hamilton, who was an aristocrat by birth and breeding, and who was connected by marriage with the wealthiest family of the landed aristocracy of New York, was a strong representative of the trading, banking and commercial element of New York City and New England, which constituted the Tory element of the Revolution.

The presence of two statesmen of such wholly antagonistic views and temperaments in the cabinet of Washington, naturally originated divisions of political sentiment, from which sprang two great political parties.

One of the first measures which received the aid and sanction of Hamilton was the act of Congress, adopted February 25, 1791, chartering the Bank of the United States.

Jefferson, whose penetrating mind perceived the vast power for mischief lodged in an institution of that nature, in a powerful communication to the President, advised him to veto the bill.

Washington, however, accepted the views of Hamilton, his Secretary of the Treasury, and signed the bill, and it became a law.

By the terms of the act incorporating the bank, its capital was fixed at ten millions of dollars. The power to issue its circulating notes as money having full legal tender quality for the payment of taxes and demands due the Government was conferred upon it. It was made the depositary of the revenues of the Government, and therefore it became the fiscal agent of the Treasury department. It was chartered for the period of twenty years.

For the extensive powers and exclusive privileges bestowed upon it by Congress, the bank paid the United States a small bonus.

This bank, therefore, was a monopoly sustained by the credit and the revenues of the United States. It had the sole power of issuing legal tender paper money, and its actual capital was trebled in its earning capacity by loaning its circulating notes at interest, and by having the control of the government revenues.

This was the first appearance of an ORGANIZED MONEY POWER in the United States.

Thomas Jefferson, by voice and pen, in language of rare power and felicity, pointed out the dangerous possibilities of the bank to influence the politics and business of the nation.

In a letter to Madison in 1793, Jefferson stated that the bank party consisted of the fashionable circles of Philadelphia, New York, Boston and Charleston (natural aristocrats). 2. Merchants trading in British capital. 3. Paper men. Against the bank were—1. Merchants trading on their own capital. 2. Irish merchants. 3. Tradesmen, mechanics, farmers and every other possible description of our citizens.

In 1811, Congress refused to re-charter the bank, and as it had during its brief career obtained the mastery over the entire business of the country by its loans of circulating notes and the public revenues, and had built up a system of credit in the commercial centers, to intimidate Congress and the people, it made a concerted contraction of the currency and brought on the great panic of 1811.

United States Senator Benton, in a speech in the senate during the administration of Jackson, thus graphically states the manner in which the bank contrived to manufacture public sentiment in its favor. He says:—

"All the machinery of alarm and distress was in as full activity at that time as at present, and with the same identical effects—town meetings, memorials, resolutions, deputations to congress, alarming speeches in congress. The price of all property was shown to be depressed. Hemp sunk in Philadelphia from $350 to $250 per ton; flour sunk from $11.00 per barrel to $7.75; all real estate fell thirty per cent.; five hundred houses were suspended in their erection; the rent of money rose to one and a half per month on the best paper; confidence destroyed; manufactories stopped; workmen dismissed and the ruin of the country confidently predicted."

The Senator goes on to show that great public meetings were held, inflammatory speeches made, cannon fired, great feasts given—all engineered by the bank. That those members of Congress who favored the bank, traveled with public honors like conquering generals returning from victorious battlefields, saluted with acclamations by the masses, escorted by processions, and that those members favoring the bank were exhibited throughout the United States as though they were some superior beings from the celestial regions.

In 1812 occurred the second war with England, and the bank threw its whole influence against the United States during that great struggle.

Evidence is not wanting to sustain the charges made that the bank element of New England planned the separation of that section from the Union.

During the continuance of this war, the United States issued its treasury notes with full legal tender power, and they were gladly received by the people.

Albert Gallatin, for twelve years Secretary of the Treasury, and one of the ablest statesmen of the day, thus bears valuable testimony to the efficiency of government paper money in carrying the United States through that war. He says:—

"The paper money carried the United States through the most arduous and perilous stages of the war, and though operating as a most unequal tax, it cannot be denied that it saved the country."

In a letter to John Tyler, May 28, 1816, Jefferson says:—

"The system of banking we have both equally and ever reprobated. I contemplate it as a blot left in all our constitutions which, if not covered, will end in their destruction, which is already hit by the gamblers in corruption, and is sweeping away in its progress the fortunes and morals of our citizens. Funding I consider as limited rightfully to a redemption of the debt within the lives of a majority of the generation contracting it; every generation coming equally by the laws of the Creator of the world to the free possession of the earth He made for their subsistence unincumbered by their predecessors. And I sincerely believe with you that banking institutions are more dangerous than standing armies, and that the principle of spending money to be paid by posterity under the name of funding is but swindling futurity on a large scale."

In a letter of March 2, 1815, written by Jefferson to the celebrated French author, Say, he said:—

"The government is now issuing treasury notes for circulation, bottomed on solid funds and bearing interest. The banking confederacy (and the merchants bound to them by their debts) will endeavor to crush the credit of these notes; but the country is eager for them as something they can trust to, and so soon as a convenient quantity of them can get into circulation the bank notes die."

It has been stated that the bank, during the war of 1812, exerted its whole influence against the United States. It was a matter of little concern to it that Great Britain had impressed into her service thousands of native born citizens of this country, and compelled them, against their will, to man British guns. What cared the bank that hundreds of American merchant vessels were confiscated, in a time of profound peace, by orders of the English government, and that repeated insults had been heaped on this republic by the insolence of British statesmen?

Although the bank was a creature of the legislative powers of congress, and had received vast financial benefits from the country, it sought to embarrass the government in its struggle against Great Britain by arraying the moneyed class against the struggling republic.

Money could not be obtained by means of loans to organize, arm, and equip the American armies and to construct vessels of war to protect American commerce. In this emergency the counsel of Jefferson was requested, and he advised the issue of treasury notes by the government in lieu of borrowing.

In a letter dated September 11, 1813, he thus stated his position: "The question will be asked, and ought to be looked at, What is to be the course if loans cannot be obtained?" There is but one—"Carthago delenda est." Bank paper must be suppressed, and the circulating medium must be restored to the nation to whom it belongs. It is the only fund on which they can rely for loans; it is the only resource which can never fail them, and it is an abundant one for every necessary purpose. Treasury bills, bottomed on taxes, bearing or not bearing interest, as may be found necessary, thrown into circulation will take the place of so much gold and silver, which last, when crowded, will find an efflux into other countries, and thus keep the quantum of medium at its salutary level. Let the banks continue, if they please, but let them discount for cash alone or for treasury notes."

The sound advice couched in this letter was heeded by the government, and the country was carried safely through the second war for independence.

Immediately after the close of the war, the bank put forth renewed efforts to secure a new charter.

At this juncture, William Cobbett, the celebrated English writer and economist, transmitted a letter to

Mr. Dallas, Secretary of the Treasury under President Madison, in which he strenuously urged him to oppose the project.

As a warning against chartering a bank of issue, Cobbett pointed out the immense power of the Bank of England to ruin the tradesmen of that country, and to dictate the political sentiments of that people. He said:—

London, January 13, 1816.

"To Mr. Secretary Dallas:

"Sir: I have read with great care and uncommon interest your proposition to congress, under date of 6th December, 1815, for the establishment of a national bank; and as a part of the reasons which you urge in support of that proposition appear to be founded on the experience of a similar institution in England, I cannot refrain from endeavoring to show you what some of these effects really have been, and what is at present the situation of this country, owing, in a great measure, to the existence of a great banking establishment closely connected with the government.

"It is the evil of a national bank, as experienced by us, to which I particularly wish to draw your attention. You profess, and I dare say very sincerely, so to frame this establishment in America that it shall be independent of the Government. It is next to impossible, indeed, that you, or any of the persons in whose hands the Government is, should have a desire to make a bank what our bank has long been; but while there is a possibility of its becoming, in any hands or at any time, anything resembling this bank, it must be a matter of serious dread to every friend of America that such an establishment is likely to take place. Sir, it is as a bank of discount that this establishment exercises the most pernicious influence. The directors, who are a chosen divan, regulate these discounts, and in so doing decide in some sort upon the rise or fall, the making or the ruin, of all men in trade, and indeed of most other men, except such as have no capital at all.

"The amount of these discounts at any given time is supposed to be about £6,000,000, as they are never for more than two months. Here is a sum of thirty-six millions lent every year to individuals. The bills for discounts are sent in; the directors consent or not, without any reasons assigned. Now, sir, consider the magnitude of the sum discounted. It is little short of half a million dollars a day, Sundays excepted. It is perfectly well known to you that in state of such things almost every man in trade is under the necessity of having a regular supply from discounting. If he be excluded from his fair share here, he cannot trade with the same advantage as other men trade. If he be in the practice of discounting, and if his discounts be cut off, he cannot go on; he stops payment and is frequently ruined forever, even while he possesses property which, with the fair chances of time, would not only enable him to pay his debts but to proceed in prosperity.

"I beseech you, then, sir, to look seriously at the extent of the dangerous power of these bank directors. You must see that they hold in their hands the pecuniary fate of a very large part of the community, and that they have it in their power, every day of their lives, to destroy the credit of many men, and to plunge their families into shame and misery. If I am asked for their motives to act like these, to pursue such partiality, to make themselves the instruments in committing such detestable injustice and cruelty, need I point out to you that they have been and must be constantly actuated by the strongest political prejudices? The fact is, however, that the Bank of England, by means of its power of granting or withholding discounts, has been, and is one of the most potent instruments of political corruption, on the one hand, and of political vengeance on the other hand."

In speaking of the great profits reaped by that bank, this writer said:—

"I have given this rough statement that you may be struck with the magnitude of the object I present to you. Diminish the amount as much as you fairly can and even then you will dwell upon the subject with a deliberation you cannot prevent. One fact will at least corroborate what I have suggested; viz., that the Bank of England had £20,000,000, or nearly $100,000,000, surplus in nineteen years, after paying bonuses and dividing 7 per cent. per annum, which was two fifths more than legal interest. I will not here allude to the United States Bank, to which I may hereafter devote an essay."

The array of facts set out by this writer, in which he exhibited the appalling power of this bank, did not deter the American statesmen of that day from their attempt to fasten a like institution on this country.

In 1816, congress chartered the United States Bank with a capital stock of thirty-five million dollars; to it was delegated the sole power of issuing notes receivable by the United States for taxes and demands due it; and designed to serve as the Treasury Department of the government by receiving and disbursing the public revenues of the nation.

Section 21 of the Bank Act was as follows:—

"That no other bank shall be established by any future law of the United States, during the continuance of the corporation hereby created, for which the faith of the United States is hereby pledged. Provided, Congress may renew existing charters for banks within the District of Columbia, not increasing the capital thereof, and may also establish any other bank or banks in said District, with capitals not exceeding, in the whole, six millions of dollars, if they shall deem it expedient."

By this section Congress surrendered its constitutional powers to legislate upon a subject within its exclusive jurisdiction for the period of twenty years.

Not satisfied with a monopoly of the currency and banking of the country, the unlimited greed of the wealthy stockholders of this bank demanded and secured from Congress, a pledge of the public faith that the essential powers of the Government should lie dormant for twenty years!

In the early days of the republic, the accursed spirit of special privileges had shorn the nation of its means of self-preservation.

For the exclusive powers conferred upon it, the government received in return for this valuable franchise a small annual bonus.

It will be ascertained from the enormous powers enjoyed by the bank, that it obtained a monopoly of the circulating medium of the country; that, in addition to its capital stock of thirty-five million dollars which constituted its primary loanable fund, it would earn interest upon the circulating notes issued by it, as well as usury upon the government revenues when used in discounts.

Therefore, by force of law, the interest earning capacity of its capital was more than doubled.

It was a colossal moneyed monopoly.

The bank rapidly obtained a practical control over the business of the nation, and it would tolerate no opposition. By its methods of conferring substantial favors upon the influential journals of the leading commercial cities, and by its loans to powerful members of both branches of Congress, it was enabled to rally to its support a coerced and manufactured public sentiment—far-reaching and wide-spread as the limits of the Union.

The financial power of the bank, under its able and

unscrupulous management, had become so dominant in its influence that it deemed itself master of the government and the people.

This monopoly believed in the Hamiltonian maxim that a "Public debt is a public blessing," and, during its career as the fiscal agent of the Government, threw every obstacle in the way of the payment of the national debt.

It may be inquired by some why the bank should oppose the payment of the debt? The reason is obvious. The larger the debt, the more revenues necessary to pay the interest charge thereon, and, therefore, the more profit to the bank from the use of the increased revenues in making loans and discounts.

From 1816 to 1828, it was the sole arbiter of the financial affairs of the nation, both public and private. Its power in politics was immense, and it swayed elections at will.

The most eloquent Senators and Representatives were continually sounding its praises in the halls of Congress as the most perfect financial institution ever devised by the wit of man. Deluded with the idea that it was invincible in its influence, and that it was a necessary part of the machinery of Government, it was confident that its charter would be renewed before its expiration by limitation of law.

The audacity of the bank was destined to receive a check in its career of uninterrupted power and success, and its astonishing abuses of its franchise were to be mercilessly exposed, and it was doomed to fall never to rise again.

In the presidential election of 1828, Andrew Jackson, the hero of New Orleans, was elected chief magistrate by a great majority, and the bank, its defenders, and retainers, were fated to run counter to a patriot and statesman of invincible will and unflinching integrity.

At the time of this election, and prior thereto, the public debt was being reduced rapidly, and it would not be long before the United States would not owe a single dollar.

As has been stated, the United States bank strongly opposed the payment of the debt for the aggrandizement of its own selfish purpose.

On the 8th day of December, 1829, President Jackson, in his first annual message to Congress, announced to that body that he was opposed to the bank, and that he would not favor a renewal of its charter. In the year 1830, a large surplus of public revenues accrued to the United States, and according to law, the money was deposited in the bank. This accumulation of revenues served to augment the power of the bank as it increased its resources, and, therefore, its facility to make additional loans and discounts in the various commercial centers of the country.

President Jackson discerned the policy of the bank, and in 1830 he advocated the passage of a law distributing these surplus revenues among the states. He again opposed the renewal of its charter.

United States Senator Benton, of Missouri, a man of great energy, extensive learning, and commanding ability, thoroughly understood the means by which the bank had obtained its mastery over the commerce and industry of the nation, and, therefore, at that session of congress, he presented a resolution in the United States senate to the effect, that the charter of the bank ought not to be renewed. The resolution was lost by a vote of twenty-three to twenty. The introduction of that resolution and the narrow majority by which it failed of passage, sounded a note of warning to the bank, and it gathered all its energies for the struggle that sooner or later was bound to come.

To arouse public sentiment in its behalf, it initiated a policy of expanding its loans until they reached the vast total of seventy-one million dollars, which were so judiciously placed among leading merchants and manufacturers, that, in the event of their being called in by the bank, a powerful pressure would be exerted upon the President and Congress by those who were borrowers of the bank.

On the 4th of July, 1832, a bill to re-charter the bank, after its passage by Congress, was sent to President Jackson for approval.

Many of the influential political friends of the President, aware of his intense hostility toward the bank and its methods, importuned him to sign the bill; large delegations of leading citizens from every trade center in the country implored him to allow the measure to become a law. Merchants and importers, who were heavy borrowers from the bank, trooped to Washington to add their appeals to the petitions already presented.

Its paid hirelings, in the halls of congress and elsewhere, predicted dreadful results to business interests, should the President not recede from his opposition to the bill continuing the existence of the bank for the period of twenty years longer.

To add to the general clamor, the bank, through its officials, avowed its purpose to precipitate a panic, and to pull down in ruins the business of the country, should its demands not be conceded. It compelled its thousands of borrowers to sign distress petitions, which it caused to be sent to the President as the apparently free expression of public sentiment.

The magazine had long been prepared by the bank, the train was laid, and Nicholas Biddle, the president of this great financial institution, sat in his luxurious office, and declared himself ready and willing to apply the match that would start the most ruinous financial explosion that had yet shook the foundations of the republic. Mr. Biddle had most able lieutenants in both branches of congress devoted to his interest.

Daniel Webster, the eloquent orator and great lawyer; Henry Clay, whose persuasive powers were unrivaled; and Calhoun, the great leader of the South, led the banking interest in congress.

In a work entitled, "Andrew Jackson and the Bank of the United States," William L. Royall thus speaks of the conduct of these three leaders:—

"In addition to all its other sources of power the cause of the bank received invaluable assistance from the coalition of these great men (Webster, Clay, and Calhoun). Each was an aspirant for the presidency, and upon the bank's cause and paper money, each found a common ground upon which all three could meet and oppose Jackson, the great enemy of both these things. All the movements of the bank were but a repetition, with a change of names and dates, of what had taken place in 1811."

On the other hand, the stalwart Benton was a stern opponent of the bank, and he was supported by an able array of statesmen of the first rank.

Webster and Clay advocated a liberal construction of the Constitution, and were eternally sounding the praises of that instrument as the noblest work of statesmanship, yet, while ascribing to it the most ample powers and authority, they strangely supported the theory that the United States Bank was absolutely necessary to the financial administration of the Federal Government.

Benton was a strict constructionist, and asserted that the general Government was inherently qualified to transact its financial operations without the aid or assistance of any bank or system of banks. He ably maintained the Jeffersonian principles of Government that bank paper should be suppressed.

In a speech delivered in the United States Senate, Benton thus truly describes the immense power of the bank over the Government and the people:—

"The Government itself ceases to be independent, it ceases to be safe when the national currency is at the will of a company. The Government can undertake no great enterprise, neither war nor peace, without the consent and co-operation of that company; it cannot count its revenues six months ahead without referring to the action of that company—its friendship or its enmity, its concurrence or opposition—to see how far that company will permit money to be scarce or to be plentiful; how far it will let the money system go on regularly or throw it into disorder; how far it will suit the interest or policy of that company to create a tempest or suffer a calm in the money ocean. The people are not safe when such a company has such a power. The temptation is too great, the opportunity too easy, to put up and put down prices, to make and break fortunes; to bring the whole community upon its knees to the Neptunes who preside over the flux and reflux of paper. All property is at their mercy, the price of real estate, of every growing crop, of every staple article in the market, is at their command. Stocks are their playthings—their gambling theater, on which they gamble daily with as little secrecy and as little morality and far more mischief to fortunes than common gamblers carry on their operations."

This unanswerable argument, built on impregnable facts, could not be met by all the eloquence and logic that could be mustered against it by the great Triumvirate—Clay, Webster and Calhoun.

In a message to Congress, President Jackson, in speaking of the banking power, said:—

"In this point of the case the question is distinctly presented, whether the people of the United States are to govern through representatives chosen by their unbiased suffrages, or whether the power and money of a great corporation are to be secretly exerted to influence their judgment and control their decisions."

These pointed shafts from the executive struck home, and rankled in the breasts of those Senators and Representatives who supported the bank and its policy.

When the bank ascertained beyond any doubt that President Jackson was firmly opposed to its further continuance, it began calling in its loans rapidly, the volume of currency was contracted greatly by the bank and its branches, merchants were mercilessly driven to the wall, mills and factories closed down everywhere, and tens of thousands of skilled workmen were thrown out of employment, and their families felt the pangs of hunger, notwithstanding there was abundance in the country.

Every day it tightened its coils around its helpless victims, while President Biddle sat in his office at the bank, and laughed at the needless ruin he wrought among his fellowmen. His course is only paralleled by that of Nero, who is said to have fiddled while Rome was burning.

The great journals of the leading cities, subsidized by loans—presumably—teemed with editorials denouncing President Jackson and defending the course of the bank.

Distress meetings at the same time and at the same points were held, fiery speeches were made, and strongly worded resolutions were adopted, requesting the President to append his signature to the bill renewing the charter of the bank.

There was a singular identity in the editorials written, in the speeches delivered, and in the resolutions adopted, that gave evidence of a concerted action. This similarity of sentiments and language in the journals, speeches, and resolutions, evinced a most remarkable talent, for combining the various means of influencing President Jackson.

But the hero of New Orleans was as immovable as the Rock of Gibralter.

Andrew Jackson was in many respects the most remarkable man in American history. A sincere patriot of the purest integrity, with a clearness of mental vision that was unsurpassed, with a profound insight into the principles upon which our Government rested, he plainly saw that the interests of the bank were wholly at variance with that of American liberty.

He well knew that to transfer to a private corporation for its gain, the issuance and control of the currency of the country, and to accumulate in its vaults the national revenues, would eventuate in building up a moneyed monopoly, ultimately controlling the press, the business interests, and the legislation of the nation.

That point was now reached.

He was utterly opposed to the Government abdicating its highest sovereign function,—the issuance and control of the currency,—and delegating it to individuals or to corporations for their gain.

He was conversant with the traitorous conduct of the bank during the war of 1812, and he concurred in the declaration of Jefferson that, "Banks of issue were more dangerous to the liberties of the people than standing armies."

In speaking of the firmness displayed by President Jackson against the arrogance of the bank, the distinguished historian Bancroft says:—

"When the period for addressing Congress drew near, it was still urged that to attack the bank would forfeit his popularity and secure his future defeat. The President replied, 'It is not for myself that I care.' It was urged that haste was unnecessary, as the bank had still six unexpired years of chartered existence. 'I may die,' he replied, 'before another Congress comes together, and I could not rest quietly in my grave, if I failed to do what I hold so essential to the liberty of my country.'"

Bancroft further says, that, upon one occasion when the bank conflict had reached its greatest height, the President and some of his friends were standing over the rocks of the Rip Raps, looking out upon the ocean, when the subject of chartering the bank was brought forward, whereupon the President remarked, "Providence may change my determination; but man no more can do it than he can remove these Rip Raps, which have resisted the rolling ocean from the beginning of time."

History fails to record a nobler sublimity of purpose than that displayed by President Jackson during the war of the bank upon the people.

Notwithstanding the immense pressure brought to bear upon him, President Jackson, on the 10th day of July, 1832, returned the bill to the Senate, whence it originated, accompanied with his veto message, which was a masterly exposition of his views upon the true principles of free Government, and it ranks in importance with the Declaration of Independence.

The first reason assigned by the President in his objections against the renewal of the charter of the bank was, that it created a monopoly under the authority of the general Government, and, therefore, it increased the value of its stock far above its par value, which operated as a gift of many millions to its stock holders.

The President laid down the fundamental principle, that a monopoly should only be granted when it returned a fair equivalent to the people.

He showed that while its capital stock was fixed at $28,000,000, to confer this privilege upon the bank would add the enormous sum of $17,000,000 to the value of the stock, and for this immensely valuable franchise the Government would receive the pitiful sum of $200,000 per annum.

The President advocated the sale of the stock to the highest bidder, and that the premium received therefrom by the Government be paid into the national Treasury to lighten the burdens of taxation in lieu of its bestowal upon a few wealthy citizens.

He stated that $8,000,000 of the stock of the present bank was held by foreigners, chiefly in England; that this was the most dangerous feature of the plan; that a majority of the shares of its stock might fall into those alien hands, and that in the event the United

States would be involved in war with that nation, thus holding a large amount of the stock of this great bank monopoly, its influence would be thrown against the United States.

The President says:—

"All its operations within would be in aid of the hostile fleets and armies without. Controlling our currency, receiving our public moneys, and holding thousands of our citizens in dependence, it would be more formidable and dangerous than the naval and military power of the enemy."

He produced figures demonstrating the sectional character of the bank, that out of $35,000,000 of stock, $8,405,500 were held chiefly by Great Britain; only $140,200 were held by the nine great western states; $3,455,598 in the four southern states, and $13,522,000 in the eastern and middle states.

That in 1831, the profits of the bank were $3,455,598; of this amount the western states contributed $1,640,048; the four southern states $352,507, and the middle and eastern states $1,463,041.

It will be ascertained that under the operations of this banking monopoly, the agricultural states of the West were paying heavy tribute to the East.

It was further pointed out by the President, that the principle of taxation involved in the bill was radically wrong in this: that only the stock could be taxed where held. Therefore, while the nine western states paid $1,640,048 in profits to the bank, only $140,200 of its stock was held there subject to taxation; that, in the year 1831, the branch bank at Mobile earned dividends of $95,140, yet the state of Alabama could not tax the property of the bank, because not a single share of its stock was owned in its jurisdiction.

The foreign stock holders could not be taxed a single penny on their holdings, as they were beyond the taxing power of the United States. The foreign stock holder would be drawing large dividends from the American people without bearing any of the burdens of government. This would tend to alien ownership of this bank, non-contribution to the burdens of Government creating this valuable privilege, and a continued drainage of specie to foreign nations.

The fourth section of the proposed law provided:— "That the bills and notes of said corporation, although the same be, on the faces thereof, made payable at one place only, shall, nevertheless, be received by the said corporation at the bank or at any of the offices thereof, if tendered in liquidation or payment of any balance or balances due to said corporation, or to such office of discount and profit from any other incorporated bank."

The right thus conferred upon state banks to pay their debts to the United States Bank, with the notes and bills of any branch bank thereof, would tend to unify the whole banking interest of the nation into a powerful combination, while at the same time, any individual who held currency issued by a branch of the United States Bank, situated at any other place than his residence, was deprived of that right, therefore, he would be compelled to discount the bills of the branch bank, or transmit them to Philadelphia to obtain the cash for them.

These were a few of the reasons assigned by the President in his famous veto message.

It is now conceded by the most eminent historians of America, that General Jackson, in throttling the corrupt and unscrupulous money power of that day, saved the nation.

On the 8th of January, 1815, General Jackson had met the veterans of Wellington at New Orleans, and inflicted upon them the most disastrous defeat ever suffered by England, and shed undying renown upon American arms. He saved America then, and he preserved its independence in 1832.

By act of Congress, June 28, 1834, a change was made in the coinage laws of April 2, 1792. By the latter act, the legal ratio of silver to gold was fixed at fifteen to one, that is, fifteen pounds of pure silver were the legal equivalent of one pound of pure gold, and this ratio was maintained until the passage of the act of June 28, 1834.

France and the other Latin States maintained a legal ratio of fifteen and one half to one. Consequently the United States over-valued silver when compared with gold. The bullion dealers, ever on the alert for a profit, sent the gold abroad and sold it at a premium. To remedy this, the act of June 28, 1834, reduced the quantity of gold in the gold eagle from 247½ grains of pure gold to 232 grains, or a reduction in the ten dollar gold piece from 270 grains of standard gold to 258 grains. A corresponding reduction was made in the half-eagle and quarter-eagle. A fraction over six per cent. of gold bullion was therefore deducted from the gold coins. This made the legal ratio of silver to gold stand at sixteen to one. By this act, silver was undervalued and gold made its appearance in circulation, and silver disappeared from the channels of trade.

The object of the passage of this law was to supersede the United States Bank bills by the substitution of gold coin as a circulating medium. The people remembered the great efforts of the bank to monopolize the entire volume of money in the country, and gladly received the two and one half, five and ten dollar gold pieces in preference to bank notes.

This substitution of gold coin for bank notes greatly diminished the profits of the bank, and it immediately declared war upon that coin. Its subsidized press, its minions and dependents denounced this species of money in terms of ridicule. The subservient tools of the bank, when offered gold coin in the ordinary transactions of business, would shudder and recoil at its appearance, and demand United States bank notes as the superior money.

In the meantime, however, in 1832, a presidential election was held. Henry Clay was put forward as the candidate of the Whigs and of the bank power. Andrew Jackson was the candidate of the Democratic party, and represented the principles of Jefferson. Jackson received two hundred nineteen electoral votes to forty-nine for Clay. The prophecies of those Democrats that Jackson had ruined the party by his contest with the bank were refuted by a decisive vote of the people.

REMOVAL OF THE GOVERNMENT DEPOSITS.

The next step taken by the President to curtail the power of the bank for mischief, was the removal of the government deposits amounting to many millions of dollars.

After the bank so signally failed to obtain a renewal of its exclusive banking privileges, it did not deviate from its policy of inflicting distress and ruin upon the people.

From the 1st day of August, 1833, to the 30th of June, 1834, it continued its contraction of the currency by calling in its loans, giving as its reasons therefor, that the Government was harassing it on every hand. It had ample time in which to arrange its affairs without seriously crippling the business of the country and its excuse was not valid.

Although many millions of public revenues were under its sole charge, constituting a loanable fund for the benefit of the bank, its hireling press teemed with abuse against the administration of President Jackson.

The President, in view of all the facts within his knowledge, entertained the opinion that the bank was insolvent, and an unsafe depository for the public moneys. He had previously communicated his belief to Congress as to the unsafe condition of the bank, but such was its influence in that body, that the House of Representatives, by a practically unanimous vote, declared its confidence in the institution.

In the lawful exercise of his powers, the President ordered the Secretary of the Treasury, through the five government directors, to investigate its financial condition. The directors made a demand upon the bank for an inspection of its books, but they were denied access to them. In the face of the obstacles thrown in their way to ascertain its true condition, the directors made an investigation with astonishing results.

To obtain a full, true, and complete statement of the expenditures of the bank for political purposes, the official directors submitted a resolution to the full board of the bank, requesting the cashier to furnish a statement to the board, as early as possible, showing what amount was paid out for certain purposes, the sums of money paid to each person, the quantity and names of documents furnished by him, and his charges for the distribution of them. Similar statements were requested from the various branch offices of the bank. The resolution was voted down by the board of directors, and a substitute was adopted expressing implicit confidence in the course of its president—Nicolas Biddle.

Subsequent events gave satisfactory explanation why the officials of the bank pursued that course in refusing an inspection of the books. Upon a report of the government directors setting forth these facts, the President assumed the responsibility of removing the public moneys from the bank, and distributed them among the various state banks.

In this course he met decided opposition to this order in his cabinet. The Secretary of the Treasury, William J. Duane, peremptorily refused to obey the command of his chief, and for this act of insubordination he was summarily removed from his office.

Attorney General Taney was appointed to fill the vacancy occasioned by Duane's removal, and the order was executed to the letter.

The bold stand taken by the President in the removal of the deposits, stirred up the wrath of the bank party in Congress, and Henry Clay offered a resolution in the United States Senate as follows:—

"Resolved, That the President in the late executive proceeding in relation to the public revenue, has assumed upon himself authority and power not conferred by the constitution and laws, but in derogation of both."

This resolution censuring President Jackson was adopted by the Senate on the 28th of March, 1834.

The bank pointed to this action of the senate as proof of its great power.

On the 15th day of April, 1834, President Jackson transmitted a message to the Senate, respectfully protesting against this implied impeachment of his official acts. His communication to that body was a magnificent exposition of constitutional law, and he severely arraigned the senate for passing judgment upon him without granting him an opportunity to be heard in his defense.

Three years afterward the resolution of Clay was expunged from the journals of the senate.

The President was fated to emerge triumphant from every contest with the banking power.

The bank still continued its warfare upon the people. It avowed its purpose to precipitate a wide spread panic. It announced its intention to crush the business of the nation, unless the order of removal was recalled, and the deposits restored. The pressure brought to bear by the bank was directed at the chief commercial and industrial centers. The havoc wrought by it was as broad as the range of its operations, and its course was sustained by politicians as one of self-defense.

Public men who were deeply indebted to it openly upheld its conduct. One of these purchasable demagogues owed the bank the great sum of $100,000, and his defense of his owner was in direct proportion to his obligation to his master—the bank. One loan of $1,100,000 was made by it to a broker in New York City, at which time it was steadily contracting the currency at every point where it was represented by an office. The broker to whom this immense loan was made, accumulated a fortune by speculating with this money upon the misfortunes of others.

Distress meetings were held everywhere under the auspices of the bank, resolutions were adopted, and memorials were presented to the President, requesting him to rescind his order of removal, but without avail.

The presidents, vice-presidents, and various other officers of the so-called distress meetings were selected from those who had supported Jackson for the presidency, which fact was always announced to the people. The petitions, memorials, and remonstrances presented to the President but served to strengthen his determination to crush the bank, and the last fangs of the oppressors were pulled by the removal of these deposits amounting to $40,000,000.

It must be borne in mind, that during the administration of Jackson, a controversy arose between the United States and France with reference to the depredations committed upon our merchant marine by the latter nation during the Directory. A treaty had been concluded by the administration with the kingdom of France on the 4th of July, 1831, by the provisions of which, the latter power agreed to pay the United States the sum of $5,000,000, as indemnity for such depredations.

The French authorities failed to pay the first installment thereof, and the Secretary of the Treasury, under the direction of the President, drew a bill of exchange upon France for the amount. The bill was transmitted to Paris through the United States Bank as the fiscal agent of the Government. The authorities of France refused to honor the bill, and it was protested, whereupon the bank seized upon the Government funds in its possession to the amount of $170,040 which it claimed as damages for the protestation of the bill. This high handed procedure was clearly illegal on the part of the bank, and violative of the Constitution which provides that no money shall be drawn from the treasury, except through appropriations made by Congress.

To force a suspension of specie payments by state banks of issue, it drew immense bills of exchange on Paris, where it had no money, for the payment of them, then drew vast sums of specie out of the banks of New York City, and transmitted it to Paris to meet the bills so drawn by it.

In speaking of the course of the bank, in attempting to force a suspension of specie payments by the state banks of issue, Mr. Royall says:—

"It was certainly not too good to do so, and in the year 1841, just before it finally expired, it is proved to have attempted to create a general suspension, by forcing the banks of the city of New York to suspend. The manner of this attempt was afterward related by its cashier. It consisted in selling bills in unlimited quantities on Paris—at this time in great demand—where it had not a cent to meet them, and drawing the coin with the proceeds of these sales out of the New York banks and shipping it abroad to meet these bills as they made their appearance there. The bills, however, got to Paris before the coin, came back protested, and the great bubble was finally pricked."

This act was committed by the bank to embarrass the government, to emphasize the panic then beginning to rage, and to bankrupt the business interests of the nation.

In short, no trick, device, or artifice was too villainous or traitorous for the bank to injure the credit of the Government and the happiness of the people.

The bank again failed to obtain a charter in 1841.

The rottenness of the bank then became known, and a complete investigation into its management from 1830 to 1836, instituted by the stockholders, developed an astonishing degree of villainy, corruption, and rascality that was appalling, and the results of which more than sustained the charges brought against it by President Jackson and his supporters.

It was discovered that hundreds of thousands of dollars were expended by President Biddle in influencing elections, subsidizing the press, and bribing members of Congress.

The stockholders, on the completion of this investigation, instituted a suit against President Biddle in the United States circuit court at Philadelphia, for the sum of $1,018,000 expended by him for which no vouchers could be found.

It was further demonstrated that, from 1830 to 1836, during the struggle of the bank for a new lease of corporate life, loans, aggregating more than $30,000,000, were made by its president to members of Congress, editors of newspapers, politicians of all grades, jobbers and brokers, mostly without security.

Perhaps all the facts connected with its management were never made known, on the ground of public policy, as the reputations of many eminent men, not excepting presidential candidates, would have been utterly ruined.

In speaking of the contest between the bank and President Jackson, Parton, the biographer, says:—

"In these Jacksonian contests, therefore, we find nearly all the talent, nearly all the learning, nearly all the ancient wealth, nearly all the business activity, nearly all the book-nourished intelligence, nearly all the silver-forked civilization of the country, united in opposition to General Jackson, who represented the country's untutored instincts."

Parton further says that Jackson was called a murderer, a traitor, an ignoramus, a fool, a crook-back, a pretender, and various other vile names.

Nicolas Biddle, who, to a very large extent, was responsible for the gigantic conspiracies, bank-panics with their resultant ruin and misery, was driven in disgrace from his exalted position, and he died a shameful death almost unknown, unhonored, and unsung.

The man before whom bowed in fawning adulation, great and wise statesmen, merchant princes, editors of powerful journals, and leaders of public opinion; he, who, in the magnitude of his financial plans and undertakings, rivaled the money kings of Europe; he, who arrayed dollars against the immutable principles of justice and the rights of man, lived to see his name become a by-word, a hissing, and a reproach.

The career of the United States Bank and its president is an awful monument of warning on the highway of time to come, an object lesson to that colossal greed of power, which, to tighten its grip upon the people, scatters distress and ruin in its train, and which, from its ramparts of ill-gotten wealth obtained by monopoly and special privileges, defies the laws of man and the laws of God.

On the other hand, the fame of Jackson shines more and more with the lapse of time.

Thomas Jefferson, the founder of American Democracy, and the friend of the human race, is honored as the great constructive statesman of America; Andrew Jackson is revered as that great leader who regenerated the politics of his country, and rescued a people from financial slavery. During his administration, the public debt was wholly paid, a large surplus of public revenues accumulated to the credit of the United States, the money power was dethroned, the American nation was honored everywhere, and he retired from the presidency amid the plaudits of his countrymen.

In his farewell address to the people, March 3, 1837, he solemnly warned them against the money power, that special privileges must not be granted to any class of citizens, and that justice must be the basis of public and private conduct.

In this noble document, the President admonishes the people to be on their guard against the money power. He says:—

"But when the charter for the bank of the United States was obtained from Congress, it perfected the paper system, and gave to its advocates the position they have struggled to obtain from the commencement of the Federal Government down to the present hour. The immense capital and peculiar privileges bestowed upon it, enabled it to exercise despotic sway over the other banks in every part of the country. From its superior strength it could seriously injure, if not destroy, the business of any one of them that would incur its resentment; and it openly claimed for itself the power of regulating the currency throughout the United States. In other words, it asserted (and undoubtedly possessed) the power to make money plenty or scarce, at its pleasure, at any time, and in any quarter of the Union, by controlling the issues of other banks, and in permitting an expansion, or compelling a general contraction of the circulating medium according to its own will.

"The other banking institutions were sensible of its strength, and they soon became generally its obedient instruments, ready at all times to execute its mandates; and with the other banks necessarily went also that numerous class of persons in our commercial cities who depend altogether on bank credits for their solvency and means of business, and who are therefore obliged, for their safety, to propitiate the favor of the money power by distinguished zeal and devotion in its service. The result of the ill-advised legislation which established this great monopoly, was to concentrate the whole moneyed power of the Union, with its boundless means of corruption, and its numerous dependents, under the direction and command of one acknowledged head; thus organizing this particular interest as one body, and securing to it unity of action throughout the United States, and enabling it to bring forward, upon any occasion, its entire and undivided strength to support or defeat any measure of the government. In the hands of this formidable power, thus perfectly organized, was also placed unlimited dominion over the amount of circulating medium, giving it the power to regulate the value of property, and the fruits of labor in every quarter of the Union; and to bestow prosperity, or bring ruin upon any city or section of the country as might best comport with its own interests or policy.

"We are not left to conjecture how the moneyed power, thus organized, and with such a weapon in its hands, would be likely to use it. The distress and alarm which pervaded and agitated the whole country, when the Bank of the United States waged war upon the people in order to compel them to submit to their demands, cannot yet be forgotten. The ruthless and unsparing temper with which whole cities and communities were oppressed, individuals impoverished and ruined, a scene of cheerful prosperity suddenly changed into one of gloom and despondency, ought to be indelibly impressed on the memory of the people of the United States. If such was its power in a time of peace, what would it not have been in a season of war, with an enemy at your doors. No nation but the freeman of the United States could have come out victorious from such contest; yet, if you had not conquered, the Government would have passed from the hands of the many to the hands of the few; and this organized money power, from its secret conclave, would have dictated the choice of your highest officers, and compelled you to make peace or war, as best suited their own wishes. The form of your Government might for a time have remained, but its living spirit would have departed from it."

The wise counsel couched in these golden words of President Jackson are now more applicable than when uttered by him.

In the election of 1836, Martin Van Buren succeeded Jackson in the presidency. The panic engineered by the bank enveloped the people, and the whole system of credit built up by it fell with a crash. In fact the bank had so shrewdly manipulated the volume of money, and so absolute was its control over it, that society had resolved itself into two classes, a creditor class, small in numbers, but powerful in influence; a debtor class, constituting a great majority of the people, but helpless in the grasp of the creditor class.

One was the master, the other the servant.

During the administration of Van Buren, the Independent Treasury Bill became a law.

Thus the work begun by Jackson in crushing the bank, was consummated by the separation of the public moneys from those of the banks—a most salutary reform.

CHAPTER II.

ORIGIN OF THE PRESENT NATIONAL BANKING SYSTEM.

"She is not dead, but holding her capital and stock holders together under a state charter, she has taken a position to watch events and also to profit by them. The Royal tiger has gone into the jungle; and, crouching on his belly, he awaits the favorable moment of emerging from his covert and springing on the body of the unsuspicious traveler."—Thomas H. Benton.

"Bank paper must be suppressed and the circulation restored to the nation to whom it belongs.

"The power to issue money should be taken from the banks and restored to congress and the people.

"I sincerely believe that banking establishments are more dangerous than standing armies.

"I am not among those who fear the people. They, and not the rich, are our dependence for continued freedom. And to preserve their independence, we must not let our rulers load us with perpetual debt.

"Put down the banks and if this country could not be carried through the longest war against her most powerful enemy without ever knowing the want of a dollar, without dependence upon the traitorous class of her citizens, without bearing hard upon the resources of the people or loading the public with an indefinite burden of debt, I know nothing of my countrymen."
—Thomas Jefferson.

In the preceding chapter, the career of the United States Bank was traced from its origin to its downfall.

It was there shown that the United States, by transferring its sovereign power of issuing currency to circulate as money among the people, and delegating it to a private corporation, had, in a period of less than fifty years, built up a monopoly that threatened to pull down the pillars of the republic.

That the panics of 1811, 1833, and 1837-41, with their consequent ruin of tens of thousands of industries, with the attendant circumstances of hunger, suffering, and starvation, were designedly produced by the bank to overawe Congress and the President.

That it secured the powerful political influence of Webster, Clay, and Calhoun on the floor of the United States senate as the champions of its interests.

That the press of the country, to a very large extent, succumbed to its moneyed influence.

That it attempted to crush the beneficient administration of President Jackson.

We now come to consider a system of national banking, compared with which, the old United States Bank was a pigmy.

In 1861, when the Southern states attempted to withdraw from the Union, the result was that great conflict known in history as the civil war. Throughout its progress, the mass of the people were intently engaged with the gigantic operations constantly carried on during that period, and, therefore, little attention was paid by them to the financial legislation, enacted by Congress.

When the North and the South were marshaling their respective armies to determine the question of military supremacy, the weight of foreign influence was thrown to the southern cause. Great Britain, from her antipathy to the people of the United States, early recognized the Confederacy, and her course was followed by France and Spain, but the latter powers did not resort to the extreme measures of England.

During the early period of the war, immense sums of money were needed by the Federal Government to arm, equip, and maintain her numerous armies and fleets necessary for the suppression of the rebellion.

Heavy taxes of various kinds were levied and collected for the payment of the extraordinary expenses incurred by the war, but this was insufficient to meet the expenditures. Resort was had to borrowing money on the credit of the United States by the sale of bonds.

At that time as at present, New York City was the financial center of the country. August Belmont & Co. were the American agents of the Rothchilds, and the former advised this great banking house that there would be much risk in purchasing American bonds.

The Rothchilds were located in the city of London, England, with branch banks at Paris, Frankfort, Berlin, and Vienna.

From the year 1800, up to the outbreak of the civil war, the United States had made astonishing progress as a commercial nation, our commerce had rapidly grown to be the second largest in the world, and it promised, ere long, to surpass that of Great Britain, who had long looked with jealous eye on the remarkable growth of the American merchant marine. She had for centuries prided herself as the "Mistress of the Seas," and had long feared that this republic would snatch its supremacy from her, and thus relegate her to a second rate power.

Hence, upon the outbreak of the war, the rejoicing in England was immense, and British statesmen predicted the success of the Confederacy. Nor was this all. England aided the South by money, munitions of war, by the recognition of her belligerency, and by her moral support.

It was evident that no money could be secured from England by the United States to maintain the supremacy of the Constitution, for nations, like men, are governed in their money transactions largely by their likes and dislikes.

In 1861, the money in circulation in the United States consisted of gold and silver coins, and state bank currency. As the expenses of the Government in 1861-62 were many millions of dollars in excess of its income, and as but little money could be had by the sale of its bonds, recourse was had to issuing paper money.

By the acts of July 17th, and August 5, 1861, the Secretary of the Treasury was authorized to issue demand notes to the amount of fifty millions of dollars, and these notes were made full legal tender for all debts and demands, both public and private. This was not the first time that the Federal Government had issued its notes to circulate as money. It will be remembered that during the war of 1812, the Government had resorted to this means, a precedent followed by the administrations of Van Buren, Polk, and Buchanan.

These notes so issued at these various times were maintained at a parity with gold and silver coin, and were a favorite money of the people. History records the fact that no less than twenty issues of paper money were emitted by the general Government prior to the year 1862; that the people never questioned its value and efficiency as a medium of exchange. These various issues of currency were uniformly receivable by the Government in payment of its taxes and revenues.

During the perilous times of the nation, when bankers and financiers refused to loan money to it, the issue of full legal tender paper money never failed to come to the rescue, while cowardly gold fled to the rear.

Therefore, the fifty millions of demand notes issued under the authority of the acts of July 17th and August 5, 1861, having unlimited legal tender power for the payment of all demands, never depreciated a farthing.

Subsequent to the passage of this act, a bill was introduced in Congress providing for the issue of non-interest bearing treasury notes to the amount of $150,000,000 with full legal tender power for the payment of all debts and demands, public and private. Immediately, from the leading cities of the country, a horde of bankers, or as Hon. Thaddeus Stevens aptly termed them, "A delegation of bankers and coin venders," hastened to Washington, organized themselves, and requested the Committee on Ways and Means of the House, and the Finance Committee of the Senate to meet with them at the office of the Secretary of the Treasury. Their request was complied with on the 11th day of February, 1862.

Owing to some peculiar and powerful influence, then and there exerted by these organized bankers on these committees, the legal tender clause was modified to read as follows:—

"That the amount of the two kinds of notes together shall at no time exceed the sum of $150,000,000, and such notes herein authorized shall be receivable in payment of taxes, internal duties, excises, debts, and demand of every kind due to the United States, except duties on imports, and of all claims and demands against the United States of every kind whatsoever, except for interest upon bonds and notes which shall be paid in coin, and shall also be lawful money and a legal tender in the payment of all debts, public and private, within the United States, except duties on imports and interest as aforesaid."

This proposed amendment was severely criticised by Mr. Stevens, of Pennsylvania, and by Mr. Spaulding, of New York. During the debate upon the bill as amended, Mr. Stevens denounced the demands of the bankers and said:—

"A doleful sound came up from the caverns of the bullion brokers and the saloons of the associated banks. Their cashiers and agents were soon on the ground, and persuaded the Senate with but little deliberation to mangle and destroy what it had cost the House months to digest, consider and pass.

"Instead of being a beneficent and invigorating measure, it is now positively mischievous. It has all the bad qualities which its enemies charged on the original bill and none of its benefits. It now creates money and by its very terms declares it a depreciated currency. It make two classes of money—one for banks and brokers and another for the people. It discriminates between the rights of different classes of creditors; allowing the rich capitalist to demand gold and compelling the ordinary lender of money on individual security to receive notes which the Government had purposely discredited."

Mr. Stevens further said:—

"Who is this favored class? The bankers and brokers and nobody else. But how is this gold to be raised? The duties and public lands are to be paid for in United States notes, and they or bonds are to be put up at auction, to get coin for these very brokers, who would furnish the coin to pay themselves by getting twenty per cent. discount on the notes thus bought."

While on his death bed, the Great Commoner, as his friends loved to call him, recalled the action of Congress in demonetizing the greenback at the instigation of the banks.

In speaking of the bankers he said:—

"We were foolish to grant them gold interest, and now they unblushingly demand further advantages. The truth is we can never satisfy their appetite for money."

The amendment of Mr. Stevens to place officers and soldiers of the army and navy, and those who should furnish them with provisions upon the same standing as the bankers and brokers, was defeated by a vote of 72 to 67.

In denouncing the amendment striking out the legal tender clause, Senator John Sherman spoke as follows:—

"If you strike out this legal tender clause you do it with the knowledge that these notes will fall dead upon the money market of the world; that they will be refused by the banks; that they will be a disgraced currency that will not pass from hand to hand; that they will have no legal sanction; that any man may decline to receive them, and thus discredit the obligations of the Government. I ask again if that is just to the men to whom you have contracted to pay debts? When you issue demand notes and announce your purpose not to pay any more gold and silver coin, you tender to those who have furnished provisions and services this paper money. What can they do? They can not pay their debts with it, they can not support their families with it, without a depreciation."

He further said in this speech of February 13, 1862, that "I much prefer the credit of the United States, based as it is upon all the productions and property of the United States, to the issues of any corporation, however guarded and managed."

This language of Senator Sherman was that of undoubted patriotism, and it is strongly condemnatory of his subsequent public career, during which he became the active ally of the national banks.

Mr. Kellogg, of Illinois, thus scored the greed of these men. He said:—

"I am pained to sit in my place in the House and hear members talk about 'the sacredness of capital,' that the interests of money must not be touched. Yes, sir, they will vote six hundred thousand of the flower of the American youth for the army to be sacrificed without a blush, but the great interests of capital, of currency, must not be touched."

In referring to the grand struggle made by Mr. Stevens for full legal tender currency, Judge Kelley said:—

"I remember the grand old Commoner with his hat in his hand and his cane under his arm, when he returned to the House from the final conference, shedding bitter tears over the result. 'Yes,' said he, 'we have had to yield. The Senate was stubborn. We did not yield until we found that the country must be lost or the banks be gratified; and we have sought to save the country in spite of the cupidity of its wealthiest citizens.'"

The bankers thus succeeded in limiting the legal tender power of the Treasury note, or as it is commonly called, the greenback, and from this time on the bankers, brokers, and speculators have, with few exceptions, dictated the financial legislation in the United States.

This amendment, by which the debt paying power of the Treasury note was restricted within such narrow limits, was a most dishonest act on the part of the government.

It drew distinctions between the various kinds of money issued by the United States. It made the bankers and bond holders a privileged class, and it inflicted a wound upon the nation from which it has not yet recovered. It made gold and silver coin the money of the privileged classes, who composed that traitorous element so justly denounced by Jefferson.

By force of this amendment, coin went to a premium, thereby greatly enhancing the wealth of the bankers and bullion brokers.

Moreover, the principle involved in that act greatly weakened the most powerful element of sovereignty that can reside in a nation, by placing the control of the value of money in the hands of organized greed, in this case the gold gamblers of Wall street.

It laid the foundation of a stupendous public debt, which the holders thereof would strive to perpetuate by every means in their power, and it was the first step to fasten on the people the most powerful and merciless tyranny that ever cursed a free people—the centralized money power known as the national banking system.

The bill, as amended, became a law on July 11, 1862, and, from that time, began the depreciation of the greenback currency.

The banking power, which had succeeded in inducing Congress and the President to cripple that currency, which eventually saved the Union, afterward pointed the finger of scorn at this money as a debased currency, and they, therefore, impliedly damned their own nefarious conduct by denouncing it as "rag-baby" money.

As a result of this act as amended, the merchant who

paid duties on merchandise imported from abroad was compelled to pay the taxes levied thereon, in coin. To obtain that kind of money he must proceed to the bullion broker, and pay him a large premium for the coin to make his payment of the customs levied on his merchandise. The bond holder was paid his interest on government bonds in gold, which was afterward sold by him to the importer, at a high premium.

This legislation was the result toward which the bullion brokers and gold gamblers of Wall street bent all their energies to procure, when they induced the government to rob the greenback of its full legal tender debt-paying power. It was the consummation of the most dishonest financial scheme ever perpetrated upon a heavily taxed and patriotic people.

Immediately following the visit of these bankers to Washington, a circular was issued by the London bankers, and distributed by one Hazard, who was their representative in this country at that time.

The contents of this famous circular are as follows:—

"Slavery is likely to be abolished by the war power and chattel slavery destroyed. This I and my European friends are in favor of; for slavery is but the owning of labor and carries with it the care of the laborer, while the European plan, led on by England, is capital control of labor by controlling wages. This can be done by controlling the money. The debt, that capitalists will see is to be made out of the war, must be used as a measure to control the volume of money. To accomplish this the bonds must be used as a banking basis. We are now waiting for the Secretary of the Treasury to make his recommendation to Congress. It will not do to allow the greenback (as it is called) to circulate as money any length of time, for we cannot control it."

The existence of this remarkable circular has been strenuously denied time and again by the national banking money power. Notwithstanding these denials, the line of action indicated in that circular has been consistently pursued from that day to this.

The advice of said Hazard was at once acted upon by the organized banks, and they proceeded to make known their demands to Congress.

Therefore, a bill was speedily brought forward by Senator Sherman in the United States Senate, providing for the incorporation and organization of the present system of national banks as banks of issue—a bill whose passage meant the creation of moneyed institutions, whose interests would be, or could be made, antagonistic to the nation.

Is it not exceedingly strange, that Senator Sherman, who, in his able speech of February 13, 1862, advanced powerful arguments in behalf of Government legal tender currency, or greenbacks, in which he stated that he preferred the credit of the United States, based, as it was, upon all the productions and property of the people, to the issue of any corporation however well guarded and managed, would thus suddenly change his position?

In less than a year from the time he so ably defended legal tender greenback currency, he reversed his position, and fathered a financial measure which brought into being a dangerous rival to the Government when it was engaged in a death struggle.

In substance, this act provided for the incorporation of banking companies, by which not less than five persons could, under certain restrictions, organize a bank, by depositing with the Secretary of the Treasury

United States bonds to secure the circulation of national bank notes as currency.

The capitalists thus organizing themselves into a national bank association, were required to enter into articles of association which should specify, in general terms, the object for which the association was formed. These articles were to be signed by the persons uniting to form the association, and a copy of them was to be forwarded to the Comptroller of the Currency to be filed and preserved in his office.

No association could be organized as a national bank with a less capital than one hundred thousand dollars; except that banks with a capital of not less than fifty thousand dollars could, with the approval of the Secretary of the Treasury, be organized in any place having a population not exceeding six thousand inhabitants.

Upon a deposit of United States bonds, the banking associations were entitled to receive from the Comptroller of the Currency, circulating notes, of different denominations, in blank, registered or countersigned, equal in amount to ninety per centum of the amount of the current market value of the bonds so deposited by the association with the Comptroller, but in any case the circulating notes were not to exceed ninety per centum of the par value of the said bonds, if bearing interest at a rate of not less than five per cent. per annum; and the amount of circulating notes to be furnished to each association shall be in proportion to its paid-up capital as follows, and no more:—

1. To each association whose capital does not exceed five hundred thousand dollars, ninety per centum of such capital.

2. To each association whose capital exceeds five

hundred thousand, but not exceed one million of dollars, eighty per centum of such capital.

3. To each association whose capital exceeds one million of dollars, but not exceed three millions of dollars, seventy-five per centum of such capital.

4. To each association whose capital exceeds three millions of dollars, sixty per centum of such capital.

The law further provided that after any association receiving circulating notes under this act, and has caused its promise to pay such notes on demand to be signed by the president, or vice-president, and cashier thereof in such manner as to make them obligatory promissory notes, payable on demand, at its place of business, such association may issue and circulate the same as money. And such notes shall be received at par in all parts of the United States in payment of taxes, excises, public lands, and all other dues to the United States, except duties on imports, and also for all salaries and other debts and demands owing by the United States to individuals, corporations, and associations within the United States, except interest on the public debt, and in redemption of the national currency.

This act also provided that, in lieu of all existing taxes, each association should pay a duty of one per cent. per annum upon the average amount of its notes in circulation, and one-half of one per cent. per annum upon the average amount of its deposits, and a duty of one-half of one per cent. per annum on the average amount of its capital stock beyond the amount invested in United States bonds.

Furthermore, these national banking associations were authorized to institute suits at law in the United States courts as courts of orginial jurisdiction.

This provision gave the national banks an advantage over the ordinary citizen, and placed these associations beyond the jurisdiction of the State courts; in other words, these banks could select whatever court their interest dictated.

It will at once be ascertained, from a study of the national banking law, that the capital of the associations was nearly doubled by act of Congress.

In the first place, bonds, deposited by them to secure their circulation drew interest payable in gold, at this time at a high premium. Second, the circulating notes issued to them by the United States, although promissory notes payable on demand and therefore debts of the banks, were nominally money, and were loaned out at a high rate of interest to the customers of the national banks.

The United States Government gave the wealthiest men of the country, in the time of its greatest peril and distress, a gratuity equal to ninety per centum of their banking capital.

This scheme engineered through Congress by the money power, greatly tended to centralize the currency in the large cities, and, therefore, made it master of the productive energies of the American people, as the vast majority of the bonds were held in New York City and other centers of wealth and population.

It made the circulating notes of these banks a rival to the greenback currency, and it would be to the interest of the national bankers, by every means in their power, to drive out and destroy the paper money issued by the Government.

This law placed it in the hands of the money power to contract or expand the volume of money at its pleasure, and, therefore, enhance or depreciate the value of stocks, bonds, and all other forms of property in the United States.

The far-reaching influence of this act of Congress, chartering national banks, becomes apparent, when the true principles and functions of Government are considered in all their relations to the people.

Pre-eminent among the various powers conferred upon, or assumed by a sovereign state, are those of taxation, of raising armies, and of coining, issuing, and controlling the volume of money.

The first named power, that of taxation, is only limited by the necessities of the State, and of the amount of property upon which it operates.

A citizen of a state may become the owner of a home through arduous toil and life-long rigid economy, yet, the state, when invoking the power of levying and collecting taxes, may sweep away this property, not leaving a vestige for the man whose labor and privations created a shelter for himself and family.

In a great case before the highest tribunal of the nation, Justice Samuel F. Miller said that "The power of taxation is the power to destroy."

No man who is endowed with a modicum of intelligence would advocate a transfer of this immense power to a private corporation for its gain.

It would amount to the self-destruction of a nation.

The power of raising and maintaining armies is inherent in a sovereign state, and is absolutely necessary for its self-defense, and therefore its self-preservation.

The strong arm of the Government can reach every fireside in the land, and can drag from thence the father, husband, or son, tear him away from the family circle, force him to don the national uniform, to bear arms, and to lay down his life for his country.

No citizen can resist the imperative call of his country when involved in war.

No sane man would advocate the delegation of this high attribute of sovereignty to a corporation for its individual gain, as such transfer of power would inevitably result in frightful oppression.

The power of coining, issuing, and controlling the volume of money is a far more important function of government than the foregoing.

All commerce, exchange, the existence of Government, of civilization itself, hinges upon this mighty function of Government. The power of issuing and controlling money exercises an imperial sway over all productive industry as universal as the law of gravitation upon all matter.

The value of all property, whether of the present time, or of that resulting from the earnings and accumulations of all past generations, depends upon the control of the volume of money.

The power of levying and collecting taxes for the support of the nation, of raising and maintaining armies for its preservation, is dependent upon the control of the currency.

The former is subordinate to the last named power, and consequently involves the very life of the nation.

Yet, in time of the greatest need of the nation, when everything most valuable to man was at stake, this necessary power of Government was delegated to the most traitorous and rapacious system of corporations that ever cursed the people.

By this transfer of sovereign power to the national

banking system, the Federal Government divested itself of that never failing resource which secured the independence of the colonies, and which successfully enabled the administration of James Madison to chastise the overweening pride of Great Britain in 1812.

The alienation of this highest function of the nation to the national banking money power was a high crime against the welfare of the country, and it created a powerful moneyed interest antagonistic to the United States.

More than one hundred years ago, the illustrious Jefferson clearly pointed out the dangers of banks of issue. Time and again, he exerted his voice, his pen, and his influence, in warning the people of the consequences that would inevitably flow from such selfish schemes as the transfer of national powers to corporations.

The extreme danger of a sovereign power, in transferring its absolute right of coining and issuing money in whole, or in part, to a private individual, or corporation, has been clearly pointed out by the ablest thinkers of all ages. Such transfers of the powers of a state have universally resulted in extortion and oppression by those to whom this privilege is granted.

Vattel, the great authority on the law of nations, instances several cases. He places the right of coining money among the prerogatives of majesty, and he relates that Sigismund, king of Poland, having granted this privilege to his vassal, the Duke of Prussia, in the year 1543, the Estates of that country passed a decree in which it was asserted that the king could not grant that privilege, it being inseparable from the crown.

The kings of France granted the privileges of coining money to lords and bishops, and these grantees having used that power as an instrument of great oppression, these privileges were cancelled by the crown on account of the great abuses practiced on its subjects.

The history of England furnishes a notable example, for in 1723, one Wood, an Englishman, obtained a royal patent for the coinage of copper half-pence. Wood at once proceeded to flood Ireland with this base coin, and robbed the down-trodden people of that country out of thousands of pounds sterling.

This gross outrage upon that nation aroused the indignation of Swift, and in his "Drapier's Letters" he attacked the Government with such bitter satire, that, in 1725, the patent to Wood was withdrawn.

Parliament, however, granted the scoundrelly Wood an annuity of fifteen thousand dollars per annum for the period of twelve years as an indemnity! The presumption is, that this great sum of money was given to Wood on the ground that he had surrendered a "vested right."

Our Government, in the enactment of this national banking law, gave away its greatest resource in time of peace or war; viz., the power to issue legal tender paper money, a resource that had time and again come to the rescue of the people while the capitalists held aloof.

The principal excuse offered by those who procured the passage of this law was, that it would create a market for bonds, and would aid in the maintainance of the public credit; that, for the consideration of receiving these circulating notes to loan out at interest as money, the bankers, who were the beneficiaries of this law, would lend their assistance to the Government by aiding it to maintain a high price for its obligations.

The very reason advanced by the originators of that system of banking and currency for its creation, became the strongest reason why the Government credit sunk to its lowest point, because, the national bankers, to obtain these bonds as low as possible, would combine to depress the market value of the United States bonds which formed the basis of bank currency.

In fact, the market price of Government bonds rapidly fell to the lowest mark ever known, after the passage of this act, and the national banking money power consequently reaped a harvest reaching into scores of millions.

The same power depreciated the value of greenbacks for the avowed purpose of increasing the premium on gold.

Not satisfied with the immense advantages thus obtained from the Government, during the most critical period of the war, the money power, on the 17th day of March, 1864, succeeded in securing the passage of a resolution through Congress, authorizing the Secretary of the Treasury to pay the interest upon bonds, in advance, not exceeding one year, either with or without rebate for such prepayment, according to his discretion.

The bond holders and bankers were thus enabled to draw their interest in gold one year in advance, dispose of it at a high premium to the government and to those who paid duties on imported merchandise.

In July, 1864, gold rose to a premium of $2.85, and the bond holder, national banker, and gold gambler fleeced the people out of millions; while the soldier, who was sacrificing his life for his country, was paid in greenbacks purposely depreciated by the government for whose existence he fought.

During the Forty-fifth Congress, Hon. James B. Weaver introduced the following resolution in the House of Representatives:—

"Resolved, That the Secretary of the Treasury be and is hereby directed to report to this house whether he has at any time anticipated the payment of interest on the public debt; if so, how much has been paid in advance, and to whom."

This resolution was referred to the Committee on Ways and Means, and the chairman thereof sent the resolution to the Secretary of the Treasury, Sherman, with a request to state when he could report.

The Secretary, in reply, stated:—

"That there was no public document that would give the information required. The department has been in the habit for five years of paying the interest in advance without charging anything."

This remarkable admission will attract attention for the reason, that the head of the Treasury Department distinctly states that interest had been paid in advance to the bond holders and bankers without any deduction for the use of the money, and that there was no public docment that would give the information required. The obvious reason why there were no public documents in the treasury department, containing a record of the interest on bonds paid in advance was this, that it would show a gigantic robbery of the government by the banks and bond holders, and that it would awaken the just wrath of the people at the subservience of congress to the demands of the gold gambling money power.

In a speech delivered by Senator Sherman in advocacy of the national banking law, he said:—

"We are about to choose between a permanent system, designed to establish a uniform national currency, based upon the public credit, limited in amount, and guarded by all the restrictions which the experience of man has proved necessary and a system of paper money without limit as to amount, except for the growing necessities of war."

In this declaration of the senator, he expressly admits that the circulating notes of these banks were based on the credit of the Government.

The truth is, that no safe system of bank currency has ever yet been devised by the wit of man, but that its credit is based upon that of the Government, and the credit of a government rests upon its taxing power, which is its means of self-preservation.

To give an excuse for his change of front from an advocate of a legal tender Government currency, to a champion of the national banking system, the senator uses the following language:—

"It is asked, why look at all to the interests of the banks; why not directly issue the notes of the Government, and thus save the people the interest on the debt represented by the circulation? The only answer to this question is that history teaches us that the public faith of the nation alone is not sufficient to maintain a paper currency. There must be a combination between the interests of individuals and the Government."

This astonishing declaration of Senator Sherman is proven absolutely false by the provisions of his own act, the national banking law, which makes United States bonds the sole security for national bank notes, and compels the Government to act as a redemption agency for the notes of insolvent banks.

As the next step to secure the perpetuation of this robbery of the people, Congress, on the 3d of March,

1863, authorized the Secretary of the Treasury to issue $900,000,000 in bonds, drawing interest at six per cent., and redeemable in not less than ten nor more than forty years. These bonds could be purchased by lawful money, thereby meaning United States notes and treasury notes.

There was a lapse of six days between the passage of the national banking act and the passage of this act authorizing said bond issue.

There was yet one rival in the field which the national banks desired to crush, and this was the state banks of issue, which, at this time, had a circulation of $238,677,218 in state bank currency.

To destroy the state banks as banks of issue, and to drive out of circulation that species of paper money, the national banking money power prevailed upon congress to call into requisition the taxing power of the nation to clear the field of these competitors.

In compliance with their demands, Congress enacted the following law, viz:—

"That every national banking association, state bank, or state banking association, shall pay a tax of ten per centum on the amount of notes of any person, or of any state bank or state banking association used for circulation and paid by them."

This great tax thus imposed by Congress upon the issues of state bank currency was effectual in successfully accomplishing its purpose.

The state banks, therefore, were driven to the necessity of organizing themselves into national banks, and this tended to a further consolidation of the moneylending interests of the country.

During the early part of the year 1864, after the

organized banks had secured the passage of the law depriving greenbacks of their legal tender power, and after the passage of the national banking law, one James Buell, secretary of the New York bankers' committee, issued the following circular to the bankers of the country at large:—

"Dear Sir: It is advisable to do all in your power to sustain such daily and prominent weekly newspapers, especially the agricultural and religious press, as will oppose the issuing of greenback money, and that you withhold patronage and favor from all applicants who are not willing to oppose the Government issue of money. Let the Government issue the coin and the banks issue the paper money of the country, for we can better protect each other. To repeal the law creating national banks or to restore to circulation the Government issue of money will be to provide the people with money, and will therefore seriously affect your individual profit as banker or lender. See your member of Congress at once and engage him to support our interest that we may control legislation."

The appearance of this infamous circular stirred up the wrath of the people, and a wave of indignation swept over the land. The nefarious schemes of the money power were set out in this circular with startling distinctness.

The bankers of the country were urged to combine their power; the press of the country was to be corrupted, and legislation was to be controlled, to effect the purpose of transferring the control of the money of the country to the dictation of the money power.

The associated banks of New York City, in order to conciliate the people who were strongly denouncing the scheme set forth in the circular of Buell, announced that this document was issued without their knowledge or authority. However, Mr. Buell, whose name was appended to this circular, was rewarded by an election to the presidency of the Importers' and Traders' National bank, of New York City, a position which has given him much power and prestige as one of the money kings of Wall street.

The evidence is positive that this circular was issued with the approval, and by the orders of the associated banks of New York City. In the first place, the advice tendered to the various banks of the country was in complete harmony with the intentions of the money power, and secondly, the national banks, from that day to this, have carried into execution the baleful plan outlined in that document, as the various acts of congress and subsequent history abundantly prove.

It was during the corrupt period of the war that immense grants of public lands were made to railway corporations, that donations of United States bonds, amounting to nearly one hundred million of dollars were made to the Pacific railway companies, and this was done during a time when the government was in need of funds to suppress the rebellion.

It was during this period that Congress passed the notorious foreign contract labor law, through the operation of which, the mills, factories and mines of the United States were flooded with the Slavs, Huns, Bohemians, Poles, and various other nationalities of Europe, thereby laying the foundation for the countless race and labor riots, that have disgraced and cursed the manufacturing and mining states of the Union.

After the suppression of the state banks of issue, the next step of the national bank was directed toward the destruction of the greenbacks and United States notes, and, therefore, on the 12th of April, 1866, an act of Congress was duly signed by the President providing for the withdrawal and cancellation of the United States notes and treasury notes.

This act provided that, within six months after the passage thereof, the Secretary of the Treasury was authorized to retire from circulation United States notes to the amount of ten million dollars, and for every month thereafter a sum not to exceed four million dollars.

At the time of the passage of the act of April 12, 1866, Hon. Hugh McCulloch, a national banker, and a bitter opponent of the legal tender currency, was Secretary of the Treasury. He had gone so far in his opposition to the United States notes and treasury notes as to denounce them as "disreputable, dishonorable money."

Secretary McCulloch immediately proceeded to remorselessly contract the volume of legal tender notes, until $94,000,000 of them were withdrawn from circulation by the issue of interest bearing bonds in exchange therefor.

On the 2d of March, 1867, an act was adopted by Congress providing for the redemption and retirement of the compound interest notes, which, at this time were outstanding to the amount of $159,000,000 and which circulated as money.

The method of redemption was the substitution of temporary loan certificates in lieu of these notes. The amount of such certificates was fixed at $50,000,000, and they bore interest at the rate of three per cent. per annum, and national banks were authorized to count such certificates as part of the Reserve Fund provided in the national banking law.

On July 25, 1868, the Secretary of the Treasury was authorized to issue additional loan certificates to the amount of $25,000,000.

The acts of March 2, 1867, and July 25, 1868, made a further contraction of money to the amount of $75,000,000.

It will be seen, therefore, that the scheme set forth in the circular of James Buell was being carried out to the letter.

Step by step, the national banking money power was gradually succeeding in driving the legal tender currency out of circulation, in perpetuating the public debt by the issue of long time bonds, and usurping the functions of government by the issue of bank notes.

On the 18th of March, 1869, a bill entitled, "An Act to Strengthen the Public Credit," was signed by President Grant.

The provisions of the Credit Strengthening Act declared that the public faith is solemnly pledged to the payment of the interest and non-interest bearing obligations of the government in coin or its equivalent, except where the law authorizing the issue of such obligations has expressly provided that the same may be paid in lawful money, or other currency than gold and silver. Furthermore, the United States solemnly pledged its faith to make provisions at the earliest practical period for the redemption of the United States notes in coin.

This so-called Credit Strengthening Act, by force of its provisions, made every dollar of the bonded debt of the United States payable in gold and silver coin. It was estimated by the ablest public men of the day that this rascally piece of legislation added six hundred million dollars to the wealth of the national banks and bond holders.

Let it be remembered that this bonded debt was purchased, to a very large extent, with treasury notes purposely depreciated by act of Congress, and that a very large portion of these bonds were bought with greenbacks when the latter were worth but forty cents on the dollar in gold.

It should further be borne in mind, that for more than three years prior to the passage of this act, peace had been restored, the Federal authority was re-established over the South, slavery, the cause of the war, was abolished, the treasury notes and United States notes were appreciating in value every day since the establishment of peace, which, it was admitted, were continually adding wealth to the holders of United States bonds, therefore, those members of Congress who voted for that measure could not even urge necessity—the last plea of tyrants—as an excuse for voting hundreds of millions of dollars to the least patriotic of American citizens.

Owing to the enormous revenues collected by the Federal Government, the public debt was being rapidly paid, which exceedingly alarmed the national banking money power, who desired the perpetuation of the bonded debt of the United States, for without bonds, there would be no national banks.

Therefore, the national banks sought by every means in their power to secure the perpetuation of the national debt, and this result could be obtained in two ways, first—by a heavy reduction of the public revenues; second—by funding the present debt into long time bonds.

During the war heavy duties were laid upon imported goods, taxes were levied on incomes, railway companies, insurance companies, manufacturers, and excises were collected on tobacco and spiritous liquors.

The manufacturing interests of the country were protected from the competition of foreign goods, wares, and merchandise by a very high tariff, while at the same time they were enabled, under the provisions of the foreign contract labor law of July 4, 1864, to import cheap labor by the wholesale from China, Germany, Belgium, Italy, Russia, Austria, and other foreign nations. It was a matter of prime interest to the manufacturers to maintain the present high rate of duties on imports, and at the same time secure the removal of the taxes on incomes, manufactures, and various other forms of internal revenue. Moreover, the manufacturers desired the perpetuation of a huge public debt which would necessitate the raising of large revenues to meet the interest charged thereon. Furthermore, it would be to the interest of the national banks and manufacturers that Congress should make extravagant appropriations for the support of the Government.

The subsequent action of these two interests taken in connection with the legislation procured by them from congress, abundantly prove that the foregoing statements are true.

Hon. William D. Kelley, member of Congress from Pennsylvania, was the outspoken advocate of the manufacturing interests on the floor of the house. In 1867, he offered the following resolution:—

"Resolved, That the Committee on Ways and Means be instructed to inquire into the expediency of immediately repealing the provisions of the internal revenue law, whereby a tax of five per cent. is imposed on the mechanical and manufacturing interests of the country."

The resolution was unanimously adopted.

At the same time, Jay Cooke, the head of a great banking firm in Philadelphia, was the agent of the United States Treasury, and as such agent had negotiated the sale of government bonds in England and America to the amount of several hundred million dollars, and he, therefore, assumed the position of spokesman for the national banking interests.

As early as 1867, Mr. Cooke declared that the income tax should "Be scornfully abandoned and that right speedily."

He laid down the following monstrous principle:—

"We lay down the proposition that our national debt, made permanent and rightfully managed, will be a national blessing.

"The funded debt of the United States is the addition of $3,000,000,000 to the previously realized wealth of the nation. It is three thousand millions added to the available active capital. To pay this debt would be to extinguish this capital and lose this wealth. To extinguish this capital and lose this wealth would be an inconceivably great national misfortune."

We can easily concevie why Jay Cooke, the alleged great financier, should give utterance to such an absurd statement. Mr. Cooke is an interested witness in the support of the ridiculous maxim "That a public debt is a public blessing." He was realizing millions in the way of commissions by negotiating the sale of bonds.

To attract the support of the manufacturers, he says:—

"The maintenance of our national debt is protection. The destruction of it by payment is bondage again to the manufacturers of Europe."

In his appeal to the national banking money power, he says:—

"That is not a hazardous opinion which declares that in less than twenty years our national bank circulation will be $1,000,000,000. The currency that sixty-one millions of people, unequaled in industry and untrammeled in enterprise, will require, has got to have the basis of a national debt. There is no other foundation for it to stand on that will impart to it at once safety and nationality."

It will be well to state here, that the man who gave utterance to these vicious propositions was overtaken with calamity, and the gigantic failure of his banking house heralded the great panic of 1873.

The national banks at once joined hands with the manufacturing interests, and brought their combined influence to bear upon congress.

On the first day of the session of Congress in 1867, Representative Kelley, known as "Pig Iron" Kelley, introduced the following resolution in the House:—

"Resolved, That the war debt of the country should be extinguished by the generation that contracted it, is not sustained by sound principles of national economy, and does not meet the approval of this house."

This resolution was adopted.

As a result of the combined influence of the national banking money power and the manufacturing interests, congress eventually repealed the tax on incomes, manufactures, railroads, insurance companies, and the tax on perfumes, bank checks, and reduced the excise tax on whisky and tobacco.

In all, the total taxation remitted by the general government, at the behest of the sordid wealth of the country, amounted to $227,000,000 per annum.

Such was the process by which ill-gotten accumulated wealth escaped taxation.

The national banking money power was not yet satisfied; its greed was insatiate; the more it received from the hands of the government the more ravenous its demands; and on the 14th of July, 1870, it procured the passage of the Funding Act through a venal and corrupt congress.

This act was supplementary to the Credit Strengthening Act of March 18, 1869, and it went one step farther by providing that the 5-20 bonds should be payable in coin. It authorized the Secretary of the Treasury to issue bonds to the amount of $200,000,000 in denominations of fifty dollars, or some multiple of that sum, redeemable in coin of the present standard value, at the pleasure of the United States, after ten years from the date of their issue, and bearing interest at the rate of five per cent. per annum, payable semi-annually in coin; also a sum not exceeding $300,000,000 of like bonds, the same in all respects, but payable at the pleasure of the United States, after fifteen years from their issue, and bearing interest at the rate of four and one-half per cent. per annum; he was further authorized to issue bonds to the amount of $1,000,000,000, the same in all respects as the others, but payable at the pleasure of the United States after thirty years from the date of their issue, and bearing interest at the rate of four per cent. per annum.

We quote from a portion of the law as follows:—

"All of which said several classes of bonds and the interest thereon shall be exempt from the payment of all taxes or duties of the United States, as well as from taxation in any form by or under state, municipal or local authority; and the said bonds shall set forth and express upon their face the above specified conditions, and shall, with their coupons, be made payable at the treasury of the United States."

The Secretary of the Treasury was authorized to sell these several classes of bonds, at not less than par, for coin, and to redeem the 5-20 bonds, hitherto exempted from payment in coin by the Credit Strengthening Act; or he was authorized to exchange the 5-20 currency bonds, at their face value for the coin bonds provided for by the Funding Act of July 14, 1870.

To exhibit the powerful influence exerted upon that congress which passed the Funding act of July 14, 1870, we will refer to a few facts that have become history.

When the Funding bill was originally introduced, section eight provided that on and after the 1st day of October, 1870, national banks should deposit registered bonds of any denomination not less than one thousand dollars, issued under the provisions of this Funding act, and no other, with the Treasurer of the United States as security for notes issued to national banking associations for circulation under the act of June 3, 1864. The banks were given one year in which to take advantage of this section to deposit the new bonds in lieu of the former, as security for their circulating notes. In case of failure to obey this act, their right to issue notes was forfeited.

On their failure to deposit bonds issued under the act of July 14, 1870, in lieu of the bonds then on deposit as security for their circulation, the Treasurer and the Comptroller of the Currency were authorized to call in and destroy their outstanding circulating notes, and to return the bonds held as security therefor to the association by whom they were deposited.

The bill containing this section originated in the senate, and after it passed that body and came up in the house for consideration, the national bankers swarmed in the halls of Congress and demanded that this section be stricken out.

At no one time during the history of the national banks did their combined power appear so formidable.

The house quailed in the presence of these money kings, and the section was stricken out, and the bill thus amended was sent back to the senate.

The demands and methods of the banks in seeking the defeat of this section had become so insolent that even Senator Sherman rebelled.

He said in reply to their imperious demands:—

"Mr. President, the three remaining sections of this bill apply to the national banks. That is much too great a theme for me to enter upon at this stage of the debate; but I will explain in a very few words the theory of those sections. The national banks are mere creatures of law. They hold their existence at the pleasure of Congress. We may, to-morrow, if it promotes the public interests, withdraw their authority. The franchise has been valuable to them.

"We think it right they should aid us in funding the public debt. They hold of our securities $346,000,000. Nearly all of these bear six per cent. interest in coin. We will not deprive them of any of them; we will not take from them the property they enjoy; we will not deny them even the payment of six per cent. gold interest as long as they are the owners of these bonds. But they hold the franchise of issuing paper money guaranteed by the United States, and which constitutes the circulation of our country; and we say that, enjoying this franchise, we now stipulate with them for the reduction of interest on the bonds they hold. The provisions of this bill are not arbitrary.

"We are about to retire and cancel our notes by the provisions of this act. We are about to give them the monopoly of the circulation of this country, the sole and exclusive privilege of issuing paper money. We have destroyed the state banks. And now what do we require in return? That they shall join us in reducing the burdens of the public debt; that they shall bear some little of their share of the loss of income which every holder of the public securities must suffer.

"Sir, national banks would be very unwise indeed to make issue on this question. If any man here is a friend to the national bank system, I can claim to be. I was here at its cradle, introduced the original banking bill, and advocated it, and also introduced the amendment to it, conducted it, and saw it passed. But if I believed now that the banks of the United States were unwilling to aid us in reducing the rate of interest on the public debt to the extent of the limited sacrifices they are called upon by this bill to make, I should certainly change very much my opinion of them and of the whole system.

"I wish now to record my deliberate judgment that in this conclusion to which we have been compelled to arrive by the action of the house we are doing the national banks a great injury, which will impair their influence and power among the people, and that the opposition of the national banks to this provision which would have required them to aid in the funding of the public debt, will tend more to weaken and destroy them than anything that has transpired since their organization. I do not see how we can go before the people of the United States and ask them to lend us gold at par for our bonds, when we refuse to require agencies of our own creation to take them; when we even refuse to require new banks not yet organized to take these new bonds, and when we refuse to require old banks, which have made on the average from fifteen to twenty per cent. annually upon the franchise. But, sir, the vote of the House shows the power of the national banks."

The Senate gave way to the banks, and these monopolies compelled Congress to submit to their will.

It would be presumed that Senator Sherman, judging from the vigor of his speech against these monopolies on this occasion, would subsequently oppose their future demands. Not so, however. He became a more devoted servant than ever in furthering the ambition of the national banking money power to monopolize the issue of paper money.

By an amendatory act of January 20, 1871, the secretary of the Treasury was authorized to increase the issue of five per cent. bonds, for which provision was made by the Funding Act, from $200,000,000 to $500,000,000, making a total interest charge upon the $1,500,000,000 of bonds so authorized to be issued, of $62,500,000 per annum.

The outrageous legislation embodied in this Funding Act becomes apparent to the reader.

In the first place, the 5-20 bonds, to the amount of $722,205,500, purchased with treasury notes, purposely depreciated by the Government at the demand of the gold gamblers of Wall street, were made redeemable in coin.

This resulted in a gratuity of many millions of dollars to the holders of these bonds, which was nothing more nor less than robbery under form of law.

Second, it created a vast debt, making an annual charge upon the industries of the people of $62,500,000, all of which, both principal and interest, was exempt from taxation, national, state, county, and municipal, creating a special privileged class who could not be compelled to contribute a farthing toward the expenses of that Government which gave them protection.

Not only were these bond holders expressly exempted from taxes, but these non-taxable bonds opened a wide door for extensive frauds upon the revenues of state and municipal authorities.

The process by which states, cities, counties, townships, and school districts were swindled out of taxes and revenues was by the shifting of the ownership, nominally at least, of these bonds around the various banks and capitalists who returned them as non-taxable.

For instance, banks and capitalists, when the time came for them to return their assessments of personal property, would report large holdings of these non-taxable bonds, which were obtained for the occasion, and since 1870, this resulted in swindling the various local governments out of countless millions of dollars in taxes.

The same process by which non-taxable greenbacks were shifted from hand to hand, to avoid the payment of taxes during the period required by law for the return of assessment lists for taxation, was adopted on a larger scale in the case of these non-taxable bonds. It set a premium on perjury.

As these bonds were held to a very large extent in the great cities of the country where taxation is very high, in some cases equalling four per cent. on the dollar, it will be seen that the actual rate of interest on these bonds ranged from seven to nine per cent. per annum.

Thus far the national banking money power succeeded in inducing Congress to grant every demand made by it. Not satisfied with the enormously valuable privileges bestowed upon it, this subtile power continued to appear at the opening of each session of the national legislature, and make new appeals for additional legislation in its interests.

Each new demand of the national banks met with prompt compliance from Congress, and the decrees of this organized, voracious money power were registered upon the statute books of the nation by the most corrupt legislative body in the world.

On January 20, 1871, a bill was rushed through Congress by which the Secretary of the Treasury was authorized, in his discretion, to pay the interest on the national debt every three months.

Notwithstanding the fierce opposition displayed by the national banks against the United States notes and treasury notes, in spite of the efforts of Congress to withdraw from circulation the war money of the country by funding this currency into interest-bearing, non-taxable, long-time bonds, this paper money directly issued by the United States was so popular with the people that a very large amount remained in the channels of trade.

The people revered the greenback and United States note, as that money which came forward in time of deadliest peril; which armed, equipped and paid more than two million patriots, whose magnificent bravery won the greatest battles of modern times, and whose heroism secured the perpetuity of American institutions; while gold, the money of kings, the loaded dice of stock gamblers, fled at the first approach of danger; gold, whose value appreciated with every defeat of the Union cause; gold, that vulture which fattened and thrived upon the carnage of the great civil war, laughed the appeals of the nation to scorn.

In consequence of the further demands of the national banks, Congress, on the 20th of June, 1874, amended the National Banking Act, which permitted these banks to withdraw the bonds deposited by them to secure the circulation of bank notes, and deposit, in lieu thereof as security, the non-interest-bearing notes issued by the Government. Prior to the passage of this amendment, United States bonds had risen to a premium in consequence of the various acts of Congress culminating in the Credit Strengthening Act, and, therefore, this act was adopted by Congress to enable the banks to withdraw the bonds deposited by them, and make a large profit by selling them for the premium, many of which had been originally purchased for less than sixty cents on the dollar.

The operation of the amendment effectually contracted the legal tender currency of the country, for the substitution of United States notes and treasury notes in lieu of the bonds, diminished the volume of legal tender currency afloat to an extent equal to the bonds so withdrawn.

During this period, the national banking money power began to advance the argument that the character and volume of money should be determined, not by the legislative power of the nation, but by what was called the "Business interests of the country."

It sought to educate the people to accept the doctrine, that it was dangerous to permit congress "To interfere with the dearest interests of the country," and that the solution of the money question must be settled by the national bankers, who assumed to hold the key to all monetary science.

President Grant was wonderfully impressed with this great discovery of the bankers and, in his message to congress, December 3, 1874, he gave utterance to this statement:—

"The experience and judgment of the people can best decide how much currency is required for the transaction of the business of the country. It is unsafe to leave the settlement of this question to Congress, the Secretary of the Treasury or the Executive."

The President, therefore, as far as lay in his power, tacitly surrendered the constitutional power of Congress and of the Executive to deal with questions of finance, and conferred it upon the national banks.

The people to whom reference is made in this quotation from the President, were the national bankers, and the chief executive was willing to transfer the power of issuing and controlling money to that class of men, whose sole ambition was the extortion of the highest rates of interest, and who loved to shave notes and bonds when they purchased, and exact a premium when they sold.

On the 24th of January, 1875, after the congressional election of 1874, which returned a great Democratic majority in the House of Representatives, the specie resumption act became a law.

The enactment of this measure carried into execution that part of the Credit Strengthening Act where the United States solemnly pledged its faith to make provisions for the redemption of the United States notes in coin, which now legally meant gold.

One section of this law provided for the substitution of fractional silver coins for the fractional currency; a subsequent section abolished the charge of one sixth of one per cent. for converting gold bullion into coin, thereby providing for the free coinage of gold at every United States mint.

The most important section of the Resumption Act is as follows:—

"That section 5777, of the Revised Statutes of the United States, limiting the aggregate amount of the circulating notes of the National Banking Associations, be, and is hereby repealed, and each existing banking association may increase its circulating notes in accordance with the existing law, without respect to said aggregate limit; and new banking associations may be organized in accordance with the existing law without respect to said aggregate limit; and the provisions of the law for the withdrawal and re-distribution of national bank currency among the several states and territories are hereby repealed; and whenever and so often as circulating notes shall be issued to any such banking association, so increasing its capital or circulating notes, or so newly organized as aforesaid, it shall be the duty of the Secretary of the Treasury to redeem the legal tender United States notes in excess of only $300,000,000 to the amount of eighty per centum of the sum of national bank notes so issued to any such banking association as aforesaid, and to continue such redemption as such circulating notes are issued until there shall be outstanding the sum of $300,000,000 of such legal tender United States notes, and no more. And on and after the 1st day of January, A. D., 1879, the Secretary of the Treasury shall redeem in coin the United States notes then outstanding on their presentation for redemption at the office of the assistant-treasurer of the United States, in the city of New York, in sums of not less than $50. And to enable the Secretary of the Treasury to prepare and provide for the redemption in this act authorized or required, he is authorized to use any surplus revenues from time to time in the treasury not otherwise appropriated, and to issue, sell, and dispose of, at not less than par in coin, either of the description of bonds of the United States described in the act of Congress approved July 14, 1870, entitled, 'An Act to Authorize the Re-Funding of the National Debt,' with like privileges and exemption, to the extent necessary to carry this act into effect, and to use the proceeds thereof for the purpose aforesaid."

A critical examination of the Resumption Act will disclose the sinister purpose of the organized national banking money power to carry into execution, to the letter, the instructions couched in the Hazard circular. One of the strange features of this act which assumes to restore specie payments, is found in the express language of this statute. While Congress, by its solemn legislative decree, provided for the redemption of United States non-interest legal tender notes in gold, it did not require the national banks to redeem their circulating notes in anywise whatever.

On the contrary, the so-called Resumption Act provided for the substitution of national bank notes for the non-interest-bearing legal tenders issued by the government, although the national banking law made the United States notes a fund to redeem national bank notes.

Again: it was a contraction of non-interest-bearing legal tender notes, and expansion by the additional issue of national bank notes, which were mere promissory notes of the banks, the latter to be loaned by the bankers at a high rate of interest to the business men of the country. These circulating bank notes cost the bankers one cent on the dollar, and the Government was the redeemer of this currency. It was gold redemption of the greenbacks by the nation, an inflation of paper money by the banks at a cost to them of one cent on the dollar.

It was a shrewd scheme to discredit the legal tender currency of the country, that the national banking money power might inherit that rich estate of issuing paper money.

Next, it repealed that part of the original National Bank Act which provided for the due distribution of the currency throughout the states and territories, West, as well as East, South, as well as North. And it speedily resulted in the absolute control of the volume of money by the opulent bankers of the East, for the great capitalists of New York City, Boston, Baltimore, Philadelphia, and other large eastern cities held ninety per cent. of the United States bonds, without which there could be no national bank circulation. The domicile of the bond holder determined the location of the national bank, and the location of the national bank fixed the point at which the currency of the country could only be obtained, and therefore, the productive energies of the West and South were at the mercy of the national banks. The two places fixed by this act for the redemption of legal tender notes were in New York City—the arena of gold gamblers, stock speculators, railroad wreckers—and San Francisco. No sum less than fifty dollars in United States notes would be redeemed.

The reason of this limitation is very apparent. The banks of New York City are the reserve agents for the many thousand banks scattered over the country, and, therefore, hold hundreds of millions of dollars in deposits.

By hoarding the legal tender notes received in the

ordinary course of business, the banks of New York City were enabled to accumulate many millions of United States notes, and present them for redemption at the sub-treasury; but the plain citizen who could not command fifty dollars of these notes was barred from the benefits of the Resumption Act.

The United States presented the key of the National Treasury to the national banks, with an implied invitation to help themselves to every thing in sight. It was a Government of national banks, for the national banks, and by the national banks.

Provision was made for the issue of bonds to obtain gold to redeem these legal tenders, and this was a part of the scheme to perpetuate the national debt, and as Jefferson said: "To swindle futurity on a large scale."

At the time of the passage of the laws upon which comment is made, General Grant was President of the United States.

The career of President Grant is one of the most unique and instructive in history. Of comparatively humble, but respectable origin, he did not, prior to the civil war, give any indications of winning that world-wide fame which has become the heritage of the American people.

That fratricidal strife was the tide that carried General Grant from obscurity to the highest pinnacle of renown. It was in the character of soldier that he gained an illustrious name.

In his character as a man, he gave abundant proof of many admirable traits, among which were magnanimity toward the vanquished, unimpeachable personal integrity, and lasting tenacity in his friendships, in which latter attribute he bore a striking resemblance to General Jackson.

Yet this distinguished man of iron nerve became as plastic as wax in the hands of those to whom he attached himself, and his confidence in his trusted advisers was shockingly abused for the furtherance of many selfish and dishonest schemes. It is this latter fact that gave birth to those shameless abuses and scandals which have sullied the pages of political history.

Many eminent public men are of the opinion that his administration of civil affairs did not tend to the enhancement of his fame.

A summary of the war legislation, in so far as it relates to the finances of the Government, exhibits these remarkable facts as to the existence of a remorseless money power:

First, Congress at the demand of the bullion brokers and gold gamblers of New York City and Boston, purposely depreciated the currency issued by the government by striking out its legal tender qualities, by refusing to receive its own money in payment of its taxes. It was high priced gold for the bond holder, and depreciated greenbacks for the patriotic soldier who offered up his life for his country.

Second, The passage of the national banking law, by which the government delegated its highest sovereign power—that of issuing money—to private corporations for private gain, resulting in a privileged class of capitalists, whose interests were wholly antagonistic to the welfare of the United States, thereby making a permanent creditor and debtor class, one the master, the other the servant.

Third, An alliance, offensive and defensive, of the national banking money power and the manufacturers, whose combined interests have dominated the legislation of Congress, by which the banks have practically secured a monopoly of the medium of exchange, and by which the manufacturers have secured a high protective tariff for their immediate benefit, and at the same time flooded their mills and factories with cheap foreign labor.

Fourth, The passage of laws, the effect of which was to enormously increase the untaxed wealth of a privileged class, who extort heavy tribute from the productive energy of the American people.

Fifth, The creation of a money power, foretold by Andrew Jackson, whose unlimited greed has appropriated to its own use the greatest portion of the wealth of the United States.

Sixth, A matured plan to perpetuate the public debt of the United States for the purpose of holding the people in subjection to the money power.

Seventh, An enormously extravagant administration of the Federal Government, as a part of the plan to fix a permanent debt on the nation.

Eighth, Senator Sherman, during all this period, was the chairman of the Finance Committee of the Senate, and he was the influential agent of the money power who shaped and molded that legislation, upon which was reared that imperial combination of moneyed influence which, to a very large extent, rules the press, the pulpit, the legislative bodies, and the courts of the country.

In view of the various financial measures enacted by Congress from 1865, to the passage of the Resumption Act of 1875, all of which tended to greatly appreciate stocks and bonds, and to divest the Government of its undoubted power to issue full legal tender United States notes, or greenbacks, the following significant extract from the most influential journal of Great Britain, the London Times, is hereby subjoined.

In 1865 the Times editorially stated:—

"If that mischievous financial policy which had its origin in the North American Republic during the late war in that country should become indurated down to a fixture, then that Government will furnish its money without cost.

"It will have all the money that is necessary to carry on its trade and commerce.

"It will become prosperous beyond precedent in the history of the civilized nations of the world. The brain and wealth of all countries will go to North America. That Government must be destroyed or it will destroy every monarchy on this globe."

CHAPTER III.

NATIONAL BANKS AND SILVER.

"The high-handed career of this institution imposes upon the constitutional functionaries of this government, duties of the gravest and most imperative character—duties which they can not avoid, and from which I trust there will be no inclination on the part of any of them to shrink."—Andrew Jackson.

The success of the national banking money power in securing control of Congress, and, through that body, an oppressive monopoly of the currency of the country, met the most sanguine expectations of the men who hoped to rule the industries of the people with an iron hand.

The outlines of that great scheme of the national banks, which aimed to throw the entire business of the country on a credit basis, were now plainly apparent, and it became patent that the plan was to be consummated by placing the entire volume of currency in the hands of the bankers.

Under the workings of the national bank system, all circulating bank notes, before they would reach the hands of the mass of the people and thus be thrown into the channels of trade, must first pass through the toll gates erected over the counters of the bankers, making them at once the lenders of money, and the great majority of our citizens, borrowers of that currency, gratuitously bestowed by the government upon the wealthiest moneyed corporations of the United States.

All the industries were compelled to pay usury to the most traitorous class of our citizens. The banks were enabled to lay the foundations of that colossal structure of credit, which has plunged the people into an abyss of indebtedness from whence they will not emerge for generations.

Up to the time of the passage of the Resumption Act, the banking monopoly saw no difficulty standing in its way to keep it from being the master of all the property and industry. While corrupt congresses, notorious for the infamous scandals which smirched the reputations of some of the foremost men of the Republican party, bartered away the most precious rights of the people, nature came to the rescue by affording a great supply of that most precious metal—silver.

The bank monopoly at once caught the alarm, and the plan was matured in London and Wall street to assassinate the silver dollar.

Under the free coinage of gold and silver, the national banks could not control the volume of money, and, therefore, the position taken by this monopoly was an essential part of that gigantic conspiracy to demonetize silver, and thus maintain its grasp on the property of the people; furthermore, a fight must be waged against the standard silver dollar as a part of the scheme to sustain the supremacy of New York City as the great money center of the country.

Moreover, an adequate supply of silver meant the freedom of the agricultural districts of the West and South from the financial domination of the cent per cent. men of the East.

The national bank autocrats saw, in the rich deposits of silver in the Western States, the danger that menaced their power, and they made haste to strike down the silver dollar, which, in their fears, would become the regenerator of the financial condition of the people. Silver dollars meant cash, national bank notes meant credit, and therefore the bond-holders and bankers of London and New York City decreed that silver must die.

As a preliminary statement of the reason for the opposition of national banks to the coinage of silver, it must be born in mind, that prior to the adoption of the Federal Constitution, the United colonies, under the Articles of Confederation, had no power to establish mints, and, therefore, they had no national system of money.

This want of uniform coinage and currency laws was one of the urgent reasons which led to the assembling of the constitutional convention that eventually framed the national charter.

This body of able and learned men, justly celebrated for their wisdom and knowledge, provided for a uniform system of money for the people. They knew that without a national system of coinage and currency, no people could become great in commerce and industry. The power of determining what should constitute money, was lodged in the general government by that part of section eight, of article one, of the constitution, which is as follows: "Congress shall have power to coin money, regulate the value thereof and of foreign coin."

The convention which framed this great instrument contained some of the ablest political economists and financiers of that day, among whom were Benjamin Franklin, Robert Morris, the eminent banker, James

Madison, Alexander Hamilton, and Gouveneur Morris. These distinguished men knew that the essential nature of money was its function as a medium of exchange, and they knew that this function was impressed by the sovereign power of the nation.

Hence, the power to coin money and to regulate its value, was decreed to fall within the sphere of the lawmaker, rather than left to the ability of those who corner gold and silver to enhance their profits.

The absurd theory of our modern statesmen that commerce, and not law, fixes the value of money has never been recognized as sound doctrine until the national banking monopoly demanded the power of issuing currency as a vested right.

Upon the adoption of the Constitution, and after the election and inauguration of General Washington to the presidency of the United States, Congress, on the 2d of April, 1792, enacted the first coinage law under the new order of things. The system of coinage adopted by Congress, was based on the decimal plan which sprung from the imperial intellect of Jefferson, to whom belongs the honor of inventing and establishing that great reform.

The Coinage Act of April 2, 1792, is as follows:—

"That the money of account of the United States shall be expressed in dollars or units, dimes or tenths, cents or hundredths, mills or thousandths, a dime being the tenth part of a dollar, a cent the hundredth part of a dollar, a mill the thousandth part of a dollar and that all accounts in the public offices and all proceedings in the courts of the United States shall be kept and had in conformity to this regulation.

"That a mint for the purpose of a national coinage be and the same is established, to be situated and carried on at the seat of the government of the United States for the time being.

"There shall be, from time to time, struck and coined at said mint, coins of gold, silver, and copper, of the following denominations, values and descriptions; viz., Eagles, each to be of the value of ten dollars, or units, and to contain 247½ grains of pure, or 270 grains of standard gold. Half eagles, each to be of the value of five dollars, or units, and to contain 123¾ grains of pure, or 135 grains of standard gold. Quarter eagles, each to be of the value of two and one-half dollars, and to contain 61⅞ grains of pure, or 67½ grains of standard gold. Dollars or units, each to be of the value of a Spanish milled dollar, as the same is now current, and to contain 371¼ grains of pure, or 416 grains of standard silver. Half dollars, each to be of half the value of the dollar or unit, and to contain 185⅝ grains of pure, or 208 grains of standard silver. Quarter dollars, each to be of one-fourth the value of the dollar or unit, and to contain 92$\frac{13}{16}$ grains of pure, or 104 grains of standard silver. Dimes, each to be one-tenth of the value of a dollar or unit, and to contain 37⅛ grains of pure, or 41¾ grains of standard silver. Half dimes, each to be of the value of one-twentieth of a dollar or unit, and to contain 18$\frac{9}{16}$ grains of pure, or 20⅝ grains of standard silver. Cents, each to be of the value of one hundredth part of a dollar, and to contain 11 pennyweights of copper. Half cents, each to be of the value of half a cent, and to contain 5½ pennyweights of copper."

The ratio of the value of gold to silver in all coins provided for by the act of April 2, 1792, was fixed at fifteen to one, that is to say, the statute made fifteen pounds weight of pure silver equal in value in all payments to one pound weight of pure gold.

Section Fourteen of this act provided for the free coinage of gold and silver in the following language:—

"That it shall be lawful for any person or persons to

bring to the said mint gold and silver bullion, in order to their being coined; and that the bullion so brought shall be there assayed and coined as speedily as may after the receipt thereof, and that free of expense to the person or persons by whom the same shall have been brought."

The free coinage thus provided for by the act of April 2, 1792, placed gold and silver coinage directly in the hands of the people. The money thus coined would not be compelled to go through the banks as intermediaries before it reached the channels of trade.

This coinage law was the joint product of the study and research of Hamilton and Jefferson, and it made the silver dollar containing $371\frac{1}{4}$ grains of pure silver, the unit of account in the exchange of commodities and for the payment of debts.

It may be inquired why the Spanish milled dollar was taken as the basis of the American unit of account.

At that time, Spain was the great dominating power in the western hemisphere, and she exercised jurisdiction over what is now Texas, California, New Mexico, Nevada, Mexico proper, the Central American States, the greater portion of South America and the West Indies.

It was the mines of the Spanish colonies, from 1500 to 1800, that poured hundreds of millions of the precious metals into the lap of European commerce.

A single mine of South America produced silver to the amount of $600,000,000.

During the period that the Spanish colonies poured forth their streams of wealth, and saved the dying industries of Europe from total extinction, the chivalry of Christian England went forth in their piratical craft in a time of peace, and plundered the Spanish treasure ships of their rich cargoes. British historians yet gloat over the naval prowess that robbed an unoffending power in time of profound quiet.

The reasons why this young republic appropriated the Spanish milled dollar as the model upon which to base its coinage laws were these: First, a large number of Spanish coins were in circulation in this country, and these coins were of a very high standard of purity; second, the people were familiar with the Spanish milled dollar, and its adoption as money saved the expense of re-coinage; third, the United States maintained an extensive commerce with the Spanish West Indies, and the adoption of a coin similar to the Spanish dollar facilitated trade wonderfully, and gave the enterprise of this country the advantage over that of foreign nations, whose system of coinage did not correspond with that of Spain and her colonies.

To give the reader a correct understanding of the coinage laws of the United States from 1790 to 1873, the following summary of the various enactments of congress providing for the mintage of gold and silver coins will be necessary.

The act of congress of March 2, 1799, fixed the value of foreign coins, and made them legal tender.

On April 10, 1806, the gold coins of Great Britain and Portugal, as well as those of France and Spain, were made legal tender for the payment of all debts and demands within the United States. The same act of congress made the Spanish milled dollar and the crown of France, which were silver coins, legal tender and current in this country.

During the year 1805 President Jefferson suspended

the coinage of the silver dollar at the United States mint.

The reasons adduced by him in ordering the cessation of the coinage of the dollar were stated in a report made by Mr. Ingham, Secretary of the Treasury under President Jackson.

Secretary Ingham said that President Jefferson ascertained that the newly coined silver dollars, being of full weight, bright, and clean, were shipped out of the country by speculators; second, it was a useless expense to coin these dollars, when the law made the foreign silver coins full legal tender for the payment of all debts, public and private; third, it was more desirable to coin silver bullion into half dollars, quarter dollars, dimes and half dimes to serve as change.

By act of Congress, March 5, 1823, the gold coins of Great Britain, Portugal, France and Spain were received in payment by the United States on account of sales of public lands.

By act of June 25, 1834, the following silver coins were made of legal value, and passed current as money within the United States for the payment of all debts and demands at the rate of one hundred cents to the dollar; viz., The dollars of Mexico, Peru, Chili, and Central America; this act fixed the value of the Brazilian dollar, and the silver five-franc piece of France and it passed current.

By the same act, the gold coins of Great Britain, Portugal, Brazil, France, Spain, Mexico, and Columbia were made legal tender for the payment of all debts and demands within the United States.

On the 28th of June, 1834, the quantity of gold in the eagle, or ten dollar piece, was reduced from 247½ grains of pure gold to 232 grains, the amount of standard gold in that coin was reduced from 270 grains to 258 grains.

Under the act of April 2, 1792, the legal ratio of silver to gold was fifteen to one, which ratio undervalued gold.

Since 1803, France and the Latin countries adopted a legal ratio of fifteen and one half of silver to one of gold, and as a consequence, gold, being undervalued in the United States, was withdrawn from circulation here, and sold abroad at a profit by the bullion brokers who were ever on the alert for gain.

The change made the act of June, 1834, undervalued silver, the ratio of that metal to gold being fixed at fifteen and ninety-eight one-hundredths to one.

But the principal reason assigned for the overvaluation of gold by the act of June 28, 1834, was to provide coins of large denominations to take the place of the notes and bills issued by the United States Bank. In other words, President Jackson fought the United States Bank with a gold coinage as a legitimate weapon to conquer that money power.

It has become the settled policy of those financiers who so urgently advocate a single standard of gold, to point to the act of June 28, 1834, as the establishment of that system. This has been the gist of the numberless arguments of the gold standard advocates, constantly reiterated in the halls of congress and elsewhere, with a brazen disregard of truth that approaches desperation.

The congressional legislation by which a very large volume of gold coin was brought into circulation after 1834, was directly opposed to that policy which secured the demonetization of silver in 1873.

It is an absolute falsehood to assert that the single standard of gold was adopted by this nation in 1834, for the plain reason that the mints of the United States remained open to the free and unlimited coinage of both gold and silver, and the law made these coins full legal tender for the payment of all debts and demands, both public and private.

The silver dollar still remained the unit of account.

By the act of January 18, 1837, a slight change was made in the alloy in the gold and silver coins. The standard of purity was fixed at nine tenths of pure metal to one tenth of alloy.

By this alteration in the purity of the coin, the standard was raised, and, therefore, the weight of the silver dollar and fractional silver coins was slightly reduced.

The material part of that act is as follows:—

"The standard for both gold and silver coins of the United States shall hereafter be such that of one thousand parts by weight, nine hundred shall be of pure metal and one hundred of alloy, and the alloy of silver coins shall be of copper, and the alloy of the gold coins shall be of copper and silver, provided that the silver does not exceed one half of the alloy.

"Of the silver coins the dollar shall be of the weight of $412\frac{1}{2}$ grains, the half dollar of the weight of $206\frac{1}{4}$ grains, the quarter dollar of the weight of $103\frac{1}{8}$ grains, the dime or tenth part of a dollar of the weight of $41\frac{1}{4}$ grains, and the half dime or twentieth part of a dollar of the weight of $20\frac{5}{8}$ grains.

"And that dollars, half dollars, quarter dollars, dimes and half dimes shall be legal tender of payment according to their nominal value for any sums whatever.

"Of the gold coins, the weight of the eagle shall be 258 grains, that of the half eagle 229 grains, and of the quarter eagle $64\frac{1}{2}$ grains.

"And that for all sums whatever, the eagle shall be a legal tender of payment for ten dollars, the half eagle for five dollars, and the quarter eagle for two and one-half dollars."

The alloy in the silver dollar was reduced in quantity, while the pure silver of 371¼ grains, as originally fixed by the act of April 2, 1792, was retained in the standard dollar, and it remained the unit of account and was of unlimited legal tender.

This fact is borne out by the act of March 3, 1849, which provided for the coinage of double eagles and one dollar gold pieces.

We will quote the exact language of this statute, which is as follows:—

"There shall be from time to time struck and coined at the mint of the United States and branches thereof—conformably in all respects to law, and conformably in all respects to the standard for gold coins now established by law—coins of gold of the following denominations and value; viz., double eagles, each to be of the value of twenty dollars or units, and gold dollars, each to be of the value of one dollar or unit.

"For all sums whatever the double eagle shall be a legal tender for twenty dollars, and the gold dollar shall be a legal tender for one dollar."

This statute explicitly recognizes a unit, and that unit of the exchange value of money was the silver dollar, the coinage of which was provided for by the act of April 2, 1792. The value of these gold pieces were respectively fixed by referring them to a unit, and up to this time the sole unit of account in the United States from which calculations were made was the silver dollar.

By act of congress February 21, 1853, a change

was made by reducing the weight of the fractional silver coins.

The language of this statute is as follows:—

"That the weight of the half dollar or piece of fifty cents shall be 192 grains, and the quarter dollar, dime and half dime shall be respectively one-half, one-fifth and one-tenth of the weight of the half dollar.

"The silver coins issued in conformity with the above section shall be legal tenders in the payments of debts for all sums not exceeding five dollars.

"From time to time there shall be struck and coined at the mint of the United States and the branches thereof conformably in all respects to the standard of gold coins now established by law, a coin of gold of the value of three dollars or units."

This act, which was the first legislation limiting the legal tender quality of silver coins, is pointed to by the single gold standard advocates as a demonetization of silver.

In order that we may ascertain the intention of Congress in enacting this law, it will be necessary to look at contemporaneous history, the evils sought to be corrected, and the remedy applied.

The highest courts of the land have adopted this principle as the cardinal rule in the interpretation and construction of statutory law, and it is a safe one for the ordinary individual.

At the time of the passage of this act of Congress, the bullion in the silver was more valuable as a commodity than the bullion in the gold dollar, consequently the silver dollars were withdrawn from circulation and sold as bullion in the European markets at a profit.

To remedy this, Congress reduced the weight of the

fractional silver coins, and limited their legal tender debt-paying power, but left the coinage of the silver dollar free and unlimited.

Congress correctly foresaw that the owners of silver bullion, from motives of self interest, would not coin their bullion into silver dollars, when they would be gainers by its coinage into light weight fractional coins.

It would require 412½ grains of standard silver for a one dollar piece, or unit, but it would need only 384 grains for the coinage of two half dollar pieces.

The limitation of legal tender power of the fractional silver coins under the act of 1853, was embodied in that law for the express purpose of preventing their exportation to foreign countries.

Another reason for the enactment of this statute arose from the fact that the miners of California and Australia were pouring hundreds of millions of dollars of gold into the arteries of commerce, and a number of leading financial writers of France and Germany urged their respective countries to demonetize gold, for the express purpose of increasing the value of bonds and annuities.

Michel Chevalier, a member of the Council of State of Napoleon III. at this time, published a work entitled, "The Probable Fall in the Value of Gold."

In this volume he strongly urges the demonetization of gold, giving as his reason for this position that it was becoming too abundant, and that its purchasing power had greatly fallen.

Chevalier says:—

"If we would particularize the persons who would be more or less deeply affected by the fall in gold, we have only to select those whose income will not find itself augmented naturally and by a self-adjusting process, in exact proportion to the fall, in gold. The national creditor is the characteristic type of this class of sufferers. All those persons whose incomes, expressed in monetary units, remain the same would be injured by the change to the extent of the half of their income, all other things being equal.

"All commodities excepting gold and every kind of property excepting that of which the income is, from the present, fixed, as is the case with government funds, ought, from the moment that the monetary crisis is terminated, to have attained in a gold currency double the price which they are at present worth. It will be the same eventually with wages (that is to say wages would double), and with all personal services, whether rendered in the factory or on the farm, or from the liberal professions."

In summing up his arguments in favor of the demonetization of gold, Chevalier states the following conclusions:—

"Thus as a definite analysis, the properties of lands, houses, and other real estate, manufacturers, merchants, and their auxiliaries of every kind; public functionaries of all ranks; and also those who follow the different learned professions, will all find themselves in the end compensated in the new state of things with advantages which they now enjoy, all other things being equal. It is another class of persons, the national creditor, whom we have previously defined in a general way who have to submit to a sacrifice in the proportion to the fall in the precious metal."

In his plea for the bond holders, Chevalier, unlike those American financiers who worship a single standard, displays one admirable trait. He truthfully states the reasons why he urges the destruction of gold as money. He says that the coinage of those large amounts of gold from the mines of California and Australia will double the volume of money, and therefore diminish its purchasing power one-half, and that the bond holder would suffer loss.

Finally, Chevalier sums up the effect of a change from falling prices to rising prices, in which he said:—

"In time the change will profit those who live by present labor; it will injure those who live on the fruits of past labor, be it their own or that of their fathers. In this respect it will act in the direction with the greater part of those evolutions which are accomplished in virtue of the great law of civilization to which ordinarily we assign the noble name of Progress.

"It remains to add that in society as it is at present organized, the number is very small of those whom it can truly be said that they live on the fruits of past labor. Real property, rents, and the interest of investment depend in such a degree on the present labor of those who pay them, that in an important sense those who receive them live rather on the present labor of others than upon past labor."

Chevalier positively admits that a small volume of money benefits a very small number, and those are the most undeserving.

The American gold standard advocate is not so frank in his reasons for a single standard. Every national banker, and single gold standard financier is in favor of that system of finance, because the laboring man, the widow, and the orphan will be the sole beneficiaries of a contracted volume of money?

The arguments of that class of political economists teem with figures, showing that the workingmen, widows, and orphans are the chief stock holders in national banks, loan and trust companies, and that they constitute the largest class of depositors in savings banks, hence, the fear of this philanthropic (?) class of disinterested patriots, that the poor toiler, the friendless widow and orphan must be protected by a single standard of gold!

Germany and some of the smaller European states actually demonetized gold in 1857, and adopted a silver standard.

From the action of these states in thus attempting to cripple the United States by demonetizing gold, and going on a silver basis, a great struggle arose in Germany and Austria to obtain silver.

Therefore, to prevent these countries from drawing their supplies of that metal from the United States, Congress reduced the weight and limited the legal tender power of the minor silver coins, and thus the volume of silver in circulation here was protected from exportation to the silver standard countries.

Furthermore, Congress now endeavored to supply the people with a uniform system of gold and silver coinage, and, in the execution of that policy, enacted the law of March 3, 1853, which provided that the Secretary of the Treasury should establish an assay office in the city of New York, for the assaying and casting of gold and silver bullion and foreign coin into bars, ignots, or disks, and the assistant treasurer at New York was made the treasurer of such assay office; and he was authorized, upon the deposit of gold or silver bullion or foreign coin, and the ascertainment of its net value, "To issue his certificate of the net value thereof payable in coins of the same metal as that deposited."

The certificates so issued by the assistant treasurer were made receivable at any time within sixty days from the date thereof, in the payment of all debts due to the United States at the port of New York for the full sum therein certified.

Thus the foreign importer, in the payment of the duties on goods, wares, and merchandise at the custom house, would take his foreign coin to the assay office, have its fineness determined, obtain a certificate for the amount of its value, and pay the duties imposed upon his goods with said certificate. Such foreign coins were cast into bars and transformed into coins of the United States.

By the act of February 21, 1859, Congress fixed the value of the fractional parts of the Spanish pillar dollar, and the Mexican dollar as follows; viz., "The fourth of a dollar, or piece of two reals at twenty cents, the eighth of a dollar, or piece of one real at ten cents, and the sixteenth of a dollar, or half-real, at five cents."

These coins at the valuations thus fixed by law were receivable at the Treasury of the United States, the post offices, and land offices, as legal tender for the payment of debts and demands.

The former acts of Congress, authorizing the circulation of foreign gold and silver coins, and declaring the same a legal tender for the payment of debts, were repealed.

The reason for the repeal of former laws declaring foreign gold and silver coins legal tender was based on the following facts: first, the United States had become, with the discovery of the rich gold mines of California, the greatest producer of gold in the world, and it endeavored to supply the people with a volume of coins stamped in American mints; second, nearly sixty years had elapsed since the passage of the first coinage law, and the capacity of the United States mints being greatly increased, Congress, by said repeal, aimed at a re-coinage of the foreign gold and silver coins into American coins, and by this means supply a homogeneous circulation of gold and silver.

Six years had elapsed since the passage of the law of March 3, 1853, authorizing the issuing of certificates for deposits of foreign coin, and the act of February 21, 1859, was merely an accumulative statute to that act for the transformation of foreign coin into that of the United States.

The latter act did not take away the privilege of the holder of foreign coin to receive certificates of deposit at the assay office in New York City, and the issuance of these certificates was of great convenience to the owner of bullion and such coin. From the act of March 3, 1853, dates the origin of gold and silver certificates.

From 1859 to 1873 but few changes were made in the coinage laws, and these were comparatively unimportant in their nature.

Prior to 1861, the annual production of silver in the United States never exceeded the value of $100,000, on the other hand, the amount of gold produced in the mines of California, from 1848 to the outbreak of the war, amounted to hundreds of millions of dollars. The greatest amount of gold produced from American mines in any one year was in 1853, when it reached the enormous sum of $65,000,000. The total product of gold from the mines of the United States, from 1848 to 1861 inclusive, reached the grand total of $700,000,000.

In the year 1859, that great deposit of silver, the

Comstock Lode, was discovered in Nevada, and from this period the United States is reckoned among the greatest producers of silver in the world.

In 1860 the production of silver had risen to $150,000, which, up to this period, was the greatest amount produced in the United States in any one year. In the same year the production of gold in California alone was $45,000,000 in value.

In 1863, the value of the product of silver had risen to $8,500,000.

In 1867, silver to the amount of $13,500,000 was produced from the mines of the west—chiefly in Nevada.

The production of gold for the same year was $51,725,000.

At this period, the national debt had reached the enormous sum of $2,700,000,000, the interest of which was payable in coin.

The whole annual product of the gold mines in the United States would scarcely suffice to pay one-half of the annual interest charge upon the national debt held by the national banking money power.

Therefore, the control of the gold supply of the country was in the firm grasp of the national banks and bond holders.

It is much easier for the money power to manipulate the volume of gold than that of silver, in as much as gold contains a much greater value in a proportionately smaller bulk than silver.

Again, gold bullion is converted into coins of large denominations, chiefly ten and twenty dollar gold pieces; while silver is coined into dollars and fractional parts thereof.

From the foregoing facts, gold is the money of the wealthy, while silver is the money of the laborer.

It is the small coins that most actively circulate in the channels of trade; it is gold that is hoarded by the miser and the capitalist.

The small coins that are in active circulation have always eluded every effort to hoard them in large quantities.

The rapid increase in the production of silver in the United States meant the financial liberation of the people from the money power of the East. The prospects for an enormous supply of silver from the western mines threatened the supremacy of New York City and London as the money markets of the world.

The owner of silver could take his bullion to the mint, have it coined into standard silver dollars of full legal tender debt paying power, receive them after their mintage, and transact business by their means; he was not under the necessity, when in need of money, to make application to a national bank for a loan of its circulating notes, whose sole credit rested on the solvency of the United States. He was not compelled to pay TOLL to the national banks for the use of their debts as money.

The national banking money power could not control the silver dollar, as long as the law authorized its free coinage, and consequently, a gigantic conspiracy was formed in London and New York City to demonetize silver.

This great money power whose almost absolute control of the currency was surely driving all business to a credit basis, deliberately planned the destruction of that precious metal whose value has been far more stable than that of gold.

CHAPTER IV.

CONSPIRACY OF NEW YORK AND LONDON BANKERS AND BOND HOLDERS TO DEMONETIZE SILVER.

"I have before me the record of the proceedings of this House on the passage of that measure, a record which no man can read without being convinced that the measure and the method of its passage through this House was a 'colossal swindle.' I assert that the measure never had the sanction of this House, and it does not possess the moral force of law."—William S. Holman.

Prior to the demonetization of silver in the United States, England and Portugal were the only nations whose standard of monetary value was based on gold.

After the great Napoleonic wars which convulsed Europe for so many years, finally ending in the overthrow of the military power of France at Waterloo in 1815, the national debt of England reached a colossal figure, exceeding four billions of dollars.

This vast debt was created by the efforts of Great Britain in her struggle to crush Napoleon.

The greater portion of this immense burden on the industries of the people of that country was purchased at a very heavy discount by the bond holders.

At this time England was the great naval power of the world, and her merchant vessels entered the ports of every civilized and semi-civilized nation; and she made good her boast that she was "Mistress of the Seas."

In 1816, England adopted a single gold standard as the basis of her financial system. Silver was made a legal tender to an amount not exceeding forty shillings for any one payment.

This act of parliament was procured through the influence of the immensely wealthy bankers and fund holders, with the sole aim of enhancing the value of the vast debt held by them, and with the avowed purpose of perpetuating its existence.

Sir Moreton Frewen, an eminent writer and financier of London, charges that this measure was instigated by the capitalists of England, and that it was class legislation of the worst type.

The financial system thus adopted by parliament during the ministry of Lord Liverpool consisted of gold as the standard of value, silver as subsidiary coin used in the small transactions of business, and notes issued by the Bank of England, the latter being a credit currency redeemable in gold by the bank.

In 1844, the charter of the Bank of England was amended by act of parliament, by which that corporation must pay for all gold bullion or mutilated coins offered at its counter, the sum of three pounds, seventeen shillings, and nine pence for each ounce of gold tendered to it. This price was equivalent to eighteen dollars and ninety-two cents in money of the United States.

This act of parliament was the matured result of the policy of Sir Robert Peel, at that time the Prime Minister of England, and it fixed the price of gold throughout the British empire in every part of the world, and it gave notice to the owners of gold bullion everywhere, that this great bank stood ready, at all times, to pay the price fixed by the law of its creation. Gold would never go below that price, although there was no limitation in the law by which the bank was forbidden to pay more for that precious metal.

The evident purpose of that policy fixing the minimum value of gold was the prohibition of speculation in it by bullion brokers. Another important object of the passage of this law was to make London the money market of the world, and therefore the center of exchange.

Moreover, at the time of the parliamentary act of 1844, the colossal debt of England was payable in gold, and the fund-holding class of Great Britain was instrumental in procuring the passage of this act, fixing the minimum price of gold by law with the avowed intention of enhancing its purchasing power over all other forms of property.

The policy embodied in the Peel Act is the basis of the financial system of England.

After the close of the civil war in America, Great Britain had become a large holder of United States bonds, railway stocks, and securities, and other obligations of this country, to the amount of many hundreds of millions of dollars, the great majority of which were purchased for a pittance.

The great banking houses of New York City and Boston are the agents of the money lending classes of Great Britain, and are the mere echoes of Lombard street, London.

Since the discovery of the enormously rich gold mines of Australia, which rivaled those of California, she ranks as one of the leading producers of gold, while the mines of the latter are giving indications of exhaustion.

The production of silver in the British empire was

comparatively small, while that of the United States was rapidly increasing in value.

The amount of English capital invested in the national banking system is unknown, but is undoubtedly very large, and it was the bankers of London who suggested the scheme of the present national banking law, as shown by the circular issued by James Hazard, of which mention was made in the second chapter of this work.

It must be borne in mind that, from 1862 to 1873, United States Senator John Sherman was the Chairman of the Finance Committee of the national Senate, to which was referred, and which framed and moulded the various financial measures placed upon the statute books of the nation. He was the great predominating power in the financial legislation of Congress.

In 1867, the great International Exposition at Paris was held, to which the nations of the world were invited by the Emperor of France.

Secretary of State Seward, on behalf of the United States, appointed Samuel B. Ruggles as the commissioner to represent this country at that magnificent undertaking.

Napoleon III, the Emperor of France, on the 4th of January, 1867, extended an invitation to all the powers, including the United States, to hold a conference in Paris, for the purpose of extending the principles of the Latin Union throughout the commercial world. This Union was originally formed December 23, 1865, by and between France, Italy, Greece, Belgium, and Switzerland, whereby these five nations agreed to establish for themselves jointly a system of common coinage, weights, and measures, as a means for the promotion of commerce.

The monetary system adopted by the Latin Union provided for the free coinage of both gold and silver at a ratio of fifteen and one-half to one.

It also made provision in its articles by which any other nation could become a member of the convention.

Article 12 of the union was as follows; viz.,—

"Any other nation can join the present convention by accepting its obligations and adopting the monetary system of the union in regard to gold and silver coins."

The invitation of the French Emperor was accepted by the commercial nations of Europe and America, and Mr. Ruggles was appointed as the representative of the United States.

Senator Sherman, who was the Chairman of the Committee on Finance of the Senate, on information of the receipt of the invitation of the Emperor, visited London in the spring of 1867, prior to the convening of this monetary conference. After consulting with the London bankers and capitalists, he hastened to Paris where the conference was to convene in the near future, and in reply to a note of Ruggles, sent a communication to that gentleman in which he advocated the adoption of a single gold standard.

The material part of this remarkable letter to Mr. Ruggles is as follows:—

"Hotel Jardin des Tuileries, May 18, 1867.

"My Dear Sir: Your note of yesterday, inquiring whether Congress would probably, in future coinage, make our gold dollar conform in value to the gold 5-franc piece, has been received.

"There has been so little discussion in Congress upon the subject that I cannot base my opinion upon anything said or done there.

"The subject has, however, excited the attention of several important commercial bodies in the United States, and the time is now so favorable that I feel quite sure that Congress will adopt any practical measure that will secure to the commercial world a uniform standard of value and exchange.

"The only question will be how this can be accomplished.

"The treaty of December 23, 1865, between France, Italy, Belgium, and Switzerland, and the probable acquiescence in that treaty by Prussia, has laid the foundation for such a standard.

"If Great Britain will reduce the value of her sovereign 2 pence, and the United States will reduce the value of her dollar something over 3 cents, we then have a coinage in the franc, dollar, and sovereign easily computed, and which will readily pass in all countries; the dollar as 5 francs, and the sovereign as 25 francs.

"This will put an end to the loss and intricacies of exchange and discount.

"Our gold dollar is certainly as good a unit of value as the franc, and so the English think of their pound sterling. These coins are now exchangeable only at a considerable loss, and this exchange is a profit only to brokers and bankers. Surely each commercial nation should be willing to yield a little to secure a gold coin of equal value, weight, and diameter, from whatever mint it may have been issued.

"As the gold 5-franc piece is now in use by over 60,000,000 of people of several different nationalities, and is of convenient form and size, it may well be adopted by other nations as the common standard of value; leaving to each nation to regulate the divisions of this unit in silver coins or tokens.

"If this is done France will surely abandon the impossible effort of making two standards of value. Gold coins will answer all the purposes of European commerce. A common gold standard will regulate silver coinage, of which the United States will furnish the greater part, especially for the Chinese trade."

It will be seen from the statements volunteered by Mr. Sherman in his letter to Mr. Ruggles, that he was endeavoring to leave the impression upon this conference, that the United States was in favor of a single standard of gold; and that the effort of France in making two standards of value was impossible; and that a common gold standard would regulate silver coinage.

The position assumed by Senator Sherman had immense influence, for at that time he held the most important position on the leading committee of the United State Senate.

He spoke as one having authority, and gave his moral influence to that financial policy which has finally destroyed one-half of the money metals of the world.

While in England Mr. Sherman was evidently ascertaining the views of influential persons and bodies upon this proposed change of the coinage laws. We quote further from his letter to Mr. Ruggles in which he says:—

"In England many persons of influence and different chambers are earnestly in favor of the proposed change in the coinage. The change is so slight with them that an enlightened self-interest will soon induce them to make it, especially if we make the greater change in our coinage."

This letter is an important link in the chain of evidence that tends to prove a concerted plan on the part of British and American financiers to effect a momentous change in the coinage laws of the United States, a change that resulted in the demonetization of silver.

Senator Sherman furnished the best of evidence, that, "Many persons of influence and different chambers" of a foreign country were taking deep interest in the coinage laws of a nation to which they owed no allegiance.

Mr. Sherman was a leading member of the United States Senate, and it is deducible from his writings that, after ascertaining the views of these "influential persons and chambers" as to what system of coinage would be satisfactory to them, he immediately proceeded to carry them into effect by introducing a bill to that end.

The phrase, "Many persons of influence and different chambers," undoubtedly signifies the bankers and other fund holding classes of Great Britain, who were interested in securing legislation that would enhance the value of stocks and bonds.

This letter of the Senator to Commissioner Ruggles is a voluntary confession from Mr. Sherman, that he was in London in conference with influential interests which were earnestly in favor of the proposed change in the standard of money.

On the 30th of May, 1867, Mr. Ruggles transmitted a communication to Secretary of State Seward, in which he states that the letter of Senator Sherman urging the adoption of a single standard of gold was laid before the International Committee having the question of uniform coin under special examination.

In this communication, Mr. Ruggles informs the Secretary of State of an interview held with Napoleon, with reference to the coinage of gold and silver, in the course of which the French emperor propounded the following significant question: "Can France do anything more in aid of the work?"

We here quote the reply of Mr. Ruggles to the question of the emperor in his own language; viz.,—

"To which it was replied, France can coin a piece of gold of twenty-five francs, to circulate side by side on terms of absolute equality with the half eagle of the United States and the sovereign, or pound sterling, of Great Britain, when reduced, as they readily might be, precisely to the value of twenty-five francs. The emperor then asked, 'Will not a French coin of twenty-five francs impair the symmetry of the French decimal system?' To which it was answered, 'No more than it is affected, if at all, by the existing gold coin of five francs;' that it was only the silver coins of France which were of even metric weight, while every one of its gold coins, without exception, represented unequal fractions of the meter.

"It was then stated to the Emperor that an eminent American statesman, Mr. Sherman, Senator from Ohio, Chairman of the Finance Committee of the Senate of the United States, and recently in Paris, had written an important and interesting letter, expressing his opinion that the gold dollar of the United States ought to be and readily might be reduced by Congress, in weight and value, to correspond with the gold 5-franc piece of France; that the letter was now before the International Committee having the question of uniform coin under special examination, to which letter, as being one of the best interpretations of the views of the American people, the attention of the public authorities of France was respectfully invited. The emporer then closed the audience by repeating the assurances of his gratification that the important international measure in question was likely to receive active support from the United States.

"The letter of Mr. Sherman, above referred to, dated the 18th of May, 1867, originally written in English, was presented in a French translation a few days afterward to the International Committee in full session, where it was received with unusual interest and ordered by the committee to be printed in both languages. A copy is herewith transmitted for the information of the Department of State."

Upon a final vote in the conference, the influence of England and John Sherman succeeded in defeating the adoption of a bi-metallic standard, and a single standard of gold was agreed upon by the conference with but a single dissenting vote. Hence, it will be seen that John Sherman and Samuel B. Ruggles were the two eminent persons whose influence was exerted against the adoption of the sagacious policy of the Emperor of France, which had for its object an international standard of both gold and silver at a ratio of fifteen and one-half to one.

It is evident that Senator Sherman exerted his great influence in defeating international bi-metallism, the adoption of which would have resulted in untold benefits, not only to the United States, but to the world at large.

As the first step for carrying into execution the scheme outlined in his Paris letter, Senator Sherman, during the second session of the Fortieth Congress, introduced Senate bill 217, entitled, "A bill in relation to coinage of gold and silver."

The material parts of this proposed measure are contained in sections one, two, and three, which are as follows:—

"Be it enacted by the Senate and House of Representatives of the United States of America in Congress assembled, That, with a view to promote a uniform currency among the nations, the weight of the gold coin of five dollars shall be $124\frac{9}{20}$ troy grains, so that it shall agree with a French coin of twenty-five francs, and with the rate of thirty-one hundred francs to the kilogram;

and the other sizes or denominations shall be in due proportion of weight, and the fineness shall be nine-tenths or 900 parts fine in 1,000.

"Section 2. And be it further enacted, That, in order to conform the silver coinage to this rate and to the French valuation, the weight of the half dollar shall be 179 grains, equivalent to 116 decigrams; and the lesser coins be in due proportion, and the fineness shall be nine-tenths. But the coinage of silver pieces of one dollar, five cents, and three cents shall be discontinued.

"Section 3. And be it further enacted, That the gold coins to be issued under this act shall be a legal tender in all payments to any amount; and the silver coins shall be a legal tender to an amount not exceeding ten dollars in any one payment."

The language of these sections expressly demonetizes the standard silver dollar of 412½ grains as the unit of account by omitting to provide for its coinage.

The only silver coins that could be issued from the mints of the United States, should this bill become a law, would be the half dollar, the quarter dollar, and ten cent piece, which would be legal tender for the payment of debts to any amount not exceeding ten dollars in any one payment; while gold coin would be unlimited legal tender to any amount.

The bill was referred to the Finance Committee, of which Mr. Sherman was Chairman, and on the 9th of June, 1868, he reported it back favorably, and he advocated its passage in an elaborately written argument.

He thus spoke of the system of coinage which the bill proposed to establish as follows:—

"The second inquiry of your committee was whether the plan proposed by the Paris conference was the best mode to accomplish the end desired.

It proposes:—

1. A single standard exclusively of gold.

2. Coins of equal weight and diameter.

3. Of equal quality of fineness—nine-tenths fine.

4. The weight of the present 5-franc gold piece to be the unit.

5. The coins of each nation to bear the names and emblems prepared by each, but to be legal tenders public and private in all.

"The single standard of gold is an American idea, yielded reluctantly by France and other countries, where silver is the chief standard of value. The impossible attempt to maintain two standards of value has given rise to nearly all the debasement of coinage of the last two centuries. The relative market value of silver and gold varied like other commodities, and this led first to the demonetization of the more valuable metal, and second to the debasement or diminution of the quantity of that metal in a given coin."

This was the first effort ever attempted to fasten a single gold standard upon the American people, and the declaration of Senator Sherman that, "The single standard of gold is an American idea," was misleading, as he well knew at the time when he used this language in the report quoted.

The single gold standard is of British origin, as the parliamentary acts of 1816 and 1844 conclusively prove beyond any doubt whatever.

Mr. Sherman also used the following language in that report:—

"France, whose standard is adopted, makes a new coin similar to our half eagle. She yields to our demand for the sole standard of gold, and during the whole conference evinced the most earnest wish to secure the co-operation of the United States in the great object of unification of coinage."

The report above quoted is proof positive, that Senator Sherman and Mr. Ruggles had placed the United States in a false light before the Paris conference.

The distinguished Senator avers that France yielded to "Our demand for the sole standard of gold"—an astonishing piece of intelligence to his colleagues.

For, be it remembered, Mr. Ruggles was a mere appointee of the President, and Congress had not, either by bill or resolution, authorized Mr. Ruggles to represent the United States at any monetary conference whatever.

The attitude of Mr. Ruggles on the proposed change of the coinage laws of the United States was purely voluntary, and, in fact, the views of this gentleman and Senator Sherman were distinctly repudiated by Congress at its earliest opportunity.

The same committee, by Senator Morgan, of New York, submitted a minority report against the passage of the bill. We quote at length from this powerful document:—

"In June last, while the Universal Exposition was in progress, an international monetary conference was held in Paris under the presidency of the French minister of foreign affairs.

"Delegates from the several European nations were present.

"Mr. Samuel B. Ruggles represented the United States, and his report on the subject has been communicated to Congress through the Department of State. From this it appears that a plan of monetary unification was there agreed upon, the general features of which are:

"1. A single standard, exclusively of gold.
"2. Coins of equal weight and diameter.
"3. Of equal quality, nine-tenths fine.
"4. The weight of the present 5-franc gold piece to the unit, with its multiples. The issue by France of a new coin of value and weight of 25 francs was recommended.

"5. The coins of each nation to continue to bear the names and emblems preferred by each, but to be legal tenders, public and private, in all.

"Senate bill 217 is designed to carry into effect this plan. Its passage would reduce the weight of our gold coin of $5, so as to agree with a French coin of 25 francs.

"It determines that other sizes and denominations shall be in due proportion of weight and fineness, and that foreign gold coin, conformed to this basis, shall be a legal tender so long as the standard of weight and fineness are maintained. It requires that the value of gold coin shall be stated both in dollars and francs, and also in British terms, whenever Great Britain shall conform the pound sterling to the piece of $5.

"It conforms our silver coinage to the French valuation, and discontinues the silver pieces of $1, 5, and 3 cents, and limits silver as a legal tender to payments of $10. The 1st of January, 1869, is fixed as the period for the act to take effect.

"The reduction which this measure would effect in the present legal standard value of the gold coin of the United States would be at the rate of three and a half dollars to the hundred, and the reduction in the legal value of our silver coinage would be still more considerable.

"A change in our national coinage so grave as that proposed by the bill should be made only after the most mature deliberation. The circulating medium is a matter that directly concerns the affairs of everyday life, affecting not only the varied, intricate and multiform interests of the people at home, to the minutest detail, but the relations of the nation with all other countries as well. The United States has a peculiar interest in such a question. It is a principal producer of the precious metals, and its geographical position, most favorable in view of impending commercial changes, renders it wise that we should be in no haste to fetter ourselves by any new international regulation based on an order of things belonging essentially to the past."

Further on in his report, the distinguished Senator, with rare power of fact and argument, exposes this new scheme of finance proposed to be fastened upon the American people by the bill introduced by Sherman.

He shows that the American continent produced four-fifths of the silver of commerce; that the mines of Nevada have taken high rank; and that Mexico alone supplied more than half of the world's grand total.

He points out that silver money is the key to the commerce of the western hemisphere, and of the trade of China, Japan, India, and other Oriental countries.

The Senator says:—

"The American continent, too, produces four-fifths of the silver of commerce. The mines of Nevada have already taken high rank, and Mexico alone supplies more than half the world's grand total. Our relations with the silver-producing people, geographically most favorable, are otherwise intimate.

"Manifestly our business intercourse with them can be largely increased, a fact especially true of Mexico, which, for well-known political reasons seeks the friendliest understanding. This must not be overlooked.

"These two streams of the precious metals, poured into the current of commerce in full volume, will produce perturbations marked and important. Other countries will be affected, but the United States will feel the effect first and more directly than any other.

"The Pacific railway will open to us the trade of China, Japan, India, and other Oriental countries, of whose prepossessions we must not lose sight. For years silver, for reasons not fully understood, has been the object of unusual demand among these Asiatic nations, and now forms the almost universal medium of circulation, absorbing rapidly the silver of coinage. The erroneous proportion fixed between silver and gold by France, and which we are asked to copy, is denuding that country of the former metal. Our own monetary system, though less faulty, is not suitably adjusted in this respect. The silver dollar, for instance, a favorite coin of the native Indian and distant Asiatic, has well-nigh disappeared from domestic circulation, to reappear among the eastern peoples, with whom we more than ever seek close intimacy.

"As they prefer this piece we do well to increase rather than discontinue its coinage, for we must not deprive ourselves of the advantages which its agency will afford, and 'it would be useless to send dollars to Asia inferior in weight and value to its well-known Spanish and American prototype.'"

Mr. Ruggles says that nearly all the silver coined in the United States prior to 1858 has disappeared. A remedy is not to be found in the adoption of a system that undervalues this metal, for that commodity, like any other, shuns the market where not taken at its full value to find the more favorable one.

It is a favorite metal, entering into all transactions of daily life, and deserves proper recognition in the monetary system.

"It is said that 'To promote the intercourse of nations with each other, uniformity in weights, coins, and measures of capacity is among the most efficacious agencies.' Our weights, coins, and measures now correspond much more nearly to the English than to the French standard. Our commerce with Great Britain is nine times greater than with France, and if the former does not adopt the Paris system of coinage—and we have no assurance that she will—the United States would certainly commit a serious error in passing this bill. No argument is needed to enforce this. And what of the rising communities? A properly adjusted coinage would stimulate commerce with those great parts of the continent lying south and southwest of us, with the West Indies and the countless millions of trans-Pacific countries. We stand midway on the thoroughfare of traffic between these two widely-separated races. Our railways, canals, our natural highways and merchant marine may be made to control their carrying trade.

"But here, as everywhere else, a well-adjusted coinage becomes a wand of power in the hand of enterprise. Tokens are not wanting to mark the favor in which the United States are held by China. The unusual honor recently conferred by that government upon a citizen of this country was not alone because of his fitness as an ambassador at large, but was a mark as well of a friendly disposition toward this country. Future harmony of intercourse is assured, too, by their adoption as a text-book in diplomatic correspondence of a leading American authority on international law. Much might also be said about the growing partiality of Japan towards this country, but it is enough that the recent opening of certain ports indicates an enlightened change in the politics of these two old empires, of which commerce, especially our own, is availing itself."

This patriotic document pilloried the rascality of that scheme, which would destroy the immense mineral wealth of the western hemisphere by the destruction of silver money.

Further on in the same report, Senator Morgan exposes the fallacy of this so-called international system of coinage embodied in the Sherman bill. The genuine Americanism of his nature is finely illustrated by the concluding language of that celebrated report.

He continues:—

"Our coinage is believed to be the simplest of any in circulation, and every way satisfactory for purposes of domestic commerce; it possesses special merits of every-day value, and should not, for light reasons, be exchanged where the advantages sought to be gained are mainly theoretical, engaging more properly the attention of the philosopher than the practical man. The instincts of our people lead them to believe that we are on the eve of important business changes, and we may therefore safely hold fast for the present to what experience has proven to be good, following only where clear indications may lead, and a future of great prosperity opens to our country.

"The war gave us self-assertion of character, and removed many impediments to progress; it also proved our ability to originate means to ends. Its expensive lesson will be measurably lost if it fails to impress upon us the fact that we have a distinctive American policy to work out, one sufficiently free from the traditions of Europe to be suited to our peculiar situation and the genius of our enterprising countrymen.

"The people of the United States have been quick to avail themselves of their natural advantages. Not only the public lands and the mines of precious metals, but our political institutions, have likewise powerfully operated in our favor, and will continue to do so with increasing force."—(Senate Report, Com. No. 117, 40th Congress, 2d Sess., Page 13.)

Judging from the language of the report just quoted, the great Senator from the Empire state was a firm believer in the power of the American people to legislate upon domestic financial questions without the aid or consent of foreign powers and potentates.

Were he alive at the present day, how his indignation would be aroused at the successive journeyings to England by American monetary commissioners, who have humiliated our national self-respect by getting down on their knees before the "Old Lady of Thread Needle Street," London, and begging for her assistance in the solution of our financial problems.

The report of Senator Morgan was the death knell of

the bill, and no attempt was made to bring it up again while Mr. Morgan was a member of the Senate.

After the retirement of Mr. Morgan from the United States Senate, March 4, 1869, a revision of the mint laws was undertaken.

Mr. Boutwell, Secretary of the Treasury, John J. Knox, Deputy Comptroller of the Currency, and Mr. Linderman, Director of the mint, all of whom were devoted adherents of the national banking system, and a single standard of gold, framed a bill containing seventy-one sections, the object of which was ostensibly a revision of the mint laws of the United States.

On April 25, 1870, this bill, prepared by the Treasury clique, was transmitted by Secretary Boutwell to John Sherman, chairman of the Finance Committee, with a recommendation that it be adopted by Congress.

Nowhere in the report of Secretary Boutwell, which accompanied this bill, was any mention made of any change in the system of coinage, but he called it, "A bill revising the laws relative to the mint, assay office, and coinage of the United States."

This proposed measure, which purported to be a mere codification of the mint laws, in reality provided for the demonetization of the silver dollar.

On the 28th of April, 1870, the bill was introduced into the United States Senate by Mr. Sherman, and was referred to the Committee on Finance.

On December 19, 1870, it was reported back to the Senate with amendments.

On January 9, 1871, the bill came up in the Senate and was discussed in Committee of the Whole.

That the reader may understand the process by which legislation can be surreptitiously pushed through Congress, it must be borne in mind that the various committees of the Senate and House of Representatives have immense power to control the passage of laws.

A measure is introduced into either branch of Congress, it is referred to the appropriate committee which takes charge of the bill, considers it in all its phases, and makes a report for or against its passage. The report of the committee, in a majority of cases, is the foundation of the action of that branch where it was originally proposed.

Therefore, it is the various committees of Congress which exert a powerful influence upon the fate of bills, as such reports are generally taken to be absolutely true by the members of that body.

The bill as amended passed the Senate on the 10th of January, 1871; and on the 13th of the same month it reached the House and was ordered to be printed.

On February 25, 1871, Mr. Kelley, chairman of the Committee on Coinage, reported the bill back with an amendment, in the nature of a substitute, when it was again printed and re-committed.

The bill was never heard of at that session and it never was debated in the House for a single moment.

On March 9, 1871, Mr. Kelley introduced a bill in the Forty-second Congress, when it was ordered to be printed, and referred to the Committee on Coinage when appointed.

On January 9, 1872, the bill was reported by Mr. Kelley, chairman of the Coinage Committee, with the recommendation that it pass.

In the report made by Mr. Kelley to the House, the general objects of the bill were pointed out by him.

He informed the House that it had been prepared in the Treasury Department for the purpose of codifying and simplifying the mint laws. He stated to the House that the most important change made by the bill was that creating a Director of the mint, with headquarters in the Treasury Department. Mr. Maynard, a member of the Committee on Coinage, made the following statement of the scope of the bill; viz. :—

"This bill is symmetrical in all its parts; it is a mere revision of the mint laws, suggested by the Secretary of the Treasury, and concurred in by every man who sees the difficulty of managing mints and assay offices, scattered over this country as they are, without having a responsible head. Its sole function is to so codify the laws, and to appoint a responsible head under the Secretary of the Treasury."

On the 10th of January, 1872, the House resumed consideration of the bill, and it was finally re-committed to the Committee on Coinage, Weights, and Measures for a report. The committee reported the bill to the House on April 9, 1872.

Mr. Hooper, of Massachusetts, who was in charge of the bill, made a lengthy explanation of its provisions, and the only allusion made by him with reference to the silver dollar is the following; viz. :—

"Section 16 re-enacts the provisions of existing laws defining the silver coins and their weights, respectively, except in relation to the silver dollar, which is reduced in weight from 412½ to 384 grains; thus making it a subsidiary coin in harmony with the silver coins of less denomination, to secure its current circulation with them. The silver dollar of 412½ grains, by reason of its bullion and intrinsic value being greater than its nominal value, long since ceased to be a coin of circulation, and is melted by manufacturers of silverware. It does not circulate now in commercial transactions with any country, and the convenience of those manufacturers in this respect can better be met by supplying small stamped bars of the same standard, avoiding the useless expense of coining the dollar for that purpose. The coinage of the half dime is discontinued, for the reason that its place is supplied by the copper-nickel 5-cent piece, of which a large issue has been made, and which, by the provisions of the act authorizing its issue, is redeemable in United States currency."— (See Cong. Globe, Part 3, Page 2,306, 2d Sess., 42d Congress.)

Mr. Hooper correctly stated the weight and fineness of the dollar contained in the bill pending, and as it finally passed the House, but he does not state that it was a legal tender for only five dollars. From the tenor of his remarks and the character of his argument, it could have been justly inferred that the purpose of this bill was to reduce the weight of the silver dollar so that it would circulate on a parity with that of gold, as at this time the value of the silver dollar exceeded that of gold by a fraction over three per cent.

During the debate on the bill, Hon. Clarkson N. Potter, member of Congress from New York, opposed its passage in a speech of great length.

The speech of Mr. Potter excited a very warm controversy, and those who were urging the passage of the bill, seeing the determined and aggressive opposition brought to bear against it, professedly abandoned it, and brought in a substitute which they asserted was entirely free from the objections brought against the original measure.

On the 27th of May, 1872, Mr. Hooper obtained the floor and made a statement as follows; viz.:—

"I desire to call up the bill (H. R., No. 1,427) revising and amending the laws relative to mints, assay offices, and coinage of the United States. I do so for the purpose of offering an amendment to the bill in the nature of a substitute, one which has been very carfully prepared, and which I have submitted to the different gentlemen in this House who have taken a special interest in the bill. I find that it meets with universal approbation in the form in which I offer it. I move that the rules be suspended and that the substitute be put on its passage."

Mr. Brooks: I ask the gentleman from Massachusetts [Mr. Hooper] to postpone his motion until his colleague on the committee, my colleague from New York [Mr. Potter] is in his seat.

Mr. Hooper, of Massachusetts: It is so late in the session that I must decline waiting any longer.

Mr. Brooks: I would again suggest to the gentleman that he should wait until my colleague comes in.

Mr. Hooper, of Massachusetts: I cannot do so.

Mr. Holman: I suppose that it is intended to have the bill read before it is put on its passage.

The Speaker: The substitute will be read.

Mr. Hooper, of Massachusetts: I hope not. It is a long bill, and those who are interested in it are perfectly familiar with its provisions.

Mr. Kerr: The rules can not be suspended so as to dispense with the reading of the bill?

The Speaker: They can be.

Mr. Kerr: I want the House to understand that it is attempted to put through this bill without being read.

The Speaker: Does the gentleman from Massachusetts [Mr. Hooper] move that the reading of the bill be dispensed with?

Mr. Hooper of Massachusetts: I will so frame my motion to suspend the rules that it will dispense with the reading of the bill.

The Speaker: The gentleman from Massachusetts moves that the rules be suspended and that the bill pass, the reading thereof being dispensed with.

Mr. Randall: Can not we have a division of that motion?

The Speaker: A motion to suspend the rules cannot be divided.

Mr. Randall: I should like to have the bill read, although I am willing that the rules shall be suspended as to the passage of the bill.

The question was put on suspending the rules and passing the bill without reading; and (two-thirds not voting in favor thereof) the rules were not suspended.

The Congressional Record from which he have quoted is proof that it was a cunning move on the part of Mr. Hooper to push a measure through the House during the closing hours of its session, and that he sought to do this during the temporary absence of those members who were aware of his plan, and who were opposed to the consummation of the scheme. This unscrupulous tool of the money power did not even want this bill read so that its contents would become known, as that would defeat its passage.

In this dilemma, Mr. Speaker Blaine came to the rescue of Mr. Hooper, and suggested to the latter that he move the suspension of the rules, so that the bill could be passed without reading.

The suggestion of Speaker Blaine was promptly acted on by Mr. Hooper, but the motion to suspend the rules and pass the bill without reading failed for want of a two-thirds vote.

Mr. Hooper thereupon moved that the substitute be read, that the rules be suspended and the bill passed, which action had been prompted by Speaker Blaine.

We give the proceedings of the House verbatim; viz.:

Mr. Hooper, of Massachusetts: I now move that the rules be suspended, and the substitute for the bill in relation to mints and coinage passed; and I ask that the substitute be read.

The clerk began to read the substitute.

Mr. Brooks: Is that the original bill?

The Speaker: The motion of the gentleman from Massachusetts [Mr. Hooper] applies to the substitute, and that on which the House is called to act is being read.

Mr. Brooks: As there is to be no debate, the only chance we have to know what we are doing is to have both the bill and the substitute read.

The Speaker: The motion of the gentleman from Massachusetts being to suspend the rules and pass the substitute, it gives no choice between the two bills. The House must either pass the substitute or none.

Mr. Brooks: How can we choose between the original bill and the substitute unless we hear them both read?

The Speaker: The gentleman can vote "aye" or "no" on this question whether this substitute shall be passed.

Mr. Brooks: I am very much in the habit of voting "no" when I do not know what is going on.

Mr. Holman: Before the question is taken up on suspending the rules and passing the bill, I hope the gentleman from Massachusetts will explain the leading changes made by this bill in the existing law, especially in reference to the coinage. It would seem that all the small coinage of the country is intended to be recoined.

Mr. Hooper of Massachusetts: This bill makes no changes in the existing law in that regard. It does not require the recoinage of the small coins."—(Cong. Globe, Part 5, Page 3,883, 2d Sess., 42d Congress.)

The question being taken upon the motion of Mr. Hooper, the rules were suspended by an aye and nay vote and the bill passed.

The scheme was forced through the House by the

downright falsehoods of Samuel Hooper, a banker of Boston, aided by the trickery and the manipulation of parliamentary rules by Mr. Speaker Blaine.

The facts in the case were, that the provisions of the original bill abandoned by Mr. Hooper, and those of the substitute afterward passed, were practically the same.

The bill was now transmitted to the Senate where it went into the hands of the Finance Committee, which, on December 16, 1872, reported the bill back with amendments.

On January 7, 1873, additional amendments were reported which were ordered to be printed with the bill.

Section 16 of the substitute passed by the House was in the following language, viz.:—

"That the silver coins of the United States shall be a dollar, a half dollar or 50-cent piece, a quarter dollar or 25-cent piece, and a dime or 10-cent piece; and the weight of the dollar shall be 384 grains; the half dollar, quarter dollar, and the dime shall be, respectively, one-half, one-quarter and one-tenth of the weight of said dollar, which coins shall be a legal tender, at their nominal value, for any amount not exceeding five dollars in any one payment."

This section of the substitute was identical with that of the original bill which was withdrawn by Mr. Hooper; and it will be seen that silver was demonetized by its provisions, by which the free and unlimited coinage thereof was taken away from that metal, and its legal tender debt paying power limited to the insignificant sum of five dollars for any one payment.

Section 15 of the substitute passed by the House was stricken out by the Finance Committee of the Senate in the way of amendment. When the question on the amendment striking out section 15 was before the Senate it was agreed to by that body. The next amendment was to strike out the word seventeen in the 17th section of the substitute, and this amendment made section 17 of the substitute, read 16 of the bill as amended by the Senate.

The number of each succeeding section was changed accordingly.

The several sections of the substitute were taken up in their changed numeral order until section 19 of the substitute as passed by the House was reached, which, by the striking out of section 15 of said substitute, became section 18 of the amended Senate bill.

This latter section provided for the inscription and mottoes to be impressed upon the coins to be issued under this bill.

A debate arose upon this question, and Senator Casserly, of California, called attention to the omission of the eagle upon the gold dollar, three dollar gold piece, the silver dollar, half dollar and quarter dollar.

Senator Sherman gave the following explanation; viz. :—

Mr. Sherman: "If the Senator will allow me, he will see that the preceding section provides for coin which is exactly interchangeable with the English shilling and the 5-franc piece of France; that is, a 5-franc piece of France will be the exact equivalent of a dollar of the United States in our silver coinage; and in order to show this wherever our silver coin shall float— and we are providing that it shall float all over the world —we propose to stamp upon it, instead of our eagle, which foreigners may not understand, and which they may not distinguish from a buzzard or some other bird, the intrinsic fineness and weight of the coin."—(Cong..

Globe, Part 1, Page 672, 3d Sess., 42d Congress, 1872-73.)

This public declaration of Senator Sherman, in reply to the question of Senator Casserly, is one of the mysteries of this transaction. He had charge of this bill, and the Congressional Globe shows that what afterward became section 15 of the bill as amended by the Senate was never read nor acted upon by that body.

The French 5-franc piece, about which Mr. Sherman spoke in his reply to Senator Casserly, was the equivalent of a silver dollar containing 384 grains of silver, mentioned in section 16 of the substitute, now section 15 of the amended bill before the Senate.

In 1874, upon the discovery of the demonetization of silver, said section 15 of the amended Senate bill, which was now the law, was ascertained to read as follows:—

"The silver coins of the United States shall be a trade dollar, a half dollar, or 50-cent piece, a quarter dollar, or 25-cent piece, a dime, or 10-cent piece; and the weight of the trade dollar shall be 420 grains troy; the weight of the half dollar shall be 12 grams and one-half of a gram; the quarter dollar and the dime shall be, respectively, one-half and one-fifth of the weight of said half dollar; and said coins shall be a legal tender at their nominal value for any amount not exceeding five dollars in any one payment."

That this section of the coinage law, providing for the mintage of a trade dollar containing 420 grains of silver, was not in the bill when the debate arose upon the inscriptions and mottoes designed to be placed upon the coins provided for by this act, is evident from the answer made by Sherman to the inquiry of Mr. Casserly; for the reason that the debate arose over section 18 of the amended bill, while the provision for the coinage of silver was embraced in the preceding section 15 of the amended act. Said section 15 was formerly 16 of Mr. Hooper's substitute.

The parliamentary procedure in the consideration of bills in both Houses of Congress is to read each section separately, take a vote upon its passage, and thus act upon each section consecutively.

The bill so amended went to the House of Representatives for its concurrence in the Senate amendments.

Speaker Blaine appointed Messrs. Hooper and Stoughton as the Committee of Conference on the part of the House; Senators Sherman, Scott, and Bayard, three of the most radical single gold standard men in Congress, were appointed conferees on the part of the Senate.

The Conference Committees met, and, with the exception of a few trifling amendments, agreed to the provisions of the bill as it came from the Senate. They made their reports to their respective Houses, and the bill became a law on the 12th of February, 1873.

We now come to a singular act on the part of Sherman when the bill came up for final passage in the Senate.

During his career as chairman of the Finance Committee of the Senate, we have seen him in the city of London, in 1867, next he appears at Paris in the same year, and throws his influence in behalf of the single standard of gold, then he introduces a bill in Congress in 1868 for the demonetization of silver. Afterward, during the year 1870, he brings forward the bill framed by Secretary Boutwell, of which mention has been made heretofore. He reports bill after bill for the adoption of a single standard of gold, and now he votes against the act of February 12, 1873, which was finally the fruition of his efforts.

This incomprehensible action is the strangest episode in the long public career of the Great Demonetizer, and many explanations have been volunteered for this apparently inconsistent conduct.

In a speech in the United States Senate, Mr. Sherman attempted the following explanation of his course which led to the demonetization of the silver dollar, he says:—

"The old silver dollar was dropped out, in the revision, and why? Simply because it was not in use. No law repealed the silver dollar; it was simply dropped out—there was no such coin in use. It could not circulate because, in 1872 and 1873, the silver dollar was worth more than the gold dollar. As it had not been coined for twenty years it was dropped out from among the coins of the United States."

With his consistent and usual disregard of facts, Senator Sherman avers that no silver dollars had been coined for the period of twenty years prior to the demonetization act of February 12, 1873. This statement was made in the face of the official report of the director of the United States mint for the year 1873, in which it is shown that 1,117,136 standard silver dollars were coined in the calendar year of 1871, that 1,118,600 were coined in the year 1872, and in the one month and twelve days from January 1, 1873, to February 12, 1873, 296,000 of standard silver dollars were coined.

The excuse tendered by Mr. Sherman for the passage of the act of February 12, 1873, is that the silver dollar was worth more than the gold dollar. The silver dollar so "dropped out" contained 412½ grains of silver. Now, if the reasons stated by Mr. Sherman for the omission of the coinage of the silver dollar by that act were valid and controlled his action, why did the honorable Senator amend that act in committee by increasing the number of grains in the silver dollar to 420, thus making its bullion value greater than before the passage of this act?

His strange logic is as follows: First, prior to its demonetization, the silver dollar was more valuable than that of gold, hence it would not circulate; therefore, as a remedy to increase its circulation, the value of the bullion in the silver dollar must be made greater.

In other words, the silver dollar was worth three and one-fourth cents more than that of gold and the former was hoarded or sold abroad; therefore, to obviate this difficulty in the way of increasing the circulation of that dollar, the weight was increased from 412½ to 420 grains, and its overvaluation from three and one-fourth cents to five cents.

With such sophistry as the above, Mr. Sherman sought to delude the American people.

The manner in which the act of February 12, 1873, was slipped through both Houses of Congress has excited endless controversies which rage even to this day.

Senator Sherman, in his speech of August 30, 1893, made a labored defense of his conduct during the passage of the bill demonetizing silver. He asserts that the measure was fully and thoroughly debated, but the Congressional Globe of that period conclusively proves that such was not the fact.

On the other hand, many Senators and Representatives of long service in Congress, including the sessions of 1870-71-72-73, renowned for their ability and integrity, have declared time and again that false statements were made by those having charge of the bill, that these statements were relied on by the various members, and that those who voted for the measure never knew or even suspected that silver would be demonetized by its passage.

The public men making these statements bear such high reputation for truth and integrity, that their testimony does not require the sanction of an oath to carry conviction.

One exceedingly strong circumstance that adds great weight to the charge of fraud in the passage of the act of February 12, 1873, lies in the fact that Senators Nye and Stewart, who represented the state of Nevada—the greatest silver producing territory in America—voted in favor of the bill.

Will any sane person suppose that these two Senators would knowingly vote for a measure which would ruin the immensely rich silver mines of that state that had honored them by an election to the United States Senate?

It is preposterous.

The following statements of leading members of Congress furnish a solution to this memorable controversy.

Mr. Holman, in a speech delivered in the House of Representatives July 13, 1876, said, with reference to the act of February 12, 1873:—

"I have before me the record of the proceedings of this House on the passage of that measure, a record which no man can read without being convinced that the measure and the method of its passage through this House was a 'colossal swindle.' I assert that the measure never had the sanction of this House, and it does not possess the moral force of law."—(Cong. Record, Vol. IV, Part 6, Appendix, Page 193, 1st Sess., 44th Congress.)

This is the statement of a man renowned as the "Watch Dog of the Treasury," and whose vigilance during his long career in Congress has saved the nation hundreds of millions of dollars.

Mr. Birchard, a republican member of Congress from Illinois, in a speech in the House on July 13, 1876, said:—

"The coinage act of 1873, unaccompanied by any written report upon the subject from any committee, and unknown to the members of Congress, who without opposition allowed it to pass under the belief, if not assurance, that it made no alteration in the value of the current coins, changed the unit of value from silver to gold."—(Same Cong. Record, Page 4,560.)

Mr. Cannon, a republican member of Congress from the same state, in a speech on July 13, 1876, said:—

"This legislation was had in the Forty-second Congress, February 12, 1873, by a bill to regulate the mints of the United States, and practically abolish silver as money by failing to provide for the coinage of the silver dollar. It was not discussed, as shown by the Record, and neither members of Congress nor the people understood the scope of the legislation."—(Same Cong. Record, Appendix, Page 197.)

Again on August 5, 1876, Mr. Holman in speaking of that bill said:—

"The original bill was simply a bill to organize a Bureau of mines and coinage. The bill which finally passed the House and which ultimately became a law was certainly not read in this House."

On the same day in the course of the same speech he said:—

"It was never considered before the House as it was passed. Up to the time the bill came before this House for final passage the measure had simply been one to establish a bureau of mines; I believe I use the term correctly now. It came from the Committee on Coinage, Weights, and Measures. The substitute which finally became a law was never read, and is subject to the charge made against it by the gentleman from Missouri [Mr. Bland], that it was passed by the House without a knowledge of its provisions, especially upon that of coinage.

"I myself asked the question of Mr. Hooper, who stood near where I am now standing, whether it changed the law in regard to coinage. And the answer of Mr. Hooper certainly left the impression upon the whole House that the subject of coinage was not affected by that bill."—(Cong. Record, Vol. IV, Part 6, Page 5,237, 1st Sess., 44th Congress.)

Mr. Bright, of Tennessee, said of this law:—

"It passed by fraud in the House, never having been printed in advance, being a substitute for the printed bill; never having been read at the Clerk's desk, the reading having been dispensed with by an impression that the bill made no material alteration in the coinage laws; it was passed without discussion, debate being cut off by operation of the previous question. It was passed to my certain information, under such circumstances that the fraud escaped the attention of some of the most watchful as well as the ablest statesmen in Congress at that time. '. . . Aye, sir, it was a fraud that smells to heaven. It was a fraud that will stink in the nose of posterity, and for which some persons must give account in the day of retribution."— (Cong. Record, Vol. VII, Part 1, Page 584, 2d Sess. 45th Congress.)

Senator Allison, on February 15, 1878, when House bill 1,093, to authorize the free coinage of the standard silver dollar, and to restore its legal tender character was under consideration, stated:—

"But when the secret history of this bill of 1873 comes to be told, it will disclose the fact that the House of Representatives intended to coin both gold and silver, and intended to place both metals upon the French relation instead of on our own, which was the true scientific position with reference to this subject in 1873, but that the bill afterward was doctored, if I may use that term, and I use it in no offensive sense of course—"

Mr. Sargent interrupted him and asked him what he meant by the word "doctored."

Mr. Allison said:—

"I said I used the word in no offensive sense. It was changed after discussion, and the dollar of 420 grains was substituted for it."—(Cong. Record, Vol. VII, Part 2, Page 1,058, 2d Sess. 45th Congress.)

General Garfield, in a speech made at Springfield, Ohio, during the fall of 1877, said:—

"Perhaps I ought to be ashamed to say so, but it is the truth to say that, I at that time being Chairman of the Committee on Appropriations, and having my hands overfull during all that time with work, I never read the bill. I took it upon the faith of a prominent democrat and a prominent republican, and I do not know that I voted at all. There was no call of the yeas and nays, and nobody opposed that bill that I know of. It was put through as dozens of bills are, as my friend and I know, in Congress, on the faith of the report of the chairman of the committee; therefore I tell you, because it is the truth, that I have no knowledge about it."—(Cong. Record, Vol. VII, Part 1, Page 989, 2d Sess., 45th Congress.)

Senator Howe, in a speech delivered in the Senate on February 5, 1878, said:—

"Mr. President, I do not regard the demonetization of silver as an attempt to wrench from the people more than they agree to pay. That is not the crime of which I accuse the act of 1873. I charge it with guilt compared with which the robbery of two hundred millions is venial."—(Cong. Record, Vol. VII, Part 1, Page 754, 2d Sess., 45th Congress.)

Senator Thurman, on the 15th of February, 1878, in debate said:—

"I can not say what took place in the House, but know when the bill was pending in the Senate we thought it was simply a bill to reform the mint, regulate coinage, and fix up one thing and another, and there is not a single man in the Senate, I think, unless a member of the committee from which the bill came, who had the slightest idea that it was even a squint toward demonetization."— (Cong. Record, Vol. VII, Part 2, Page 1,064, 2d Sess., 45th Congress.)

Mr. Kelley, a republican member of Congress from Pennsylvania, in a speech delivered in the House in 1879, in speaking of the act of February 12, 1873, said:—

"All I can say is that the Committee on Coinage, Weights, and Measures, who reported the original bill, were faithful and able, and scanned its provisions closely; that as their organ I reported it; that it contained provision for both the standard silver dollar and the trade dollar. Never having heard until a long time after its enactment into law of the substitution in the Senate of the section which dropped the standard dollar, I profess to know nothing of its history; but I am prepared to say that in all the legislation of this country there is no mystery equal to the demonetization of the standard silver dollar of the United States. I have never found a man who could tell just how it came about or why."—(Cong. Record, Vol. IX, Part 1, Page 1,231, 1st Sess., 46th Congress.)

President Grant was also ignorant of the demonetization of silver. Eight months after the passage of the bill, he wrote a letter to Mr. Cowdrey, from which the following extract is taken:—

"The panic has brought greenbacks about to a par with silver. I wonder that silver is not already coming into the market to supply the deficiency in the circulating medium. When it does come, and I predict that it will soon, we will have made a rapid stride toward specie payments. Currency will never go below silver after that. The circulation of silver will have other beneficial effects. Experience has proved that it takes about forty millions of fractional currency to make small change necessary for the transaction of the business of the country. Silver will gradually take the place of this currency, and, further, will become the standard of values which will be hoarded in a small way. I estimate that this will consume from two to three hundred millions, in time, of this species of our circulating medium.

"It will leave the paper currency free to perform the legitimate functions of trade and will tend to bring us back where we must come at last, to a specie basis. I confess to a desire to see a limited hoarding of money. It insures a firm foundation in time of need. But I want to see the hoarding of something that has a standard of value the world over. Silver has this, and if we once get back to that our strides toward a higher appreciation of our currency will be rapid. Our mines are now producing almost unlimited amounts of silver, and it is becoming a question, 'What shall we do with it?' I suggest here a solution that will answer for some years, and suggest to you bankers whether you may not imitate it: To put it in circulation now; keep it there until it is fixed, and then we will find other markets."—(McPherson's Hand Book of Politics for 1874, Pages 134-135.)

It has been charged time and again, that Ernest Seyd, the emissary of the London money power, was in this country at the time of the demonetization of silver, and that he used the vast sum of $500,000 with which to corrupt Congress and to secure its demonetization.

On the 30th of August, 1893, Senator Sherman, in a speech urging the repeal of the purchasing clause of the Sherman Law of July 14, 1890, took occasion to severely denounce the charge as utterly false.

But as evidence that some mysterious influence was brought to bear upon certain members of Congress, we produce the following language taken from the report upon the bill which demonetized silver. This report was written by Mr. Hooper who was in charge of that bill, and who was so persistent in engineering its passage through the Forty-Second Congress. That report contains the following statement; viz.:—

"The bill was prepared two years ago, and has been submitted to careful and deliberate examination. It has the approval of nearly all the mint experts of the country and the sanction of the Secretary of the Treasury. Ernest Seyd, of London, a distinguished writer and bullionist, is now here, and has given great attention to the subject of mints and coinage, and after examining the first draft of the bill made various sensible suggestions, which the committee accepted and embodied in the bill. While the committee take no credit to themselves for the original preparation of this bill, they have no hesitation in unanimously recommending its passage as necessary and expedient."

Here is a direct admission that Ernest Seyd, a citizen of England, was in this country at the time that the first steps were taken in the drafting of that bill which aimed at the striking down of the time-honored silver dollar, and the passage of which meant the destruction of the valuable silver mines of the United

States, together with those of Mexico and South America.

Mr. Seyd was not here merely as a spectator, as the language of Mr. Hooper shows, for he says that this Englishman, "After examining the first draft of the bill made various sensible suggestions, which the committee accepted and embodied in the bill."

It will strike the average American citizen as singular that public men of the prominence of Samuel Hooper and John Sherman, members of the National Congress, should submit a great measure of such importance as this bill to the inspection and for the correction of its provisions by an alien who owed allegiance to Great Britain.

It is a remarkable coincidence that foreign nations, especially England, should exert such influence in the preparation and enactment of financial measures that came solely within the constitutional powers of an American Congress.

These striking coincidences of the constant meetings and consultations of Senator Sherman with the financiers of Great Britain, from the time of his visit to London, in 1867, down to the passage of that infamous act demonetizing silver, were not the results of mere accident.

It has been affirmed, time and again, by the ablest Senators and Representatives of Congress, statesmen of unblemished honor, that the demonetization of silver in 1873 was the premeditated act of the combined money power of England and America.

This charge of a deeply laid and successful conspiracy has been openly and fearlessly made in the halls of Congress, and has not been met and overthrown The Congressional Records, published by authority of Congress, affords ample justification for this statement.

It is a historical fact that the financiers of Great Britain were mainly influential in procuring that great change in the coinage laws of this country, and Senator Sherman, who introduced the first bill providing for the demonetization of silver, and who ever since 1873 has exerted his immense prestige and influence against every measure providing for its restoration, in whole or in part, gives most conclusive evidence that such was the case.

To support this statement, we quote from his speech delivered before the Chamber of Commerce, of New York City, March 6, 1876, in which he made an elaborate argument against the resolution of that body in favor of repealing the Resumption Act of 1875.

In the course of his remarks, adverse to that course of the Chamber of Commerce, he said:—

"Our coinage act came into operation on the 1st of April, 1873, and constituted the gold one dollar piece the sole unit of value, while it restricted the legal tender of the new trade dollar and the half dollar and subdivisions to an amount not exceeding five dollars in one payment.

Thus the double standard previously existing was finally abolished, and the United States as usual was influenced by Great Britain in making gold coin the only standard. This suits England, but does not suit us. I think with our large silver producing capacity we should return to the double standard, at least in part, and this will constitute one of the means by which we will be enabled to resume specie payments."
—(Cong. Globe, Vol. IV, Part 2, Page 1,481, 1st Sess., 44th Congress.)

Is this not a plain admission by the chairman of the Finance Committee of the United States Senate, that Great Britain had wielded a great influence in procuring the demonetization of silver in 1873?

In connection with this deliberate public admission of Senator Sherman, let it be borne in mind that Samuel Hooper stated on the floor of the House of Representatives, that a citizen of England assisted in framing the bill which demonetized silver.

This speech of Senator Sherman was clothed with official authority, and he distinctly stated that, "The double standard previously existing was finally abolished, and the United States as usual was influenced by Great Britain in making gold coin the only standard. This suits England, but does not suit us."

In his elaborate address to the leading commercial body of America, Mr. Sherman avers that British influence was successful in securing legislation from an American Congress favorable to that country, and that "This suits England but does not suit us." This is equivalent to a charge of treason against Congress and the President, and implies corruption; for what American law-maker, however base, would voluntarily prostitute his power to the influence of a foreign state?

He makes an implied charge against the patriotism of that party of which he is a leader, for it held the presidency and a great majority of both Houses of the Federal legislature at the time the act which demonetized silver was placed upon the statute books. And nowhere during the debates upon that measure does he denounce those whom he alleges voted a bill through Congress to "suit England;" nowhere had he censured those who were influenced by Great Britain. The query naturally presents itself—Did Great Britain influence Sherman to present the bill of June 9, 1868, which sought to demonetize silver? Was that to suit England?

Mr. Sherman knew whereof he spoke. It will be remembered that the first bill introduced in Congress to demonetize silver was that of the 9th of June, 1868, and it came fresh from the hands of Mr. Sherman.

Furthermore in his report advocating the passage of this bill, Mr. Sherman stated that "The single standard of gold is an American idea."

In his address to the Chamber of Commerce he asserts that the United States was influenced by Great Britain in adopting the single standard of gold.

No living man can reconcile the utterly inconsistent statements of this alleged statesman.

It was during this period, beginning with the year 1862 down to the year 1873, that so many gigantic scandals smirched the legislative record of Congress.

During the time covered by these years, the Federal legislature gave away more than 200,000,000 acres of the public domain to great railway corporations, in addition to a gratuity of United States bonds to the amount of $65,000,000; the Credit Mobilier rascality resulted from an exposure of the corruption of many distinguished members of Congress who sold their votes outright; the great whisky ring was all-powerful, and, in collusion with the treasury officials and revenue officers, swindled the government out of untold millions; the President, it is true, ordered Secretary Bristow "To let no guilty man escape," and then he nullified all prosecutions of the scoundrels by the exercise of his pardoning power; Boss Shepherd reigned supreme at Washington; the "Salary Grab" and "Back Pay" schemes of plunder were brazenly pushed through Congress, while the Freedman's Bureau robbed the negro of his savings.

It would require pages to briefly summarize the history of the congressional and departmental scandals rife at the national capital.

The Washington correspondent of that leading republican journal, the Chicago Tribune, of the date of February 21, 1873, thus described the corruption prevalent at Washington. He says: "Turkish corruption under the pashas and beys, or Russian official rottenness, could scarcely be worse than it is here."

The public conscience was so aroused by these exposures and proofs of the boundless official corruption and debauchery, that, in the congressional elections of 1874, the republican party met with an overwhelming defeat, and the democracy carried the House of Representatives by a great majority.

Immediately after the demonetization of silver by the United States, Norway, Sweden, and Denmark closed their mints to silver and adopted the gold standard.

The Latin Union, however, still continued the unlimited coinage of silver for a brief period.

On September 6, 1873, the French government limited the amount of silver to be accepted at the mints for coinage.

To afford the reader an explanation of the closing of the mints to silver by France, we refer to the great Franco-Prussian war of 1870-71, brought on by the folly of Emperor Napoleon, who, to restore his waning influence over the French nation, declared war against Prussia, July 15, 1870.

In the brief period of two hundred and ten days, the armies of France were destroyed; her territory was over-run by the victorious Germans, and the nation lay prostrate under the heel of her bitterest enemy—Prince Bismarck.

In the treaty of peace negotiated by Theirs on behalf of France, and Bismarck, on the part of Germany, the latter succeeded in imposing the most enormous burdens upon the French people.

The treaty of peace as finally agreed upon by France and Germany provided that the former should pay the latter the immense sum of 5,000,000,000 francs ($1,000,-000,000), in gold as an indemnity for the expense of the war, payable in three installments, the last of which would fall due March 1, 1875.

In the meantime the French authorities were to support a German army of occupation until the money was paid.

Not satisfied with the exaction of this enormous indemnity, Bismarck compelled the French to cede to the German empire the two splendid provinces of Alsace and Lorraine.

It is said that the venerable and patriotic Theirs shed bitter tears when he signed this treaty, and that Bismarck smiled in derision at the humiliation of the Frenchman.

Up to the time of this treaty the German empire was on a silver basis, but, upon the payment of this enormous war indemnity, Bismarck, in the execution of his policy to cripple France as much as lay in his power, procured the passage of a law through the German parliament which provided for the demonetization of silver.

This measure became a law July 9, 1873, and it established a national gold standard throughout Germany, and it further provided that the aggregate issue of silver coin should not, until further orders, exceed ten marks ($2.50), for each inhabitant of the empire, and that the silver in excess of this amount should be withdrawn from circulation and sold.

The evident object of this measure was the enhancement of the value of the vast war indemnity received from France, and, by throwing a large amount of non-legal tender silver on the market, to force down its price, which, in effect, would depreciate the silver coinage of France and the other members of the Latin union, whose mints still remained open to the free and unlimited coinage of silver at a ratio of fifteen and one-half to one.

The shrewd statesmen of France at once penetrated the scheme of the wily Bismarck to debase the French coinage, and, therefore, on the 6th of September, 1873, the French government in a treasury order limited the amount of silver to be accepted by the mints.

In February, 1874, the Latin union states jointly closed their mints to the free coinage of silver, agreeing, however, to coin on government account such quantities as were fixed upon from time to time.

Such were the reasons that moved France to suspend the unlimited coinage of silver.

During the years of 1868, 1869, 1870, 1871, 1872, and 1873, the production of silver in the United States rapidly increased, while that of gold largely diminished.

In the last named year the production of silver reached the great sum of $35,750,000, the use of which as money was destroyed by the act of February 12, 1873.

Shortly after the demonetization of silver in the United States, a distinguished political economist of Europe urged this country to readopt the bi-metallic law, and he forcibly stated that it would, "Not only save the world at large from an abyss, and prevent the accomplishment of a stupid general crime, whose authors humanity would some day learn to curse, but that she would advance her own material interests more than may be supposed possible, and that she may perchance take the lead in the intelligent and prudent organization of firm monetary systems."

The destructive effects of the demonetizing act of 1873 upon the value of property was so great, that Hon. Alexander Stephens, one of the ablest and most conservative of American statesmen, declared that it was more disastrous to the American people than the total cost and destruction of that bloody and protracted war between the North and the South. He said:—

"A careful calculator told me the other day that shrinkage of values in this country after the fatal act was more than the whole expense of our war. That fatality was worse than war. There is no remedy for us now except in re-establishing the value of silver and its free coinage. We want $900,000,000 in circulation, at least. We have now only fourteen dollars per capita in circulation, including all the hoarded gold and silver. We want at least twenty-five dollars per capita, or as much as we had before the crash of 1873. People fear the silver flood; I would let it come from all the world until we have a thousand millions in circulation."

The enormity of this crime, as stated by Mr. Stephens, can only be adequately gauged when it is borne in mind that the cost of the war of the Rebellion up to the time that he made that statement aggregated $8,000,000,000.

The process by which the value of bonds and of public debts was increased by legislation, both here and in Europe, and the value of other property was correspondingly depreciated, as measured by the exchange power of money, was shown by a paper read before the Society of Arts of London, by J. Barr Robertson, the value of which was so highly recognized by the United States government, that it was published on page 354 of the coinage laws of the United States.

Mr. Robertson says:—

"While it would take too much space to enter into details regarding the practical effects of this appreciation of gold, it will suffice to give some indication of the enormous injury it has inflicted, if it is stated that the transfer of wealth from the landed and propertied classes and from the mercantile, manufacturing, and producing classes generally in the United Kingdom to the holders of securities, mortgages, annuities, etc., can not be less than £2,000,000,000, due solely to the appreciation of gold.

"It is already a question how much further the holders of securities are to receive the assistance of a continually contracting currency to enable them to go on absorbing further and further the wealth of the producing classes. If no other relief can be obtained, it may be necessary to fix a commodity standard instead of a money standard for long-dated payments, as has been recommended by the principal economists of the last hundred years. Such a colossal unearned increment as has accrued to the holders of securities valued in gold during the last twenty years in Europe and the United States, amounting to not less than from £7,000,000,000 to £9,000,000,000, is entirely unparalleled in the history of the world, and all other public questions sink into utter insignificance compared with it."

Think of it! The demonetization of silver by the United States and Europe so enhanced the exchange value of gold over other forms of property that it added $10,000,000,000 to the wealth of the creditor classes of England; and from $35,000,000,000 to $45,000,000,000 to the accumulations of the creditor classes of Europe and the United States.

In speaking of the effects of the demonetization of silver, initiated in England by Lord Liverpool in 1816, later followed by the United States and Germany, and in describing the artificial increase of the value of money over all other species of property, and in pointing out the class who are the sole beneficiaries of that infamous system, Sir Moreton Frewen well said:—

"It may, indeed, be affirmed without fear of contradiction, the legislation arranged in the interest of a certain class, first by Lord Liverpool in this country, and again by Sir Robert Peel at the instigation of Mr. Jones Loyd and other wealthy bankers, which was supplemented recently by simultaneous anti-silver legislation in Berlin and Washington at the instance of the great financial houses. This legislation has about doubled the burden of all national debts by an artificial enhancement of the value of money.

"The fall of all prices induced by this cause has been on such a scale that while in twenty years the national debt of the United States quoted in dollars has been reduced by nearly two-thirds, yet the value of the remaining one-third, measured in wheat, in bar iron, or bales of cotton, is considerably greater, is a greater demand on the labor and industry of the nation than was the whole debt at the time it was contracted.

"The aggravation of the burdens of taxation induced by this so-called "appreciation of gold," which is no natural appreciation, but has been brought about by class legislation to increase the value of gold which is in few hands, requires but to be explained to an enfranchised democracy, which will know how to protect itself against further attempts to contract the currency and force down prices to the confusion of every existing contract.

"Of all classes of middle-men, bankers have been by far the most successful in intercepting and appropriating an undue share of produced wealth. While the modern system of banking and credit may be said to be even yet in its infancy, that portion of the assets of the community which is to-day in the strong boxes of the bankers, would, if declared, be an astounding revelation of the recent profits of this particular business; and not only has the business itself become a most profitable monopoly, but its interests in a very few hands are diametrically opposed to the interests of the majority. By legislation intended to contract the currency and force down all prices, including wages, the price paid for labor, the money owner has been able to increase the purchase power of his sovereign or dollar by the direct diminution of the price of every kind of property measured in money."

CHAPTER V.

EFFORTS TO REMONETIZE SILVER AND PRESERVE THE GREENBACK.

"According to my views of the subject, the conspiracy which seems to have been formed here and in Europe, to destroy by legislation and otherwise, from three-sevenths to one-half, of the metallic money of the world, is the most gigantic crime of this or any other age."—John G. Carlisle, in 1878.

"It is the monometallists who are the authors of the depreciation which they point to as a proof of the unworthiness of the metal they cry down. They resemble the people who, having tied the legs of a horse, call out for him to be killed because he does not gallop."—Henri Cernushi.

In the preceding chapter, the writer faithfully endeavored to give a true history of the legislation culminating in the act of February 12, 1873, which struck down the standard silver dollar as the unit of account.

Step by step, the money power successfully attained its great end in the halls of Congress, and, with the downfall of silver, nothing apparently stood in its way for the complete control of the currency of the nation, and consequently an oppressive mastery over all other property.

The financial legislation, up to this period, was dictated by the national banks and their firm allies, the money lenders of London.

Congress merely registered the demands of this money power upon the statute books as the law of the land.

EFFORTS TO REMONETIZE SILVER.

Since April 1, 1873, we have ascertained that a single standard of gold was fastened upon the nation by the combined influence of England and her ally—the national banking system.

The passage of the so-called specie resumption act of 1875 planted this country upon a gold standard, and practically gave the banks a monopoly of the currency.

This was the policy planned and matured by the money power to place the vast business interests of the nation upon a bank credit basis as the sole method of carrying on all trade and commerce.

The way was apparently clear to substitute a national bank credit currency in lieu of legal tender silver and greenbacks, force all business to be tributary to the banks, and to perpetuate a huge national debt.

This system of finance was the exact counterpart of that of England—in fact, it was borrowed from that country.

That the scheme of finance embodied in the national banking act was imported from England by John Sherman—the author of the original bill providing for its creation—is indisputable.

In one of his reports as Secretary of the Treasury, Mr. Sherman refers to this fact and says: "Both England and the United States have settled upon a bank currency secured by government bonds."

This language of Mr. Sherman, in thus speaking of England and the United States, signifies a unity of purpose to fasten on this country the British system.

To illustrate the immense power of the Bank of England over the people of Great Britain, we quote from a report made by the Chamber of Commerce of the city of Manchester, England, in 1859, which says:—

"Although it scarcely comes within the scope of their present object, the board will add a reflection upon the subject of the undue privileges assumed by the Bank of England. That such a power over the property and even over the lives of the people of this country can be allowed to exist is one of the phenomena of our civilization. That their directors, twenty-six in number, can in secret session, without the consent of their constituents, decide the value of all property, is to be regarded as one of the greatest crimes against modern civilization."

In the face of this indictment against the Bank of England, Mr. Sherman appropriated its plan as the model of his scheme — the national banking act of February 25, 1863.

After the demonetization of silver in 1873, the most disastrous panic ever known in history up to that time, swept over this country, tens of thousands of failures occurred, entailing losses of hundreds of millions of dollars of capital.

The extent of the loss wrought by that great crash cannot be described by the language of man. Resource must be had to figures to convey an adequate idea of the magnitude of the disaster flowing from this wide spread ruin and wreckage of values.

In 1873, the number of failures was 5,183, with liabilities of $228,500,000; in 1874, the failures were 5,830, and the liabilities, $155,239,000; in 1875 the failures were 7,740, and liabilities of $201,000,000; in 1876, the number of failures was 9,092 with a loss of $191,000,-000; in 1877, the failures were 8,872 and liabilities were $190,669,000; in 1878, the failures reached 10,478 with the vast aggregate of $234,383,000 in liabilities—a total of failures numbering 45,195, with liabilities of $1,110,-

906,000—exceeding the enormous war indemnity paid by France to Germany.

Exclusive of this immense loss to business, the amount of suffering borne by the people will never be known to the historian.

Hundreds of thousands of skilled and unskilled workmen were thrown out of employment, although the crops were abundant, and the number of consumers was larger than ever before known.

Then, for the first time in the history of the United States, appeared that phenomenon—the American tramp—whose appearance and permanency, as an established institution in civil society, is a problem that must be solved some time in the near future.

Then occurred an universal reduction of wages in all the leading industries throughout the United States, and in many cases skilled workmen received a wage of less than one dollar per day. Hundreds of thousands of American citizens, the flower of the industrial class, struck against these starvation wages, and these strikes spread all over the United States, resulting in tumults, riots, and bloodshed, assuming the proportions of a civil war.

The United States troops were called out to put down the workingmen at the point of the bayonet, and their just grievances were quenched by the regular army.

It was during this period that a celebrated divine, in a sermon delivered from his pulpit, said:—

"Is not a dollar a day enough to buy bread? Water costs nothing! And a man who cannot live on bread is not fit to live. A family may live, laugh, love, and be happy, that eats bread in the morning with good water, and good water and bread at noon, and water and bread at night."

This humane discourse was uttered by a minister of the gospel who received the princely salary of $25,000 per annum.

Jay Gould, the great railroad wrecker, said: "We shall shortly find ourselves living under a monarchy. I would give a million dollars to see Grant in the white house."

The New York Times, a republican journal, said:—

"There seems to be but one remedy, and it must come—a change of ownership of the soil and the creation of a class of land-owners on the one hand and of tenant farmers on the other—something similar to what long existed in the older countries of Europe."

Hon. J. C. Burrows, a republican member of Congress from Michigan, gave utterance to the following language in a speech delivered by him on the question of finance:—

"To-day, the best that could happen to the financial interests and the business interests would be for Congress to pass a law, at its very next session, to punish with death any member of Congress that would make a speech on finance for the next twenty years. What we want is to be let alone, and we are on the high road to prosperity."

Rev. Joseph Cook, of Boston, a divine and public lecturer, used this remarkable language in a speech delivered by him:—

"The strongest of this generation wants a dictator. I say come on with your schemes of confiscation and forced loans, and graded income taxes, and irredeemable currency, under universal suffrage, and if you are sufficiently frank in proclaiming the doctrines of your ringleaders, then, under military necessity, and even here in the United States, we must get rid of universal suffrage, and we shall. Rather than allow these things we will have one of the fiercest of civil wars."

The Nevada Chronicle, the organ of the millionaire Senator Sharon, editorially said:—

"We need a stronger government. The wealth of the country demands it. Without capital and capitalists our government would not be worth a fig. The capital of the country demands protection; its rights are as sacred as the rights of the paupers who are continually prating of the encroachments of capital and against centralization. We have tried Grant, and we know him to be a man for the place above all others. He has nerve. As President he would be commander-in-chief of the army and navy, and when the communistic tramps of the country raise mobs to tear up railroad tracks, and to sack cities on the sham cry of 'bread or blood,' he would not hesitate to turn loose upon them canister and grape. The wealth of the country has to bear the burden of government and it should control it. The people are becoming educated up to this theory rapidly, and the sooner the theory is recognized in the constitution and laws, the better it will be for the people. Without blood, and rivers of it, there will be no political change of administration. The moneyed interests, for self-preservation, must sustain the republican party. The railroads, the banks, and the manufacturers, the heavy importers, and all classes of business in which millions are invested, will sustain the supremacy of the republican party.

"To avert fearful bloodshed, a strong central government should be established as soon as possible."

These are but a few of the many expressions of the sentiments entertained by a corrupt and subsidized press, clerical hypocrites, and gigantic knaves.

United States Senator Sharon was one of the most notorious corruptionists and libertines that ever disgraced the name of man. Statesmen and financiers of the stamp of Gould and Sharon are libels on the human race, and their influence was a standing menace against the liberties of the people.

This panic hung over the people like a pall for seven long years. The extent of the suffering throughout the duration of this panic is eloquently expressed by Colonel Ingersoll, who said:—

"No man can imagine, all the languages of the world can not express what the people of the United States suffered from 1873 to 1879. Men who considered themselves millionaires found that they were beggars; men living in palaces, supposing they had enough to give sunshine to the winter of their age, supposing that they had enough to have all they loved in affluence and comfort, suddenly found that they were mendicants with bonds, stocks, mortgages, all turned to ashes in their hands. The chimneys grew cold, the fires in furnaces went out, the poor families were turned adrift, and the highways of the United States were crowded with tramps."

Of course the wise men of that day, in their conceit, discovered a reason for the panic of 1873. In their learned dissertations on the origin of this financial breakdown, they asserted that over production was the moving cause that so fearfully multiplied failures, threw workmen out of employment, and made hundreds of thousands of men, women, and children feel the pangs of hunger and starvation.

The reasoning of these financial wiseacres took the form of the following syllogism: Panics, want and starvation are results of the production of large quantities of wheat, corn, and other agricultured products; prior to 1873 and several years after that date the American people produced immense crops of farm products; therefore, these immense crops were the cause of panics, bankruptcies, loss of employment, hunger, and starvation. Such was the theory gravely announced by so-called learned professors of political economy.

This doctrine was taken up and echoed in the halls of Congress by alleged statesmen, reiterated in the press, and formed the burden of the stump speeches of designing politicians who sought political preferment. This absurd, sophistical argument had some weight with the unthinking. Ordinarily, instances of such suffering that were prevalent during the panic of 1873, usually proceeded from failures of crops.

It is a historical fact that all great panics that had occurred in the United States up to this time, were during periods when nature exerted herself to the utmost to make bounteous provision for the wants of man.

The scarcity of money, the want and suffering became so great that, in 1876, the Chamber of Commerce of New York City adopted a resolution urging the immediate repeal of the specie Resumption Act of January 24, 1875.

It was on this occasion that John Sherman met with this body, and gave utterance to the statement quoted in the preceding chapter that, "The United States as usual was influenced by Great Britain in making gold coin the standard. This suits England but it does not suit us."

One great cause of the panic originating in 1873, was the natural result of that financial policy, which had persisted in a long continued contraction of the currency, a policy initiated by Hon. Hugh McCulloch, who had been appointed Secretary of the Treasury in 1865.

Upon his appointment as the head of the Treasury Department, he at once took measures, in pursuance of the various acts of Congress, to fund the currency of the nation into interest-bearing bonds, and to create a permanent public debt.

Under the act of April 12, 1866, the Secretary of the Treasury was authorized to exchange interest-bearing bonds for the notes circulating as money, whether said notes were interest-bearing or otherwise.

Secretary McCulloch, a national banker by profession, proceeded to carry out this policy of a merciless contraction of the currency to the full extent of his power.

At the time he began this policy of funding the currency into long time interest-bearing bonds, the entire volume of the various notes performing the functions of money amounted to the sum of $1,983,000,000, exclusive of gold and silver coin. This volume of currency consisted of greenbacks, temporary loan certificates, one and two-year treasury notes, certificates of indebtedness, postal currency, compound interest treasury notes, fractional currency, 7-30 notes of August and September, 1864, 7-30 notes of 1864-65, state bank circulation, and national bank notes.

The two classes of 7-30 treasury notes alone amounted to $845,553,000.

It has been denied that these treasury notes circulated as money, but General Logan and numerous other public men of that day, declared that these notes formed a very material part of the volume of currency.

With this large volume of circulation the national banking money power saw that it was impossible to obtain control of the currency of the nation.

Money being plentiful, business was transacted on a cash basis, and, therefore, the people were not compelled to borrow the circulating notes of the national banks at a high rate of interest, and thus be placed in the power of these banks.

These conditions were so apparent, that, in his report as Secretary of the Treasury for the year 1865, Mr. McCulloch said:—

"The country as a whole, notwithstanding the ravages of war and the draught upon labor, is by its greatly developed resources, far in advance of what it was in 1857. The people are now comparatively free from debt."

Hence it was the policy of the national banking money power, by this funding of the ready cash of the country into bonds, and substituting the national bank circulation for the currency issued by the government, to control the business of the nation, and ultimately the votes of the people who were obligated to the banks as borrowers.

The national banks desired that all business should be done upon credit; that this credit should be given to them by the government in the form of national bank notes, the latter form of currency to be loaned by the banks to the business interest of the country.

Secretary McCulloch carried out this policy so energetically, and contracted the volume of legal tender currency so rapidly, that strong protests went up from the people, and, on the 3d of February, 1868, Congress forbade the further destruction of the legal tenders, which had been reduced to $346,000,000. The total contraction of all forms of notes circulating as money, reached the enormous sum of $1,000,000,000, during the administration of Mr. McCulloch. We include in these last figures, all government obligations utilized as money by the people, whether legal tender or otherwise.

In a speech delivered in the Senate in 1874, General Logan stated that the contraction of the volume of money up to that time was more than one billion dollars.

It was this murderous policy of contraction, initiated by Secretary McCulloch and followed by his successors, that eventually led to the panic of 1873, from which dates a universal stagnation of business lasting seven long years.

During this panic, the democracy was successful in the elections of 1874, and for the first time since 1860, the Lower House was controlled by the party of Jefferson and Jackson.

It was then ascertained that silver had been demonetized by the act of February 12, 1873, and the House at once endeavored to enact measures to undo the wrong.

During the Forty-fourth Congress, which came into existence March 4, 1875, and continued in power until the 4th of March, 1877, the President was republican. In the Senate there were 46 republicans, 29 democrats, and one vacancy. The House of Representatives was composed of 186 democrats and 107 republicans.

This Congress convened on the 6th of December, 1875.

On March 27, 1876, the Committee on Appropriations brought forward House bill 2,450, which appropriated money for a deficiency for the Bureau of engraving and printing, and section 2 provided for the issue of subsidiary silver.

Mr. Reagan, of Texas, offered an amendment making the trade dollar legal tender for any amount not exceeding fifty dollars, and the silver coins less than one dollar for any amount not exceeding twenty-five dollars. This was agreed to. Yeas 124—99 democrats, 22 republicans, 1 independent; nays 94—28 democrats, 65 republicans, 1 independent. As amended the bill passed. Yeas 122—50 democrats, 70 republicans, and 2 independents; nays 100—80 democrats, 18 republicans, and 2 independents.

The bill was transmitted to the Senate, and it was referred to the Finance Committee, of which Mr. Sherman was chairman.

On April 10, 1876, Mr. Sherman, from the Finance Committee, reported the bill with amendments; one amending section 3 so as to authorize the coinage of a silver dollar of 412.8 grains—a legal tender not exceeding twenty dollars in any one payment except for customs, dues, and interests on public debt, and stopped the coinage of trade dollars. Another—a new section 4—authorized the exchange of silver dollars for an equal amount of United States notes to be retired, canceled, and not reissued; and also for coining silver bullion at its market value. The amended bill thus reported by Senator Sherman, authorized the coinage of a silver dollar of 412.8 grains, which, while it would increase its legal tender debt-paying power from five dollars to twenty dollars, could not be received for custom dues, and could not be utilized for the payment of interest on the public debt.

These silver dollars were to be exchanged for an equal amount of United States notes, which were thus to be permanently retired from circulation.

The propositions of the amended bill, as reported by Senator Sherman, should it become a law, would not increase the volume of money a single dollar, for the reason that the silver dollar would be solely used to retire an equal amount of legal tender currency.

The most vicious part of the amended bill was that which limited the legal tender debt-paying power of the silver dollar to twenty dollars; the legal tender currency, for which the silver dollars were to be substituted, was an unlimited legal tender, except for duties on imports and interest on the public debt.

Therefore, the adoption of this measure would be the substitution of a limited legal tender silver dollar for a full legal tender currency, leaving gold the sole unlimited legal tender for the payment of all debts, public and private, including duties on imports and interest on the public debt.

The amended bill was discussed in the Senate, and, on motion of Mr. Sherman, sections 3 and 4 of the amended bill were stricken out, and that motion carried out of the bill the House amendment offered by Mr. Reagan which proposed to make trade dollars legal tender to the amount of fifty dollars, which, by the act of February 12, 1873, were limited to five dollars for any one payment.

By this parliamentary device with the House bill, Mr. Sherman succeeded in killing that measure, the passage of which would have conferred an enlarged debt-paying power on the trade dollar.

On June 10, 1876, Mr. S. S. Cox, from the Committee on Banking and Currency, reported a joint resolution to issue the silver coins in the Treasury to an amount not exceeding $10,000,000 in exchange for an equal amount of legal tender notes, to be kept as a special fund, to be reissued only upon the retirement of fractional currency; which was passed without a division.

June 21, 1876, in the Senate, the House joint resolution was amended by adding a section prohibiting the coinage of the trade dollar except for export trade; thus striking down the trade dollar, the only dollar authorized by the coinage law of 1873.

Again, the fine Italian hand of the money power was visible in the Senate amendment to this joint resolution.

On June 10, 1876, Mr. Cox, from the Committee on Banking and Currency, reported a resolution in three sections, providing for an increased coinage of silver. It was passed without division, and was transmitted to the Senate.

In the Senate June 27, 1876, the bill was considered on the report of the Finance Committee to strike out all after the enacting clause and insert four new sections. This was a substitute proposed by the Senate Committee on Finance, headed by the distinguished senior Senator from Ohio.

Section 1 provided for the coinage of silver dollars of 412.8 grains, to be legal tender for sums not exceeding twenty dollars.

Section 2 provided for exchanging such dollars and minor coins for legal tenders to be canceled and not reissued or replaced.

Section 3 provided for purchasing silver bullion at market rates for such coinage, to be made without loss in coinage and issue.

Section 4, prohibiting legal tender of the trade dollar and limiting its coinage to export demand. This was before the law of July 22, 1876, had been enacted.

Again the scheme to substitute a limited legal tender silver dollar for United States notes and treasury notes was brought forward in these amendments.

The continued efforts of the Senate to retire permanently the government legal tender notes were a part of the plan of the national banking money power to force the business of the country to be transacted by a credit money.

This bill also aimed at the coinage of silver on government account alone, hence, should the silver so coined out of the bullion purchased by the government decline in bullion value as compared with gold, the national banking money power would demand that the silver dollar be redeemed in gold. It furthermore took away all legal tender debt-paying power of the trade dollar, and limited its coinage to export demand.

On June 28, 1876, Senator Bogy moved to amend section 1 of the Senate bill by striking out the words "Not exceeding twenty dollars," the effect of which would be to make the silver dollar a full legal tender for the payment of all debts. The amendment was agreed to by a vote of 18 to 14.

On June 29, 1876, the bill as amended was recommitted to the Finance Committee, where it slept the sleep that knows no waking.

On July 19, 1876, in the House of Representatives, Mr. Bland, from the Committee on Mines and Mining, reported resolution 3,635, authorizing the free coinage of gold and silver. This resolution was carried over to the next session of Congress, and, on December 13, 1876, Mr. Bland offered a substitute for the resolution of July 19, 1876, which provided for the free and unlimited coinage of the silver dollar of 412½ grains, with full legal tender power.

This substitute, which restored silver to the position it occupied prior to 1873, was passed by a vote of 168 yeas to 53 nays. It was sent to the republican Senate, referred to the Finance Committee where it was smothered by John Sherman.

On August 15, 1876, a joint resolution was adopted by Congress which provided for the creation of a Monetary Commission, "To consist of three Senators, to be appointed by the Senate, three members of the House of Representatives, to be appointed by the Speaker, and experts not exceeding three in number, to be selected by and associated with them." Congress instructed the commission to make an examination into the money question, and to give its opinion as to "The best means for providing for facilitating the resumption of specie payments."

On March 2, 1877, the commission made its report, or more strictly speaking, several reports. The majority report signed by five of its members, gave a history of the bi-metallic laws in force previous to 1873, together with their effects on the value of commodities, trade, and commerce, and, as its conclusion, advocated an immediate return to the bi-metallic standard of sixteen to one.

In speaking of the effect of the volume of money on values, and the baleful influences of falling prices on society, the majority report says:—

"At the Christian era the metallic money of the Roman empire amounted to $1,800,000,000. By the end of the fifteenth century it had shrunk to less than $200,000,000. During this period a most extraordinary and baleful change took place in the condition of the world. Population dwindled, and commerce, arts, wealth, and freedom all disappeared. The people were reduced by poverty and misery to the most degraded conditions of serfdom and slavery. The disintegration of society was almost complete. The conditions of life were so hard that individual selfishness was the only thing consistent with the instinct of self-preservation. All public spirit, all generous emotions, all the noble aspirations of man shriveled and disappeared as the volume of money shrunk and as prices fell.

"History records no such disastrous transition as that from the Roman empire to the dark ages. Various explanations have been given of this entire breaking down of the framework of society, but it was certainly coincident with the shrinkage in the volume of money, which was also without historical parallel. The crumbling of institutions kept even step and pace with the shrinkage in the stock of money and the falling of prices. All other attendant circumstances than these last have occurred in other historical periods unaccompanied and unfollowed by any such mighty disasters. It is a suggestive coincidence that the first glimmer of light only came with the invention of bills of exchange and paper substitutes, through which the scanty stock of the precious metals was increased in efficiency. But not less than the energizing influence of Potosi and all the argosies of treasure from the new world were needed to arouse the old world from its comatose sleep, to quicken the torpid limbs of industry, and to plume the leaden wings of commerce.

"It needed the heroic treatment of rising prices to enable society to reunite its shattered links, to shake off the shackels of feudalism, to relight and uplift the almost extinguished torch of civilization. That the disasters of the dark ages were caused by decreasing money and falling prices, and that the recovery therefrom and the comparative prosperity which followed the discovery of America were due to an increasing supply of the precious metals and rising prices, will not seem surprising or unreasonable when the noble functions of money are considered. Money is the great instrument of association, the very fiber of social organism, the vitalizing force of industry, the protoplasm of civilization, and as essential to its existence as oxygen is to animal life. Without money civilization could not have had a beginning; with a diminishing supply it must languish, and, unless relieved, finally perish."

The report sets out the reason why silver was demonetized in 1873. It says:—

"Manifestly the real reason for the demonetization of silver was the apprehension of the creditor classes (money lending classes) that the combined production of the two metals would raise prices and cheapen money unless one of them was shorn of the money function. In Europe this reason was distinctly avowed."

This conclusion has been abundantly verified, inasmuch as every attempt made by Congress for the restoration of silver as legal tender money has been denounced as a scheme to rob the public creditors—a charge which has been reiterated thousands of times in the press, in the halls of Congress and elsewhere.

Professor Bowen, of Massachusetts, and Representative Gibson handed in a minority report, in which it was stated that every attempt made previous to 1873 to establish a double standard "has been a total failure."

Senator Boutwell, in his minority report as a member of the commission, stated his conclusions in effect as follows; he said:—

"A successful use of gold and silver simultaneously in any country can be effected only by their consolidation upon an agreed ratio of value, or by the concurrence of the commercial nations of the world."

He, therefore, advocated a postponement of the free coinage of silver by the United States, "Until the effort to secure the co-operation of other nations has been faithfully tried.''

On the 4th of March, 1877, Rutherford B. Hayes was inaugurated President of the United States. He was the beneficiary of that fraud—the Returning Board of Louisiana. In the formation of his cabinet he selected John Sherman for the responsible post of Secretary of the Treasury.

During the time he was at the head of that great department, the national banking money power became more imperious in its demands upon the government. The United States Treasury was made wholly subservient to the clearing house of New York City.

The immense resources of the Treasury were practically placed at the disposal of the banks, which fact became so notorious, that United States Senator James B. Beck and other members of Congress denounced Secretary Sherman for bestowing such munificent favors upon a few great banks.

During the session of the Forty-fifth Congress, which came into power March 4, 1877, and which was in control until March 4, 1879, the President was republican; the House was democratic by a vote of 156 to 136; the Senate consisted of 39 republicans, 36 democrats and 1 independent.

In the first or called session of the Forty-fifth Congress, November 5, 1877, Mr. Bland, of Missouri, introduced a bill in the House of Representatives entitled, "An act to authorize the free coinage of the standard silver dollar and to restore its legal tender character."

The text of the bill was as follows:—

"Be it enacted by the Senate and House of Representatives of the United States of America in Congress assembled, That there shall be coined at the several mints of the United States, silver dollars of the weight of 412½ grains troy of standard silver, as provided in the act of January 18, 1837, on which shall be the devices and superscriptions provided by said act; which coins, together with all silver dollars heretofore coined by the United States of like weight and fineness, and shall be a legal tender, at their nominal value, for all debts and dues, public and private, except where otherwise provided by contract; and any owner of silver bullion may deposit the same at any United States coinage mint or assay office, to be coined into such dollars, for his benefit, upon the same terms and conditions as gold bullion is deposited for coinage under existing laws.

"Section 2. All acts and parts of acts inconsistent with the provisions of this act are hereby repealed."

The rules were suspended by a vote of 164 yeas to 34 nays, and the bill was passed and transmitted to the Senate.

On November 21, 1877, Mr. Allison, from the Finance Committee, reported the bill to the Senate with amendments to strike out the clause beginning "And any owner of silver bullion," and to insert in lieu thereof a purchasing clause, and to add section 2 for an international monetary conference.

From 1862 up to 1875, the legislation of Congress tended wholly for the benefit of the East. Almost every law was enacted with the view of giving the New England states, New York, and Pennsylvania a great preponderance over the rest of the nation; exorbitant tariffs were levied on imported goods for the benefit of Eastern manufacturers, the burdens of which fell upon the consumer; foreign contract labor laws were adopted to afford these highly-protected manufacturers an abundant supply of cheap labor as a means for crushing the various labor organizations; out of the billions of money appropriated by Congress during that period, by far the greater portion was expended in those few states lying along the Atlantic; Eastern corporations received subsidies of public money to the amount of millions; the great railway corporations, burdened with liabilities far exceeding their assets, robbed the west and south of hundreds of millions of dollars by the imposition of heavy transportation charges, and these railways were owned by Eastern capitalist; while the rich silver mines of the West were practically rendered valueless by the demonetization of silver.

During the debate in the Senate on this silver bill, Hon. John J. Ingalls, a republican Senator from Kansas, in a speech delivered on the 14th of February, 1877, used the following strong language:—

"If by any process all business were compelled to be transacted on a coin basis, and actual specie payments should be enforced, the whole civilized world would be bankrupt before sunset. There is not coin enough in existence to meet in specie the one-thousandth part of the commercial obligations of mankind. Specie payments, as an actual fact, will never be resumed, neither in gold nor silver in January, 1879, nor at any other date, here nor elsewhere. The pretense that they will be is either dishonest or delusive."

The Senator in the same speech points to the fact that the Eastern section of the country had subordinated all Federal legislation to their demands, he thus arraigns the greed of the East:—

"The Senator from Wisconsin was right. It is not the east against the west.

"It is the east against the west and south combined. It is the corn and wheat and beef and cotton of the country against its bonds and its gold; its productive industry against its accumulations. It is the men who own the public debt against those who are to pay it, if it is to be paid at all. If the bonds of this government are ever paid, they will be paid by the labor of the country, and not by its capital. They are exempt from taxation and bear none of the burdens of society.

"The alliance between the west and the south upon all matters affecting their material welfare hereafter is inevitable. Their interests are mutual and identical. With the removal of the causes of political dissension that have so long separated them, they must coalesce, and united they will be invincible. The valleys of the Mississippi and Missouri, with their tributaries, form an empire that must have a homogeneous population and a common destiny from the Yellowstone to the Gulf.

"These great communities have been alienated by factions that have estranged them only to prey upon them and to maintian political supremacy by their separation. Unfriendly legislation has imposed intolerable burdens upon their energies; invidious discriminations have been made against their products; unjust tariffs have repressed their industries. While vast appropriations have been made to protect the harbors of the Atlantic, and to erect beacons upon every headland to warn the mariner with silent admonition from the "merchant-marring rocks," the Mississippi was left choked with its drifting sands till the daring genius of Eads undertook the gigantic labor of compelling the great stream to dredge its own channel to the sea. The opening of this avenue of commerce marks the epoch of the emancipation of the west and south from their bondage to the capital of the east. In asking the passage of this bill they are asking less than they will ever ask again. When I reflect upon the burdens they have borne, the wrongs they have suffered, I am astonished at their moderation."

The charges made by Mr. Ingalls against the cupidity of the East were true, and at the same time it was a bitter condemnation of the record of the republican party.

During the same speech on this bill, the brilliant Kansan had recourse to metaphor to upbraid those who advocated a single standard of gold, and at the same time he paid a glowing tribute to the monetary properties of the silver dollar as the money of the people.

He said:—

"No enduring fabric of national prosperity can be builded on gold. Gold is the money of monarchs; kings covet it, the exchanges of nations are effected by it. Its tendency is to accumulate in vast masses in the commercial centers, and to move from kingdom to kingdom in such volumes as to unsettle values and disturb the finances of the world. It is the instrument of gamblers and speculators, and the idol of the miser and the thief. Being the object of so much adoration, it becomes haughty and sensitive and shrinks at the approach of danger, and whenever it is most needed it always disappears. At the slightest alarm it begins to look for a refuge. It flies from the nation at war to the nation at peace. War makes it a fugitive.

"No people in a great emergency ever found a faithful ally in gold. It is the most cowardly and treacherous of all metals. It makes no treaty that it does not break. It has no friend whom it does not sooner or later betray. Armies and navies are not maintained by gold. In times of panic and calamity, shipwreck and disaster, it becomes the chief agent and minister of ruin. No nation every fought a great war by the aid of gold. On the contrary, in the crisis of greater peril it becomes an enemy more potent than the foe in the field; but when the battle is won and peace has been secured, gold reappears and claims the fruits of victory. In our own civil war it is doubtful if the gold of

New York and London did not work us greater injury than the powder and lead and iron of the rebels. It was the most invincible enemy of the public credit. Gold paid no soldier nor sailor. It refused the national obligation. It was worth most when our fortunes were lowest. Every defeat gave it increased value. It was in open alliance with our enemies the world over, and all its energies were evoked for our destruction. But as usual when danger has been averted and the victory secured, gold swaggers to the front and asserts the supremacy. But silver is the money of the people. It is the money of wages and retail. Its tendency is toward diffusion and dissemination. It enters into the minute concerns of traffic, and is exchanged day by day for daily bread. It penetrates the remotest channels of commerce, and its abundance, bulk, and small subdivisions prevents its deportation in sufficient amount to disturb or unsettle values. If it retires at the approach of danger, or from the presence of an inferior currency, it still remains at home ready to respond to the first summons for its return."

The characteristics which he attributes to gold in this beautiful figure of speech, were those which belonged to its owners, and thus he scathingly denounced the greed of the gold gamblers and bullion brokers of the East, who, during the war, rejoiced at every reverse of the northern armies, for, with the sinking of the fortunes of the Union cause, the more valuable became gold proportionately.

The silver bill as amended by the Senate was returned to the House for concurrence and passage. The manner in which the House bill was mutilated by the Senate aroused the anger of the House, and a fierce debate arose between the friends of silver and its opponents. Some of those who most strongly opposed the bill as a concession to the West and South were men who were notorious for the scandals that blackened their reputations as public men. Those members of Congress, who opposed the remonetization of silver in any form whatever, had, in their past careers, shown a remarkable inclination for Credit Mobilier stock, and other corrupt deals which had so deeply disgraced preceding Congresses.

Yet these Credit Mobilier statesmen were the ones who prated the loudest for the "public credit," "the public faith," and "honest money." It was Satan preaching against sin.

Among other powerful advocates of the coinage of silver was John G. Carlisle, who was recognized on the floor of the House as its ablest logician. Mr. Carlisle charged that the demonetization of silver was brought about by a conspiracy of the money power.

He said:—

"I know that the world's stock of precious metals is none too large, and I see no reason to apprehend that it will ever be so. Mankind will be fortunate indeed if the annual production of gold and silver coin shall keep pace with the annual increase of population, commerce, and industry. According to my views of the subject, the conspiracy which seems to have been formed here and in Europe to destroy by legislation and otherwise from three-sevenths to one-half of the metallic money of the world is the most gigantic crime of this or any other age. The consummation of such a scheme would ultimately entail more misery upon the human race than all the wars, pestilences, and famines that ever occurred in the history of the world.

"The absolute and instantaneous destruction of half the entire movable property of the world, including houses, ships, railroads, and other appliances for carrying on commerce, while it would be felt more sensibly at the moment, would not produce anything like a prolonged distress and disorganization of society that must inevitably result from the permanent annihilation of one-half the metallic money of the world."

This terrific arraignment of the money power was followed by an appeal to the House, in which he advised the blocking of the wheels of government by a refusal to appropriate money for its support should the President veto the bill. He said:—

"The struggle now going on cannot cease, and ought not to cease, until all the industrial interests of the country are fully and finally emancipated from the heartless domination of syndicates, stock exchanges, and other great combinations of money grabbers in this country and in Europe. Let us, if we can do no better, pass bill after bill, embodying in each some substantial provision for relief, and send them to the executive for his approval. If he withholds his signature, and we are unable to secure the necessary vote, here or elsewhere, to enact them into laws notwithstanding his veto, let us, as a last resort, suspend the rules and put them into the general appropriation bills, with the distinct understanding that if the people can get no relief the government can get no money."

After a long debate the House finally acquiesced in the senate amendments. It was the bill as amended by the Senate or nothing, for at that time the upper house was the stronghold of the money grabbers, syndicates, and combinations of capital, whose greed was so severely denounced in the powerful speech of Mr. Carlisle.

The bill as amended by the Senate finally passed both houses, and was presented to President Hayes, who returned it to the House with his veto and a message stating his reasons for refusing to sign the measure.

In his veto message, the President states that one of the reasons why the bill does not meet his approval arose from the fact that the proposed dollar would be worth but ninety or ninety-two cents, as compared with the standard gold dollar.

It will be remembered that the sole reason advanced by John Sherman, at this time Secretary of the Treasury, for the demonetization of the silver dollar in 1868 and subsequent years, was, that the silver dollar was more valuable than the gold dollar.

President Hayes, and presumably his Secretary of the Treasury, urged as a reason for the veto of this bill providing for the coinage of silver, that it was worth less than the gold dollar.

The President says:—

"The right to pay duties in certificates for silver deposits will, when they are issued is sufficient amount to circulate, put an end to the receipt of revenues in gold, and thus compel the payment of silver for both the principal and interest on the public debt."

The future receipts of revenues have shown that this prophecy of President Hayes fell to the ground. After the passage of this bill over his veto, the volume of gold in circulation and in the banks increased in the course of a few years to many millions of dollars.

The President further says:—

"The standard of value should not be changed without the consent of both parties to the contract. National promises should be kept with unflinching fidelity. There is no power to compel a nation to pay its just debts. Its credit depends on its honor. The nation owes what it has led or allowed its creditors to expect. I cannot approve a bill which, in my judgment, authorizes the violation of sacred obligations. The obligation of public faith transcends all questions of profit or public advantage. Its unquestionable maintenance is the dictate as well of the highest expediency as of the most necessary duty, and should ever be carefully guarded by the executive, by congress, and by the people."

This plea for the poor bond holder, that noble patriot who originally bought bonds as low as thirty-five cents on the dollar, bearing gold interest the equivalent in currency to eighteen per cent., payable a year in advance, and used by him as loaded dice to gamble on the public credit, was the dear object of the President's solicitude.

The bond holders who secured the passage of the Credit Strengthening Act of March 18, 1869, an act which enhanced the value of his bonds enormously, had become sacred in the eyes of the weak Hayes.

The veto message of the President angered Congress, and, on the same day, it rode rough shod over his veto by more than the necessary two-thirds vote, and the bill became a law on the 28th day of February, 1878.

To enable the reader to fully understand the coinage law of 1878, we incorporate the text of the act in full.

It is as follows; viz. :—

"An act to authorize the coinage of the standard silver dollar, and to restore its legal tender character.

"Be it enacted, etc., That there shall be coined, at the several mints of the United States, silver dollars of the weight of 412½ grains troy of standard silver, as provided in the act of January 18, 1837, on which shall be the devices and superscriptions provided by said act; which coins, together with all silver dollars heretofore coined by the United States, of like weight and fineness, shall be a legal tender, at their nominal value, for all debts and dues, public and private, except where otherwise expressly stipulated in the contract. And the secretary of the treasury is authorized and directed to purchase, from time to time, silver bullion at the market price thereof, not less than $2,000,000 worth per month nor more than $4,000,000 worth per month, and cause the same to be coined monthly, as fast as so purchased, into such dollars; and a sum sufficient to carry out the foregoing provision of this act is hereby appropriated out of any money in the treasury not otherwise appropriated. And any gain or seigniorage arising from this coinage shall be accounted for and paid into the treasury, as provided under existing laws relative to the subsidiary coinage: Provided, That the amount of money at any one time invested in such silver bullion, exclusive of such resulting coin, shall not exceed $5,000,000; And provided further, That nothing in this act shall be construed to authorize the payment in silver of certificates of deposit issued under the provisions of section 254 of the Revised Statutes.

"Section 2. That immediately after the passage of this act the President shall invite the governments of the countries comprising the Latin union, so called, and of such other European nations as he may deem advisable, to join the United States in a conference to adopt a common ratio between gold and silver, for the purpose of establishing, internationally, the use of bi-metallic money and securing fixity of relative value between those metals, such conference to be held at such place, in Europe or the United States, at such time within six months, as may be mutually agreed upon by the executives of the governments joining in the same, whenever the governments so invited, or any three of them, shall have signified their willingness to unite in the same.

"The President shall, by and with the advice and consent of the senate, appoint three commissioners, who shall attend such conference on behalf of the United States, and shall report the doings thereof to the President, who shall transmit the same to congress.

"Said commissioners shall each receive the sum of $2,500 and their reasonable expenses, to be approved by the secretary of state, and the amount necessary to pay such compensation and expenses is hereby appropriated out of any money in the treasury not otherwise appropriated.

"Section 3. That any holder of the coin authorized by this act may deposit the same with the treasurer or any assistant treasurer of the United States, in sums not less than ten dollars, and receive therefor certificates of not less than ten dollars each, corresponding with the denominations of the United States notes. The coin deposited for or representing the certificates shall be retained in the treasury for the payment of the same on demand. Said certificate shall be receivable for customs, taxes, and all public dues, and, when so received, may be reissued.

"Section 4. All acts and parts of acts inconsistent with the provisions of this act are hereby repealed."

A comparison drawn between the provisions of the original bill introduced by Mr. Bland and passed by the House, and those of the act of February 28th, will be instructive.

The House bill was a free coinage measure, and it placed silver as a money metal on the same footing as gold. It proposed to restore silver to the same position which it held, in law, prior to its demonetization in 1873.

Free coinage of gold created an unlimited demand for it as money. Under free coinage, the owner of gold bullion had the right of entry to any mint of the United States, he could have his bullion transformed into gold coin without charge, and returned to him as full legal tender money. Therefore, the law which conferred the right of free coinage upon the owner of gold bullion created an unlimited demand of the use of that precious metal as money; the Government had never restricted the amount of gold coinage.

Free and unlimited coinage of silver likewise would have created a demand for it as money as extensive as its production.

In all ages, the chief use of the precious metals arose from their utility as a medium of exchange—money.

The demand for the use of these metals has always exceeded their supply.

By the Bland-Allison law, the coinage of silver dollars was limited, and that coinage was on Government account alone.

At the time of the passage of the Bland-Allison law, the production of silver from the mines of the United States amounted to more than $45,000,000 for that year.

Since the demonetization of silver in 1873, its total production in the United States amounted to $210,000,000.

This law provided for the purchase of not less than $2,000,000 of silver nor more than $4,000,000 per month.

The bullion so bought by the Government was to be coined into dollars as fast as purchased, and the gain or seigniorage arising from this coinage was to be paid into the Treasury.

It will be seen that the Secretary of the Treasury was not legally compelled to purchase more silver per month than the minimum amount ($2,000,000).

A purchase of the minimum amount of silver would afford a market for only one-half of the yearly production, and this would result in an accumulation of a large surplus for which there would be no demand. This surplus would fix the price of every ounce of silver mined in the United States, causing a fall in its bullion value.

This result would afford an opportunity for the national banking money power to point to the silver dollar as a "dishonest dollar," a "90-cent dollar."

Mr. Sherman held the Treasury portfolio, and it was averred that he would use all the influence of his office to discredit the new coinage. He was known to be an unrelenting enemy of the free coinage of silver, and his subsequent speeches and writings gave abundant proofs of that fact.

It was further provided in that act, that the amount of money at any one time invested in such silver bullion, exclusive of such resulting coin, should not exceed $5,000,000.

By this restriction the Secretary of the Treasury could limit the annual purchase of silver to $29,000,000. He was not compelled to purchase silver exceeding $2,000,000 per month, or $24,000,000 per annum, and this policy which was carried out by the Secretary, made the Government a "bear" in the silver market.

This law gave rise to a new form of contracts based upon the legal tender clause which contained the following language, "Except where otherwise expressly stipulated in the contract."

This exception was the most absurd provision ever embodied in a monetary law. It declared the silver dollar to be legal tender, yet it conferred upon money lenders the power to demonetize it by private contract. It made the mere will of an individual superior to the collective will of the nation. It placed the greed of the shylock above the power of the constitution. Every usurer was permitted to constitute himself a Congress and a President to demonetize silver at will. While the powerful Government of the United States was compelled to receive these silver dollars for debts and demands due it, the holders of mortgages could exact gold obligations. It transferred to the hands of the national banking money power the right to loan Government credit in the form of bank notes, costing it one cent on the dollar, at a high rate of interest, exact a note payable in gold, with the "vested privilege" of making war against the currency of the United States.

It built up a powerful privileged class, whose interests would be antagonistic to any future legislation of Congress, having for its object an enlarged use of silver as money.

In his uncontradicted evidence before the British gold and silver commission, on June 24, 1887, J. Barr Robertson stated that "The French law makes it criminal to act on the basis of premium on money or discount on money. It always did so."

The policy of France, which has the most scientific system of money in the world, makes it a crime for any one of its citizens to attempt to demonetize its money by private contract.

In that nation, the sovereign power of the State over the legal value of money cannot be impaired by the greed of money changers, bullion dealers, and bankers. After the enactment of this law a new system of written contracts providing for the payment of money came into vogue, denominated "gold contracts," all of which contained a stipulation that the obligation should be payable in "Gold coin of the present weight and fineness or its equivalent."

Railroad bonds and mortgages containing gold clauses, aggregating many hundreds of millions of dollars, were fastened upon this species of property, and real estate mortgages and promissory notes amounting to immense sums were made payable in gold coin.

This plan of the money-lending class actually made an enormous indebtedness payable in gold, a coin constantly appreciating in value, and it practically made the single standard of gold the financial policy of the country.

Not a single United States bond expressed an agreement to pay in gold, and yet the Government turned the great majority of its citizens over to the tender mercies of the money-lenders of the East and Great Britain, by authorizing them to exact gold payments.

The legality of contracting against any part of the legal tender money of the nation is extremely doubtful; and it seems that, on the plainest principles of justice, and on the highest grounds of public policy, a contract in which it is sought to demonetize legal tender money is utterly void, and is therefore unconstitutional.

Section 2 of the Bland-Allison Act authorized the President to invite the countries of Europe to join the United States in a conference to secure the adoption of a common ratio between gold and silver, and for the purpose of establishing an international bi-metallic money, and securing fixity of relative value between these metals.

The President was authorized to appoint three Commissioners to represent the United States at such conference, if any should be held. The Commissioners were to report the doings of the conference and he was to transmit the same to Congress.

This section marked the beginning of those successive pilgrimages of so-called international monetary commissions, who, as the representatives of the United States, humiliated the American people by begging the aid of European monarchies to assist in the establishment of a financial system for this republic.

Section 3 provided for the issue of silver certificates to any person who deposited with the Treasurer or any Assistant Treasurer of the United States silver dollars in sums of not less than ten dollars.

The coin deposited for these certificates was to be retained in the Treasury for the payment of the said certificates on demand. These certificates were receivable for customs, taxes and all public dues, and when so received could be reissued.

The object of this section in providing for the issuance of silver certificates was to obviate objections against the use of silver because of its weight. The certificate was a credit money based on the silver dollars so deposited, which latter constituted a trust fund as a means for redeeming the certificates.

To Senator Booth, of California, belongs the honor of suggesting the provisions of section 3 of this law.

Section 4 repealed all former laws inconsistent with the act.

When this bill was up for consideration before Congress, the national banking money power and its subsidized press continually prophesied that if the silver bill should become a law, the gold of the nation would take flight to Europe, leaving this country upon a silver basis. The leading national bank presidents of New York City were especially active in denouncing the bill, and numerous predictions were made by them that it would be impossible to resume specie payment if it became a law.

George S. Coe, President of the American Exchange National Bank of New York City, publicly stated that he would give $50,000 to be at the head of the line of those who would present themselves at the sub-treasury on the 1st day of January, 1879, to offer greenbacks for gold, should President Hayes not veto the bill.

So far as is known, Mr. Coe still retains his $50,000, which he publicly stated that he would offer for the privilege of having the first opportunity to present greenbacks for redemption in gold, and for the plain reason that greenbacks were at par with gold—that yellow divinity of the money changers—before the 1st day of January, 1879, approached.

One of the reasons urged against the passage of the Bland-Allison law, as stated heretofore, was that it would endanger the resumption of specie payments, and that it would result in placing the country on a silver basis.

On the 19th of March, 1878, three weeks after the law was in force, Senators Morill, Dawes, Ferry, Jones, Allison, Kernan, Wallace, Bayard, and Voorhees, composing the Finance Committee of the Senate, had a conference with Secretary Sherman to obtain his views upon the effect of the new silver coinage law upon resumption.

During this conference the following statements were made by the Secretary to the committee in answer to the inquiries of its members:—

"CHAIRMAN: What effect has the silver bill had, or is likely to have, upon resumption?

"SECRETARY SHERMAN: I do not want to tread on delicate ground in answering that question, Mr. Chairman. I shall have to confess that I have been mistaken myself. Now, as to the silver bill, I have watched its operations very closely. I think the silver bill has had some adverse effects, and it has had some favorable effects, on the question of resumption. Perhaps the best way for me to proceed would be to state the adverse effects first. It has undoubtedly stopped refunding operations. Since the agitation of the silver question, I have not been able largely to sell bonds, although I have made every effort to do so.

"Now, another adverse effect the silver bill has had is to stop the accumulation of coin. Since the 1st of January we have accumulated no coin, except for coin certificates, and except the balance of revenue over expenditure. The revenues in coin being more than enough to pay the interest of the debt and coin liabilities, we accumulate some coin.

"Another effect that the silver bill has had is to cause the return of our bonds from Europe. Although the movement of our bonds in this direction has been pretty steady for more than a year, yet it is latterly largely increased, how much I am not prepared to say.

"On the other hand, I will give the favorable effects. In the first place, the silver bill satisfied a strong public demand for bi-metallic money, and that demand is, no doubt, largely sectional. No doubt there is a difference of opinion between the West and South and the East on this subject, but the desire for remonetization of silver was almost universal. In a government like ours it is always good to obey the popular current, and that has been done, I think, by the passage of the silver bill. Resumption can be maintained more easily upon a double standard than upon a single standard. The bulky character of silver would prevent payments in it, while gold, being more portable, would be more freely demanded, and I think resumption can be maintained with a less amount of silver than of gold alone.

"SENATOR BAYARD: You are speaking of resumption upon the basis of silver, or of silver and gold?

"SECRETARY SHERMAN: Yes, sir; I think it can be maintained better upon a bi-metallic, or alternative standard, than upon a single one, and with less accumulation of gold. In this way remonetization of silver would rather aid resumption. The bonds that have been returned from Europe have been readily absorbed —remarkably so. The recent returns in New York show the amount of bonds absorbed in this country is at least a million and a quarter a day. We have sold scarcely any from the Treasury since that time. This shows the confidence of the people in our securities, and their rapid absorption will tend to check the European scare.

"SENATOR VOORHEES: That shows, Mr. Secretary, that this cry of alarm in New York was unfounded. Then, this capital seeks our bonds when this bi-metallic basis is declared?

"SECRETARY SHERMAN: Yes; many circumstances favor this. The demand for bonds extends to the West and to the banks.

"SENATOR JONES: Then, in its effect upon the return of the vast amount of bonds you refer to, would there not be an element of strength added in favor of resumption, in that the interest on these bonds returned would not be a constant drain upon the country?

"SECRETARY SHERMAN: Undoubtedly.

"SENATOR JONES: Would the fact that they come back enable us to maintain resumption much easier?

"SECRETARY SHERMAN: Undoubtedly.

"SENATOR BAYARD: You speak of resumption upon a bi-metallic basis being easier. Do you make that proposition irrespective of the readjustment of the relative values of the two metals as we have declared them?

"SECRETARY SHERMAN: I think so. Our mere right to pay in silver would deter a great many people from presenting notes for redemption who would readily do so if they could get the lighter and more portable coin in exchange. Besides, gold coin can be exported, while silver coin could not be exported, because its market value is less than its coin value.

"SENATOR BAYARD: I understand that it works practically very well. So long as the silver is less in value than the paper you will have no trouble in redeeming your paper. When a paper dollar is worth ninety-eight cents nobody is going to take it to the Treasury and get ninety-two cents in silver; but what are you to do as your silver coin is minted? By the 1st of July next or the 1st of January next you have eighteen or twenty millions of silver dollars which are in circulation and payable for duties, and how long do you suppose this short supply of silver and your control of it by your coinage will keep it equivalent to gold—when one is worth ten cents less than the other?

"SECRETARY SHERMAN: Just so long as it can be used for anything that gold is used for. It will be worth in this country the par of gold until it becomes so abundant and bulky that people will become tired of carrying it about; but in our country that can be avoided by depositing it for coin-certificates."

Such was the testimony given by Secretary Sherman in reply to the questions propounded to him by these distinguished men, and it demonstrated the real reason why a single standard of gold was preferred by the national banking money power. Gold, from its portability, could be more easily exported than silver, and large quantities of the former metal could be readily shifted back and forth between New York City and London as a means to create temporary panics, and thus afford the gold gamblers and stock speculators opportunities to depress or raise the price of bonds, stocks, and securities whenever it subserved their interests.

In 1878, after the passage of the Bland-Allison law, Secretary Sherman authorized the sub-treasury at New York City to become a member of the Clearing House Association, whose membership consisted of sixty-six national banks of that city.

This association was the most powerful financial body in the United States, and it was the head and front of the money power.

This act of Secretary Sherman was an exceedingly shrewd move on his part to add an official sanction to the war that was to be waged against the use of silver and silver certificates by the Clearing House Association.

To afford a consecutive statement of the various financial measures of Congress, we must retrace our steps to the 16th day of January, 1878.

At and prior to this time a controversy arose as to whether United States bonds were payable in gold solely.

To set this question at rest forever, Senator Matthews, of Ohio, submitted a concurrent resolution in the Senate, declaring that all United States bonds issued under the Refunding Act of July 14, 1870, and the Resumption Act of January 14, 1875, could be paid at the option of the government in standard silver dollars of 412½ grains without violation of the public faith.

All proposed amendments were voted down, and the resolution was agreed to by a vote of 43 yeas to 22 nays.

On January 29, 1879, the House agreed to the resolution in the form in which it came from the Senate by a vote of 189 yeas to 79 nays.

Divested of its preamble which merely recited the facts in controversy, the resolution is as follows:—

"Resolved by the Senate (the House of Representatives concurring therein), That all the bonds of the United States issued under the said acts of Congress hereinbefore recited are payable, principal and interest, at the option of the government of the United States, in silver dollars of the coinage of the United States, containing $412\frac{1}{2}$ grains each of standard silver; and that to restore to its coinage such silver coins as a legal tender in payment of said bonds, principal and interest, is not in violation of the public faith nor in derogation of the rights of the public creditor."

It is in force to this day as declaratory of the financial policy of the United States.

On December 9, 1878, Mr. Fort moved that the House suspend the rules and pass a resolution, declaring any discrimination against standard silver dollars by National Banking Associations a defiance of law, and instructing the Committee on Banking and Currency to report a bill for withdrawing their circulation.

The resolution received a majority, but not the necessary two-thirds vote, and it failed to pass.

The republican members of the House voted almost solidly against the resolution.

This resolution was brought forward in the House as a warning to the Clearing House Association of New York City, composed largely of national banks, for its refusal to accept silver dollars and silver certificates in settlement of balances due from the various banks.

Although the Bland-Allison law was in effect but a few months, the traitorous national banking money power at once begun a war upon the lawful money of the United States, and this was done with the open consent of the Secretary of the Treasury, who had made the sub-treasury at New York City a member of the Clearing House Association as an aid to the consummation of its schemes.

This action of the national banks in thus deliberately conspiring to nullify a law of the United States, gave origin to a warm debate in Congress, during which Secretary Sherman was severely criticised for giving official sanction to the acts of the associated banks.

During the session of the Fifty-first Congress, at which time Mr. Sherman was a member of the Senate, Senator Morgan, of Alabama, in a debate upon the money question, recalled this fact and asserted that the former had, while Secretary of the Treasury, been cognizant of the designs of the clearing house banks to refuse silver in payment of balances, and that those banks were emboldened to pursue that course by the acquiescence of the Secretary.

He proceeded to quote from a statement made by Mr. Weston, Secretary of the Monetary Commission of 1886, in which the latter said:—

"On the 8th inst. [November, 1878,] a committee of these banks [New York Clearing House Association] had a conference at Washington with the Secretary of Treasury [Mr. Sherman], at which were present the Attorney-General and some minor officials.

"The result was a plan submitted by the banks on the 12th inst., and agreed to, only one bank representative [Mr. Colgate] objecting. The leading features of it, are first, that the banks will reject silver deposits, except as re-payable in kind; second, that silver shall not be allowed as clearing house money except for small fractional sums not exceeding $10; and third, that in respect to all payments by government drafts on the New York banks or on the United States assistant treasurer at New York, they shall be cleared at the clearing house in New York, at which a desk is to be assigned to a representative of the United States Treasury. At the bank meeting on the 12th Mr. Colgate objected to the plan, that it could only mean 'To fly in the face of Congress and to declare the silver dollar that has been declared a legal tender to be worthless."

In spite of the immense power of the banks, aided by the official power of Secretary Sherman, to discredit the legal tender silver dollars and silver certificates, Congress, at its very next session, after this exposure of the conduct of the Clearing House Association and that of Secretary Sherman, passed a law requiring that no national bank should become a member of any clearing house, or exercise any privilege therein to any kind whatever, unless it agreed to accept silver on deposits and receive silver certificates as money through which the balances might be settled.

Although the organized banks still continued their aggressions upon the rights of the people, and although they exerted their utmost power to degrade the silver dollar and its representative, this money became so popular with the people that they exchanged gold coin for silver certificates at the Treasury of the United States.

This exchange of gold coin for silver began in November, 1880, and continued until the Treasury made a gain in gold aggregating $78,000,000. Thus the absurd predictions set forth in the veto message of President Hayes, and echoed by the senseless clamors of the national banks, were answered by the common sense and patriotism of the people of the United States.

In 1878, the year that the Bland-Allison bill became a law, the number of failures were 10,478, with liabilities of $234,383,000; in the following year of 1879 the list of failures were only 6,658, with liabilities of $98,149,000—a remarkable decrease.

According to the provisions of the Resumption Act of 1875, greenbacks were redeemable in specie on and after the 1st day of January, 1879. Prior to this time greenbacks and United States notes were on a parity with gold, and hence on May 31, 1878, Congress enacted a law forbidding the further destruction of these legal tenders, and the Secretary of the Treasury was authorized to re-issue them for the payment of demands against the United States. Senator Thurman introduced this bill in the Senate, and against the combined opposition of the national banks, secured its passage through Congress, thus preserving this currency to that amount.

In the meantime, however, prior to January 1, 1879, Secretary Sherman issued a circular to the collectors of the various ports throughout the United States, directing them to receive United States notes and Treasury notes in payment of duties on imported goods.

The act of July 11, 1862, which provided for the issue of Treasury notes, prohibited the Secretary of the Treasury from receiving them for duties on imports.

Nevertheless Secretary Sherman, by a mere executive order, nullified this part of that act by ordering the collectors of custom duties to receive them. This order made the Treasury notes, in this respect, the equal of gold.

The object of the Secretary in adopting this policy

excited considerable discussion in Congress, but the order was acquiesced in by the people, for the reason that the discrimination so long exerted against the greenback was withdrawn. The government honored its own currency by receiving it for taxes—the best form of redemption ever adopted by a nation.

CHAPTER VI.

THE NATIONAL BANKS WAGE WAR UPON THE CREDIT OF THE UNITED STATES.

"The wisdom of the whole nation can see farther than the sages of Westminster Hall. The collective knowledge and penetration of the people at large are more to be depended on than the boasted discernment of all the bar. The reason is clear: Their eyes are not dazzled by the prospects of an opposite interest. The Crown has no lure sufficiently tempting to make them forget themselves and the general good."— Edmund Burke.

The profoundest thinkers upon the subject of free government have always maintained that the common people are inspired by nobler sentiments of justice than that select class who arrogate to themselves all virtue and knowledge.

History has affirmed, time and again, that the collective wisdom of the people is the safest guide for a nation.

The celebrated Edmund Burke, in that splendid defense of Woodfall, the publisher of the letters of Junius, goes so far as to declare, in the august presence of the highest court of England, that the sense of justice prevalent among the common people is truer than that entertained by those learned in the law.

The reason why the common people seldom err in their instincts of justice is, that they are not the highly favored subjects of special privileges, and that they are not continually seeking unearned advantages over their fellow-men.

On the other hand the moving reason why the

wealthy, privileged, and aristocratic portion of mankind is not animated and governed as largely by the plain principles of justice, as the great majority of common people, is very apparent, as it is an established fact that the possession of great wealth and privileges render its possessors eager for added accumulations, and this results in a selfishness from which springs by far the larger part of the unnecessary evils of government.

With this latter class the desire of heaping up great wealth develops into a controlling passion—in many cases it degenerates into a mania.

This observation is true of the national banking money power. Notwithstanding it received a gift of the most valuable and profitable franchises ever conferred upon organized capital, it was continually demanding new concessions at the hands of Congress. It was insatiable.

This money power persevered in its vindictive warfare against the people, its subsidized press publicly threatened Congress with a visitation of wrath, and it utilized its control of the currency to oppress.

It asserted that the country needed a king, and that a strong government should be erected upon the ruins of American liberty.

The national banks continued their opposition to the coinage of silver, but without avail.

On April 16, 1879, the Committee on Coinage, Weights, and Measures, by Hon. A. H. Stephens, of Georgia, reported House bill No. 4, which provided that fractional silver coins should be a legal tender for any sum not exceeding ten dollars in any one payment.

On April 19, 1879, Mr. Springer moved an amendment to the third section of the bill, increasing the legal tender debt-paying power of fractional silver coin to twenty dollars in any one payment.

The bill so amended in its third section passed the House on the 22d day of April, 1879, and it was transmitted to the Senate, where, on May 28th, an amendment offered by the Committee on Finance was adopted, striking out the word "twenty" and inserting the word "ten" in lieu thereof.

The bill thus amended passed the Senate, was concurred in by the House, and became a law June 9, 1879.

The effect of this measure increased the legal tender power of fractional silver coins from five dollars to ten.

On the same day the House passed a bill providing for the exchange of trade dollars for legal tender standard silver dollars.

It was sent to the Senate but that body buried it by a reference to the Finance Committee.

Had this proposed measure been enacted into law, a large volume of full legal tender silver dollars would have been added to the circulation, increasing the amount of money at least thirty millions, and it would have removed a large mass of non-legal tender trade dollars as a disturbing element in the silver market.

The national banks opposed this bill, and hence it was smothered in the republican Senate.

On June 27, 1879, Mr. Vest, of Missouri, offered the following resolution in the Senate:—

"Resolved by the Senate (the House of Representatives concurring), That the complete remonetization of silver, its full restoration as a money metal, and its free coinage by the mints of the United States are demanded alike by the dictates of justice and wise statesmenship."

On June 30th this resolution was referred to the Committee on Finance on motion of Mr. Allison, by a vote of 23 yeas to 22 nays.

This resolution was never reported from this committee back to the Senate.

One singularity which will attract the attention of the reader is, that every measure adopted by the House providing for the restoration of silver, was, on reaching the Senate, uniformly referred to the Finance Committee, from whence it never returned.

As it was then constituted, the Finance Committee was composed largely of Eastern Senators, and this fact affords an explanation of the wonderful facility with which this committee nullified all efforts of the House for remedial legislation.

In the meantime Secretary Sherman was administering the Treasury Department with a view of throwing discredit upon the silver coinage, and he persisted in the policy of refusing to pay out silver dollars, except where specific demands were made for that money. His object in following out this line of policy, aimed at a large accumulation of silver dollars in the Treasury, and this condition would supply him with arguments to convince Congress, if possible, that no one desired silver as money. This intention was evidenced by a communication to Congress by him, in which he requested an appropriation for the construction of additional vaults for the storage of standard silver dollars.

At this period United States bonds were at a very

high premium, and this fact led to a severe contraction of the currency by the national banks.

It will be remembered that the original National Banking Act of February 25, 1863, provided for a distribution of circulating bank notes, and as a consequence of that provision the power to suddenly contract or expand the volume of circulating notes was withheld from the banks.

This salutary provision was repealed by section 4 of the act of June 20, 1874, which authorized the national banks at any time, and for any reason which they chose to consider sufficient, to deposit United States notes and treasury notes to secure their circulating bank notes, and contract the currency to the extent of the substitution of government legal tenders for the bonds deposited as security by the national banks; these banks then withdrew their bonds and sold them for the high premium which they then commanded.

This power conferred on the national banks, by which they could contract the volume of currency, was a standing menace against the prosperity of the country; and armed with this destructive weapon they could, without any notice to the people, prostrate every industry in the country.

The extent to which this sudden contraction and expansion was practiced by the banks was clearly stated in a report made by Mr. Gilfillan, United States Treasurer, for the year 1880. Mr. Gilfillan says:—

"Under the construction placed upon the law, banks which have thus reduced their circulation have been permitted to increase it again as often and as largely as they chose, whether their legal tender deposits were exhausted or not. An example will better illustrate these operations. In January and February,

1875, a certain bank reduced its circulation from $308,490 to $45,000 by deposits of legal tender notes. Between September 26, 1876, and May 26, 1877, and before that deposit was exhausted, it increased its circulation to $450,000. Between August 14th and September 10, 1877, it again reduced its circulation to $45,000. On September 19, 1877, nine days after completing the deposits for this reduction, it again began to take out additional circulation, although $402,550 of prior deposits remained in the Treasury, and by the 26th of that month its circulation had again been increased to $450,000. July 22, 1878, it, for the third time, reduced its circulation to $45,000, and in August and September, 1879, again increased it to $450,000, at which it now remains, the balance of its former legal tender deposit then in the Treasury being $112,615."

This report exhibits the dangerous power placed in the hands of the national banks to unsettle values, disturb business, and inflict panics whenever it was to the interests of the national banking money power to exhibit their strength over the legitimate business of the people.

Mr. Gilfillan further says:—

"No one will contend that this was a legitimate and proper method of conducting business under the national banking system, and yet it can be resorted to every-day by every bank in the United States as long as the fourth section of the act of June 20, 1874, remains unrepealed. It disturbs values, affects the money market, and subjects the government to unnecessary expense, merely to gratify a spirit of speculation and gain on the part of the managers of the bank, and it ought to be peremptorily forbidden in the future."

This last extract clearly demonstrates that it was in the power of the thousands of national banks to effect a combination, or trust, for the contraction of the volume of currency whenever such policy would be decided upon by them to influence the legislation of Congress.

During 1880 and 1881, a large amount of the national debt would fall due, and provision must be made for the payment of bonds aggregating $800,000,000. These bonds bore interest at the rate of 4, 4½ and 5 per cent. per annum.

During the session of 1879, Representatives Garfield, of Ohio, and Wood, of New York, both introduced bills in the House, providing for the exchange of these maturing obligations for bonds bearing four per cent. interest, and running from twenty to forty years. These bills were referred to the appropriate committee, where they remained until the latter part of 1880.

After the presidential election of that year the committee reported a substitute for the Wood bill, providing for the funding of these maturing bonds at three and one-half per cent. interest, and running from ten to forty years.

A strenuous effort was made to push this bill through the House, but it was not successful, and it was amended by that body, making the bonds redeemable at the option of the government after the expiration of five years from their date of issue, and the rate of interest was reduced to three per cent. per annum.

The bonds were to be sold by public subscription, at not less than par, and no contract or award of these bonds should be made by the Secretary of the Treasury to any syndicate, or bankers, or otherwise, until after the expiration of thirty days from the date of the announcement that public subscriptions would be opened for the sale of said bonds.

The Secretary was authorized to designate banks to receive subscriptions for bonds so offered.

Section 5 of this Funding Act was as follows:—

"From and after the 1st day of July, 1881, the three per cent. bonds authorized by this act shall be the only bonds receivable as security for national bank circulation, or as security for the safe-keeping and prompt payment of the public money deposited with such banks: Provided, That the Secretary of the Treasury shall not have issued all the bonds herein authorized, or so many thereof as to make it impossible for him to issue the amount of bonds required: And provided further, That no bond upon which interest has ceased shall be accepted or shall be continued on deposit as security for circulation or for the safe-keeping of the public money; and in case bonds so deposited shall not be withdrawn, as provided by law, within thirty days after the interest has ceased thereon, the banking association depositing the same shall be subject to the liabilities and proceedings on the part of the Comptroller provided for in section 5234 of the Revised Statutes of the United States: And provided further, That section 4 of the act of June 20, 1874, entitled 'An act fixing the amount of United States notes, providing for a redistribution of the national bank currency, and for other purposes,' be, and the same is hereby, repealed; and sections 5159 and 5160 of the Revised Statutes of the United States be, and the same are hereby, re-enacted."

This section was by far the most important part of the funding bill, and its provisions aimed to curtail the immense powers of the national banks. It required them to substitute the new three per cent. bonds, authorized by this bill, as security for their circulating notes, in lieu of the maturing bonds.

The feature of this measure which the national banks regarded as the most dangerous to their existence, was in that part of the bill which made the bonds redeemable, at the option of the government, after the expiration of five years from the date of their issue.

This would place the power in the hands of the government to discipline the national banks whenever these corporations would refuse to obey the laws, or conspire against the interests of the people. The bonds being redeemable, at the option of the government, after the expiration of five years, the latter could at any period after the lapse of the minimum time, call in those bonds deposited by the national banks to secure their circulation, and thus eventually rid the country of this gigantic money power.

Furthermore, this section would not permit national banks to deposit bonds, upon which interest had ceased, to secure their circulating notes. Neither would it allow them to continue bonds on deposit upon which interest had ceased. Were it otherwise, the national banks could perpetuate their existence against the will of the government, by continuing on deposit bonds that were past due. In case of failure on the part of the banks to withdraw their bonds which were due, and upon which interest had ceased, within thirty days after these bonds matured, the Comptroller of the Currency was authorized to call in the circulation of those banks refusing to obey this provision, and wind up their affairs according to the provisions of section 5,234, of the Revised Statutes of the United States.

Furthermore, the unlimited power of the banks to contract or expand the currency conferred upon them by section 4, of the act of June 20, 1874, was taken away by the proposed re-enactment of sections 5,159 and 5,160 of the Revised Statutes of the United States.

The re-enactment of these two sections would place the control of the circulating bank notes in the hands of the Comptroller of the Currency.

When this three per cent. funding bill was before the House, the greatest pressure was brought to bear upon that body by the combined efforts of the national banks to secure the defeat of the measure. The halls of Congress swarmed with the agents, lobbyists, and attorneys of the money power who attempted to intimidate Congress and defeat the bill. Threats were openly made by these venal scoundrels, that, unless the measure was withdrawn, the national banking money power would punish the country by inflicting a monetary panic upon it.

The New York Tribune, the leading organ of this money power, thus described the vast power of the banks of the East, and hinted at its possible exercise. It said:—

"The time is near when they (the banks) will feel compelled to act strongly. Meanwhile a very good thing has been done. The machinery is now furnished by which, in any emergency, the financial corporations of the East can act together on a single day's notice with such power that no act of Congress can overcome or resist their decision."

In its zeal to serve the purpose of the financial corporations of the East, it exposed the traitorous sentiments of the financial magnates of New York City. It said:—

"It is astonishing, yea, startling, the extent to which faith prevails in money circles in New York that we ought to have a king."

The banks of the East, in their efforts to coerce Congress into submission, at once commenced a rapid contraction of the currency during the time the bill was under consideration by the House.

In the short period of thirteen days, the banks of New York City surrendered their circulating notes to the extent of $18,722,340, and conspired to precipitate a panic upon the country, with its accompaniments of bankruptcy, financial ruin, and suffering.

This concerted action of the New York banks produced such a flurry in the money market, that prices fell five, ten, and fifteen per cent. in a few moments; and interest at the rate of 472 per cent. per annum was exacted for the use of money by these infamous conspirators against the human race.

The situation in New York City became so acute, that the Secretary of the Treasury relieved the condition of the people by purchasing a large amount of bonds, and thereby increasing the volume of money by many millions; while the Canadian banks forwarded $8,000,000 to be thrown on the money market.

This course of the banks led to a severe denunciation of their policy in Congress.

In a speech in the House on the 1st of March, 1881, Hon. John G. Carlisle, strongly arraigned the New York banks as the bitterest enemies of the government and the people; he said:—

"But, Mr. Speaker, by far the most dangerous feature yet introduced into the national banking system is contained in that part of the fourth section of the act of June 20, 1874, which authorizes the banks at any time, and for any reason which they may choose to consider sufficient, to deposit lawful money with the Treasurer, contract the currency to that extent and withdraw their bonds; and, sir, it is not going too far to say that until this feature is wholly eliminated or materially modified there can be no assurance of safety to any legitimate investment or business enterprise in this country. If there was ever a doubt as to the dangerous character of the power which this part of the law gives to the banks over the business and property of the people, the arbitrary and unjustifiable proceedings of the last week ought to dispel it forever. The power was conferred in the first instance, as I have said, for a special and temporary purpose, the equalization of the national bank circulation, but when the Resumption Act of January 14, 1875, was passed, which removed all restrictions as to the amount of such currency and made the system entirely free, there was no longer any necessity for this clause, and it should have been instantly repealed. It is a standing menace against the prosperity of the country. Armed with this destructive weapon the banks may at any time, without a moment's notice or a shadow of provocation, strike down every industry and every commercial enterprise of the people.

"The banks, or some of them at least, first began to pervert this section of the statute from its original purpose and abuse the power which it conferred upon them by depositing lawful money and withdrawing their bonds from time to time, in order to speculate upon them in the market. They thus withdrew large amounts of their circulation and contracted the currency, not because the reduced demands of business made the outstanding volume of circulation unnecessary or unprofitable, but simply because they wanted to realize the high premiums on their bonds and speculate in the securities upon which the Government had already delivered to them 90 per cent. in notes. These notes would be left outstanding for the time being, but an equal amount of Treasury notes would, of course, be withdrawn from circulation and held at the Department to redeem the bank notes as they might come in. The Treasurer, in his last annual report, describes this process by reference to actual transactions in his office; and as his statement on this subject cannot be condensed without impairing its force, I give it in his own words."

After quoting from the report of 1880, made by Treasurer Gilfillan, Mr. Carlisle continued:—

"Under this section the banks have it in their power to contract the currency and produce financial distress, involving every interest in the country and embarrassing the operations of the Government itself, whenever they may think it will promote their special interests to do so. If they do not like proposed legislation in Congress or elsewhere; if they are opposed to the success of a particular political party; if they conclude that they ought to be exempt from all taxation, State and Federal; if they want additional privileges conferred upon them in respect to any matter connected with their business; in short, if their opinions and interests are not consulted in all cases, whatsoever, they can resort at once to this tremendous power over the fortunes of the people and thus bring the timid to terms and ruin all who refuse to accede to their demands. A plausible pretext can always be found or invented for the exercise of such a power as this, and powerful influences can always be brought to justify and sustain it.

"The two Houses of Congress, representing the aggregate interests of fifty millions of people, have, after mature deliberation, passed a bill which the banks have chosen to consider obnoxious to them, and forewith—within thirteen days—they have contracted the currency to the extent of $18,722,340 and precipitated a crisis which would have been disastrous to the country had it not been met by measures which they had no power to prevent. The prompt action of the Secretary of the Treasury in purchasing a large amount of bonds at the city of New York, and the course of the Canadian banks in throwing seven or eight million dollars of their loanable capital on the market, alone prevented a catastrophe from the effects of which we might not have entirely recovered for many years.

"When Secretary McCulloch, several years since, in pursuance of his contraction policy, began to retire and cancel legal tender notes at the rate of $4,000,000,000 per month, it produced such consternation in business circles that Congress was forced to intervene at once and arrest the process by the passage of a joint resolution; but now we have seen nearly $19,000,000 of circulation withdrawn in less than half a month, not by the Government, but by institutions in the management of which the Government has no voice, and still gentlemen here insist that the power under which this has been done, and under which it may at any time be repeated, shall not be taken away. Why, sir, the whole contraction of legal tender Treasury notes under the provisions of the Resumption Act, from January 14, 1875, to May 31, 1878, when it was prohibited by law, was only $34,318,984, not twice as much in more than three years as the bank contraction had been in less than two weeks.

"This experience warns us that we cannot safely permit this great power to remain in the hands of these institutions unchecked by legal restrictions. It is an engine of destruction standing in the very narrowest part of the way to permanent industrial and commercial prosperity in this country; for there can be no such prosperity anywhere, in the midst of sudden and enormous contractions of the currency; nor will prudent and experienced business men embark in large and expensive enterprises when the power to make such contractions is held by private and interested parties who acknowledge no restraints except public sentiment and their own views of the public welfare.

"By law the volume of legal tender notes is limited to $346,681,016, while under the policy of the Government nearly $150,000,000 in gold and silver coin are permanently withheld from circulation and hoarded in the Treasury. Of the $454,000,000 gold coin in the country the Government and the banks held, on the 1st day of November last, $254,000,000, and the people only $200,000,000. The circulation of State banks is taxed out of existence; the coinage of silver is limited by statute to $4,000,000 per month; and so it appears that by statute or public policy every form of currency which the people can use in the transaction of their business is restricted, except national bank notes. They alone are perfectly free from all restictions, legal or otherwise, and upon them the people are compelled to rely under existing circumstances for the additional facilities of exchange necessary to enable them to carry on their growing industries and conduct their rapidly increasing commercial enterprises.

"What a fatal policy it is, in view of these considerations, to retain on the statute book as part of our currency system a law which subjects all these great interests to the arbitrary will or mistaken judgment of two thousand corporations."

The dangerous powers conferred upon the national banks were so clearly pointed out by Mr. Carlisle in his magnificent speech that the bill passed the House by a decisive vote.

In the meantime, the policy of the banks in making war upon the public credit received criticism from many journals which were friendly to the national bank system.

We will quote a few extracts:—

"It is a question whether a clique of bankers is to dictate to Congress and the country what is for the best interest of the country, and to manipulate the money market in order to depress the stock market."
—New York Advertiser.

"It is rule or ruin with the national banks. When Congress gets down on its honorable knees to the national banks everything will be lovely. Fattening on the Treasury for years, the national banks have entered into a conspiracy to wreck the business of the country rather than submit to what they consider unfavorable legislation. The people will remember this against them, and the day of reckoning is not as far off as they imagine."—Chicago News.

"Some of the national banks of this city have played a very contemptible part in the flurry of yesterday and to-day. It is not the first time that they have acted in this way against the public credit. In one instance, which we do not care to name at present, but which will be understood by most Wall street people, the want of loyalty to the public credit has shown itself on all occasions, from the outbreak of the civil war in 1861 down to the present time."—New York Commercial.

"It is understood that there is to be an amendment offered in the House to the bill providing for the issue of greenbacks to take the place of bank circulation that may be withdrawn. If this sensible precaution is taken it will instantly restore confidence and take permanently away from the banks this fearful power to withdraw in one day all their bills from circulation, or, what is worse, lock up an equal amount of gold and legal tenders and leave the street utterly without means of doing business. Such terrible power no set of men should for one instant possess."—New York Graphic.

The New York Tribune uttered the following implied threats against Congress should the bill pass. It said:—

"The country knows that it has escaped a great disaster. Everywhere there is a feeling of intense relief and thankfulness, as substantial people come to realize how terrible a revulsion the enactment of the Carlisle section would have caused. But it is not well to forget that the danger has been escaped only upon condition that the fatal section is defeated. If Congress or the President is led to believe that disaster has been and can be averted by any action of the Treasury Department, so that the pending bill can now be passed without causing a great calamity, the consequences of that error may be incalulably disastrous. Let the situation be fully understood."

The toryism of the Tribune always shone forth conspicuously when it defended the lawless banks of New York City.

"The trade and general business of the country has been subjected to a strain during the past week more severe than any which has been put on them since 1873. This deplorable state of affairs was brought about by the selfish conspiracy of a certain number of national banks bent on opposing the national will in the matter of establishing a lower national rate of interest by such duly chosen representatives of the people of the United States as they have thought proper to adopt. Our Government and people who maintain it have submitted to great sacrifices to afford all reasonable support to national banks. But the banks have not kept within the reasonable limits of their demand for compensation for such financial services as they have been able to render the country.

"A few of these banks have not hesitated to invite the destruction of the whole system and provoke popular anger by pursuing a course which must inevitably force on American citizens the question whether legislative and executive officers chosen to represent the people or a few bank officers are to administer the financial destinies of this country. It is not probable the natural resentment of the legislature against the attempted conspiracy will extend to the condemnation of the whole national system. But we have no doubt at the same time that when the indignation has cooled off, those conspirators against the prosperity and credit of the Republic will be subjected to such temperate and wholesome discipline as shall be a warning to them and their kind for years to come."—New York World.

"It strikes us that the gentlemen in Wall street, who are trying to prevent the Senate Funding Bill from becoming a law, rather make a mistake. Undoubtedly they have a right to express their opinions about the bill, but when it comes to threatening that, unless it is modified to meet their views, they will wreck the trade of the entire country, they go a step too far. The average Congressman has no such fear of banks and bankers as to make him alter his vote to avoid their displeasure, and as to any possibility of the mischief they may do, he will soon find a way to prevent it. If the officers of the banks should attempt, as some foolish men here say they will do, to withdraw their circulation unless certain provisions in the bill are stricken out, it would be very easy to supply the deficiency with an additional issue of greenbacks, and if they try by underhand means to thwart the negotiation of the new bonds because the rate of interest is not high enough to please them, they can be deprived of the privilege of issuing circulation altogether.

"It is a dangerous thing for the tail to attempt to wag the dog, for if the dog gets angry he can switch the tail about in a very unpleasant way for the tail. The truth is, that in matters of national interest there is no set of people as stupid as the Wall street financiers. Absorbed in the business of buying and selling stocks and lending money, they only consider what immediately effects to-day's markets, without a foresight of the future or regard for what is going on elsewhere. In the present case they are evidently in blissful ignorance of the general hostility of the people of the West and Southwest to the national bank system and the slender thread of toleration on which it hangs. It needs only a good pretext to secure the sweeping of the whole thing out of existence, and the substitution for it of any exclusive national currency. That pretext all the Wall street bankers seem bent on furnishing, and Washington will, we fear, be only too glad to seize upon it."—New York Sun.

On March 1, 1881, the Chicago Express, which opposed the pretensions of the national banks, editorially spoke as follows:—

"The funding bill, as it passed both Houses of Congress, was, in the language of a Washington dispatch, 'The most serious blow the national banks ever received from Congress since the organization of the national banking system.'

"The act of January, 1875, clothed the national banks with the power of unlimited and unrestricted contraction and expansion of the currency. It gave them absolute control over the volume of money, and consequently over the market value of labor and all kinds of property. It gave them power to inflate the currency when they could make money through the inflation of prices, and when their interests could be better served by panic, depressed prices and general business stagnation and bankruptcy, they had power to accomplish their end through the contraction of their circulating notes.

"The provisions of the new funding bill materially interfere with their nicely-planned scheme, and deprive them of nearly all their power over sudden contractions and inflation. It puts a limit to their privileges, and bounds to their unwarranted powers.

"Without waiting even for the concurrence of the House in the slight Senate amendments, a large and powerful bank lobby from Wall street and the clearing house association at once bore down upon the White House armed with magazines, Gatling guns and infernal machines of dire calamities, which they threatened would surely explode in the very heart of the nation's business and industries from spontaneous ignition, in case he did not interpose his prerogative to save. They were armed with authority from the national banks represented by the American Bankers' Association to inform his Excellency that in case he withheld his veto they would immediately retire their circulation, in which case a money stringency would follow which would be terribly disastrous to every business interest producing the most ruinous financial crash which ever befell the country."

Senator Plumb, who was one of the three republican Senators that voted for the bill, stated his opinion as follows:—

"I am a national bank president, so I can speak without prejudice. I tell you the crisis has come when we shall see whether the banks run the Government or the Government the banks. I think the Government has a right to fix the rate of interest it will pay, and it is no business of any set of men. It makes no difference to the people if Wall street gamblers do lose money, or railroad stocks stop rising. It would make a difference if the hoes in western cornfields should stop, and it is with the producers that the prosperity of the country rests. Let the bottom fall out of it if it will. It is an artificial movement to coerce the Government."

The funding bill passed Congress, and was presented to President Hayes, who, on March 3, 1881, returned the bill to the House of Representatives with his veto, accompanied by a message stating his objections to the measure.

The following extracts from the message will give the reader a correct opinion of the influence that forced the President to veto this measure, which was the result of the matured labor of Congress. The President says:—

"While in my opinion it would be wise to authorize the Secretary of the Treasury, in his discretion, to offer to the public bonds bearing 3½ per cent. interest in aid of refunding, I should not deem it my duty to interpose my constitutional objection to the passage of the present bill if it did not contain in the fifth section provisions which, in my judgment, seriously impair the value, and tend to the destruction of the present national banking system of the country.

"This system has now been in operation almost

twenty years. No safer or more beneficial banking system was ever established. Its advantages as a business is free to all who have the necessary capital. It furnishes a currency to the people which for convenience and the security of the bill holder has probably never been equaled by that or any other banking system. Its notes are secured by the deposit with the government of the interest-bearing bonds of the United States."

Further on in his veto message, President Hayes makes vigorous objections to section 5 of the act, on the grounds that it jeopardized the existence of the national banks, and there would be no inducement for the organization of additional ones.

He says:—"In short, I cannot but regard the fifth section of the bill as a step in the direction of the destruction of the national banking system."

Again he says:—"Under this section it is obvious that no additional banks will hereafter be organized, except, possibly, in a few cities or localities where the prevailing rates of interest in ordinary business are extremely low."

The extreme solicitude manifested by the President for the national banks is apparent.

Thus the timid Hayes quaked before this august banking monopoly, and vetoed this beneficial measure at the insolent command of an organized clique, whose greed was not even satiated with 472 per cent. usury.

Furthermore, this bill would have resulted in a saving to the Government of many millions per annum by a reduction of the rate of interest.

It will subsequently appear that these bankers who threw the country into a state of panic; who threatened Congress; who forced the weak Hayes to veto this bill; who wanted a king, will, in the near future, constitute themselves the special guardians of that most sacred object—the public credit!

These conspirators, who prevented a reduction in the interest on the public debt, will, in a few years from this period, assume the championship of the public faith!

In the meantime, that powerful ally of the money power, the Secretary of the Treasury, was throwing the weight of his official influence against the silver dollar.

In one of his reports to Congress, he makes the following recommendation with reference to the silver dollar; he says:—

"The Secretary believes that all the beneficial results hoped for from a liberal issue of silver coin by issuing this coin, in pursuance of the general policy of the act of 1853, in exchange for United States notes, coined from bullion purchased in the open market, by the United States."

An analysis of this recommendation, in view of the resumption act of 1875, will illustrate the enmity of Secretary Sherman toward the use of silver as a standard money.

First, He would limit all silver coins, whether dollars or otherwise, as. a legal tender, to the amount of five dollars. Second, With this limited legal tender silver coin he would redeem and retire the United States legal tender notes. Third, He would redeem said silver coin in what?—In gold. And that would be the sole redemption money.

This policy of the Secretary aimed at the complete withdrawal and cancellation of $346,000,000 of legal tenders, by a redemption in silver coin, the latter redeemable in gold.

This scheme of contraction would be followed by continual issues of bonds to secure gold for a redemption fund for this silver.

It will be noticed that this man, who was so anxious to make United States notes and silver coin redeemable in gold, never, during his public career, once intimated that national banks should redeem their circulating notes in gold.

In 1880, Secretary Sherman again inflicted one of his usual recommendations on Congress, asking for the passage of a law to prohibit the further coinage of silver.

We quote his exact language in which he avers:—

"First, It is too bulky for large transactions, and its purpose is confined mainly for payments for manual labor, and for market purposes for change. The amount needed for these purposes is already in excess of the probable demand.

"Second, It is known to contain a quantity of silver of less market value than the gold in gold coin.

"This fact would not impair the circulation of such limited amount as experience shows to be convenient for use, but it does prevent its being held or hoarded as reserves, or exported, and pushes it into active circulation, until it returns to the Treasury, as the least valuable money in use.

"For these reasons the Secretary respectfully but earnestly recommends that the further compulsory coinage of the silver dollar be suspended."

The phrase "compulsory coinage" clearly indicates the hostility of the Secretary toward silver.

An examination of his reasons, urging the suspension of the coinage of the silver dollar, furnishes the strongest argument against his position.

In the first place, the silver dollars are too heavy for large transactions, therefore this fact places them beyond the control of the national banking money power.

The gold gamblers and bullion brokers of Wall street found it difficult to obtain control of those coins whose largest denominations were one dollar pieces.

At the very time that Secretary Sherman urged this objection against the silver dollar, the inconvenience, if any, of its size and weight was obviated by the issuance of silver certificates in denominations of from ten to one thousand dollars.

He says that it was the money of small transactions, such as the payment of wages to labor, and the purchase of provisions.

This is one of the strongest reasons that could be advanced for the continued coinage of the silver dollar. This money that paid the wages of labor was worth one hundred cents on the dollar.

Again, he says that it was of less market value than the gold in the gold dollar. This is true of it as a mere commodity, but as a legal tender, a medium of exchange, it was the equal of gold anywhere on the face of the earth.

But the true animus of the Secretary against the silver dollar sprung from the fact that it was not held, or hoarded, or exported, but that it was in active circulation.

This is the first time that an American Secretary of the Treasury advocated a theory as absurd as the one urged by Mr. Sherman.

The principle upon which a true monetary system is based is that of circulation.

Mints are not established to coin money for the purpose of hoarding it up in the vaults of banks. It performs its true functions when it passes from hand to hand in exchange for the commodities and necessaries of life.

One hundred and fifty years ago the celebrated historian and philosopher, David Hume, in speaking of the effects of hoarding money, said: "As regards prices, money locked up in chests is as if it were annihilated."

He says, "It is not exported."

Just why Secretary Sherman desired a coin that can be readily exported to some foreign country, is not stated by him in his report and recommendations to Congress.

The objections urged against silver because of non-export of that coin, shows that it could not be readily shipped and re-shipped across the Atlantic, at the nod and beck of the stock gamblers, bullion brokers and panic breeders of the New York clearing house and London.

The Secretary said, "It is in active circulation."

This constitutes no crime on the part of silver. All money is coined or issued to subserve the purposes of man by being thrown into active circulation as a medium of exchange.

These weak and puerile reasons of Secretary Sherman against the continued coinage of silver dollars had no effect upon Congress. They were contemptuously ignored by that body.

The childish spite exhibited by Secretary Sherman against silver, his petty slanders against the standard dollar, and his slavish devotion to the traitorous money power, disgusted many of the best men of the party to which he belonged; and, on March 30, 1880, the Chicago Tribune administered a stinging rebuke to his policy. It said:—

"Since the passage of the silver law Mr. Sherman has done everything to disparage silver; he has limited the coinage to the minimum; he refused to exercise the Government's option to pay out silver in any considerable amounts; he has restricted the issue of silver certificates; he made the Treasury Department a member of the New York Clearing House, from which silver is excluded; and has by word and letter and act done all in his power to discourage the use of silver in the United States."

The Tribune denounced his truckling policy on the financial question in the following language:—

"At the opening of the present Congress he made the extraordinary recommendation that Congress strike from $350,000,000 of the greenback currency of the country its legal tender character. It was a high bid for the support of Wall street, but a fatal one addressed to the producing and industrial classes of the country."

In the same editorial the Tribune says:—

"It is highly improbable that Mr. Sherman would receive an electoral vote from any State between the Alleghany and Rocky Mountains upon the issues of abolition of silver money and demonetization of greenbacks which would involve a contraction of the coin and paper legal tender currency exceeding $400,000,000, which would produce ruin to every industrial interest and every legitimate enterprise."

The public career of John Sherman is the most remarkable in the annals of the nation.

When a young man, he turned his attention to the profession of the law, in which he earned but meager fame and fortune. At this time he was a comparatively poor man. After a brief, or rather briefless experience as a lawyer, he determined to enter public life and was elected to the Thirty-fourth Congress in 1854. After serving in the lower House until the outbreak of the war, he was elected to the United States Senate. During the fore part of his career in that body, he served as Chairman of the Committee on Finance, the most important and influential position that can be conferred upon a member of the Senate.

He is the author of the present system of national banks, and he has left his impress upon the various financial measures of the Government from 1861 to 1875.

On the accession of Hayes to the Presidency, he was appointed Secretary of the Treasury at a salary of $8,000 per annum.

During his term of office at the head of that great department, he was a firm friend of the national banking money power which continually waged a war of extermination upon the currency of the United States.

As Secretary of the Treasury he executed those great funding operations, by which it was alleged the people had been saved a vast sum in interest, notwithstanding the singular fact that, during his incumbency, the national banks persuaded President Hayes to veto the funding bill, which reduced the rate of interest upon the national debt.

During these funding operations, he selected various national banks as depositories for the money received from the sale of bonds. One of these banks was known as the First National, situated on Broadway, in New York City. It had a capital of $500,000 and occupied offices that were humble compared with the palatial quarters of the great financial institutions of that city. According to the sworn statement of the officials of this bank, its total capital was $500,000 on the 31st day of December, 1879; on January 1, 1878, the undivided profits, after the payment of dividends, were $142,670; on April 4th of the same year the undivided profits were $339,095.60; on June 14th, after the lapse of two months, the undivided profits were $579,018.88; on October 2d, these profits reached the sum of $804,-511.26; on December 12, 1878, they were $267,700.84. The amount of dividends paid by this bank to its stockholders, during this time, has never been ascertained or disclosed, but that it was very large admits of no doubt.

Here is a single national bank, the special protégé of Secretary Sherman, that, in the short space of ten months, accumulated undivided profits which exceeded its capital stock by more than three hundred thousand dollars.

On January 1, 1878, this pet bank of the Secretary was the custodian of Government funds amounting to $24,759,948.50. On April 4th, of the same year, it held Government funds amounting to $69,927,704.43; on June 14th, these deposits were increased to $128,-109,071.04; on October 2d, they were $3,601,550. It was from these deposits of Government funds that the bank accumulated those enormous undivided profits. Why this comparatively small bank should be made the depository of Government funds to two hundred and fifty-six times its capital has never been explained by Secretary Sherman.

At this time, the sub-treasury of the United States was situated in the same city as this pet bank, and could have been utilized as a depository for this money. It will be seen that this bestowal of official favor upon this bank was worth the immense sum of twenty-one thousand dollars per day.

The figures with reference to the amount of undivided profits of the bank, and the amounts of public money deposited therein, are taken from the report of the Comptroller of the Currency for the year 1880.

On January 1, 1880, Senator Beck, of Kentucky, called the attention of the Senate to these astonishing facts, and in the course of his speech said:—

"I came to the conclusion, looking over these statements, that the best banking capital a man can have is the good will of the Secretary of the Treasury. Suppose the Senator from New York were the best banker and I were to go to him and say, 'I want to go into partnership with you,' and the Senator should say to me, 'What capital have you got?'—'None.' 'What do you propose to do?'—'I propose to bring you the good will and the deposits of the Secretary,' I think the Senator would take me into partnership, and he would make more money by doing it than he ever made in his life, and we would contribute largely to any campaign fund desired by the Secretary."

At the time when this bank was made, the custodian of these fabulous sums of public money, John Thompson, a large stockholder, was its vice-president. He was informed that this bank with a capital of only $500,000 had subscribed as a purchaser of four per cent. bonds to an amount exceeding thirty millions of dollars. When acquainted with this fact, Mr. Thompson protested against the assumption of such a risk, and said:—

"If these bonds were to fall in value one per cent. it would wipe out three fifths of our capital. If they should fall two per cent., it would absorb more than the entire capital of the bank."

Mr. Thompson was assured by its president that there was no danger incurred, because of an agreement with the Secretary of the Treasury that the bank, in that case, would not be compelled to pay for the bonds. Mr. Thompson was astounded at this information, and he sold his stock in the bank, withdrew from its directory and organized the Chase National.

During the administration of Secretary Manning, the Treasury Department deposited sixty-three million dollars with the various national banks of New York City. At that time Mr. Sherman was in the Senate and denounced the act of Mr. Manning in the strongest language. Yet, Secretary Sherman had, while he was at the head of the Treasury, deposited more than four times that sum in a single bank.

During the entire public career of Mr. Sherman as Representative in Congress, as United States Senator, and as Secretary of the Treasury, he was not engaged in any other business. With the exception of the four years that he was Secretary of the Treasury, during which he received eight thousand dollars per annum, his official yearly income never exceeded five thousand dollars.

In a letter to one of his political friends in the State of Ohio, Mr. Sherman details the immense sacrifices he had made for the public during the forty years that he was its servant. He stated that his living expenses annually averaged ten thousand dollars during that time, and that his official income never equaled his expenditures.

At the time of the writing of that letter, his residence in Washington was a palace whose sumptuousness rivaled that of the crowned heads of Europe. In addition, he was one of the most extensive owners of real estate at the capital. He is a very large holder of stocks in national banks and railroad corporations. The miraculous process by which a high official of the Government can expend twice the amount of his salary for ordinary expenses during the early part of his political career—at which time he was a poor man—and yet accumulate a magnificent fortune out of the surplus, has long been a mystery, for the solution of which Mr. Sherman has volunteered no explanation. His accumulation of millions evinces a degree of thrift that is wonderful; and the facts in the career of Senator Sherman surpass the fabulous story of King Midas, whose touch turned everything to gold.

Yet this man is revered by the national banking money power and its satellites as the ablest American financier of the age.

Since 1861, he has been on every side of nearly every political and financial question that has agitated the country.

To illustrate the facility with which he can change his position on public questions, we refer to his late action on the policy of the United States toward the recognition of Cuban Independence. In the month of January, 1897, he introduced a fiery resolution in the Senate demanding the speedy recognition of Cuban belligerency. He out-jingoed the Jingoes. Three days afterward, he withdrew said resolution, with the lame explanation that its adoption would be inexpedient at that time.

The profits of the national banking system up to and including the year 1880 were immense.

In a report of the Comptroller of the Currency for 1881, this official states that the net earnings of the national banks for the preceding twenty years were $512,825,325, besides a surplus of $130,000,000—the whole aggregating $642,825,325; and that this enormous profit was earned upon an average capital of $500,000,000,—a net profit of over twelve per cent. annually above all expenses, including the princely salaries paid to the executive officers of the respective banks.

It will be asked, why should these financial institutions so often seek to bring on stringencies in the money market? The reason is clear to those who understand what class of men are at the head of the powerful national banks of New York City and other speculative centers. An examination of the directories of these great banks exhibits the startling fact, that the executive officers, directors, and heavy stockholders of these institutions are the largest operators on the Stock Exchange.

Having control of almost unlimited amounts of money, they are enabled to depress the value of stocks, bonds, and other securities when they are buyers on the market; and can enhance the value of stocks held by them when desirous of selling. Thus they are empowered to wreck the fortunes of the smaller operators.

The entire property of the nation, both real and personal, is at the absolute mercy of these national bank money kings. The men, or combination of men, who control the volume of money of a nation are its masters, whether it is an absolute, or a constitutional monarchy, or a republic.

It is a recognized principle of finance, that the volume of money afloat in a country fixes the general level of prices of commodities; it is true that there are some exceptions to this general rule, but they arise from unusual and unforeseen circumstances.

The power of the national banks to suddenly contract the circulating medium of the country, and the tyrannical manner in which they have exercised that privilege in the past, has awakened the gravest apprehension of the thinking men of the nation.

In his report of 1880, Treasurer Gilfillan stated that the national banks since the 20th of June, 1874, up to the time of his report of 1880, had surrendered their circulation in a sum exceeding $85,000,000, by depositing legal tender notes for the redemption of their circulating notes.

In addition to this contraction spoken of by the Treasurer in this report, the national banks possessed additional means of creating a sudden scarcity of money. Besides the circulating notes which these banks were authorized to loan as money, they controlled deposits of more than a billion dollars.

Therefore the loanable funds of these banks could be transformed into a most deadly weapon against the legitimate enterprise of the nation.

All that was necessary to bring on a monetary panic was a concerted plan on the part of these banks to call in their loans, and this action would be followed by a crisis as surely as night follows the day.

CHAPTER VII.

NATIONAL BANKS SECURE A CONTINUATION OF THEIR EXISTENCE.

"The abandonment of silver will result in the enhancement of the burden of all debts and fixed charges, acting as a drag upon production, and suffocation, strangulation, are words hardly too strong to express the agony of the industrial body when embraced in the fatal coils of a contracting money."—Francis A. Walker.

"Many of our rich men have not been content with equal protection and equal benefits, but have besought us to make them richer by act of Congress. By attempting to gratify their desires we have, in the results of our legislation, arrayed section against section, interest against interest, and man against man in a fearful commotion which threatens to shake the very foundation of our union.

"It is time to pause in our career; to review our principles, and, if possible, to revive that devoted patriotism and spirit of compromise that distinguished the sages of the Revolution and the fathers of our union. If we cannot at once, in justice to interests invested under improvident legislation, make our Government what it ought to be, we can at least take a stand against all new grants of monopolies and exclusive privileges; against any prostitution of our Government to the advancement of a few at the expense of the many, and in favor of compromise and gradual reform in our code of laws and system of political economy."—Andrew Jackson.

In the presidential campaign of 1880, the two great political parties arrayed themselves against each other in this contest with the utmost zeal.

The National Republican Convention met in Chicago

on the 2d of June, 1880. Among the leading candidates striving for the nomination for President were John Sherman, General Grant, and James A. Garfield. After a long contest, lasting seven days, the latter received the nomination. The Vice-Presidential candidate was Chester A. Arthur, of New York.

The Republican nominee for President had seen long service in the House of Representatives, where he was conspicuous as the champion of the national banking system, and as an advocate of the single standard of gold.

On the 27th of June, 1880, the Democratic National Convention met in Cincinnati, and its deliberations resulted in the nomination of Major-General Winfield S. Hancock for President, and William H. English, of Indiana, for Vice-President.

The Democratic nominee was one of the most illustrious soldiers in American history.

During the late civil war he was the most conspicuous corps commander in the Northern armies, and with his command, the famous Second corps of the Army of the Potomac, met and vanquished the flower of the Confederate armies on many hard fought fields.

General Hancock had endeared himself to the Democratic party by his manly course as military governor of Texas, during which he patriotically maintained the rights of the people of that State against the rapacity of the notorious Pease—the civil governor.

His private character was absolutely unassailable.

During the campaign the organized national banking money power joined its forces with all other privileged interests, and thus a mighty influence was exerted to secure the election of Garfield to the Presidency.

The battle cry of the Republican party in this notable contest was "A solid South against a solid North."

The money power joined in the senseless hue and cry, and by playing upon the smouldering prejudices of the people growing out of the late war, and by seeking to reopen the festering wounds of sectional hate, aimed to control the election and consequently the financial policy of the Government.

Owing to the dissensions of the New York State democracy, which grew out of the gubernatorial election of 1879, and which were not healed, and the lavish use of money, the Republican candidates were successful.

After the 4th of March, 1881, the Republicans had full control of the Government, and there was no obstacle in their way to hinder or obstruct the execution of their policy.

William Windom, of Minnesota, was selected by President Garfield for the post of Secretary of the Treasury.

After the adjournment of Congress in the early part of 1881, Secretary Windom and the bond-holders mutually agreed that the bonds bearing five and six per cent. interest then maturing, should be refunded at three and one-half per cent., payable at the option of the Government.

This action of Secretary Windom had no authority in any law then existing, and was an unwarranted assumption of the constitutional power of Congress by an executive officer.

The usurpation of legislative power by the Secretary of the Treasury was tolerated for the reason that it saved the Government a large amount of interest;

nevertheless, Congress, at its next session, sharply criticised Mr. Windom for this exercise of arbitrary power.

The action of the bond-holders in voluntarily accepting a lower rate of interest than their contracts called for excited a great deal of comment at the time.

The supporters of the national banking money power never wearied of pointing at this sacrifice by the national creditors as a remarkable example of patriotism, and asserted that the bond-holders and national banks were not as dangerous to the liberties of the people as their opponents declared them to be.

This apparent sacrifice of millions of interest annually was a rare stroke of policy on the money power. The shrewd men at the head of the national banking system were thoroughly acquainted with those traits of character which distinguished the American people from all others of modern times.

They knew that we, as a people, look to the events of to-day and do not worry with apprehensions for the future. Moreover, the country had entered upon a career of prosperity, the tendency of which was to make the people forgetful of the wrongs heaped upon them in the past by the present banking system.

According to the provisions of the national banking law of 1863, the charters of the national banks would expire in 1884, and the time seemed propitious for this money power to carry into execution the next step of its policy—which was to obtain the passage of a law through Congress extending the franchises of the national banks.

Therefore, during the time that the fears of the people were temporarily allayed by the voluntary acts of the bond-holders and banking interests in accepting a lower rate of interest on their bonds, the national banking money power seized this golden opportunity to secure an extension of their system.

Hence, at the next session of Congress, in 1882, Mr. Crapo, of Massachusetts, introduced a joint resolution authorizing national banking associations to extend their corporate existence for the period of twenty years. The speeches made against its passage were very able, notably those of Representatives Carlisle and Culberson.

So powerful was the opposition against an extension of the national banking system that the Democratic minority succeeded in engrafting a section upon the resolution, by which the circulating notes of national banks could not be surrendered to an amount exceeding $3,000,000 per month.

This curtailed the power of the banks to suddenly contract the volume of currency, by surrendering up for cancellation large amounts of their circulating notes, a practice to which they had resorted many times in the past twenty years.

During the debate upon this resolution it was shown by the opponents of the national banking system that the New York Clearing House Association had conspired against the constitutional power of Congress, by refusing to accept silver dollars and silver certificates; that this association of national banks held themselves superior to the law, and arrayed themselves in solid phalanx against the financial interests of the people.

It was further shown that the power of the national banks was so great that they had the means to unsettle business throughout the country, and that every panic, from which the country suffered since the close of the war, was originated by these banks.

By an additional amendment to the resolution it was made compulsory on the part of the clearing house associations to accept silver certificates in settlement of balances.

Again, the privilege of the national banks to institute suits at law in the Federal courts, as courts of original jurisdiction, was taken away, and this means of dragging litigants hundreds of miles from their homes at immense sacrifice of time and money, was denied to these corporations, which heretofore was one of their most tyrannical means of harassing individuals.

Therefore it will be seen that the sturdy opposition of the Democratic minority in the House had succeeded in extracting a few of the sharpest fangs of the greedy national banking money power.

As amended, the resolution passed the House and was transmitted to the Senate.

During the Senate debate on the joint resolution to renew the charters of the national banks, Senator Voorhees eloquently and truthfully depicted the vast bounties that had been bestowed upon these creatures of the Government.

He pointed out the overshadowing influence of the national banking power.

On June 19th, 1882, he said:—

"A brief glance at the conduct of the banks during the last year and a half is all that I can indulge in at this time, but it is sufficient to prove the truth of what I say.

"In the closing days of the last Congress and of the last Administration the banks precipitated an issue upon the people which ought not to be forgotten on an occasion like this; an issue so full of danger to constitutional liberty that it ought to be faithfully remembered now that they are asking a new and indefinite lease of power.

"It is now twenty years ago that this Government first engaged in building up, fostering, and encouraging the present vast and overshadowing system of national banking.

"No favor ever demanded by the banks has ever been withheld, no privilege denied, until now they constitute the most powerful moneyed corporations on the face of the globe. Congress has heretofore on nearly all occasions abdicated its powers under the Constitution over the finances of the banks, except when called upon to legislate in their favor. They have demanded the violation of legislative contracts with the people, and the demand has been granted, whereby their own gains and the people's burdens have been increased a thousand fold beyond right and justice. They have demanded the remission of all taxation on their bonds, and it has been conceded, thus leaving the poor to pay the taxes of the rich. They have been fortified in their strongholds of moneyed caste and privilege by double lines of unjust laws, supplemented with here a redoubt and there a ditch, to guard them from the correcting hand of popular indignation, until now, deeming themselves impregnable, they bully and defy the Government."

He continued as follows:—

"Sir, with full and unrestricted power over the volume of the currency and, consequently, over all values conceded to the banks, together with ample machinery by which in an emergency they can defy the passage of any act of Congress, what is left to the Government except an abject submission? This Government could not, to-morrow, go to war in defense of its flag, its honor, or its existence without first asking permission to do so of the great financial corporations of the country. If there was an invading force on our soil this hour, Congress could not with safety or show of success declare war to repel it without first supplicating cowardly and unpatriotic capital, engaged in banking, not to contract the currency, withhold financial aid, and leave the country to starve. In fact, there is no measure of this Government, either in peace or in war, which is not wholly depending on the pleasure of the banks.

"This Government is at the mercy of its own creatures. It has begotten and pampered a system which is now its master. The people have been betrayed into the clutches of a financial despotism which scorns responsibility and defies lawful restraint."

At the present time the government is a submissive instrument in the hands of this money power.

After a full discussion in the Senate, during which many amendments were added to the resolution, it was returned to the House. The House agreed to the amended bill with the exceptions of a few of the Senate amendments, in which it refused to concur.

The bill then went back to the Senate, which refused to recede from its amendments.

Upon this disagreement, both Houses appointed Committees of Conference, who were to reconcile the differences existing between the two Houses with reference to the resolution as amended.

After these committees had held several meetings an agreement was reached, the resolution was reported back to the Senate and House and the measure was adopted.

This act was approved by the President on the 12th of July, 1882.

Hence, this gigantic moneyed monopoly received a new lease of life for the period of twenty years longer.

From this time on, it was the constant purpose of the

national banks to build up a colossal system of bank credit that would make the entire business interests of the country tributary to its power.

In the congressional election of 1882 the Republicans were overwhelmingly defeated, and the House became Democratic by a large majority.

On February 12, 1884, Senator McPherson, of New Jersey, a millionaire and national banker, introduced a bill to permit national banks to increase their circulating notes up to the par value of the bonds deposited by them to secure their circulation.

The Senate passed the bill, but it was defeated in the House.

In this same month the sub-treasury at New York City, through the Assistant Treasurer, addressed an inquiry to the President of the New York Clearing House as to the effect of the government paying its balances in silver money.

This action of the Sub-Treasurer was clearly for the purpose of renewing the agitation against silver, and it had the further intention of giving an excuse to the national bankers to precipitate a panic, and thus lay the foundation for a new demand for more legislation in favor of the banks.

This cowardly act of the sub-treasurer was an implied admission that the Clearing House Association was more powerful than Congress, and that it was above all law.

On February 18, 1884, a bill for the retirement and re-coinage of the trade dollar was taken up by the House.

At this time the number of trade dollars afloat in the country approximated 36,000,000, and they had no legal tender debt-paying power whatever. They were mere bullion.

On April 1, 1884, the Committee on Banking and Currency, to whom the bill had been referred, reported it back to the House.

This bill authorized the government to receive these trade dollars for all dues to the United States; they were to be received in exchange for standard silver dollars coined under the Bland-Allison law; after such exchange the trade dollars were to be coined into standard dollars.

Section 4 of the act provided that the trade dollars so exchanged should be coined under the act of February 28, 1878.

On motion of Mr. Bland, section 4 was stricken out, and the bill as thus amended, should it become a law, would add nearly forty million legal tender silver dollars to the volume of money.

In its amended form it passed the House by a vote of 198 yeas to 45 nays, and it was transmitted to the Senate.

In the meantime, after its passage by the House, the New York national banks had taken their cue from the letter addressed to them by the Sub-Treasurer, and at once began a vigorous contraction of the currency by refusing to loan money to the West and South, and calling in outstanding loans.

This action of the New York banks, with the tacit permission of the Treasury Department, brought on the great panic of 1884, in which year alone there were 10,968 business failures, with liabilities aggregating $226,343,427.

At the same time money commanded three per cent.

interest and commission per day on call. This was usury at the annual rate of eleven hundred per centum!

It is asserted that while the banks refused to loan money, and were surrendering their circulating notes by depositing United States legal tenders with the Comptroller of the Currency, that the chief stock-holders in these banks were using the deposits of these institutions in making loans at those exhorbitant rates of usury.

It may be inquired by some, why did not the Comptroller of the Currency exercise his lawful powers, and proceed against these banks for these notorious violations of law?

The facts were that every Comptroller of the Currency, since the creation of that office, has been a willing instrument in the hands of the national banks, and the Comptrollers, time and again, authorized these banks to violate the national banking law whenever it was to the financial interests of these corporations.

The open and notorious infractions of law practiced by these banks found ready apologists in Congress, who audaciously asserted that the banks were the best judges of the policy to be carried out by them, and that to enforce the law would close these institutions, and deprive the people of the benefits flowing from this beneficient system.

The history of the past thirty years exhibits this remarkable fact, that each and every Comptroller of the Currency, for his slavish subserviency to the national banks, has been rewarded by an election to the presidency of some one of these great financial institutions.

Upon the appearance, in the Senate, of the House

bill, providing for the recoinage of the trade dollars, it was referred to the Finance Committee, who reported a substitute of five sections.

Section 1 authorized the exchange of trade dollars for standard dollars, the time of exchange to be limited to July 1, 1885.

Section 2 provided that these trade dollars were to be coined as part of the bullion under the Bland-Allison law.

Section 4 provided for a renewal of that farce, an International Monetary Commission.

Section 5 provided that if no treaties could be ratified with foreign nations for free coinage of silver before August 1, 1886, then a suspension of the further coinage of silver dollars by the United States should take place by a repeal of the Bland-Allison law.

No action was taken upon this bill by the Senate, and the efforts of the House to legitimize the trade dollar by making it legal tender, and to increase the volume of silver coin were again thwarted.

In his annual message to Congress, in December, 1884, President Arthur recommended the cessation of the coinage of the silver dollar, and gave as his reasons for such recommendation that nearly 185,000,000 had been coined, of which only a little over 40,000,000 were in circulation.

We quote his language in full. He says:—

"It appears that annually for the past six years there have been coined in compliance with the requirements of the act of February 28, 1878, more than $27,000,000. The number now outstanding is reported to be nearly $185,000,000, whereof but little more than $40,000,000, or less than twenty-two per cent., are in actual circulation. The mere existence of this fact seems to me to furnish of itself a cogent argument for the repeal of the statute which has made such a fact possible."

President Arthur sought to convey the impression to Congress that only 40,000,000 silver dollars were in circulation.

At the time he penned this message the records in the Treasury Department showed that 133,940,121 silver dollars were in active circulation through their paper representative, the silver certificate, and that there were actually but 12,000,000 silver dollars lying idle in the Treasury.

One striking fact which attracts attention is the following: That the leading opponents to the coinage of silver dollars have never yet agreed upon the facts, and the arguments which they advance against the use of silver as money.

In his message of December 1, 1884, President Arthur urged as a weighty reason for the discontinuance of the coinage of silver dollars, that less than twenty-two per cent. of them were in actual circulation.

In his report of 1880, in which he advised the cessation of the coinage of the silver dollars, Secretary Sherman gave his reason why silver should not be coined, in which he says that it was not held, or hoarded, or exported, but it was pushed into active circulation.

In this same message President Arthur made the following reference to the trade dollar:—

"While the trade dollars have ceased, for the present at least, to be an element of active disturbance in our currency system, some provision should be made for their surrender to the Government. In view of the circumstances under which they were coined and of the fact that they never had a legal tender quality, there should be offered for them only a slight advance over their bullion value."

This statement of the President with reference to the legal tender power of the trade dollar is evidence of those inaccuracies that occur many times in the state papers of high officials. The President averred that trade dollars were never legal tender, while the fact is that by the law of February 12, 1873, they were made legal tender for any one payment not exceeding five dollars.

The law which conferred upon them this legal power continued in force until July 22, 1876, when the legal tender quality was taken away.

A further inaccurate statement of the President appears, when he speaks of the amount of standard dollars in circulation, which he places at a little over 40,000,000. While the actual facts were that the volume of silver dollars in circulation was 174,000,000.

Secretary Sherman had urged as an insuperable objection against the further coinage of silver dollars that they were not held, or hoarded, but were kept in active circulation. President Arthur asked the suspension of the Bland-Allison law of 1878 on the ground that they did not circulate actively enough.

This is not the first time that these two distinguished gentlemen disagreed during their public careers, for while Sherman was Secretary of the Treasury, and President Arthur was collector of the Port of New York, they had a notable controversy, with which the public were doubtless familiar.

While President Arthur was requesting Congress to suspend the coinage of the silver dollar, the banks of New York City combined to make a raid on the Treasury by presenting greenbacks for gold. That this was done with the connivance of Secretary of the Treasury, McCulloch, is evident from the acts of that official. He had dispatched a telegram to the Sub-Treasurer, in New York City, stating that the country would be on a silver basis in thirty days.

It was nothing less than a plot formed by the bankers and the Secretary to frighten Congress into repealing the Bland-Allison law of 1878.

In the meantime, the presidential campaign of 1884 had resulted in the election of Grover Cleveland, of New York, over the Republican candidate, James G. Blaine.

Prior to his election to the Presidency, Mr. Cleveland had held the office of Mayor of Buffalo, and was Governor of the State of New York, in which positions he had won much distinction as an honest and capable executive.

Some time previous to his inauguration, the report became current that the President-elect was opposed to the further coinage of silver.

In order to ascertain the views of Mr. Cleveland upon this phase of the financial issue, Congressman A. J. Warner and ninety-four members of the House, on the 11th day of February, 1885, joined in a letter to the in-coming President, requesting that he outline his future policy on the silver question, then agitating the country.

On February 24th, eight days before Mr. Cleveland was inaugurated, he gave out an open letter to the press in reply to that of Hon. A. J. Warner.

In the course of that remarkable document occurs the following statement:—

"I hope that you concur with me, and with a great

majority of our fellow-citizens, in deeming it most desirable at the present juncture to maintain and continue in use the mass of our gold coin as well as the mass of silver already coined. This is possible by a present suspension of the purchase and coinage of silver. I am not aware that by any other method is it possible. It is of momentous importance to prevent the two metals from parting company; to prevent the increasing displacement of gold by the increasing coinage of silver; to prevent the disuse of gold in the custom houses of the United States in the daily business of the people; to prevent the ultimate expulsion of gold by silver."

To state that the expectations of the Democratic party were rudely shattered by the position assumed by Mr. Cleveland, in his reply to the letter of Mr. Warner, would be putting it very mildly.

The mass of the party expressed great astonishment, not to say indignation, at the bold stand taken by the President-elect, in which he aligned himself with the single gold standard.

In his zeal for the suspension of the coinage of the silver dollar, Mr. Cleveland was led into erroneous statements of facts as to the alleged disuse of gold in the custom houses and in the business of the people.

It is a matter of public record that, in 1880, the imports of gold exceeded the exports thereof by $77,119,371; in 1881, the excess of imports of gold over exports were $1,789,174; in 1883, $6,133,261; in 1884 the exports of gold over imports were $18,250,640, leaving a great balance of imported gold over exports during those five years of more than $150,000,000.

This great gain of gold took place during the time the Bland-Allison law was in operation.

Upon the appearance of this reply of Mr. Cleveland

to the communication of Hon. A. J. Warner and others, the Wall street clique and their allies seized their opportunity.

They swooped down on Congress and endeavored to force a repeal of the silver law.

The members of the House were besieged by these hordes of coin venders and bullion brokers; the national banking money power threatened to visit another panic upon the people, and predictions were freely made that gold would go to a premium if the silver law was not repealed.

The Democratic members of Congress were informed by the thousand per cent. men of New York City that it was the wish of President-elect Cleveland that the law authorizing the coinage of silver dollars be repealed.

The New York Herald, one of the greatest journals of the East, constantly kept in a prominent place in its columns, the legend, "We are still coining the 70 and 75 per cent. dollars."

Every means and all possible influences were brought to bear upon Congress to force it to repeal the Bland-Allison law, but without avail.

A single attempt was made to carry into effect the wish of the President-elect, but it failed so ignominiously by such a decisive vote that no further effort was made in that Congress. It was as follows: On February 26, 1885, House bill 8256, being the sundry civil appropriation bill, was pending before the House. A clause was tacked to this bill, providing for the suspension of the operations of the law of February 28, 1878,—the Bland-Allison law.

Mr. Randall, an Eastern Democratic member of the

House, moved to suspend the rules and consider said clause.

This motion was disagreed to by a vote of 118 yeas to 152 nays, and this clause was abandoned and stricken from the bill.

The letter of Mr. Cleveland was regarded by the House as an open and manifest attempt to influence Congress against the continued coinage of silver, and, if such was the intention of the President-elect, he promptly received a well-deserved rebuke for his attempted interference with the legislation of Congress.

One feature of the conduct of Mr. Randall, in his effort to engraft upon an appropriation bill a clause to repeal the Bland-Allison law, exhibits the avidity of the money power to seize every opportunity, however slight, to gain its ends by legislative sanction, and that is—immediately upon the appearance of the Warner letter, it presumed that the mere *ipse dixit* of Grover Cleveland would coerce Congress into submission to his views.

The infamous nature of the financial legislation from 1862 to 1875, in so enormously enhancing the value of the public debt, and in enriching the bond-holders at the expense of the productive energy of the country, will be shown by the following figures, taken from a work entitled, "The Philosophy of Price," quoted in the Daily News Almanac and Political Register for 1891.

The time covered by "Philosophy of Price" is from July 1, 1866, up to and including 1885. "Philosophy of Price" says:—

"Here is a table showing the debt of the United

States on the 1st of July, 1866 and 1885, including non-interest bearing greenbacks, expressed in dollars, and also in the things working folks have to produce in order to get the dollars with which to pay debts and interest:—

	National Debt 1866.	National Debt 1885.
Debt in dollars	$2,773,000,000	$800,000,000
Beef, barrels	129,000,000	135,000,000
Corn, bushels	2,000,000,000	3,000,000,000
Wheat, bushels	800,000,000	1,740,000,000
Oats, bushels	3,262,000,000	4,357,000,000
Pork, barrels	82,000,000	96,000,000
Coal, tons	213,000,000	400,000,000
Cotton, bales	12,000,000	34,000,000
Bar iron, tons	24,000,000	40,000,000

"Almost every product of labor shows the same result. We paid from 1866 to 1884 on the public debt: Interest, $1,870,000,000, and principal about $1,200,000,000; yet we find that what there is left of it when measured by labor, or the product of labor, is fifty per cent. greater than the original debt."

This colossal robbery of the nation, and consequently of the people, was planned and matured by the national banking money power. It is true that the idea of this system of banking had its origin in England, and it is also a fact that the scheme of legislating increased value into the bonded debt was suggested by the influential bankers of London.

Each one of the series of enactments which legally confiscated billions of property of the tax-payers, and which handed it over to a few individuals, was placed upon the statute-books under the false and misleading plea of maintaining the "Credit of the nation untarnished."

. That distinguished historian, Prof. J. C. Ridpath, eloquently described the legislative process by which the value of the public debt was vastly increased. He said:—

"It is the hardship of war that brings debt upon the country which engages in it. In our own case we piled up a debt mountainwise. The prodigious pile reached the clouds. In any old nation there would have remained no hope at all of paying it. It would simply have been laid upon posterity as an everlasting tax. The principal question, however, with Congress and with the people of the United States, was how they should measure and manage this debt. Gold and silver had disappeared. Paper money prevailed and abounded. The premium on coin arose to almost two hundred per cent. The dollar of the law and the contract became a paper dollar, which, as measured by the standard of gold, was, for a considerable period, worth less than fifty cents.

"But what was the equity of this situation? One class of statesmen, backed up and instigated by the creditor classes, held that the dollar was always the gold and silver dollar. Practically this was not so. Theoretically and even constitutionally it was probably so. For many years together the dollar of the law and the contract was, to all intents and purposes, a dollar of paper. During the same period the modicum of gold and silver remaining in the country—though it was stamped and branded with the names of coins—was really merchandise. At length the bottom was reached—or the top, as the case may be—and the readjustment became necessary.

"Then came on the warfare between the advocates of the so-called 'honest dollar' and the paper dollar with which, and on the basis of which, the business of the country had been so long transacted. The advocates of high payment took the 'honest dollar' as their catch-word, and, to make a long narrative brief, they won with it, and by a series of legislative enactments, entailing the greatest hardships on the producing interests of the country, succeeded in twisting up, turn by turn, the standard unit in the financial mill, until the so-called resumption of specie payment was finally, after fourteen years from Appomattox, effected.

"Thus the value of the national debt was augmented from year to year as rapidly as it was paid away. As fast as payment was made the value of the dollar in which it was expressed was increased. To the debtor class all this was the labor of Sysiphus. The toiler laboriously rolled the stone to the top of the hill; but ever, when near the crest, it got away with him and returned with thundering and the roar of bankruptcy to the bottom. To the present day the process has been kept up, and, notwithstanding the multiplied billions upon billions which the American people have paid in principal and interest upon that patriotic war debt, which expressed their devotion and sacrifice, it is the truth of history, that the debt itself, is at the present time, worth virtually as much to the holders as it was when it reached its nominal maximum—in August, 1865."

In his effort to convey an adequate idea of the nature of that legislation, which had plundered the American people of billions of dollars, this renowned scholar and writer had recourse to the sublime imagery of Homer.

Prof. Ridpath demonstrates that the public debt was not decreased at all, although billions had been applied to its payment.

Not only is this true of the public debt, but the same process of depreciating the value of property has likewise enhanced the value of private debts.

The amount of property that has been transferred from debtors to creditors, as a necessary result of the enormous appreciation of money brought about by contraction of its volume, is beyond computation.

In a great speech, Wendell Phillips, illustrates the means by which the money power absorbed the wealth of the country, by juggling with the currency. He said:—

"In other words, it was the currency, which, rightly arranged, opened a nation's well springs, found work for willing hands to do, and filled them with a just return, while honest capital, daily larger and more secure, ministered to a glad prosperity. Or it was currency, wickedly and selfishly juggled, that made merchants bankrupt and starved labor into discontent and slavery, while capital added house to house and field to field, and gathered into its miserly hands all the wealth left in a ruined land.

"The first question, therefore, in an industrial nation is, Where ought control of the currency to rest? In whose hands can this almost omnipotent power be trusted? Every writer of political economy, from Aristotle to Adam Smith, allows that a change in the currency alters the price of every ounce and yard of merchandise and every foot of land. Whom can we trust with this despotism? At present the banks and the money kings wield this power. They own the yard-stick, and can make it longer or shorter, as they please. They own every pound weight, and can make it heavier or lighter as they choose. This explains the riddle, so mysterious to common people, that those who trade in money always grow rich, even while those who trade in other things go into bankruptcy."

On the 3d of February, 1886, Hon. R. Q. Mills, of Texas, in the heat of righteous indignation eloquently arraigned that unlimited avarice that was continually besieging Congress to enhance the value of bonds and securities at the expense of the producers. He said:—

"But in all the wild, reckless, and remorseless brutalities that have marked the footprints of resistless power there is some extenuating circumstance that mitigates the severity of the punishment due the crime. Some have been the product of the fierce passions of war, some have come from the antipathy that separate alien races, some from the superstitions of opposing religions.

"But the crime that is now sought to be perpetrated on more than fifty millions of people comes neither from the camp of a conqueror, the hand of a foreigner, nor the altar of an idolator. But it comes from those in whose veins runs the blood of the common ancestry, who were born under the same skies, speak the same language, reared in the same institutions, and nurtured in the principles of the same religious faith. It comes from the cold, phlegmatic, marble heart of avarice,— avarice that seeks to paralyze labor, increase the burden of debt, and fill the land with destitution and suffering to gratify the lust for gold,—avarice surrounded by every comfort that wealth can command, and rich enough to satisfy every want save that which refuses to be satisfied without the suffocation and strangulation of all the labor of the land. With a forehead that refuses to be ashamed, it demands of Congress an act that will paralyze all the forces of production, shut out labor from all employment, increase the burden of debts and taxation, and send desolation and suffering to all the homes of the poor."

In his first annual message to Congress, December 8, 1885, the President took a decided stand against the continued coinage of silver. In this document he says:—

"The necessity of an addition of the silver currency of the nation as is compelled by the silver coinage act is negatived by the fact that up to the present time only about fifty millions of the silver dollars so coined have found their way into circulation, leaving more than one hundred and sixty-five millions in the possession of the Government, the custody of which has entailed considerable expense for the construction of new vaults for its deposits. Against this latter amount there are outstanding silver certificates amounting to about ninety-three millions of dollars."

Further on in this same message he said:—

"At times during the past six months fifty-eight per cent. of the receipts for duties have been in silver or silver certificates, while the average within that period has been twenty per cent."

A comparison of the statements in his message with the predictions ventured in the Warner letter will be instructive. In the latter he desired "To prevent the disuse of gold in the custom houses of the United States;" in his message of December 8, 1885, he shows that instead of silver displacing gold in the payment of duties, only about twenty per cent. of the latter were paid in silver or silver certificates.

Just why the payment of twenty per cent. of the duties in silver should arouse the apprehensions of the President is not very apparent.

Furthermore, the very purpose of coining these silver dollars was to enable people to transact business, to pay their debts to each other, and to the Government.

Mr. Cleveland further says:—

"The condition in which our Treasury may be placed by a persistence in our present course, is a matter of concern to every patriotic citizen who does not desire his Government to pay in silver such of its obligations as should be paid in gold."

Again he says:—

"We have now on hand all the silver dollars necessary to supply the present needs of the people and to satisfy those who from sentiment wish to see them in circulation, and if their coinage is suspended, they can readily be obtained by all who desire them. If the need of more is at any time apparent their coinage can be renewed."

The President then recommends the suspension of the coinage of silver dollars coined under the law of 1878.

According to the President's theory and reasoning, the most effective means of supplying the volume of money needed by the people would be a suspension of its coinage.

In this message President Cleveland came out squarely in favor of perpetuating the national banking system. In this course he allied himself with the money power, and earned the unenviable distinction of being the first Democratic President that advocated the policy of delegating the power of issuing money to private corporations.

In this course he was sustained by a few Eastern Democratic members of Congress, but he could not lead the great body of the Western and Southern Democracy to accept that Tory-Republican system of finance that had been imported from London in 1863.

During the following year, the use of silver and silver certificates increased from $143,000,000 to $167,000,000, which indicated the great popularity of this form of money with the people.

Notwithstanding these facts, the President in his next annual message, December 6, 1886, said:—

"I see no reason to change the views expressed in my last annual message on the subject of compulsory coinage."

On December 17, 1886, Senate bill No. 199, providing for the redemption of the trade dollars for standard silver dollars, the trade dollars so redeemed to be sent to the mints for coinage as part of the bullion to be purchased under the Bland-Allison law of February 28, 1878, passed the Senate.

On February 12, 1887, Senate bill 199 was pending before the House, and it was amended to authorize the receipt of trade dollars for government dues, and in exchange for standard dollars, and for coining the said trade dollars into standard dollars, not as part of the bullion and coinage under the Bland-Allison law.

The bill, as amended, passed by a vote of 174 yeas to 36 nays; both Houses appointed a Committee of Conference, which reported a substitute that fixed the period of six months from date of the act for the exchange of trade dollars for standard dollars, or for fractional silver coin. The trade dollars so exchanged were to be recoined and not counted as part of the silver to be purchased under the Bland-Allison law of 1878.

This act became a law without the approval of the President.

Be it said to the eternal honor of the House of Representatives, which was Democratic, the advice and recommendations of the President fell on deaf ears, and this co-ordinate branch of the Government would not be coerced into repealing the Bland-Allison silver law.

In spite of the fears of President Cleveland that gold would be displaced by the increased coinage of silver, the net gain of gold during his administration was increased many millions.

In the meanwhile the monetary stringency of 1884 continued in all its severity, and even the banks of New York City felt the effects of the panic, which was the direct result of their concerted action.

These great financial institutions of New York City called upon the Government for assistance; whereupon Secretary of the Treasury Manning, a national banker, came to their relief by depositing with these banks government money to the amount of $63,000,000 without interest for the use of that enormous sum, which had been wrung from the people by a burdensome system of taxation.

Had the farmers of Kansas, or Nebraska, requested the Federal Government to loan them the public funds to assist them in agricultural pursuits, the millionaire beggars and paupers of Wall street would have emitted a loud and prolonged howl that would have been heard to the nethermost parts of the earth.

The people of Kansas and Nebraska would have been assailed by every epithet that could have been coined from the English language.

The national bank monopoly, the gold gamblers, stock speculators, railroad wreckers, the Shylocks, who gladly exacted a thousand per cent. usury, with the subsidized press and its satellites, would have denounced the hard working farmer of Kansas or Nebraska as a "long whiskered hay-seed," a "socialist," a "dangerous anarchist," or a "crank."

The Nasts and the Gillams, famed in caricature, would have expended all their genius in holding him up to ridicule.

While it would be dangerous socialism for the Government to assist the farmer during his calamities, it was the highest essence of patriotism to save the panic-breeders of New York City from the consequences of their own traitorous conduct by donating them the use of $63,000,000 in government funds.

In the meantime, notwithstanding the aid received from the Federal Government, the banks of New York City organized a clique with the intention of making a raid upon the gold in the Treasury.

The base ingratitude of the New York banks aroused the ire of Secretary Manning, and he called upon those banks who had organized a corner against the Treasury gold, and informed them of what would follow if they persevered in that course. He said:—

"You may precipitate a panic. The Government is strong; the Government can stand a panic, but you will have the panic if you continue to embarrass the Government as you have done."

He continued:—

"Here are twenty million dollars in round silver dollars, not certificates. Give me your gold for it and stop this raid upon the Treasury, or else you shall have the panic."

The heroic treatment of Secretary Manning was a warning to these scoundrels, who would willingly sink the Government if money could be made by the operation.

The stern threats of the Secretary frustrated this attempt to loot the Treasury of its gold, and to coerce Congress into repealing the Bland-Allison silver law.

In his annual message of December, 1887, President Cleveland relegated the financial question to the rear, and pushed the tariff issue to the front.

This document is justly regarded as one of the strongest state papers that ever eminated from the pen of the President.

In this message the President urged the necessity of a complete reformation of the then existing tariff, and he took strong grounds in favor of suppressing the trusts.

Upon the appearance of this message, the leaders of the Republican party charged the President with having committed the Democracy to the policy of British free trade.

Mr. Blaine, who was in Paris at the time when the contents of the message were made public, availed himself of the opportunity to answer the President by a counter blast, in the form of an extended interview held with a representative of the New York Tribune.

Meanwhile, since 1883, the national banks steadily continued their policy of contracting the currency, by substituting government legal tender notes for the United States bonds deposited with the Comptroller of the Currency to secure their circulating notes.

This policy, to a large extent, neutralized the benefits derived from the increased use of silver.

The object of the banks, in thus withdrawing their bonds deposited to secure their circulating notes, was for the avowed purpose of obtaining the great premium which they brought in the market—a premium which ranged as high as twenty-nine per cent. on the dollar.

Beside the contraction brought about by the process of depositing legal tender notes to redeem the circulating notes of national banks, the latter form of currency was surrendered by the banks, and the bonds deposited to secure these bank notes were taken up by the depositors and sold for the premium. This worked a double contraction of the currency.

During this time the Government was redeeming its bonds, and this process of redemption was carried on by the payment of a large premium to the bond-holders and national bankers.

In his report for the year 1892, the Comptroller of

the Currency showed the extent to which this system of contraction was carried on from 1883 to 1888 by these fiscal agencies of the Government.

From October 31, 1883, to October 31, 1884, the national banks surrendered their circulating notes to the amount of $24,170,676; from October 31, 1884, to October 31, 1885, the banks surrendered $15,545,461; from October 31, 1885, to October 31, 1886, national bank notes were contracted $56,590,533; from October 31, 1886, to October 31, 1887, the banks surrendered up their notes to the amount of $50,495,589; from October 31, 1887, to October 31, 1888, a further decrease was made by cancelling national bank notes to the amount of $16,848,739.

It will be ascertained that the total voluntary contraction of national bank currency, from 1883 to 1888, reached the great sum of $163,000,000.

Although the Bland-Allison law was in operation, and the Government was throwing vast sums of money into circulation by the redemption of bonds, yet the volume of money in circulation was not increased.

For nearly every dollar emitted by the Treasury Department for the redemption of bonds, the national banks surrendered up almost an equal amount of their circulating notes.

On February 29, 1888, House bill No. 5034 was pending in the House of Representatives.

This measure authorized the Secretary of the Treasury to apply the surplus in the Treasury to the purchase or redemption of United States bonds. The bill passed.

The object of this measure aimed at relieving the money market of its stringency by the purchase of bonds, and the consequent increase of the volume of currency.

On March 26, 1888, House bill 5034 came up in the Senate, and Senator Spooner offered a substitute, declaring section 2 of the sundry civil appropriation law of June 30, 1882, a permanent provision. The substitute was agreed to by the Senate.

Senator Beck offered an amendment, directing the Secretary of the Treasury, on the retirement of national bank circulation, and on failure of other banks to take out an equal amount, then to purchase an equivalent amount of silver bullion in excess of the minimum, required under the law of February 28, 1878, to be coined and used as provided in said act.

The amendment was agreed to by a vote of 32 yeas to 13 nays.

During the debate on the amendment offered by Senator Beck, Senator Plumb made the following remarks:—

"It is estimated that there are in circulation, including that which is locked up in the Treasury and held in the banks as a reserve fund, about $1,600,000,000, of all kinds of currency of the United States, gold and silver, the overplus of gold and silver certificates, greenback notes and national bank notes, all told, and there are more than $60,000,000,000 of property which must finally be measured by this volume of currency. It has been contracted during the last year more than five per cent. in addition to all that has occurred by reason of abrasion and loss. No man can tell the volume of greenbacks outstanding. Nominally it is $346,000,000 and a fraction, but that volume has been subject to all the accidents which have occurred during the past twenty-five years, whereby money has been consumed, worn out, lost, and it is doubtful if the amount is really over $300,000,000 to-day.

"But say nothing about that, the retirement of the national banking circulation during the past twelve months has been five per cent. of the total amount of the currency outstanding. There has been during that period a phenomenal depreciation of the prices of property. There has been the greatest depreciation of the price of agricultural products the country has ever known."

In speaking of the effects of contraction of the currency in depreciating the value of property, he said:—

"The contraction of the currency by five per cent. of its volume means the depreciation of the property of the country $3,000,000,000. Debts have not only increased, but the means to pay them have diminished in proportion as the currency has been contracted. Events based upon nonlegislation have proved of advantage to lenders, but disastrous to borrowers."

The bill then went to the House, but as it was near the close of the session, it did not receive any consideration.

Meanwhile the panic of 1884, as it was called—but which really began in 1882—raged throughout the entire administration of President Cleveland.

The aggregate number of failures for the years 1885, 1886, 1887 and 1888 were 51,748, and the liabilities were $756,597,883.

It was during this period of business failures and general depression everywhere, with the consequent sacrifice of property at ruinous prices, that the holders of United States bonds were obtaining a premium for their bonds ranging as high as twenty-seven per cent.

In his annual message of December, 1888, President Cleveland again urged the repeal of the Bland-Allison law. He said:—

"The Secretary recommends the suspension of the

further coinage of silver, and in such recommendation I earnestly concur."

Up to November 30, 1888, 312,570,990 silver dollars had been coined, of which 60,970,990 were in active use, not including silver certificates to the amount of $237,418,346—making a total of $298,389,336 in silver dollars and certificates that were in active circulation.

It will be observed that the many predictions of President Cleveland, as to the capacity of the country to use silver as money, were utterly discredited by these facts.

The determined opposition of the President to the coinage of silver was one of the strange features of an otherwise highly successful administration.

With the exception of his hostile attitude to silver as money, and his advocacy of the perpetuation of the national banking system, Mr. Cleveland gave the people an administration of public affairs that shed honor upon himself, and its efficiency was not surpassed by any in the annals of American history.

During the four years that he directed the public affairs of the nation, the public debt was reduced in the magnificent sum of $341,448,449.

It is true that this vast decrease of the public debt in the short period of four years resulted in an immense profit to the bond-holders and national bankers who surrendered their bonds for payment.

The amount of premium on the bonds so surrendered was $59,000,000, and this measured the profit obtained by the banks and bond-holders in the process of redeeming the debt.

In addition to this vast decrease of the public debt,

a surplus of $83,269,220 was accumulated in the Treasury over and above the gold reserve of $100,000,000.

In addition to this vast sum of money, the result of a frugal and honest administration, a bank security fund of $82,597,250 in legal tenders was accumulated as a trust fund for the redemption of national bank notes.

The total amount of cash in the Treasury on the 4th of March, 1889, when his successor was inaugurated, was $265,846,441.

His administration of other departments of the Government was notably successful.

Tens of millions of acres of the public lands, fenced in by great corporations, were restored to the public domain, and the usurpers driven off by the vigorous policy of the President.

Land grants embracing many millions of acres were forfeited and throw open for settlement.

For the first time since 1861, the Indian Department was honestly managed, and the red man received just and humane treatment at the hands of the United States.

Nevertheless the ultimate baleful results of his influence in favor of the national banks, and a single standard of gold, eventually more than counteracted an honest, economical management of the public affairs of the country.

CHAPTER VIII.

THE NATIONAL BANKING MONEY POWER SECURES COMPLETE CONTROL OF THE TREASURY.

"Resolved, That Congress has no power to charter a United States bank; that we believe such an institution to be one of deadly hostility to the best interests of the Government, dangerous to our republican institutions and the liberties of the people, and calculated to place the business of the country within the control of a concentrated money power and above the laws and the will of the people."—Democratic Platform, 1840.

"The right of issuing paper money as currency, like that of issuing gold and silver coins, belongs exclusively to the nation, and cannot be claimed by any individuals."—Albert Gallatin.

In the presidential campaign of 1888, General Benjamin Harrison was the successful candidate for the presidency.

The national Republican platform, on which Mr. Harrison stood, vigorously charged the administration of President Cleveland with having attempted to demonetize silver.

The active opposition of President Cleveland to the use of silver as money gave some color to this charge. On the 4th of March, 1889, General Harrison was duly inaugurated.

For Secretary of the Treasury he selected the Hon. William Windom, of Minnesota.

In addition to having the Presidency, the Republicans had control of both branches of Congress.

John Sherman occupied his old position of Chairman of the Finance Committee of the Senate.

In his first annual message to Congress, December 3, 1889, President Harrison paid special attention to the coinage of silver under the Bland-Allison law of 1878. He said:—

"The total coinage of silver dollars was, on November 1, 1889, $343,638,001, of which $283,539,521 were in the Treasury vaults and $60,098,480 were in circulation. Of the amount in the vaults $277,319,944 were represented by outstanding certificates, leaving $6,219,577 not in circulation and not represented by certificates."

In this message, President Harrison gave Congress and the people the clearest and fairest statement with reference to the number and circulation of silver dollars that was yet presented by any President up to his time.

Every one who would avail himself of the facts stated in this document knew, that, of the silver dollars coined under the Bland-Allison law of 1878, all were in active use and circulation except the small sum of $6,219,577.

The facts stated by President Harrison amply proved that the predictions and apprehensions of President Cleveland and others, with reference to the continued coinage of standard silver dollars, were absolutely groundless.

This remarkable absorption of silver in the channels of trade and commerce, evinced the great popularity of this money with the people.

The President further says:—

"The evil anticipations which have accompanied the coinage and use of the silver dollar have not been realized. As a coin it has not had general use, and the public Treasury has been compelled to store it.

But this is manifestly owing to the fact that its paper representative is more convenient. The general acceptance and use of the silver certificate shows that silver has not been otherwise discredited."

It seems from the opinion of President Harrison, as expressed in this message, that the use of the silver certificate in lieu of the coin it represents, was the only evidence by which it was shown that silver was discredited.

If the issuance of silver certificates operates to discredit the silver dollar, then, by a parity of reasoning, the use of gold certificates as a substitute for gold coin discredits gold.

At the time the President stated that silver was discredited by the use of certificates, there were outstanding gold certificates aggregating $165,000,000.

If the holder of silver dollars deposits that coin in the Federal Treasury, and receives therefor silver certificates, and thus discredits the silver dollar, then the owner or holder of gold coin, or bullion, who deposits his coin or bullion in the Treasury, and accepts gold certificates, also discredits gold.

The partial eulogy bestowed by President Harrison upon silver was intended as a reflection upon those public utterances of Mr. Cleveland, in which the latter opposed the use of silver as money.

Further on in the same message the President said:—

"I think it is clear that if we should make the coinage of silver at its present ratio free, we must expect that the difference in the bullion values of gold and silver dollars will be taken into account in commercial transactions, and I fear the same result would follow any considerable increase of the present rate of coinage."

President Harrison was an able lawyer, and was trained "To make the worse appear the better reason."

From the tenor of the language of President Harrison first quoted, he delicately ridicules the severe strictures of President Cleveland upon silver as money, and he seeks to cast reproach upon the late administration.

In the language last quoted, the President, with the ability of a skilled special pleader, uses innuendo against free coinage, and he speaks of the difference in the bullion value respectively of gold and silver coin, as a great obstacle in the way of free coinage of the latter metal.

Having thus cunningly stated his objections to the free coinage of silver, he carried his fears from that subject into the system of government purchase of bullion, and its coinage into dollars under the Bland-Allison law, and he suggested that there is peril in the further continuation of the coinage of silver dollars.

At this time, Secretary Windom recommended his plan to Congress, which provided that any owner of silver bullion could deposit it in the Treasury, and receive therefor silver certificates upon the bullion value of the silver so deposited.

When Mr. Windom recommended this plan, the bullion value of the silver dollar was only seventy per cent. of the bullion value of the gold dollar, and the adoption of his plan by Congress would have created two classes of silver money and silver certificates.

The silver certificate issued under the Bland-Allison law would have represented far less bullion value than the certificate issued under his plan. It can be seen that the object of the Windom plan was to disparage the silver dollars and their paper representatives issued under the Bland-Allison law, and to supply the national banking money power with an opportunity to denounce the standard silver dollar as a "cheap dollar," a "dishonest dollar," a "70-cent dollar."

Then demands would be made upon the Government to protect its credit by redeeming the standard silver dollars in gold.

This would compel the issue of nearly $400,000,000 in interest-bearing bonds to secure gold for redemption purposes; and would have resulted in a contraction of the currency equal to the amount of standard silver dollars coined since February 28, 1878.

The Windom plan was transmitted to Congress, where it was introduced as House bill 5381.

On June 5, 1890, House bill 5381, known as the Windom Silver Bullion Purchase Bill, was pending in the House. Mr. Bland moved to recommit, with instructions to the committee to report back a bill for the free coinage of silver.

The motion was defeated by a vote of 116 yeas to 140 nays.

A substitute offered by Mr. Conger was then passed, and was known as House bill 5381.

On June 17th, House bill 5381 was reported by the Finance Committee of the Senate with sundry amendments; while it was pending, Mr. Plumb, of Kansas, offered an amendment for free and unlimited coinage of silver; which was agreed to by a vote of 43 yeas to 24 nays. The bill as amended into a free coinage measure was then passed by the Senate.

On June 25th, the Senate bill came up in the House, and, after long wrangling, the Senate free coinage amendment was defeated.

Both Houses appointed a Conference Committee which, after long deliberation, brought in a conference report.

In a speech on this conference report, Hon. R. P. Bland exposed the trickery of the Republican members of that committee in holding secret meetings to prevent the free coinage members from participating in its deliberations. He said:—

"Now, Mr. Speaker, the gentleman from Iowa [Mr. Conger] says this bill is the result of a free and fair conference. I deny it. We had but one meeting in which all the conferees were represented. That was the meeting appointed for last Thursday. We were to have another meeting of the conferees, but before the date of the meeting arrived, I was notified that my presence was no longer needed and that when my services were required, I would be notified. In the meantime, secret meetings or caucuses were held by the Republican members of that conference and this bill was concocted and prepared by them; and I never received a notice to attend another meeting of this conference until this bill was agreed to and the report was ready to be signed; and I was simply asked whether I agreed to it or not."

In the Senate debate on the bill reported by the Conference Committee, Senator Cockrell, of Missouri, pointed out that this measure was designed for the degradation of silver as a money metal, and that the Secretary of the Treasury was invested with such great powers that he could practically demonetize silver by refusing to pay it out for the redemption of the Treasury notes, which, under this act, would be issued to buy the silver bullion out of which silver dollars were to be coined.

In reply to these remarks of Senator Cockrell, Senator Sherman stated, that, if the Secretary should thus discriminate against the use of silver, he ought to be impeached.

On July 10th, the report was agreed to in the Senate by a vote of 39 yeas, all Republicans, and 26 nays, all Democrats.

On July 12th, the House concurred in the conference report by a vote of 122 yeas, all Republicans, except one independent, and 90 nays, all Democrats.

Thus the so-called Sherman Silver Purchasing Law of July 14, 1890, found its way upon the statute-books.

It will be noticed that in the vote of both Houses upon this bill, not a single Democratic member favored its passage.

They knew that in the hands of a Secretary of the Treasury hostile to the use of silver, this law would become the most formidable weapon of the national banking money power to strike a deadly blow against the continued coinage of that metal into money.

The full text of this act is as follows:—

"An act directing the purchase of silver bullion and the issue of Treasury notes thereon, and for other purposes."

"Be it enacted, That the Secretary of the Treasury is hereby directed to purchase, from time to time, silver bullion to the aggregate amount of 4,500,000 ounces, or so much thereof as may be offered in each month, at the market price thereof, not exceeding $1 for 371.25 grains of pure silver, and to issue in payment for such purchases of silver bullion Treasury notes of the United States to be prepared by the Secretary of the Treasury, in such form and of such denominations, not less than $1 nor more than $1,000, as he may prescribe, and a sum sufficient to carry into effect the provisions of this act is hereby appropriated out of any money in the Treasury not otherwise appropriated.

"Section 2. That the Treasury notes issued in accordance with the provisions of this act shall be redeemable on demand, in coin, at the Treasury of the United States, or at the office of any assistant treasurer of the United States, and when so redeemed may be reissued; but no greater or less amount of such notes shall be outstanding at any time than the cost of the silver bullion and the standard silver dollars coined therefrom, then held in the Treasury, purchased by such notes; and such Treasury notes shall be a legal tender in payment of all debts, public and private, except where otherwise expressly stipulated in the contract, and shall be receivable for customs, taxes, and all public dues, and when so received may be reissued; and such notes, when held by any National Banking Association, may be counted as a part of its lawful reserve. That upon demand of the holder of any of the Treasury notes herein provided for, the Secretary of the Treasury shall, under such regulations as he may prescribe, redeem such notes in gold or silver coin, at his discretion, it being the established policy of the United States to maintain the two metals on a parity with each other upon the present legal ratio, or such ratio as may be provided by law.

"Section 3. That the Secretary of the Treasury shall each month coin 2,000,000 ounces of the silver bullion purchased under the provisions of this act into standard silver dollars until the 1st day of July, 1891, and after that time he shall coin of the silver bullion purchased under the provisions of this act as much as may be necessary to provide for the redemption of the Treasury notes herein provided for, and any gain or seigniorage arising from such coinage shall be accounted for and paid into the Treasury.

"Section 4. That the silver bullion, purchased under the provisions of this act, shall be subject to the requirements of existing law and the regulations of the mint service governing the methods of determining the amount of pure silver contained, and the amount of charges or deductions, if any, to be made.

"Section 5. That so much of the act of February 28, 1878, entitled 'An act to authorize the coinage of the standard silver dollar and to restore its legal tender character,' as requires the monthly purchase and coinage of the same into silver dollars of not less than $2,000,000 nor more than $4,000,000 worth of silver bullion, is hereby repealed.

"Section 6. That upon the passage of this act the balances standing with the Treasurer of the United States to the respective credits of national banks for deposits made to redeem the circulating notes of such banks, and all deposits thereafter received for like purpose, shall be covered into the Treasury as a miscellaneous receipt, and the Treasurer of the United States shall redeem from the general cash in the Treasury the circulating notes of said banks which may come into his possession subject to redemption; and upon the certificate of the Comptroller of the Currency that such notes have been received by him and that they have been destroyed and that no new notes will be issued in their place, reimbursement of their amount shall be made to the Treasurer, under such regulations as the Secretary of the Treasury may prescribe, from an appropriation hereby created, to be known as the national bank note redemption account; but the provisions of this act shall not apply to the deposits received under section 3 of the act of June 20, 1874, requiring every national bank to keep in lawful money with the Treasurer of the United States a sum equal to five per cent. of its circulation, to be held and used for the redemption of its circulating notes; and the balance remaining of the deposits so covered shall, at the close of each month, be reported on the monthly public debt statement as debt of the United States bearing no interest.

"Section 7. That this act shall take effect thirty days from and after its passage."

This silver purchasing law, as it finally passed Congress, was the offspring of the fertile brain of John Sherman, and future events demonstrated that it was so cunningly planned that it terminated in making silver a credit money.

Senator Sherman, who, as chairman of the Committee on Finance of the United States Senate, succeeded in getting this bill through Congress, afterward publicly stated that this measure was for the express purpose of defeating the free coinage of silver.

On August 30, 1893, Senator Sherman delivered a speech urging a speedy repeal of the law for the passage of which he had bent all his energies to secure in 1890. He said:—

"Our Democratic friends have denounced this purchasing clause as a miserable makeshift. It was a makeshift, but I think a good one to defeat the free coinage of silver on the ratio of 16 to 1. I believe in this respect it has rendered the country an enormous service."

With unparalleled brazen effrontery, he stated in his Memoirs, lately published, that he would have voted for the repeal of this law within ten days after its passage, after he had by this means defeated the free coinage measure proposed by the Senate.

An examination of the provisions of the act of July 14, 1890, in connection with the circumstances attending its passage, will exhibit some remarkable facts.

In substance, the Secretary of the Treasury was authorized to purchase, from time to time, silver bullion to the aggregate amount of 4,500,000 ounces, or as much thereof as would be offered in each month at the market price, not exceeding $1 for each 371.25 grains of pure silver. And in payment of such bullion, Treasury notes of the United States were to be prepared by the Secretary of the Treasury in denominations of not less than $1 nor more than $1,000. That the Treasury notes so issued should be redeemable on demand, in coin, at the Treasury of the United States, or at the office of any assistant treasurer of the United States, and, when so redeemed, could be reissued.

That no greater or less amount of such notes should be outstanding at any time than the cost of the silver bullion and the standard silver dollars coined therefrom, then held in the Treasury, purchased by such notes. That such Treasury notes should be a legal tender in payment of all debts, public and private, except where otherwise expressly stipulated in the contract. That such notes should be receivable for customs, taxes, and all public dues, and when so received could be reissued. That such notes could be counted a part of its lawful reserve by any National Banking Association. That, upon demand of the holder of any of the Treasury notes so issued, the Secretary of the Treasury should redeem such notes in gold or silver coin, at his discretion. That it was the established policy of the United States to maintain the two metals on a parity with each other upon the present legal ratio, or such ratio as may be provided by law.

Section 3 of this act was so cunningly contrived that it operated to hoard up the silver dollars coined under this law.

This section to which we direct the attention of the reader is as follows:—

"That the Secretary of the Treasury shall each month coin 2,000,000 ounces of the silver bullion purchased under the provisions of this act into standard silver dollars until the first day of July, 1891, and after that time he shall coin of the silver bullion purchased under the provisions of this act as much as may be necessary to provide for the redemption of the Treasury notes herein provided for."

The language of this section provided for the redemption of the Treasury notes in silver dollars, when not taken in connection with section 2.

The inference to be drawn from this language which we have quoted is, that for every dollar in Treasury notes emitted for the purchase of silver bullion, a sufficient number of dollars must be coined therefrom to redeem these notes. To maintain an adequate supply of such silver dollars available for the redemption of such notes, they must be kept inviolate in the Treasury for that identical purpose. This would prohibit them from going into circulation. Stored up in the Treasury vaults by a literal interpretation of this language, a large accumulation of these dollars would be inevitable, and would afford a President and Secretary of the Treasury, unfriendly to silver, an opportunity to point to them as evidence that they were not desired as money for actual circulation. This was actually done by President Cleveland in his message of August 8, 1893, in which he advised the speedy repeal of the purchasing clause of this law. In that document, he pointed out that the silver coin and bullion in the Treasury had increased more than $147,000,000 between the 1st of July, 1890, up to the 15th of July, 1893.

Hence, it will be seen that the silver dollars coined under this law could be hoarded up in the Treasury at the mere will of the Secretary, while, at the same time, he could use his discretion in redeeming such Treasury notes wholly in gold.

This policy was carried into effect by Secretaries Foster and Carlisle.

Section 3 also provided that any gain or seigniorage, which would be the difference between the coinage value of the silver so purchased and its bullion value, should be paid into the Treasury.

Section 4 provided that so much of the Bland-Allison act of February 28, 1878, in so far as it required the monthly purchase and coinage of silver bullion into silver dollars of not less than $2,000,000 nor more than $4,000,000 should be repealed.

Section 6 of this act provided that, upon its passage, the legal tender notes deposited by the national banks for the redemption of the circulating notes of such banks, and all deposits thereafter received for like purpose, should be paid into the Treasury as a miscellaneous receipt, and that national bank notes should be redeemed out of a fund to be created and known as the national bank note redemption account.

When we construe the propositions embraced in the act of July 14, 1890, we ascertain,—

"First, That the free coinage system, which had existed prior to 1873, was absolutely destroyed by this enactment; and that the purchase of silver bullion by the Government made this metal a mere commodity; while the holder of gold was granted the privilege of taking his bullion to the mints and have it coined into money of unlimited legal tender debt-paying power.

"Second, That the purchase of 4,500,000 ounces of silver per month, would not exhaust its annual production, but a large surplus would remain on the market, the presence of which would inevitably result in a depreciation of its bullion value—the value of silver produced during 1890 was, $70,464,000 and its price per ounce was $1.05."

Therefore, the production of silver for that year was not less than 70,000,000 ounces. The total amount of silver provided for by the Sherman law was 54,000,000 ounces per annum, leaving an annual surplus of 16,000,000 ounces to act as a depressing element on the price of silver.

Moreover, this surplus would accumulate year by year, gradually but surely lowering the bullion price of silver. In one respect, the policy embodied in the Sherman law was similar to that of the Bland-Allison law in this, that, while these two laws professed to solve the silver question, they aggravated the mischief by affording a greatly limited market for silver, and consequently a restricted demand for it with a resultant fall of price.

The abolition of free coinage of silver, and its purchase and coinage on government account alone, was adopted at the cunning suggestion and at the instigation of John Sherman.

The object of this policy, by which the Government purchased silver and coined it into dollars, was a shrewd scheme to make silver a mere credit money redeemable in gold alone. Should the silver dollars so coined fall in bullion value, a demand would be made upon Congress to maintain the public credit by guaranteeing the bullion parity of the silver dollar with that of gold.

Under the provisions of the Sherman law, the Secretary of the Treasury could go into the open market and buy silver from the lowest competitive bidder, and that process meant a continual fall in its price.

The Government became a "bear" in the silver market.

One feature of the Sherman law that was extremely vicious, was couched in that provision forbidding the Secretary of the Treasury to pay more than one dollar for each 371.25 grains of pure silver. A maximum price was fixed beyond which the Secretary could not go; but there was no minimum below which he could not buy. This provision was a statutory declaration of hostility toward silver.

The policy of England, in fixing the price of gold to be paid by the Bank of England, established a minimum, below which that bank could not go on penalty of forfeiture of its charter.

The financial system of the United States, as it was embodied in the so-called Sherman law, aimed at the destruction of the value of silver, of which it was the largest producer in the world; the policy of Great Britain aimed at the enhancement of the value of gold, of which it was the largest holder.

In payment for the silver purchased, the Secretary of the Treasury was authorized to issue Treasury notes, redeemable on demand, in coin, at the Treasury of the United States, or at the office of any assistant treasurer of the United States, and when so redeemed, they could be reissued.

Coin meant gold and silver at the time this law came in force. While the first part of the act declared these notes redeemable in coin, a subsequent clause of the same section provided,—

"That upon demand of the holder of any of the Treasury notes herein provided for, the Secretary of the Treasury shall, under such regulations as he may prescribe, redeem such notes in gold or silver coin at his discretion, it being the established policy of the United States to maintain the two metals on a parity with each other upon the present legal ratio, or such ratio as may be provided by law."

This last clause made the whole section ambiguous. The first clause declared the Treasury notes redeemable in coin; the last clause makes them redeemable in gold or silver coin.

The reader will notice how cunningly this redemption clause is worded. The Secretary of the Treasury was ordered to redeem the Treasury notes in gold *or* silver coin, not gold and silver coin.

Hence, the Secretary of the Treasury, in his discretion, could redeem the Treasury notes in either kind of coin.

The ablest writers on law have always pointed out the dangers of leaving the execution of laws subject to the discretion of those officers whose duty it is to carry them into effect.

Many of the most valuable rights of man have been thrown away, by vesting too much authority in the discretion of those officials whose duty requires them to properly execute laws.

That is the best law which leaves the least to the discretion of the authority appointed to execute it.

One other singular provision of this measure reads as follows:—

"It being the established policy of the United States to maintain the two metals on a parity with each other upon the present legal ratio, or such ratio as may be provided by law."

This language drew an invidious distinction between the coin and the metal of which it is composed.

The clause does not say parity of the two coins, but metals. Should this provision be construed against the United States, the Government would become the guarantor of the value of the bullion in the standard silver dollar, should its value be less than that in the gold dollar. Silver would become a mere credit money redeemable in gold.

This parity clause constituted the "endless chain" so graphically described by President Cleveland in his special message to Congress in August, 1893.

Should the Secretary of the Treasury surrender his discretion of redeeming Treasury notes in gold or silver coin, this parity clause would subserve two distinct purposes,—

First, It would convert every Treasury note into a vehicle for transferring the gold in the Treasury to the vaults of the national banks.

Second, This process of redemption in gold would give the national banking money power an opportunity to unsettle business by bringing on a panic, and to demand the withdrawal and destruction of the greenbacks and Treasury notes.

The Treasury notes issued under the law of 1890 were mere promissory notes payable on demand, and had the act which authorized their issue made them redeemable in the silver dollars coined out of the bullion purchased under that law, the national banking money power, and the gold speculators of London and New York City could not have drained the Treasury of its gold reserve.

It is unquestionable, that the so-called Sherman law was ambiguously worded by its authors with the ultimate design of seriously impairing the value of silver.

However, the large amount required under the provision of that act served to steady its bullion value, reckoning that value from a gold basis.

Moreover, the issue of Treasury notes utilized to purchase the required amount of silver added many millions to the volume of money in circulation. Consequently the prices of agricultural products were enhanced, and the power of Russian and Indian competition in the wheat markets of the world was measurably reduced.

In speaking of these facts in his report of 1890, Secretary Rusk, of the Department of Agriculture, said:—

"The recent legislation looking to the restoration of the bi-metallic standard of our currency, and the consequent enhancement of the value of silver, has unquestionably had much to do with the advance in the price of cereals. The same cause has advanced the price of wheat in Russia and India, and in the same degree reduced their power of competition. English gold was formerly exchanged for cheap silver, and wheat purchased with the cheaper metal was sold in Great Britain for gold. Much of this advantage is lost by the appreciation of silver in those countries. It is reasonable, therefore, to expect much higher prices for wheat than have been received in recent years."

Despite those ambiguities and inconsistencies that were embraced in the provisions of the so-called Sherman law, and which were craftily designed by its framers to cripple the coinage of silver as a medium of exchange, the addition of the Treasury notes to the circulation had raised prices correspondingly in the United States. Secretary Rusk admitted the fact.

So marked was this effect, that President Harrison made special reference to the matter in his message in December, 1891.

Hence, the national banks were planning to array their concentrated power against the issuance of the Treasury notes, the control of which had temporarily escaped their grasp.

Soon after the introduction of the Windom Silver Bullion Purchase Bill, the Secretary of the Treasury attended a banquet at New York City as the guest of the associated bankers. While in the act of delivering an address, Mr. Windom was suddenly prostrated by an attack of apoplexy which proved fatal.

The President chose Hon. Charles Foster, of Ohio, as his successor. The new Secretary of the Treasury was a national banker, and had earned some reputation as an adroit politician.

Prior to the appointment of Mr. Foster as Secretary of the Treasury, United States bonds were rapidly rising in value until they were worth from 25 to 29 per cent. above par.

In the meantime, the banks of New York City, Boston, and other financial centers of the East, were hoarding up gold, Treasury notes of the issue of 1890, and greenbacks.

The object of this combined action of the Eastern national banks, in thus hoarding up these various kinds of money, was for the purpose of embarrassing the Treasury of the United States. While these banks were engaged in this operation, the bond-holding syndicates of Europe had united to force Austro-Hungary to convert her immense debt of $2,400,000,000 into gold bonds, which was a part of the scheme to handcuff the whole civilized world to the single standard of gold.

While the syndicates of Europe were engaged in

carrying out their schemes against Austria, the national banking money power of the East had matured a plan to sell its bonds at a high premium, a process which would have netted them a profit ranging from 25 to 29 cents on the dollar.

The purpose of this combination was two-fold; in the first place, the bankers would gain this great premium by the redemption of their bonds, and this redemption would result in draining the Treasury of its gold; as a next step, a demand would be made by them for the issue of new bonds to replenish the gold reserve. These bonds would be purchased by the same clique who had sold the former bonds and gained millions by the operation.

During this time, the financiers of Austria had concluded to fund the bonds of that country into gold obligations, a policy to which they were forced by the Rothchilds who had her by the throat.

To effect these funding operations, gold must be secured somewhere to execute the mandates of the money kings of Europe.

The Bank of England held immense reserves of gold; the Bank of France had yet far more; Russia had a vast treasure exceeding $500,000,000.

Notwithstanding these facts the necessary gold could not be drawn from the Bank of England by Austria to effect her funding operations, for, at the first attempt of the latter to obtain gold in London, this great bank would immediately raise its price, a practice to which it had always resorted to prevent the exportation of gold from England.

Neither could it be obtained from the Bank of France, whose charter forbade it to pay out more than five per cent. in gold for export at any one time. The Bank of France was under rigid supervision of the Government, and it was the servant of the French Republic, not its master.

The immense accumulations of gold in Russia were unassailable, as that Empire would not pay out a single rouble in gold.

Hence, the only source of supply of gold, to which resort could be had by Austria, was that stored up in the United States Treasury and in the banks of New York City.

These banks had hoarded up more than $200,000,000 of gold, a fact of which they boasted. They would not pay out a dollar of their immense holdings of this coin, as it would be utilized by them to buy up any bonds that might be issued to maintain that absurd thing known as the "gold reserve."

But one great obstacle lay in the way of withdrawing gold from the Treasury for export, and that was embraced in section 2 of the Sherman law of July 14, 1890, which provided that the Secretary of the Treasury should redeem the treasury notes of 1890 in gold or silver coin at his discretion.

The option, or right, of this Government to redeem its treasury notes in either gold or silver coin was vested in the discretion of the Secretary of the Treasury.

This discretion, or option, was the sole barrier in the path leading to the Treasury of the United States.

With the object of ascertaining the policy of Secretary Foster, a grand banquet was given at the Delmonico restaurant by the New York bankers, and Mr. Foster was invited to attend as the special guest of the occasion.

The Secretary accepted the generous hospitality of these financiers, and again the Mountain journeyed to Mohammed.

After these distinguished patriots had feasted themselves on the costliest viands of the season, and had imbibed large quantities of sparkling champagne, these financiers called upon the honorable Secretary to state his position upon the redemption of the treasury notes and greenbacks. He was also requested to define his actual powers with reference to issuing bonds to maintain the gold reserve.

The eminent Secretary, inspired by these representatives of great wealth, gathered around the festal board, and buoyed up by the elevating influence of the champagne furnished by these money kings, then and there declared that he would redeem the Treasury notes and greenbacks in gold, and that he would persevere in that policy. The Secretary said:—

"The Resumption Act confers authority upon the Secretary of the Treasury to issue bonds to any extent that he may be called upon to do, and to increase, maintain, or decrease his gold reserve. The act of July 14, 1890, commands me to preserve the parity of gold and silver. It has always been the custom of this country to pay its obligations in gold, and therefore should there be any trouble about this, and the present hundred millions of gold, or the Reserve Fund, were to be called out or intrenched upon, it would be within the Secretary's power to issue bonds for gold up to five per cent. and to replace or increase that Reserve Fund."

Thus, at the banquet table of these Belshazzars of New York City, Secretary Foster transferred the option of the Government to redeem its notes in gold or silver to that horde of money lords, the presidents of the associated national banks of New York City.

These bank presidents at once communicated the decision of Secretary Foster to their allies in Europe, and an understanding was had between the money power of the United States and Europe, that the national banks of New York City would supply the Treasury notes necessary to deplete the Treasury of its gold.

The interests of the financiers of the East and of Europe were identical, and the offer of the one was accepted by the other.

At the time of this Delmonico banquet, there were eight varieties of money in circulation in the United States, exclusive of subsidiary silver, nickel, and copper coins, viz. :—

First, gold coin, with unlimited legal tender for all debts of every kind, public and private.

Second, gold certificates, limited to the amount of gold deposited in the Treasury, not legal tender, but could be counted as part of the national bank reserves, receivable for all public dues, and could be reissued by the Government. They were redeemable in gold coin alone. Gold certificates were the paper representatives of the gold as a more convenient form of that coin; and their denominations ranged from $20 to $10,000.

Third, Silver dollars, the coinage of which since 1878 had been limited, of full legal tender for all debts, except where otherwise specified in the contract, receivable for all taxes due the United States and exchangeable for silver certificates.

Fourth, Silver certificates, limited to the amount of silver dollars deposited in the Treasury by their holders, not legal tender, but could be counted as part of bank reserves, receivable for all dues by the Government, redeemable in silver dollars alone, their denominations ranged from $1 to $1,000.

Fifth, United States notes, known as greenbacks, their volume limited by the law of 1878 to $346,681,106, unlimited legal tender for all debts, public and private, except duties on imports and interest on the public debt, redeemable in coin in sums of $50 and upwards at the sub-treasuries of New York City and San Francisco. The denominations were identical with those of the silver certificates.

Sixth, Currency certificates, limited by amount of United States notes deposited therefor, not legal tender, could be counted as part of the national bank reserves, not receivable by the Government for taxes, exchangeable for United States notes, redeemable in that money at the sub-treasury where issued. Their denominations ranged from $5,000 to $10,000.

Seventh, Treasury notes of 1890, issued for the purchase of silver under the Sherman law, unlimited legal tender, unless otherwise specified in the contract, receivable for all dues by the United States, exchangeable for all kinds of money except gold certificates, redeemable in coin in sums of not less than $50 at the United States Treasury and the various sub-treasuries. Their denominations were the same as silver certificates.

Eighth, National bank notes, printed by the Government, and given to national banks, limited to ninety per cent. of the United States bonds deposited therefor in the Treasury, legal tender for payment of debts to national banks, for dues to the United States except duties on imports, are legal tender for payments by the United States, except interest on the public debt and redemption of currency, redeemable in lawful money at the issuing bank and at the Treasury. Their denominations are the same as United States notes with the exception of one and two dollar notes.

Under the redemption features of the national bank law, by which national bank notes were redeemable in greenbacks, these bank notes were really redeemable in gold. The circulating notes of national banks could be presented to the Treasury Department for redemption in greenbacks, and this latter currency could be immediately presented for redemption in gold.

Therefore, these bank notes were in reality redeemable in gold at the Treasury of the United States, and this scheme of converting these bank notes into government demand obligations, payable in gold, was systematically worked by the national banks.

Such was the heterogeneous mass of the various kinds of coin and currency afloat in the nation.

To John Sherman, the great necromancer of American finance, belongs the credit of originating this combative and incongruous state of currency. We except the silver dollar.

This system of finance was planned and adopted for the sole benefit of the national banks, as it furnished them with the means of discriminating against the government issues of currency.

In that conglomerate mass of crudities, the machinery necessary to operate the "endless chain" upon the gold reserve can be easily seen when taken in connection with the parity clause of the Sherman law, as construed by such eminent financiers as Charles Foster and Secretary Carlisle.

This explanation of the various kinds of coin and currency is given here to afford the reader a view of the means by which the money power geared up that "endless chain," and converted every greenback, treasury note, and bank note into buckets that were attached to this chain to dip the gold from the Treasury, and pass it to the control of the foreign and domestic gold gamblers.

On his return to Washington, Secretary Foster issued a circular inviting proposals for the purchase of bonds by the Government.

The bankers of New York City at once responded, and in seventy-five days the Secretary purchased bonds, the face value of which was $75,828,200, but for which was paid $86,266,730, a profit to the bankers of $10,438,530 in premiums.

The Secretary also advanced interest to the bondholders nine months before it was due. The amount of prepaid interest was $12,009,951.

The total amount donated to the New York banks by this quondam Secretary of the Treasury in the way of prepaid interest and premium on bonds was $29,000,000.

Gratuity upon gratuity, franchise upon franchise, have been heaped upon the richest men of the nation, the very men who caused panic after panic, and who, before many months would elapse, would exert their immense power to bankrupt tens of thousands of business men, throw out of employment hundreds of thousands of working men, and force the entire nation into a condition of want and misery that was appalling.

At first these money kings fawned at the feet of the Government for special privileges; before long we will see them turn upon and rend the very hand that conferred these immense pecuniary benefits upon them.

The national banks of New York City, which, from 1885 to 1892, received the tremendous sum of nearly $70,000,000 in premiums on the bonds held by them, prepaid interest to the amount of tens of millions, a gratuitous loan of $63,000,000 of the public funds without interest, now saw themselves in a position in which they determined to measure their strength against that of the Government.

Secretary Foster, who had transferred the purse of the Government into the hands of these money kings, met with what might be termed retribution for his cowardly surrender to the banking power. He became a bankrupt during that great panic of 1893, which was brought on by the concerted action of the very men who dined and wined him at Delmonico's in 1891. In his extremities, he called upon his New York banker friends for aid; they laughed in his face; he was mercilessly driven to the wall. His liabilities exceeded $1,000,000, of which he was scarcely able to pay ten per cent. on the dollar.

After the Delmonico episode, the money power matured their plans to raid the gold reserve in the United States Treasury.

The construction of the Sherman law, as publicly announced by Secretary Foster, made this scheme comparatively easy of execution.

The money kings of Europe, and the national banking money power, joined their forces to consummate a common purpose, the former to obtain gold out of the Treasury and sell it at a premium to Austria, the latter to force an issue of bonds and a suspension of silver coinage under the Sherman law.

The way was now clear for this combined money power to execute its purpose. The initial step was now taken.

On the 15th of August, 1892, the firm of Heidelbach, Ickelheimer & Co., Jewish bankers of New York City, agents of a foreign syndicate, presented $1,000,000 in treasury notes at the sub-treasury in that city, and demanded gold for them, and stated that they wanted this gold for shipment abroad.

Without any hesitation, Assistant Treasurer Roberts gave this firm the required gold. On this fact becoming known, a leading journal of New York City interviewed Assistant Treasurer Roberts with reference to this transaction. During the course of the interview, Mr. Roberts was asked what steps had been taken by the administration to obstruct or prevent the exportation of gold. He replied:—

"No steps have been taken by the administration to prevent or obstruct the export of gold. The Government stands ready to meet all its obligations in gold and will pay them in gold."

In this interview, the Assistant Treasurer gave notice that the Treasury stood ready to furnish all the gold required by the gold gamblers and foreign bond syndicates necessary to place Austria upon a gold standard. It would furnish the gold, and the speculators obtaining it would dispose of it at a premium.

Thus the promise which the associated bankers of New York City had extorted from Secretary Foster, in which he declared that he would pay out gold in the redemption of treasury notes and greenbacks, was a part of the concerted scheme to force the repeal of the Sherman law of 1890, and the issue of bonds to obtain gold.

It will be asked, why did these national banks who owed their very existence to the Government, and from whom they received those valuable franchises which earned them billions of dollars, deliberately conspire to embarrass the Treasury of the United States?

First, Because it brought to the aid of these banks the most powerful concentration of capital in the world, whose interests were identical with those of the national banks.

Second, It would drain the Treasury of its gold, and this would force an issue of long-time interest bearing bonds, which would serve as a basis for the continuance of the national banking system. These banks were accumulating gold to buy those bonds, while they were assisting the foreign gold speculators in their efforts to drain the Treasury.

Third, It afforded the banks the opportunity of demanding the permanent withdrawal from circulation and the consequent destruction of $500,000,000 in treasury notes and greenbacks, this currency to be supplanted by an equal issue of national bank notes donated outright to those institutions.

Fourth, The national banks could point to the silver dollar as depreciated coin, and demand its redemption in gold to "Maintain the parity of the metals."

Fifth, The whole volume of government legal tender notes, treasury notes, silver dollars, and silver certificates would become mere credit money, and the sole legal tender would be gold alone.

Sixth, It virtually deprived the Federal Government of its constitutional power to fix the value of money, and transferred that highest element of sovereignty to the bullion brokers of the world.

Seventh, It enabled the national banks to obtain a construction of the parity clause of the Sherman law, which virtually demonetized silver.

In the meantime, the House of Representatives had passed the iniquitous Force Bill, which went to the Senate.

On January 5, 1891, Mr. Stewart moved to consider Senate bill 4675, replacing the Force Bill. The motion was agreed to by a vote of 34 yeas to 29 nays.

On January 14, 1891, the same Senator moved a free coinage amendment to this bill, which had been laid aside up to that time.

The amendment was agreed to by a vote of 42 yeas to 30 nays.

Mr. Vest then offered a free and unlimited coinage provision as a substitute, and that was agreed to by a vote of 39 yeas to 27 nays.

On January 15, 1891, Senate bill 4675 being the substitute offered by Mr. Vest, came up in the House of Representatives, whereupon it was referred to the Coinage Committee, which, on February 21, 1891, made an adverse report on the measure and no further action was had on the bill.

In a report of the Committee on Coinage on one of these measures, providing for the free coinage of silver, the character of those who appeared before this committee at hearings given by it, and opposed the free coinage of silver, is thus described:—

"Almost every man who appeared in opposition to free coinage was a president or some other executive officer of some bank, some great insurance company or other firm, corporation or association controlling vast aggregations of capital."

With reference to those who were advocating free coinage the report says:—

"Upon the other hand, it may not be out of place for us to mention the circumstance by way of contrast, that at the conclusion of Mr. Atkinson's statement Mr. Dunning, the duly accredited agent of the Knights of Labor, and various other kindred organizations comprising nearly 4,000,000 voters, stepped forward and laid on the table the petition of these toiling millions, praying for the free coinage of silver.

"In additon to this it is proper for us to call attention to the further fact that the great organization known as the Farmers' Alliance has adopted a demand for the free coinage of silver as the cardinal feature of its creed."

In his message to Congress, December 3, 1891, President Harrison opposed free coinage, and gave his reasons for it in the following language:—

"I am still of the opinion that free coinage of silver under existing conditions would disastrously effect our business interests at home and abroad."

On July 14, 1892, Senator Sherman introduced a bill to repeal the purchasing clause of the law of July 14, 1890.

In the latter part of 1892, and in the months of January and February, 1893, the foreign gold speculators persevered in draining the Treasury of its gold for shipment abroad. While this process was being carried on, the press of New York City was issuing startling reports of the financial condition of the Treasury. Some of these journals published daily statements of the amount of gold taken out of the country, and demanded that Secretary Foster replenish the gold reserve by an issue of bonds. Mr. Foster meekly obeyed, and on the 23d of February, 1893, he issued a written order to the Chief of the Bureau of Engraving and Printing, directing him to prepare plates for the printing of bonds.

On hearing of the decision of the Secretary of the Treasury to issue bonds, the bankers of New York City formed a syndicate for the purchase of the proposed issue.

The order to prepare the plates for bonds became known to President Harrison, and it was countermanded by him, and he stated that this was a "debt-paying administration."

So the proposed issue of $100,000,000 of bonds did not materialize at this time. President Harrison graciously intended that the incoming administration of President Cleveland should bear the odium of increasing the national debt in time of peace.

It will be instructive to institute a comparison between the financial condition of the producers of the country with that of the bond-holding class.

In speaking of the enormous mortgage and other indebtedness of the West and South in 1890, Frederic C. Waite said:—

"Last year, after turning the scale at eight thousand millions, the mortgage indebtedness continued its upward flight, not being contented with an increase of 220 per cent., or nearly four times the increase in the true value of real estate.

"In a word, the total net private indebtedness of the American people equaled, in 1880, but $6,750,-000,000. Last September it amounted to nineteen thousand seven hundred millions, an increase of thirteen thousand millions in the short period of twelve years."

Congressman Walker, of Massachusetts, makes the

total indebtedness of the people of the United States reach the grand aggregate of thirty-two billion dollars.

While the producers were being eaten up by usury, the bond-holders were receiving from twenty-five to twenty-nine per cent. premium on their bonds.

In 1866, the national debt was $2,783,000,000, the gold value of which at that time did not exceed $1,100,000,000. Up to the early part of 1893, $1,756,000,000 had been paid on the principal; the payments of interest were $2,538,000,000, $58,000,000 were paid in premiums, making a total payment of $4,352,000,000. The amount due in 1893 was $1,027,450,000, and this residue of the debt would purchase more of the products of labor than the original amount. In 1866 the entire debt could have been paid with 1,007,000,000 bushels of wheat at the price it then brought.

After this vast amount of interest, principal, and premium was applied on this debt as stated above, it would require 2,054,900,000 bushels to pay the residue of the debt in 1893.

In 1867, 14,184,000 bales of cotton would have paid the total debt.

In 1893, at the price for which cotton sold, it would require 34,251,600 bales of that product to pay the remainder of the debt.

This after $4,352,000,000 were paid thereon.

The profits of the national banking money power, from 1872 to 1891, on its circulating notes donated to it by the Government were, according to the New York World Almanac, $1,081,988,586.

Such were the results of that British scheme of finance which was fastened on the American people.

Those who are wedded to the delusive idea of protection, as the panacea for the ills now seriously affecting all industries, must bear in mind that this frightful condition of the producer sprung up under the highest tariff laws since 1861.

CHAPTER IX.

MONEY POWER OF ENGLAND AND UNITED STATES COMBINED TO ANNIHILATE SILVER.

"Against the insidious wiles of foreign influence (I conjure you to believe me, fellow citizens) the jealousy of a free people ought to be constantly awake, since history and experience prove that foreign influence is one of the most baneful foes of Republican Government."—George Washington.

"Let us found a Government where there shall be no extremely rich men and no abjectly poor ones. Let us found a Government upon the intelligence of the people and the equitable distribution of property. Let us make laws where there shall be no governmental partnership with favored classes. Let us protect all in life, liberty, and property, and then say to every American citizen, with the gifts that God has given you, your brain and brawn and energy, work out your own fortunes under a just Government and equal laws."—Thomas Jefferson.

For the purpose of enabling the reader to thoroughly understand the nature of the events that would take place in 1893, and succeeding years, we will direct some attention to the silver agitation in Great Britain in 1892.

It was heretofore stated, that Great Britain was the first nation to adopt a single standard of gold, and that this financial system dates from the year 1816.

In many respects, England is the most wonderful country on the face of the earth. Her colonial possessions are immense, all of which enjoy some degree of self-government, except that of India, which is governed exclusively by a Viceroy appointed by the home Government.

India has an area of 1,500,000 square miles, inhabited by a population numbering 285,000,000 of industrious people.

Prior to June 25, 1893, India was on a silver standard.

Before the United States demonetized silver in 1873, the production of wheat and cotton in India was insignificant, and her manufactures of cotton fabrics were in their infancy.

With the demonetization of silver by the United States in the year mentioned, the production of wheat and cotton in India commenced on a large scale, and her manufactures of cotton goods developed very rapidly. Her remarkable growth in this direction was owing solely to the demonetization of silver by the United States and other nations, which action caused a tremendous fall in the bullion value of that metal.

Not only did this develop the resources of India, but the latter country became the most dangerous competitor of the United States in the wheat and cotton market of the world.

In 1866, the first fifty bales of cotton yarn were shipped from Bombay, and the growth of the trade was not very rapid until 1874.

In 1875, India exported 1,000,000 pounds of cotton yarn, the following year 5,000,000 pounds, this had increased annually until 1889, when its exportation reached 65,000,000 pounds. In 1891, the exports of cotton yarn from India were 165,000,000 pounds. Her exportations of raw cotton increased at the same ratio.

The number of cotton mills, from 1876 to 1887, increased 100 per cent., the number of spindles 105 per cent., cotton piece goods 243 per cent., and cotton yarn 1,058 per cent.

Prior to 1874, the production of wheat in India was very small, but within five years after the demonetization of silver by the United States, she exported 11,900,000 bushels.

During the succeeding years, her shipments of wheat steadily grew in magnitude, until they reached the enormous total of 59,000,000 bushels in 1891. The gold price of wheat fell enormously.

The demonetization of silver by the United States operated as an export bounty on the products of India, and the greater the fall of silver, the more beneficial to the wheat and cotton growers of that Oriental country.

The silver coins of India were of unlimited legal tender debt-paying power. She had no gold coinage.

Since 1873, the history of prices proves that the purchasing power of silver over commodities has been practically unimpaired, that is stable. This was especially true of the silver coins of India.

This fact was shown by the British Gold and Silver Commission of 1886, composed of twelve of the ablest financiers of England, six of whom were adherents of the gold standard, and the other six bi-metallists. This commission made an exhaustive examination into the cause leading to the fall of the gold price of silver.

This commission unanimously reported that the purchasing power of the rupee continued unimpaired, and that the prices of commodities measured in silver remained practically the same in that country.

On page 95 of its final report, the commission said:—

"In India, in the opinion of nearly all the witnesses whom we have examined, the purchasing power of the rupee continues unimpaired and the prices of commodities measured in silver remain practically the same. We have no evidence to show that silver has undergone any material change in relation to commodities, although it has fallen largely in relation to gold; in other words, the same number of rupees will no longer exchange for the same amount of gold as formerly, but, so far as we can judge, they will purchase as much of any commodity or commodities in India as they did before."

In a separate report, six of these commissioners made use of the following language as an answer that falling prices result from facilities for production. They say:—

"We are not insensible to the fact that facilities for production are habitually increasing, and the cost of production is constantly becoming less. But these factors have always been in operation since the world began; and while we recognize their tendency to depress the prices of commodities, they are not, in our opinion, sufficient to account for the abnormal fall in prices, which has been apparent since the rupture of the bi-metallic par, and only since that time."

The process by which the depreciation of silver built up the industries of India at the expense of those of the gold standard countries was apparent.

When the London merchant went to India to buy wheat and cotton, he ascertained that his gold would not purchase any more of her products than an equal amount of silver expressed at a ratio of fifteen and one half to one.

Therefore, the English merchant would send his gold to the United States, and purchase cheap silver with it, ship this silver to India and purchase the wheat and cotton of that country. If the price of silver in London was 65 cents per ounce, the English merchant would buy exchange on the United States to the amount of $13,000; with this he could purchase 20,000 ounces of silver bullion. This bullion, when shipped to India, would be worth the mint price of $1.33 per ounce. With this cheap silver, the wheat merchant would find it more profitable to buy Indian wheat at $1.20 per bushel, than to purchase the same product in the United States paying therefor 75 or 80 cents per bushel reckoned on a gold basis.

In a few years after the demonetization of silver by the United States, the English rejoiced at the blow which was thus dealt to American commerce.

At a meeting of the British and Colonial Chambers of Commerce, held in London in 1886, Sir Robert N. Fowler, a member of Parliament, a banker, and an ex-mayor of London, said:—

"That the effect of the depreciation of silver must finally be the ruin of the wheat and cotton industries of America, and be the development of India as the chief wheat and cotton exporter of the world."

At the same time that the export trade of India grew so rapidly, she manufactured more largely for herself. The reason was obvious.

Should she attempt to import foreign manufactured goods from gold standard countries, the rate of exchange against her would be equal to the depreciation existing between her silver compared to the gold of the nation from whom she would purchase.

To illustrate: Suppose a merchant of Bombay or Calcutta proceeded to England and purchased goods to the amount of 100,000 sovereigns, it would require gold coin for the payment of them, as the standard of value there is gold. He would find it necessary to convert his silver rupees into exchange on London, in order to obtain the gold, to pay for the goods, and the result would be that he would lose the difference between the bullion value of the silver compared with that of gold. Consequently, this loss of exchange would be an insurmountable obstacle in the way of his silver standard country purchasing from that which was on a gold basis. This would stimulate home manufactures in silver using countries, that is—those nations on a silver basis.

This difference in the loss of exchange would operate more effectively, in restricting foreign importations into silver standard countries, than the most rigid protective tariff laws ever enacted.

Another very important effect of the disparity between the value of gold and silver in the commercial intercourse of nations would be as follows:—First, Those nations on a silver basis would trade with each other, the population of which by far exceeded that of the gold standard countries; second, England would be the greatest sufferer should India continue on a silver standard.

These two conclusions were fully borne out by subsequent events. The great Oriental nations purchased immense quantities of manufactured goods from India, while there was a great falling off in the sales of the same class of merchandise heretofore supplied by England.

The statesmen and financiers of the latter entertained grave fears, that, if the United States should declare for free coinage of silver, it would unite the

Western Hemisphere and the silver using countries of Asia into a great commercial union, a result that would end in making the United States the greatest commercial and manufacturing nation on earth.

These fears were well expressed in a very significant editorial in the London Standard, which said:—

"What if the United States should now join Mexico in declaring for the free coinage of silver, and throwing over gold as too dear. What if the two American continents held out the hand to Asia and said: 'Let us have the white metal for our standard.' Chile, now hard-hit, would eagerly respond and all the states of South America and Mexico, with Japan and China and Java—in fact the whole mighty East (which cares little for Simla). It is a great danger to which the present outburst of alarm and fear must not render England oblivious."

The great cotton manufactures of the latter nation were steadily losing ground in China, Japan, and other Oriental countries, and as those valuable markets were lost to England, they were gained by colonial India.

Moreover, the cheap wheat of India was invading the markets of England, to the immense loss of the wealthy landed nobility of the mother country.

These two powerful interests combined in a memorial to the British Parliament, and on April 22, 1892, a commission was appointed by the Secretary of State for India, with instructions to take evidence upon the advisability of closing the Indian mints to the free coinage of silver.

As a striking coincidence, which undoubtedly proves that there was an understanding between the money power of England and that of the United States, having for its object the annihilation of silver as money, we point to the fact, that in a few days after the appointment of the commission to investigate free coinage of silver in India, Senator Sherman introduced a bill in the United States Senate to repeal the silver purchasing clause of the so-called Sherman law, at that time the only law recognizing silver in this country. As further proof that the national banking power of America had united with the capitalists of England against the use of silver as money, we refer to the following circumstance: During the sitting of the Herschell Commission, an international monetary conference was in session at Brussels. The United States was represented at this gathering of the nations. Ex-Governor McCreary, one of the American representatives, in a speech upon silver, said:—

"Speaking for myself only, I express the opinion that the silver law known as the act of 1890, now in force in my country, will be repealed. It is possible this will be done at the present session of Congress. If not this session, I believe it will certainly be repealed at the next session of Congress."

The foreign nations gathered at Brussels, therefore, were semi-officially notified that the sole law providing for the coinage of silver in the United States would be repealed in the near future.

Henry W. Cannon, a colleague of Mr. McCreary, and the president of the Chase National Bank in New York City, said:—

"The United States has seriously taken into consideration the idea of repealing the Silver Purchase Act of 1890; the two political parties as well as the great bankers of New York have advised this repeal, and if during this conference some arrangement is not attained, it is more than probable that America will not continue disposed to buy annually 54,000,000 ounces of silver at the market price."

Thus the people of the United States were again betrayed by their delegates to this conference, and the Herschell Commission received notice that the United States was opposed to silver.

At the time this commission was appointed to investigate the effects of free coinage of silver in India upon the British cotton export trade, England occupied a commanding position as the great creditor nation of the world, her aggregate holdings of stocks, bonds, securities, and other forms of public and private indebtedness run into the billions.

In a speech in the British Parliament, Mr. Gladstone eulogized his country as the greatest creditor nation on the face of the globe. Amid the boisterous cheers of the House of Commons, he declared that Great Britain was the creditor of other nations in a sum not less than $10,000,000,000!

Her colonies of Australia, South Africa, and Vancouver had risen to be the greatest gold producing regions of modern times. Australia alone had long surpassed California, we might say the United States, in the extent and richness of her gold resources. Hence, it was the policy of England to enhance the exchange power of gold, as she was the great creditor and the great gold producing nation of the present day.

Moreover, her imports greatly exceeded the value of her exports. Her imports of raw materials and bread stuffs far exceeded that of any other nation, and by limiting the world's volume of money, and increasing the purchasing power thereof, she would be enabled to obtain her supplies much cheaper on a single standard of gold, than under an universal bi-metallic system.

It is almost impossible to grasp the immense extent of her commercial power.

England owns more than three fourths—nearly four fifths—of the steamships afloat on the ocean, and nearly one half of the sailing fleet of the world, providing employment for 350,000 seamen. Her income from her merchant marine aggregates $400,000,000 per annum.

She aspires to monopolize the trade of Asia, Africa, and South America, and by supplying these people with the products of her manufactures, she strove to provide employment for her dense population.

The Asiatic and the South American nations were chiefly on a silver basis, and this formed a barrier to the extension of her trade and commerce.

Hence, the manufacturing, agricultural, and creditor classes of Great Britain demanded relief at the hands of the British Parliament, and they pointed to the fact that the cotton manufacturers of India were securing the control of those markets heretofore supplied by the mills and factories of Lancashire; and that the low price of English wheat resulted from Indian competition. Hence the appointment of this commission at the head of which was Lord Herschell.

Upon the organization of this commission it proceeded to take evidence relating to the cause of the decline of the British cotton trade in the Asiatic countries.

Many of the leading cotton manufacturers appeared before this body, and gave valuable testimony with reference to the causes of the depression existing in the cotton manufactures of England.

Upon the conclusion of its investigations, it made a report to Parliament, in which it was pointed out that the rise in the price of gold, beginning in 1873, the year that silver was demonetized by the United States, and the resulting depreciation of silver, had built up a large cotton-spinning trade in India. The report says:—

"Soon after the rise of gold began in 1873, a large cotton-spinning trade, begun previously in India, with English machinery, to supply India itself, felt at once the stimulus supplied by the difference in exchange. It prospered rapidly, grew, and continues growing fast and steadily, and exports to China and other silver countries. Here are comparisons of the English and Indian exports of cotton yarn, in pounds, to China, Hongkong, and Japan, which have for some time been supplied annually to the Economist by Mr. Abraham Haworth, of Manchester. They show how the product of silver wages beats the product of gold wages, and beats them more as the divergence between the metals widens.

"The quantities are given in pounds weight. The contrast between the stationary quantities from England and the rapid expansion of the Indian export indicates plainly a sad future for Lancashire trade if gold wages there must continue competing with silver wages in foreign markets. India will on the present footing beat Lancashire everywhere, meanwhile in the large class of goods made of Indian cottons, but ultimately in any material."

It then proceeds to give statistics showing that from 1876 to 1881, England annually exported to China a and Japan, cotton goods valued at $38,560,000. India exported only $19,641,000. From 1882 to 1887, the an-

nual exportations of England had fallen off to $33,682,-
000, while India had increased from $19,641,000 to
$71,319,000. In 1888, England sent to China and
Japan $44,642,600 worth of cotton goods, while the
exportations of India to these two countries increased
from $71,319,000 in 1887, to $114,707,300 in 1888. In
1889, England sent to China and Japan $35,720,200 of
these cotton goods, and India sold $126,766,800 against
$114,707,300 the preceding year.

In 1890, England exported to China and Japan $38,-
057,400. In the meantime, in the same year, the
Indian export increased from $126,766,800 to $145,-
112,800 worth of cotton manufactures, and it was time
for the English merchants to stop this rivalry. The
child had outgrown the parent. The colonial manufacturers had taken away the market in Japan and
China, and it was necessary to do away with silver in
order that the monopoly of this Eastern trade might
go back where it had originally been, to the English
manufacturer and the English merchant.

The conclusions of this commission, based on an
exhaustive investigation into the causes of the decline
of the British cotton trade, demonstrated that the
continued depreciation of the gold price of silver acted
as a rigid protective tariff against the manufactures of
gold standard England; and, that owing to the loss of
exchange which would accrue to silver standard countries trading with those on a gold basis, the former
would naturally trade with each other to the exclusion
of the latter. The only loss that would accrue to India
was in those cases in which she owed debts to England; for, by conversion of her silver coin into British
sterling exchange drawn to discharge these obligations,

she would lose the difference between the bullion value of silver and that of gold.

But for this loss, she was amply compensated by the immense growth of her trade and manufactures, through which her means of payment were proportionately increased.

During the sittings of this commission, the United States was in the midst of the presidential campaign of 1892.

For the third time Grover Cleveland obtained the Democratic nomination for President, although there was considerable opposition to his candidacy.

As he had thrown down the gauntlet to the highly protected manufacturing interests in his message of 1887, he was regarded as the leader of his party.

In the election of 1888, he had received a large plurality of the popular vote, and it seemed poetic justice that he should measure strength with his opponent of 1888.

The Democratic platform denounced the Sherman Silver Purchasing law as "A cowardly makeshift," and demanded its repeal.

The term "makeshift" in the sense in which it was used, meant that it was an obstacle to the free coinage of silver, and that this was the reason why a law of that character was adopted by the Fifty-first Congress—which became odious as the "billion-dollar Congress." In 1893, during the debate upon the repeal of the purchasing clause of the Sherman law, Senator Sherman admitted that this law was designed solely for the purpose of defeating the free coinage of silver.

The Democratic platform severely denounced the McKinley tariff law of 1890, "As the culminating atrocity" of tariff legislation.

One of the most iniquitous features of this measure was the sugar bounty clause, by which the sugar growers of Louisiana and Vermont received large sums of money from the general Government for their sugar product. This inured to the benefit of a few millionaire sugar planters, one of whom in a single year received the great sum of $464,000 as his share of the sugar bounty.

The Republican convention re-nominated President Harrison and endorsed the McKinley tariff law.

Mr. Cleveland was elected by an immense majority of the electoral vote, and his plurality of the popular vote over President Harrison was more than three hundred thousand.

Immediately after the election of Mr. Cleveland, the national banking money power began to lay plans to force the country upon a single standard of gold, and to increase the volume of their circulating notes.

On December 6, 1892, Congressman Harter, a national banker, introduced a bill in the House providing for the unconditional repeal of the Silver Purchase law, and to replenish the gold reserve of the United States Treasury.

To add to the clamor against the silver dollar, Mr. Harter, a member of Congress from Ohio, successfully endeavored to array the Grand Army of the Republic against the continued purchase and coinage of silver. He secured lists of the members of the various posts throughout the country, but more particularly addressed himself to those that were situated in Democratic Congressional districts. Circular letters, printed by the Government, were mailed by him to many thousands of pensioners, informing these veterans that their pensions would be paid in "seventy-cent dollars," and requesting them to join in memorials to their Representatives in Congress to vote for the repeal of the purchasing clause of the Sherman law.

Democratic Senators and members of Congress received thousands of these letters from their constituents, thus inspired, requesting them to vote for a single standard of gold.

This outrageous interference of Mr. Harter with the constituents of other members of Congress received scathing rebukes on the floors of Congress.

This was a part of the program of the money power, and it practically served notice on the Herschell Commission that the United States would cease the further coinage of silver, and that this country was apparently in sympathy with the financial policy of England.

The money power of England and America struck hands, and formed a compact to utterly annihilate silver as a money metal everywhere.

Upon the appearance of the Harter bill in the House of Representatives, the bankers of London cabled to the New York Evening Post, December 8, 1892, the news that "The belief is slightly growing that India will assume a gold standard sooner or later."

On December 9th, the same journal published a cablegram from London, in which it was stated, "That the silver question is still paramount. There is a belief that the India Council will refrain from making sales below some minimum. The Indian Government is alleged to be contemplating an immediate change of the silver standard to gold."

On the same day, Mr. Williams, of Massachusetts, brought forward a bill for the unconditional repeal of the purchase clause.

In the meantime, the great journals in the financial centers of the country began a crusade for the gold standard.

On December 9th, the Chicago Tribune, editorially said:—

"Let the Sherman act of July 14, 1890, be repealed at once without waiting for an extra session."

During this time that these various repeal measures were introduced into the House of Representatives, and while the American press was clamoring for the passage of those bills which would entirely cut off the further coinage of silver, the Herschell Commission was in session.

In England, this commission pointed to the efforts made in Congress to cut off the further coinage of silver as an indication of hostility toward that metal, and asserted that the passage of any such bill would result in a great depreciation of that metal.

The introduction of these various bills, seeking to repeal the sole law that in anywise recognized silver as a money metal, and which consequently steadied its bullion value, speedily became known to the Herschell Commission.

In its report the commission referred to these bills, and based its conclusions largely upon the effect of a repeal of the purchasing clause by the United States.

The report stated:—

"Moreover, a strong agitation exists in the United States with respect to the law now in force providing for the purchase of silver. Fears have been and are entertained that there may come to be a premium on gold, and strong pressure has been brought to bear upon the Government of that country with a view to bring about an alteration of that law."

Is it not self-evident, that these various bills to repeal the purchasing clause were brought forward in Congress at this time, with a view to influence the Herschell Commission against the continued coinage of silver in India?

The proposed action of the United States was strongly urged as a reason why the mints of India should be closed to free coinage.

Every movement, or proposed movement, made by the advocates of a single standard of gold in the United States, looking to the complete downfall of silver, was speedily transmitted to England.

In its report the Herschell Commission says:—

"In December last a bill was introduced in the Senate to repeal the Sherman Act, and that any such measures will pass into law it is impossible to foretell, but it must be regarded as possible; and although in the light of past experience, predictions on such a subject must be made with caution, it is certainly probable that the repeal of the Sherman Act would be followed by a heavy fall in silver."

While the people of England were being frightened by the bogy of depreciated silver, which was asserted would result from the probable repeal of the Sherman Law by the United States, the gold standard advocates of America were pointing to the probable closing down of the mints of India to the free coinage of silver as a reason for repealing the Silver Purchasing law of July 14, 1890.

In this way the money power of England and the United States played into the hands of each other.

At this time, the House of Representatives was strongly Democratic, and it was in favor of the use of silver as money, and, consequently, the repeal of the

Sherman Law was impossible as long as no better silver measure was proposed as a substitute for this "cowardly makeshift."

In the meantime President-elect Cleveland attempted to influence Congress to repeal the Sherman law.

He delegated Josiah Quincy as his envoy to visit Washington, ascertain the sentiments of Democratic members of Congress upon the silver question, and to make known to these Senators and Representatives that he desired the speedy repeal of the Sherman law.

On December 21, 1892, Senator McPherson introduced a joint resolution in the Senate, authorizing and directing the Secretary of the Treasury to suspend all purchases of silver bullions as provided for in the first section of the act of July 14, 1890.

Upon Mr. McPherson's request the bill was printed and laid upon the table, to be called up by him at some future time after the holiday recess.

With reference to the action of this Senator, the Chicago Tribune said:—

"His remarks will be listened to with great interest, being regarded as the unofficial expression of the views of the President-elect."

After the holiday recess, the House reassembled January 4, 1893, and Congressman Harter introduced a joint resolution similar to that of Mr. McPherson in the Senate.

On February 9th, House Resolution 10143, permitting national banks to issue bank notes up to the par value of bonds deposited by them was to be made the special order of the House, after the bill providing for the repeal of the purchasing clause of the Sherman Law was passed.

In every instance, each attempt to suspend the coinage of silver, and to retire the greenbacks, was followed by an effort to confer greater powers and privileges upon national banks.

These two Tory-Republican schemes of finance always went hand in hand.

It was evident that none of these measures could be forced through Congress at this time.

On February 12th, Henry Villard, a leading stock speculator of New York City, who was charged with wrecking the Northern Pacific Railway Company, made his appearance in Washington, and publicly announced that he was the envoy of President-elect Cleveland, and that it was Mr. Cleveland's wish that the Sherman law be repealed.

The efforts of Mr. Villard to influence Congress were fruitless.

Shortly after the appearance of Mr. Villard at the Capitol, Don M. Dickinson put in an appearance at Washington as the representative of President-elect Cleveland. He likewise informed Congress that the incoming President desired the repeal of the Sherman law.

The next morning after Dickinson left for Washington, the following interview with Mr. Cleveland was published in the New York Herald. He said:—

"The repeal of the Sherman act (unconditionally) is the great necessity of the hour. Continuance of the silver purchasing operation, made mandatory by the Sherman law, is a menace to the business and financial interests of the country. I am not yet without hope that this law will be repealed by the present Congress. Whatever influence I have is being exerted to that end. The date at which the repeal should become operative is immaterial, save that the sooner the better."

In its editorial comments upon this interview with Mr. Cleveland, the Herald said:—

"As a party man, as an upholder of the regular organization, as a vindicator of the machine, Mr. Cleveland will stand on firm ground when he declares that every aspirant for office patronage, favor, or any consideration, will be expected to line up for the repeal of the silver law."

A Washington special to the Chicago Tribune, February 1st, said:—

"President Cleveland is threatening an extra session if the silver purchase law is not repealed. Don Dickinson is the bearer of the news. Don has been at it all day interviewing Democratic Senators and the leaders in the House, including Speaker Crisp. He holds a big ugly club in the shape of patronage, which is expected to bring Democratic members to time."

Notwithstanding the appearance of Don Dickinson at Washington, and the implied threats of President-elect Cleveland, the Senate defeated a motion to take up the bill to repeal the silver law by a decisive vote.

In the House, the bill which had been introduced there was also defeated.

The actions of President-elect Cleveland, in his attempt to force the Legislative Department of the Government to submit to his will, met with an inglorious defeat at the hands of this Congress.

After the defeat of these various measures the Banker's Magazine, of New York City, said:—

"The tumble in the stock market during February had for one of its causes, unloading of stocks as fast as any one would buy them in anticipation that the gold reserve would not be replenished, and that an extra session would be called early, and an attempt be made to coerce its members into repealing the Silver Purchasing Act unconditionally."

The Commercial Bulletin said:—

"The quickest, if not the only way to repeal the Silver Purchase law is to precipitate a panic upon the country, as nothing short of this will convince the silver men of their error, and arouse public sentiment to a point which will compel the next Congress to repeal the Sherman law whether it wants to or not."

While the money power of the United States, aided by the press and the unprecedented conduct of President-elect Cleveland, was engaged in the scheme to totally cut off the further coinage of silver, the New York banks were withdrawing tens of millions of gold from the Treasury and shipping it abroad. At the time these banks were engaged in this transaction, they raised the rate of interest on call loans to twenty-five per cent. While plundering the Government of its gold as a part of the scheme to force an issue of bonds, they robbed the people by extorting illegal rates of interest.

Every step taken by the money power to force a repeal of the Sherman law was cabled to London with the avowed purpose of influencing England to close the Indian mints to the free coinage of silver. Every step thus far taken by the money power of the United States and of England to strike down silver was in pursuance of a well-defined plan to shackle the people to an appreciating gold standard.

CHAPTER X.

NATIONAL BANKING MONEY POWER BRINGS ON THE PANIC OF 1893.

"The greatest financial mistake of my life was in what I had to do with the passage of the present National Bank Act. It ought to be repealed; but before it can be done there will be such a contest between the banks on the one side, and the people on the other as has never been witnessed in this country."—Salmon P. Chase.

"Fifty men in these United States have it within their power, by reason of the wealth which they control, to come together within twenty-four hours and arrive at an understanding by which every wheel of trade and commerce may be stopped from revolving, every avenue of trade blocked, and every electric key struck dumb. Those fifty men can paralyze the whole country, for they control the circulation of currency and can create a panic whenever they will."—Chauncey M. Depew.

After the events narrated in the preceding chapter, Mr. Cleveland once more assumed the duties of the high office to which he was elected.

His conduct previous to his inauguration, in attempting to influence Congress before he was invested with the constitutional power to address that body, in the official capacity of President, aroused the gravest fears of the rank and file of the Democracy.

With much sorrow, the people saw their chosen idol ally himself with the national banking money power, and they perceived that he intended to use the immense patronage of his office to coerce Congress into submission to his will.

To add further to their misgivings, President Cleveland, in the appointment of editors of influential newspapers to highly-salaried offices, evidenced his plain purpose to subordinate the press to his views.

The number of leading journalists appointed by him to the most lucrative and honorable posts, far exceeded similar appointments made by any of his predecessors.

To the intense disgust of that great party which had so frequently honored him, he relegated tariff reform to the background.

He aggravated this distrust, which was now manifested against him, by appointing one of the ablest corporation lawyers of the country to the office of Attorney-General; viz., Hon. Richard Olney.

The only leading appointment made by him, which in anywise allayed this feeling of distrust, was that of John G. Carlisle for Secretary of the Treasury.

During his career in Congress, Mr. Carlisle was the ablest opponent of the national banking system and a single standard of gold that the country ever knew.

For logic, argument, and eloquence, his arraignment of the money power, in 1878, and 1882, was the most notable ever heard in Congress.

Subsequent events will show that he became the greatest apostate to a noble cause that ever appeared in American history.

President Cleveland had long recognized the splendid ability of Mr. Carlisle as an opponent to the national banking money power, and he resolved to convert him into an advocate of that merciless greed which had hitherto absorbed the wealth of the people.

Hence his appointment.

That the time had come in which to make a bold

stroke for the perpetuation of its system, this money power immediately perceived upon the accession of Mr. Cleveland to the Presidency.

This power knew that President Cleveland was a man whose firmness, energy, and ability, had been seldom equaled by any of his predecessors in office, that he was a staunch friend of the gold standard and of the national banking system, and, therefore, it determined to wreck the country, if necessary, to teach the people an "object lesson."

It resolved to bring on a panic, the like of which had never been visited upon any people.

Every monetary panic from which the American people had suffered, was the deliberate work of that class of men who pompously ascribed to themselves the sum and substance of all the financial wisdom of the nation.

The national banking money power, in planning and consummating the panic of 1893, had several objects in view.

First, The permanent withdrawal and destruction of the greenbacks and the treasury notes of 1890, amounting to $500,000,000, and the issue of an equal amount of bonds, running from fifty to one hundred years. These bonds were to serve as a basis for national bank notes, the issue and control of which would net the banks at least $40,000,000 in interest per annum.

Second, The withdrawal from circulation of more than 500,000,000 silver dollars, and the substitution therefor of an equal amount of bank notes, the loaning of which would annually bring the banks an additional profit of $40,000,000.

Bonds were to be issued to take up these dollars,

the bullion composing them to be thrown upon the market and sold as "old junk," to use the phrase of National Banker Lyman J. Gage.

Third, The wrecking of those great railway properties of the country which it did not control, by depreciating their stocks and bonds during the panic, buying such stocks and bonds at the lowest possible figure, thus securing ownership of all the means of transportation.

Fourth, An opportunity to exhibit its power over Congress and the people.

The immensity of this money power is almost beyond comprehension. The head and front of this great power is the Clearing House Association of New York City, composed of the membership of sixty-six national banks, whose deposits aggregated nearly a billion of dollars in 1893.

A large part of this vast accumulation of money, held by these associated banks, was not loaned to be invested in legitimate business enterprises. It was utilized to manipulate the price of stocks.

That accurate financial writer of the New York Sun, Matthew Marshall, in the early part of 1893, stated that one half of all the loans of these associated banks were made to the stock speculators of Wall street, those men who organized cliques and rings to wreck railroad properties.

With few exceptions, the thirteen thousand banks scattered over the land obey the dictates of the Clearing House to the minutest letter.

New York City is the seat of the most gigantic concentration and combination of capital in the Western Hemisphere. It is the home of those great banks, of the loan and trust companies, and of the majority of the enormously wealthy life, fire, and marine insurance companies of the United States. Wall street is the arena of the railway, gas, street railway, sugar, coffee, and oil magnates. It is a city where a fortune of less than ten millions is not considered worthy of public notice. The great banking house of Rothchild is ably represented by the Belmonts; Lombard street, London, has its agent there in the person of J. Pierpont Morgan.

New York City is the center of exchange of America. Thirteen thousand banks of the United States, private, state and national, continually maintain large deposits of money in her national banks for the payment of drafts.

These deposits of money from all parts of the nation amount to many millions, and tend to make money scarce in the South and West, and concentrate it in a few banks in the metropolis.

According to the provisions of the national banking law, the national banks of the great cities of the country were selected as the reserve agents of the 3,700 national banks throughout the country. By that law, these banks were required to keep in reserve from fifteen to twenty-five per cent. of the total amount of deposits in their custody; and they were authorized to deposit this great Reserve Fund in the national banks of New York City, a system which further added many millions of dollars to the holdings of those banks, with a consequent drain of money upon all other districts of the nation. The banks of New York City were thus enabled, from these immense accumulations of money, to make loans at the low rate of one per cent., upon call, to the stock gamblers of Wall street, while the rest of the country was suffering from a monetary famine.

While the legitimate interests of the nation were in great need of currency to keep the wheels of industry turning, the great banks of New York City, through their press, pointed to the great accumulations of money there, and the low rate of interest as evidence of a superabundance of currency.

These facts served to quiet the demands of those who were pointing to the scarcity of money prevailing throughout the West and South. The reserve funds, piled up in the banks of New York City, were loaned to the banks of the West and South at good rates of interest, which, in turn, were loaned by them to their customers at rates of usury ranging from eight to twelve per cent., during the season that money was needed to move the crops to the seaboard.

During the month of December, 1894, Mr. Dodsworth, editor of the New York Journal of Commerce, and George C. Williams, President of the Chemical National Bank of New York City, testified before the Committee on Currency, that the reserve banks of that city loaned this money to the depositing banks at rates of interest as high as six per cent.

Such was the legerdemain, by which the banks of that city obtained control of the money of the West and South, and exacted usury from the identical banks who were the actual owners of this money.

Closely related to this branch of the subject is the enormous amount of profits garnered by the national banks.

Up to 1894, the amount of interest paid on the bonds

deposited by these banks to secure their circulating notes, reached the magnificent sum of $419,887,111.

We do not include in this calculation the usury gathered from their currency or bank notes.

In its yearly almanac for 1892, the New York World, a journal friendly to national banks, shows that the profits of those banks, from 1872 to 1891, were the vast aggregate of $1,081,998,586.

Their average capital during that period was $500,000,000.

There are scores of these banks, which, after distributing great dividends to their stockholders, have a surplus and undivided profits exceeding their entire capital stock.

These facts are taken from the sworn reports of the officials of these banks.

At the hearing before the Committee on Currency in December, 1894, George C. Williams, President of the Chemical National Bank of New York City, gave the following sworn statement as to the profits of his bank. We here quote the evidence of Mr. Williams in reply to the questions of Mr. Warner, a member of the committee:—

MR. WARNER: So that the capital of your bank now represents how many millions of dollars?

MR. WILLIAMS: Our capital is $300,000 and our surplus is about $7,000,000.

MR. WARNER: Your stock is worth about $4,300 a share?

MR. WILLIAMS: Yes, sir; it sells for that. It sells for more than it is worth.

MR. WARNER: Forty-three times as much as its par. What is the amount of your bond deposit?

MR. WILLIAMS: The Chemical Bank has never taken out any circulation whatever. Our bond deposit is $50,000; but we have never circulated any notes.

The Chairman pursued this line of questioning, and elicited the following admissions:—

THE CHAIRMAN: Mr. Williams, some members of the committee desire to understand exactly the condition of your bank. What did you state the capital was?

MR. WILLIAMS: Three hundred thousand dollars.

THE CHAIRMAN: And the surplus?

MR. WILLIAMS: The surplus and undivided profits are about $7,000,000. The surplus is $6,000,000 and the undivided profits a little over a million dollars, making a little over $7,000,000 of surplus and undivided profits.

THE CHAIRMAN: And how much deposits?

MR. WILLIAMS: Thirty million dollars.

THE CHAIRMAN: What dividend do you pay per annum on your stock?

MR. WILLIAMS: We pay now 150 per cent. per annum.

The astonishing annual profits of that bank is shown by the following:—

THE CHAIRMAN: You stated the dividend last year was 150 per cent.

MR. WILLIAMS: Yes, sir.

THE CHAIRMAN: What were the undivided profits of that year?

MR. WILLIAMS: Well, I have not it in mind; but owing to the panic our profits last year were not as large as usual. Usually we expect to add to our surplus 100 per cent. besides the dividend we pay of 150 per cent.

THE CHAIRMAN: That is $300,000 a year?

MR. WILLIAMS: Yes, sir.

THE CHAIRMAN: And a dividend of 150 per cent besides?

MR. WILLIAMS: Yes, sir.

In the year of the panic of 1893, this institution gathered in a profit of 250 per cent.

A partial list of other banks of New York City is appended, to illustrate their unheard-of profits:—

The par value of the stock of the Mechanics' National Bank is $25 per share; it is now worth $195 per share.

The par value of the stock of the Importers' and Traders' National Bank is now worth $500 per share.

The par value of the stock of the Hanover National Bank is $100 per share; it is now worth $340 per share.

The par value of the stock of the Gallatin National Bank is $50 per share; it is now worth $300 per share.

The par value of the stock of the Broadway National Bank is $25 per share; it is now worth $250 per share.

The par value of the stock of the Chatham National Bank is $25 per share; it is now worth $300 per share.

The par value of the stock of the City National Bank is $100 per share; it is now worth $600 per share.

The par value of the stock of the Corn Exchange National Bank is $100 per share; it is now worth $300 per share.

The par value of the stock of the Fifth Avenue National Bank is $100 per share; it is now worth $3,000 per share.

The par value of the stock of the Chase National Bank is $100 per share; it is now worth $500 per share.

The par value of the stock of the Fourth National Bank is $100 per share; it is now worth $185 per share.

The difference between the face, or par value, of the stocks of these banks, and the market value thereof, results from the surplus and undivided profits, which are accumulated after the payment of large periodical dividends to the stockholders.

Not satisfied with these unparalleled incomes, these national banks, in connection with others of New York City, constitute that Clearing House, which persistently claimed the special bounties of the Government in the way of tens of millions of prepaid interest, premiums on bonds, and gratuitous loans of public money, aggregating hundreds of millions of dollars.

The money kings at the head of these banks are the most persistent and greatest beggars on earth.

They are the financiers who have brought on every panic since 1865, and, from the tumbling of stocks and wreckage of fortunes, gather in the wealth of the country.

In 1896, the great trust companies of that city held deposits of money aggregating $242,000,000; and paid dividends of 25 to 40 per cent. to their stockholders.

They were as strong in 1893.

These trust companies are the holders of hundreds of millions of dollars in bonds of railway, street railway, gas, and electrical companies, located chiefly in the West and South. The income from these stocks and bonds accelerates the flow of money to the East.

Many of these corporations, whose stocks are so held by the capitalists of New York City, are bonded from two to five times their actual value, thus operating as a heavy burden upon those communities who have granted these corporations valuable franchises. A single street railway corporation in one of the Western States was purchased by two Eastern speculators for $2,000,000; they at once proceeded to issue bonds upon this property to the amount of $4,000,000, which they sold to a trust company in New York City. They also issued stock to the amount of $4,500,000, which was disposed of by these scoundrels, making a total debt of $8,500,000 upon a property costing but $2,000,000. The people of that city pay the interest upon these bonds, and the dividends upon this stock, by submitting to exorbitant charges.

This money power, with the eyes of Argus and the

hands of Briareus, has likewise seized upon the natural gas resources of the West.

A syndicate of Eastern capitalists purchased the natural gas properties in the State of Indiana, the total outlay in cash being $3,500,000. It immediately proceeded to issue bonds thereon to the amount of $8,250,000, which were sold to a trust company in New York City. The proceeds of these bonds paid for the entire investment besides yielding a surplus or bonus of $2,600,000. In addition, stocks were issued on this property to the amount of $8,900,000. The interest and dividends on these stocks and bonds are squeezed out of the people of that State, and the money goes to increase the hoards of the millionaires of the East.

The same is true of the stock-yards of the West. A single stock-yard company of Kansas City is enormously over-capitalized. In order to make the dividends to transmit to the Eastern stockholders, corn was bought at ten cents per bushel, and sold at one dollar per bushel to those who are compelled to feed their stock shipped through those yards. Such is the robbery practiced on the West by what is called the culture and sound finance of the East.

The more than one hundred thousand miles of railways traversing the West and South, cost, on an avertage, $20,000 per mile for their construction. The average bonded indebtedness is $63,000 per mile, and the interest on these bonds is met by extortionate rates of transportation acting as a means of levying heavy tribute upon the agricultural products of these sections. These bonds are chiefly held in New York City and England.

The iniquity of this system can be faintly understood,

when it is borne in mind, that many of these railways were originally built by immense contributions of money and land by cities, townships, counties, and States, through which they run, in addition to the enormous land grants bestowed upon these corporations by the general Government, the last of which aggregated more than two hundred million acres of valuable public lands.

The wealth of the insurance companies is almost incalculable. There are single life insurance companies in that city, whose resources equal that of sovereign States. Three of these corporations have assets exceeding $600,000,000. The agents of those companies are planted over all the entire West and South, and the periodical flow of money to the East rivals the revenue of nations. This volume of money takes its origin from nearly every farm house, hamlet, village, town, and city in the Union, converges at the general agencies, and thence pours a mighty flood of dollars into the treasuries of the home companies.

From 1869 to 1889, a period of twenty years, the State of Illinois contributed $138,425,433 to the various insurance companies of the East. It received back, in the way of losses paid, only $84,929,204, leaving a surplus or profit over expenditures of $53,496,229. This drain was from a single State.

The aggregate from the West and South in the last twenty years would reach billions.

These insurance companies, in turn, loaned this money to the South and West at exorbitant rates of interest, resulting in an additional drain on those sections.

Then there are the loan and mortgage companies of

New York City and the East who make a specialty of loaning money on the farm lands of the West and South.

The holdings of these companies aggregate more than one billion dollars; and the annual flow of money to the East for interest charges is at least $150,000,000.

In speaking of the astonishing increase of the mortgage debt of the West, Frederic C. Waite said:—

"The most astonishing increase of all, however, is in the real estate mortgage indebtedness, as disclosed by the investigations of the eleventh census. Let us remember that this is largely the debt of the hardest working and the poorest paid of all our American citizens, namely, the farmers and the laborers who are trying to obtain a home of their own by honest toil. In the twenty-one States for which the mortgage indebtedness has been tabulated, the aggregate amount in force, at the close of 1889, was four thousand five hundred and forty-seven millions with the great States of Ohio, Texas, and California, and whole groups of lesser States yet to be heard from. The grand aggregate will be no less than six thousand three hundred millions. The aggregate in 1880 was only about two thousand five hundred millions."

The number of these loan and mortgage companies is very great, not only in New York City, but in other Eastern cities.

In an article upon this subject, the Political Science Quarterly, for September, 1889, said:—

"Boston numbers more than fifty agencies of farm-mortgage companies. It is computed that Philadelphia alone negotiates yearly more than $15,000,000 on Western loans. Kansas and Nebraska have one hundred and thirty-four incorporated mortgage companies. The companies organized under the laws of other States but operating in these two States increase the number at least two hundred.

"In this reckoning, no account is taken of firms and individuals, although a large amount of money is directly invested by lenders of this class."

The financial resources of Boston are a mere bagatelle, when compared with those of New York City, yet the former has more than fifty of these loan and mortgage companies.

The Forum, for March, 1890, makes the following astonishing statement:—

"It is impossible to say how much has been invested in the West in real estate securities, but the amount is enormous. Five mortgage companies at Topeka, Kans., report that the loans made by them, and still outstanding, amount to $22,000,000. Of this sum 90 per cent. has been invested in Kansas. Five companies at Kansas City, report $68,000,000 outstanding. This amount has been placed in a dozen Western States."

This remarkable state of affairs in the West and South will be considered strange, in view of the facts that these sections are the food-producing regions of the country, and, that while they feed this whole nation, they furnish more than three fourths of the exports which maintain a balance of trade in favor of the United States.

The high-handed and oppressive manner, in which these loan agencies and companies have invoked the law to foreclose their mortgages on the farms of the West, is a scandalous abuse of power.

As the improved farms were only pledged for the payment of a sum of money never exceeding in any case more than fifty per centum of the value of the naked land, the security was good.

Nevertheless, many thousands of suits for foreclosure were instituted on the slightest failure to pay the interest coupons; decrees of sale were accordingly entered, and the land sold to pay the debt, whereupon these mortgagers would bid in the entire mortgaged premises for a fraction of the claim, obtain the property for a mere nominal sum, and yet hold a large residue of the judgment over the head of the unfortunate debtor to seize what other property the mortgagor would happen to possess, and thus sweep away all into the coffers of these voracious usurers.

This iniquitous use of the process of the law to rob the debtors of the West and South of their whole substance, is a dark and damnable blot on the jurisprudence of the United States, and it would shame the hardened nature of a Bashi Bazouk.

The future historian will marvel at the patience displayed by these people under the circumstances.

Closely allied to the moneyed corporations of New York City, and having an unity of interest with them, are the 3,700 other national banks scattered over the country.

An examination of the list of officers and directors of the national banks of New York City, Boston, Hartford, New Haven, Providence, Philadelphia, Brooklyn, Baltimore, Chicago, and other leading cities, reveals some marvelous facts.

It will demonstrate that the presidents and directors of the national banks of the first-named city, control the operations of the loan and trust companies, the gigantic life insurance corporations, the sugar trust, and the Stock Exchange.

These financial magnates are heavy stockholders in what are called natural monopolies, such as street railway companies, and corporations which furnish water and light for the cities of the nation.

H. O. Havemeyer, the sugar trust king, is the heaviest stockholder in the Western National Bank. Russell Sage, the great stock speculator of New York City, is the chief owner of the Importers' and Traders' National Bank. And so the list could be indefinitely extended, showing that the great stock gamblers of Wall street, the organizers and managers of oppressive trusts, the wreckers of railroads, the heads of great insurance companies, the merchant princes, the highly protected manufacturing lords, the owners of great newspapers, are the individuals at the head of the national banking money power.

In the city of Chicago, all the members of the great packing house and stock-yard trust are heavily interested as owners and directors of national banks. Its millionaire merchants, grain gamblers, owners of street railway stocks, and gas properties, dictate the election of officers of these banks.

As another means of securing control of the entire volume of money, the national bank managers, with wonderful prescience, organized trust companies in every great city of the country to act in the capacity of receivers, trustees, executors, administrators, and guardians, with the intention of monopolizing the probate business of the courts.

Proof of the strongest nature can be produced, to show that these national banks have loaned money to flourishing manufacturing enterprises, then, at an opportune moment, forced their debtors into bankruptcy, had their trust companies appointed receivers of the trust estate, charged enormous fees for settling up the affairs of the bankrupts, while the officers of these banks, as private individuals, bought in the assets of these unfortunates at a great sacrifice.

It is said of a national bank president, who is also at the head of one of these trust companies, that he keeps himself thoroughly versed in the financial condition of the debtors of his and other banks, that he carefully watches the growth of the business of these debtors until they become ripe for plucking, and that, as a bon-vivant examines a fowl to ascertain its condition, so this great financier waits for his victim until he reaches that stage that he can be thrown into bankruptcy, when he pounces on him as the vulture pounces on its helpless prey. The receivership of his trust company does the rest.

Up to the early part of 1893, this money power had built up a system of bank credit that was stupendous in its proportions.

Under its manipulations of the volume of money it had forced nearly all business on a bank-borrowing basis.

In a report of the Comptroller of the Currency for 1893, the loanable funds of all the banks of the United States, on the 30th day of June of that year, aggregated $6,412,939,954.

It may seem a mystery to many how it can be possible, that, with a volume of money of but $1,600,000,000 in the nation, these banks have a loanable fund of four times that amount.

The process, or legerdemain, by which these financial institutions expand $1,600,000,000 of actual money to $6,412,939,954 of loanable bank credits, and exact the highest rate of interest on the latter is a matter which has confounded many students of finance.

The process of the banks, in building up this colossal system of credit, and subordinating the immense interests of the country to their dictation, is very simple. The loanable funds of the banks consists of their paid-up cash capital, deposits, and their loans to customers.

This expansion of the loanable funds of a bank can be most clearly explained by the example of the First National Bank of Chicago, of which Lyman J. Gage was President, previous to his appointment to the Secretaryship of the Treasury.

This bank has a capital of $3,000,000, loans and discounts of $17,723,727, and total assets of $39,500,000. The query arises—how can a bank with but $3,000,000 capital loan nearly $18,000,000 and have assets of nearly $40,000,000?

It makes these loans out of the money daily deposited with it, or, more clearly speaking, on what it owes to others. It not only controls its own money, but the money of the business community in which it is situated.

To further illustrate the methods of banks in swelling the amount of loanable funds, and consequently their power to reap interest therefrom, take the following case: A merchant goes to one of these great banks, and his credit being first class, he borrows $300,000 on thirty, sixty, or ninety days' time. The interest is deducted out of the loan in advance, and the balance credited to the borrower, who does not take this money out of the bank to his place of business. This borrowed money remains with the bank for the payment of checks drawn against it by the merchant. Owing to this process, the bank, while making a profit out of the loan, still has the use of the money out of which to make additional loans, and so this process goes on indefinitely.

The supply of money in the bank for the payment of checks and drafts is maintained by the daily deposits of its hosts of customers.

This is the identical process by which the system of banks have expanded $1,600,000,000 to $6,400,000,000 of loanable interest-bearing bank credits.

This loanable bank credit means an annual income of at least $400,000,000 to these institutions.

This is a substantial reason why the system of banks, throughout the length and breadth of the land, eulogize credit, and why they are opposed to a sufficient volume of money, and why exalt credit above actual cash.

This vast income of the banks operates as a tax upon the people—a tax which ultimately falls with crushing weight upon the laboring man.

The wholesale merchant borrows a large sum of money from one of these great banks at the prevailing rate of interest which is deducted in advance. He adds this payment of interest to the cost of the goods, and charges a profit upon the whole amount thus invested. The retailer buys these goods with the interest charge and the profit mingled with the price. In many cases, he borrows the money under the same process as the wholesale merchant, and he adds the interest charge to the cost of the goods so purchased, and thus he extracts a profit upon his goods from the ultimate purchaser, who is the consumer of them.

Therefore, these enormous profits of the credit system of the banks levy tribute upon every article necessary for the sustenance and comfort of life.

In this connection, let it be borne in mind that the sole class upon whom rests the enormous burdens of government, and from whom has been extorted those almost incomprehensible sums of money that found their way into the coffers of the bankers and bondholders, is the producers of wealth.

The creation of wealth arises in three ways; viz., transmutation, transformation, and transportation.

The man who plows, sows, and reaps, is engaged in the first-named process; the mechanic, or laborer, who adds value to the raw material, is an example of the second; the distribution of the products of the agriculturist, and the skilled or unskilled workman, falls in the province of the last named.

These processes are the sole means of adding to the stock of material wealth.

Bankers, merchants, and those belonging to what are called the learned professions, do not add a single penny to a nation's stock of wealth.

The banker and the money lender merely gathers toll from those who borrow the medium of exchange to carry on business.

The merchant of every description who obtains a profit on the merchandise he buys and sells, merely takes the difference between the cost and selling price of goods from the customers, and adds it to his own possessions. This process does not add a farthing to the wealth of the nation as a whole.

Lawyers, physicians, and all other members of the professions, only absorb what is produced by others.

There is no way under heaven by which these classes of persons add anything to the wealth of a people.

All township, municipal, county, State, and Federal officers, are merely consumers of what is produced by those who are engaged in the processes of transmutation, transformation, and transportation.

Every tax levied and collected by the Government, and its various political and territorial subdivisions, is a transference of wealth from the people, to be in turn, given to those who are the official organs of lawful authority.

These definitions of the producing and non-producing classes are matters of every-day observation, and are susceptible of complete demonstration.

It is upon the shoulders of the producing class that rest the crushing weight of government, the enormous gains of national banks, and other wealth-consuming elements.

These burdens are surely bearing down the people into a bottomless abyss of bankruptcy.

One of the means that greatly increased the power of the national banks of New York City, was their selection as depositories of government funds during the last thirty years.

In a speech of Comptroller Eckles, at a banquet given in his honor by these banks, he thus extols these pets of the Government. He said:—

"As government depositories the national banks have received, stored in their vaults, and accounted for $5,356,625,891 without expense to the Government. Allowing the rate of three eighths of one per cent. as a reasonable compensation for such services, which is the same as that fixed by the act of March 3, 1875, as the compensation of disbursing officers for public buildings, it would amount to $20,087,347."

Think of it! These few banks had the use of more than five billions of government money, increasing their loanable funds to that extent, and from which they gathered scores of millions of profit.

Through the agency of the railway and the telegraph, the national banking money power of to-day can reach every part of the United States in twenty-four hours. The national banks know the value of organization, and they have brought it to a perfection that would excite the admiration of a Napoleon.

Shortly after the inauguration of President Cleveland, the national banks of New York City transmitted the following infamous circular to the thousands of banks scattered throughout the United States. The contents of the circular are as follows:—

"Dear Sir: The interests of national bankers require immediate financial legislation by Congress. Silver, silver certificates and treasury notes, must be retired and national bank notes upon a gold basis made the only money. This will require the authorization of from $500,000,000 to $1,000,000,000 of new bonds as a basis of circulation. You will at once retire one third of your circulation and call in one half of your loans. Be careful to make a money stringency felt among your patrons, especially among influential business men. Advocate an extra session of Congress for the repeal of the purchasing clause of the Sherman law and act with the other banks of your city in securing a large petition to Congress for its unconditional repeal, per accompanying form. Use personal influence with congressmen and practically let your wishes be known to your Senators. The future life of national banks as fixed and safe investments depends upon immediate action, as there is an increasing sentiment in favor of Government legal tender notes and silver coinage."

While the national banks of that city were engaged in this conspiracy to wreck the business interests of the country, they were raiding the gold reserve of the United States Treasury to force an issue of bonds.

Coincident with the appearance of this circular, which advised the bringing on of this panic, the following remarkable document was put forth by the national banking money power. It is as follows:—

"Dear Sir: The present financial situation requires the following action by Congress, which should be favored by all interests, to wit:—

"1. Pass a resolution repealing purchase clauses of Sherman silver bill.

"2. Pass a bill authorizing the issue of $300,000,000 of United States 3 per cent. bonds, payable in gold, directing United States Treasurer to sell $100,000,000 immediately in Europe, with stipulation that none of them should be resold within the United States; the Treasurer to take this $100,000,000 of gold and issue $100,000,000 of gold certificates against it, and deposit them in the different national banks of the United States pro rata to their capital and circulation, upon adequate security being given to the Government securing such deposits; such deposits to be preferred liens upon all assets of each bank, etc.

"It should also direct the Treasurer to sell $100,000,000 of such bonds immediately in Europe under similar conditions, the money to be placed in the United States Treasury or left on deposit in London, Paris, and Berlin, for use by the Government in paying deficiencies between the Government's receipts and expenditures, and drawn as needed.

"The remaining $100,000,000 should be held subject to sale whenever the necessities of the Government or the financial interests of the country demand it.

"Bringing $200,000,000 of gold to this country, in addition to the balances of trade in our favor, would immediately establish confidence in our financial strength.

"3. Pass a resolution calling an international conference to establish an international agreement as to the use of silver as currency, to be held within twenty days after the passage of such resolution. Twenty days' notice by cable is amply sufficient to allow time for every govenment to appoint men who understand the subject thoroughly, and have them meet at some convenient place.

"The delegates representing the United States should be selected by Congress and named in the resolution, two of them to be Senators from the silver States and two of them equally representative of the other side of the question.

"4. Pass the act increasing national bank circulation to par of deposited bonds.

"The above legislation would immediately inspire confidence here and abroad in American finances and start again the wheels of business, now helplessly clogged.

"For the future the following action should be taken:

"5. Pass a resolution appointing a committee, to consist of five New York bankers of the highest standing and one each from Boston, Philadelphia, Chicago, St. Louis, Cincinnati, Nashville, Atlanta, Savannah, New Orleans, Galveston, San Francisco, Denver, St. Paul, Detroit, Buffalo, and Pittsburg, this committee to immediately meet, consider, and report to an adjourned session of Congress a bill incorporating a United States national bank, founded on the same lines as the national bank of England and the national bank of France, to be entirely divorced and free from politics; and it being expressly stipulated that one half of the committee shall be selected from Republican bankers and one half from Democratic bankers.

"A national bank is absolutely necessary for the future financial safety of the country. Under present conditions there is no elasticity to our currency.

"Five per cent. of our financial business is done with cash, 95 per cent. with credit.

"To-day credit is largely destroyed, which leaves us trying to do more than one half of the business of the country on the insignificant 5 per cent. cash, and a considerable proportion of this cash hoarded and taken out of circulation.

"To meet emergencies like this, we should have a

national bank, having power to make almost an unlimited issue of currency, with the same power and self-interest, when confidence returns, to take and return all this specially-issued currency and retire it.

"The bank of England and the bank of France have power to issue millions upon millions of additional currency whenever necessary to protect and conduct the finances of the country, and they exercise this power, and therefore such extreme panics as ours are unknown in those countries. When the crisis is over, this extra currency is retired.

"There is no question as to the safety of this power; it has been exercised by these great banks in these two countries for generations, and has been their financial salvation, and we can have no permanent financial safety in the United States until we create a similar national bank or else make the United States Treasury a bank and authorize and direct that in times of panic and destruction of credit the Government shall issue currency to an extent necessary to meet the emergency, and deposit it in the national banks of the country. Of the two measures, it is certainly preferable to have a great national bank, founded on almost exactly the lines of the Bank of England, thus taking financial questions and management entirely out of the influence of politics, because the government of the great National Bank of England is entirely in the hands of the greatest business men of the country, who have no interest whatever in politics, except as citizens. Yours truly,

WM. R. CONWAY."

This document was placed in the hands of members of Congress with a view of influencing their action. The first demand, couched in this circular, requested Congress to repeal the purchase clause of the Sherman law. The second demanded the passage of a bill authorizing the issue of $300,000,000 of United States bonds, payable in gold, and $100,000,000 of gold thus received, and for which interest was to be paid by the nation, should be given to the different national banks as a loanable fund.

The third demands the repetition of that farce—the calling of an international monetary conference. The fourth—the passage of an act permitting national banks to increase their circulation up to the par value of the bonds deposited by them.

Fifth, The passage of a resolution authorizing a committee of bankers to frame a bill incorporating a national bank, operating on the same principles as the Bank of England. This proposed bank to be endowed with the power of making an unlimited issue of currency, the volume of which could be contracted whenever the self-interest of the banks saw fit to curtail this volume of money.

Thus the Tory-Eastern system of finance was outlined by the money power. The historical incident of Didius Julianus bidding-in the Roman Empire, that he might absorb its entire revenues for his personal benefit, was not a circumstance compared to the monumental greed of the national banking money power.

Subsequent history has fully demonstrated that several of the demands set forth in this circular have found their way upon the statute-books of this nation, and that the remaining are gradually taking the form of proposed legislation.

This great scheme of building up a mighty system of bank credit would place seventy millions of Americans at the mercy of the money mongers of London and New York City.

This bank credit system, embodied in the national bank plan, has its center in London, and this would be true of any system of bank currency, no matter how carefully framed.

This was the case with the United States bank, and it applies more emphatically to the present system.

In a great speech on the banking question, Thomas H. Benton, more than fifty years ago, so clearly, logically, and powerfully traced this bank credit currency system to its source that it merits careful reading. He said:—

"The banks at that center to which currency flows, hold the power of controlling those in regions whence it comes, while the latter possess no means of restraining them; so that the value of individual property, and the prosperity of trade, through the whole interior of country, are made to depend on the good or bad management of the banking institutions in the great seats of trade on the seaboard.

"But this chain of dependence does not stop here. It does not terminate at Philadelphia or New York. It reaches across the ocean, and ends in London, the center of the credit system. The same laws of trade, which give to the banks in our principal cities power over the whole banking system of the United States, subject to the former, in their turn, to the money power in Great Britain.

"It is not denied that the suspension of the New York banks in 1837, which was followed in quick succession throughout the Union, was partly produced by an application of that power; and it is now alleged, in extenuation of the present condition of so large a portion that their embarrassments have arisen from the same cause. From this influence they cannot now entirely escape, for it has its origin in the credit currencies of the two countries; it is strengthened by the current of trade and exchange, which centers in London, and is rendered almost irresistible by the large debts contracted there by our merchants, our banks, and our States.

"It is thus that the introduction of a new bank into the most distant of our villages, places the business of that village within the influence of the money power of England. It is thus that every new debt which we contract in that country seriously affects our own currency and extends over the pursuits of our citizens its powerful influence. We cannot escape from this by making new banks, great or small, state or national. The same chains which bind those now existing to the center of this system of paper credit, must equally fetter every similar institution we create. It is only by the extent to which this system has been pushed of late, that we have been made fully aware of its irresistible tendency to subject our own banks and currency to a vast controlling power in a foreign land; and it adds a new argument to those which illustrate their precarious situation. Endangered in the first place by their own mismanagement, and again by the conduct of every institution which connects them with the center of trade in our own country, they are yet subjected, beyond all this, to the effect of whatever measures, policy, necessity, or caprice, may induce those who control the credits of England to resort to."

This great statesman, who so ably exposed the dangers of a bank currency which would degrade the United States into a mere dependency of the "Little Isle beyond the seas," has long since passed away, but his solemn warning still beckons to the people, and points out the folly of trusting themselves to the embrace of that boa constrictor—the banking monopoly.

In the month of April, 1893, the New York bankers had a conference with Secretary Carlisle at Washington, in which they demanded that he issue bonds to the amount of $150,000,000. Secretary Carlisle would not accede to their demands at this time.

The refusal of Mr. Carlisle to grant the demands of these bankers angered them, and they returned to

New York City determined to force an issue of bonds at all hazards.

They continued to raid the gold reserve more fiercely than ever.

In the meanwhile, with a few honorable exceptions, the banks throughout the country executed the mandates couched in that circular issued from New York City.

Loans were refused, and outstanding obligations were remorselessly called in by these tools of the money kings. As an excuse for that conduct, it was asserted that "confidence" was lost.

The press of New York City, with few exceptions, owned body and soul by the national banking money power, aided in the work by its senseless clamor.

It called attention to every shipment of gold that went out of the country as a fearful calamity.

One of these newspapers daily printed in large figures on its front page the low state of the gold reserve. They denounced the silver dollar as a "50-cent dollar," a "dishonest dollar," a "fiat dollar."

In short, the vocabulary of abuse was exhausted by them when speaking of silver as money.

The Sherman silver law was pointed to as the whole cause of the panic now raging.

The mercenary character of the New York press, and its ownership by foreign capitalists and the national banking money power, is best illustrated by that veteran journalist, Colonel Cockerill. He says:—

"The fashion of editing the more influential or the more successful daily newspapers by cablegram has completely destroyed what little virility was left in their editorial pages.

"The non-resident ownership of newspapers leads to one serious result, which, I think, has not been generally considered.

"The owner receives from his newspaper property, at stated intervals, returns in money. He is beyond the reach of proofs.

"The address of his banker is always known. Thither, on the first of every month, large sums of money must be forwarded.

"The tendency of non-resident ownership must, therefore, necessarily be to measure everything by a pecuniary test. The morale of the paper, its course of public measures, and its treatment of the interests of the people, whose trustee it professes to be, with such protestations, are considered only from the point of view of the counting room.

"The worst phase of non-resident ownership is its absolute heartlessness."

Such is the stinging indictment brought against these great journals by this able writer.

In speaking of the tyranny of that press, W. P. St. John, President of the Mercantile National Bank, an advocate of free coinage of silver, said:—

"There is a very widespread unrest of opinion on this topic and the allied topic, called the 'silver question,' even in New York and New England. Public opinion is under a newspaper terrorism in New York. Men who agree with me fully, and I know many of them of considerable wealth, prefer to keep silent for the present. Any nobody who will write at length a lot of nothingness adverse to silver money will be accorded certain newspapers' space and be dignified into great authorities. Rejoinder, if complete, and the more complete the more certainly, is denied even a limited space. Again, other men believe that until a change of administration here approaches it will merely cost them influence to speak their conclusions favorable to silver money. Then, too, certain newspapers shield their readers against intelligence and cow them out of any timid convictions they might indulge."

He added:—

"But conditions current here and elsewhere are forcing the truth upon general attention, and a rebellion against this tyranny and concealment of facts will manifest itself ere long in New York as elsewhere. I have recently been urged by commercial bodies of two important Eastern cities to address them at length upon my convictions. I declined on the ground that I have talked so much that I deem it unwise to be heard again on the topic until invited to speak by my immediate associates in the city of New York.

"The paper that I now ask the privilege of reading, was prepared for a monthly magazine of importance. I asked the space at first, but afterward withdrew the request. The editor urged my carrying out my first intention. His private secretary heard the matter in the rough and urged me the more to complete it for his magazine. I learn this morning that more acceptable matter will crowd me out, which is only another evidence of what you gentlemen, aiming to serve your country, are entitled to complain of in the Eastern press."

Among all the bankers of that city, Mr. St. John was the sole financier who urged the adoption of free coinage, and a continuance of the greenbacks and treasury notes as a part of the volume of money.

His example was a green oasis amidst the barren desert of avarice of the national banking element.

The press still continued this warfare upon silver, greenbacks, and the treasury notes; and editorially endorsed the course of the bankers in creating a monetary stringency.

In urging a repeal of the Sherman law, the Commercial Bulletin said:—

"The quickest if not the only way to repeal the Silver Purchase law is to precipitate a panic upon the country as nothing short of this will convince the silver men of their error, and arouse public opinion to a point which will compel the next Congress to repeal the Sherman law whether it wants to or not."

The New York Sun April 29, 1893, exposed this scheme of the New York banks, and charged that they sent abroad $110,000,000 of gold to assist the Rothchilds to demonetize silver in Austria and elsewhere. It said:—

"Let us point to another fact, and we are done. Never before have the large banking institutions of Chicago and the West ordered their gold in such large quantities direct from Europe, and in this fact is found one reason why our bankers are puzzled over the anomaly that, although all these millions are coming to the country, they experience little or no relief therefrom. The other reason, gentlemen, is, in order to force the repeal of the Sherman Act and to quickly establish your power over the plain people of this land, you first sent out of the country one hundred and ten millions of the people's currency in order to assist the Rothchilds to demonetize silver in Austria and elsewhere, and then let it remain there, to teach the West and South an 'object-lesson,' as the President called it, until you found it was necessary to recall it in order to save your own house from destruction. Now, you have not only taught the West and South an object-lesson, but yourselves one as well, and you can be sure of it."

The Sun is an advocate of a single standard of gold, but the scoundrelism of the New York banks aroused its indignation.

Meanwhile, President Cleveland was hand in glove with the treasonable banks, as the following from the New York Sun fully proves.

It said April 28, 1893:—

"Secretary Carlisle decided yesterday morning to have a talk with the New York bankers. Late on Wednesday evening after his arrival from Washington, he conferred with Assistant Treasurer Jordan, and ex-Assistant Treasurer James J. Canda. As a result the Secretary yesterday morning suggested that he meet the bank presidents and private bankers at four o'clock in the afternoon. The postponement in the naval review because of the storm caused some delay, as Secretary Carlisle accompanied President Cleveland on the Dolphin.

"The Secretary landed with the Presidential party at the foot of Ninety-sixth street, and was there met by the Columbian reception committee, including President J. Edward Simmons, of the Fourth National Bank.

"The Secretary and Mr. Simmons were driven to the home of President George G. Williams, of the Chemical Bank, and chairman of the Clearing House Association, at 34 West Fifty-eighth street.

"The following gentlemen were there to greet the Secretary: Mr. Jordan, Mr. Canda, President Perkins, of the Importers' and Traders'; President Sherman, of the Bank of Commerce; President Cannon, of the Chase; President Ives, of the Western; President Gallatin; President Coe, of the American Exchange, and President Woodward, of the Hanover, all national banks. The conference between the Secretary and the bank presidents lasted somewhat over an hour. There was the utmost good feeling displayed, and the Secretary said that he was there to make a free, frank, and open statement of what he believed to be the financial policy of the Government.

"In the first place, the Secretary said that an issue of bonds just at this time might be an effective remedy, but it would only be temporary, and that it would be followed by disturbances in the money market, and would in the end retard the determination of the administration to repeal the Sherman silver law. The Secretary said positively that there would be no bond issue except as a last resort. As the Secretary outlined the policy of the Government, it was that nothing would be done that in any way would retard or check the determination of the Cleveland administration concerning the repeal of the Sherman law. The Secretary went over the currency laws of the country, and said they were in bad shape and needed revision. He said the revision should start with the Sherman law. There is a determination also to show to the miners of silver the evil effects of the Sherman law on their own fortunes.

"President Cleveland's advisers have told him that the only way to induce the Western and Southwestern Senators and Congressmen to consent to a repeal of the Sherman law is to demonstrate to their constituents that they are losing money every day that this law is in operation. The missionary work in that direction has been started by a number of the bankers in the solid communities of the East. They are daily refusing credits to the South, Southwest, and West, fearing the effects of the Sherman law.

"The Chicago bankers, it was said, are carrying out the same line of policy. Secretary Carlisle, in his talk with the bank presidents, made his stand very clear. It is to be heroic treatment all the way through on the Sherman law; and possibly by the next session of Congress, the silver mine owners and the adherents of silver in the Senate and the House will be ready to consent to a repeal of the law.

"The bank presidents, replying to Secretary Carlisle, cordially informed him that they would be ready at all times to co-operate with him in the successful administration of the financial policy of the administration. Everybody shook hands, and there was harmony all round.

"In the meantime the Secretary continues to receive offers of gold from unexpected sources."

In its editorial comments upon this historical meeting of Secretary Carlisle and these bankers, the Sun of April 29th, says:—

"The conference yesterday between Secretary Carlisle and a number of the bankers of this city was of great value in that it resulted in a definite understanding of the financial policy of the administration, as indicated in this column last Tuesday. That policy is to interpose no obstacle to the natural operations and logical results of the Sherman law. In a word, the administration proposes to allow the people to reap the rewards of their own folly.

"The statement of Mr. Carlisle to the New York bankers makes it clear that, while Mr. Cleveland works in Congress, the bankers will be expected to work, not in New York only, but throughout the country, doing their utmost to pinch business everywhere in the expectation of causing a money crisis that will affect Congress powerfully from every quarter. There is an explicitness in these declarations and a boldness in making them that would be astounding were not the country too familiar with Mr. Cleveland and his methods to be astonished by anything from him."

These utterances of the Sun became prophecy, in view of the means utilized by President Cleveland in forcing a repeal of the Sherman law. He "worked in Congress" with the immense patronage at his disposal, as subsequent events demonstrated to a certainty.

On May 1st, the Sun announced that President Cleveland would soon call an extra session of Congress, and urge upon that body an immediate repeal of the Sherman law. It said:—

"There is to be an extra session of Congress to afford the opportunity of repealing the Sherman law as soon as possible. War will be opened against silver, notably the Sherman law."

During the waging of this war against silver by the national banking money power, aided by President Cleveland, the Herschell Commission was in session in London, having under deliberation the question of closing the mints of India to free coinage.

The only obstacle in the way of England forcing India to a gold standard was the existence of the Sherman law.

This commission was informed of every step taken by the national banking money power and by President Cleveland to coerce Congress into repealing that law.

Sir Reginald Welby, who appeared before that commission as an expert financier, after the speech of Secretary Foster at the Delmonico banquet was quoted by the chairman, informed that body, that "Americans calmly told him (authorities with whom he discussed the silver matter) that, law or no law, the intention is to maintain the equality with gold and to suspend the purchase of silver if necessary, that this was the permanent policy of the Treasury, and account is taken of it, and banks act upon it."

The only authority, from whom this witness could have received such information, was Ambassador Bayard, who, during his service in the United States Senate was a rigid gold monometallist, and an ardent supporter of national banks.

The Herschell Commission was informed that President Cleveland would call an extra session of Congress and force a repeal of the Sherman law.

The commission at once closed its deliberations, made a report recommending that the mints of India be closed to the free coinage of silver, which was done on the 25th of June, 1893.

On June 27th, two days after the mints of India were closed to the free coinage of silver, Henry Clews, the official mouthpiece of Wall street, published the following comment on the situation. He said:—

"There is every reason why Congress should be brought together at the very earliest possible day. The houses that were engaged until lately in shipping gold became so zealous in that enterprise that they tried to outstrip each other. The result was that more gold was actually shipped than Europe required. The natural result must appear in the return of the surplus thus exported. Exchange has now fallen, indeed, to the specie-importing point. As soon as our crops ripen, there will be inevitably a return of a good deal of gold to the country. One of the arguments in favor of the repeal of the Sherman law has been that the baser metal has driven the finer metal out of the country. In a little while, with gold returning to us, the strength of that argument will be sapped. An early session of Congress will leave the argument still in full force."

In three days after the closing of the Indian mints, silver fell twenty cents an ounce.

On the 30th day of the same month, President Cleveland issued his proclamation requesting Congress to meet in special session August 7, 1893.

CHAPTER XI.

SPECIAL SESSION OF CONGRESS REPEALS THE SHERMAN LAW.

"I cannot suppose that everybody is wise. Just think of the folly of the United States when they were a debtor nation in adopting a gold coinage. They know nothing about currency matters; they did not know that it was going to increase their debt enormously."
—Daniel Watney.

Labor is prior to and independent of capital. Capital is only the fruit of labor, and could never have existed if labor had not first existed. Labor is the superior of capital and deserves much the higher consideration.

"No men living are more worthy to be trusted than those who toil up from poverty; none less inclined to take or touch aught which they have not honestly earned. Let them beware of surrendering a political power which they already possess and which, if surrendered, will surely be used to close the doors of advancement against such as they, and to fix new disabilities and burdens upon them till all of liberty shall be lost."—Abraham Lincoln.

The substance of the proclamation issued by President Cleveland, convening the special session of Congress, is as follows:—

"Whereas the distrust and apprehension concerning the financial situation, which pervade all business circles, have already caused great loss and damage to our people, and threaten to cripple our merchants, stop the wheels of manufacture, and bring distress and privation to our farmers, and withhold from our working men the wage of labor;

"And, whereas, the present perilous condition is largely the result of a financial policy which the executive branch of the Government finds embodied in unwise laws which must be executed until repealed by Congress;

"Now, therefore, I, Grover Cleveland, President of the United States, in performance of a constitutional duty, do, by this proclamation declare that an extraordinary occasion requires the convening of both Houses of the Congress of the United States at the Capitol in the city of Washington on the 7th day of August next, at 12 o'clock noon, to the end that the people may be relieved, through legislation, from present impending danger and distress."

On the 7th of August, 1893, Congress met promptly at the hour indicated in the call. Both Houses organized and the President was notified of the fact.

On the 8th of August, he transmitted a special message to the House and Senate, respectively, in which he set forth his reasons for existing financial depressions, and urged the repeal of the Sherman law as the means to dispel the distrust which wrought such distress among the people. He said:—

"The existence of an alarming and extraordinary business situation, involving the welfare and prosperity of all our people, has constrained me to call together in extra session the people's representatives in Congress, to the end that through a wise and patriotic exercise of the legislative duty with which they solely are charged, present evils may be mitigated and dangers threatening the future may be averted.

"Our unfortunate financial plight is not the result of untoward events nor of conditions related to our natural resources; nor is it traceable to any of the afflictions which frequently check national growth and prosperity. With plenteous crops, with abundant promise of remunerative production and manufacture, with unusual invitation to safe investment, and with satisfactory assurance to business enterprise, suddenly financial distrust and fear have sprung up on every side. Numerous moneyed institutions have suspended because abundant assets were not immediately available to meet the demands of frightened depositors. Surviving corporations and individuals are content to keep in hand the money they are usually anxious to loan, and those engaged in legitimate business are surprised to find that the securities they offer for loans, though heretofore satisfactory, are no longer accepted. Values supposed to be fixed are fast becoming conjectural, and loss and failure have invaded every branch of business."

An analysis of this extract of his message adds accumulative evidence, that this panic was pre-arranged by the national banks to coerce Congress to repeal the hated Sherman law.

The President asserts that all the elements of prosperity were at hand, and suddenly distrust sprung up on every side.

In speaking of the coinage of silver, he said:—

"Between the 1st day of July, 1890, and the 15th day of July, 1893, the gold coin and bullion in our Treasury decreased more than $132,000,000, while during the same period the silver coin and bullion in the Treasury increased more than $147,000,000. Unless Government bonds are to be constantly issued and sold to replenish our exhausted gold, only to be again exhausted, it is apparent that the operation of the Silver Purchase Law now in force, leads in the direction of the entire substitution of silver for the gold in the Government Treasury, and that this must be followed by the payment of all Government obligations in depreciated silver."

A perusal of this part of his message exhibits his animus against silver.

He further says:—

"At this stage, gold and silver must part company, and the Government must fail in its established policy to maintain the two metals on a parity with each other. Given over to the exclusive use of a currency greatly depreciated according to the standard of the commercial world, we could no longer claim a place among nations of the first class, nor could our Government claim a performance of its obligation, so far as such an obligation has been imposed upon it, to provide for the use of the people the best and safest money."

With a remarkable disregard of existing facts, he speaks of a depreciated currency.

He adds:—

"The knowledge in business circles among our own people that our Government cannot make its fiat equivalent to intrinsic value, nor keep inferior money on a parity with superior money by its own independent efforts, has resulted in such a lack of confidence at home, in the stability of currency values that capital refuses its aid to new enterprises, while millions are actually withdrawn from the channels of trade and commerce to become idle and unproductive in the hands of timid owners. Foreign investors, equally alert, not only decline to purchase American securities, but make haste to sacrifice those which they already have."

The last sentence of the above extract affords a key to the reason why, in the opinion of the President, the Sherman law should be repealed, that is, with reference to the war waged by him against silver.

At the very time that the President was penning this message, in which he asserted that the stock of silver coin and bullion in the Treasury had increased more than $147,000,000, silver certificates were sold at a premium of two per cent. by the money brokers of New York City.

On the 5th of August, two days before Congress met, a great banking firm of New York City had the following advertisement inserted in the New York Times and in the Herald:—

"WANTED—SILVER DOLLARS.—We desire to purchase at a premium of ¾ per cent., or $7.50 per thousand, standard silver dollars, in sums of $1,000 or more, in return for our certified checks payable through the clearing house.

ZIMMERMAN & FORSHAY, Bankers, 11 Wall street."

The object of storing up $147,000,000 of silver coin and bullion in the Treasury, at a time when it was at a premium, and then pointing at this accumulation of money and bullion, as a reason for requesting hostile legislation against it, is a damning blot upon the administration.

It exhibits the length to which President Cleveland went, in his efforts to make silver the scape-goat for the traitorous acts of the national banking money power, in assailing the credit of the Government, and in precipitating the panic.

With reference to that part of his message, where President Cleveland sought to convey a wrong impression to the people with reference to the quantity of silver on hand in the Treasury, and in which he asserts that bonds must be constantly issued to replenish the gold reserve, and that there was danger of the Government going on a silver basis, we refer to the following resolution passed by the Senate August 16, 1893:—

"Resolved, That the Secretary of the Treasury be, and he is hereby, directed to report to the Senate what amount, if any, of the treasury notes issued under the act of July 14, 1890, commonly called the Sherman Act, have been during the present month redeemed by the

Government, at the request of the holders thereof, in silver dollars, and whether the holders of such notes were advised, at the time of such redemption, that they could have gold instead of silver if they so desired.

"The Secretary of the Treasury is also directed to inform the Senate whether gold coin has been recently presented to the Treasury Department, or any sub-treasury, and silver dollars asked in exchange therefor; and, if so, if such exchanges have been made, and whether the department would or could exchange silver dollars for gold coin if requested to do so by holders of gold."

On the 17th of the same month, the Secretary, after reciting this resolution, replied as follows:—

"In response thereto, I have the honor to say that during the present month, treasury notes issued under the act of July 14, 1890, amounting to $714,636, have been redeemed by the Government in silver dollars. While I do not pretend to have knowledge of the degree of information possessed by the holders of the notes so redeemed, I am of the opinion that they were fully advised at the time of such redemption that they could have gold instead of silver, if they so desired. I base this opinion upon the general publicity which has been given to the terms of the Act, no less than upon the instructions of this department to the Treasurer and Assistant Treasurers of the United States, which have been to the effect that such notes were redeemable in silver dollars at the option of the holders. I am also supported in my belief by the fact that in the circular of this department, issued to the public for their guidance in their dealings with the Treasury, and containing the regulations which govern the issue, redemption, and exchange of the paper currency and the gold, silver, and minor coins of the United States, there is a paragraph which reads as follows:—

"4. 'Gold coin is issued in redemption of United States notes, in sums not less than $50, by the Assistant Treasurers in New York and San Francisco, and in redemption of treasury notes of 1890, in like sums, by the Treasurer and all the Assistant Treasurers.'

"In further response to the resolution, I have to say that recently gold coin has been presented at an office of this department, and silver dollars asked in exchange therefor, and that the exchange was not made for the reason that all the silver dollars in the Treasury at the time were required under the provisions of the laws relating to the currency to be held in the treasury to cover outstanding silver certificates and treasury notes issued under the act of July 14, 1890. At present the department would not and could not exchange silver dollars for gold coin if requested to do so by holders of gold, for the same reason; but if the condition of the funds of the Treasury were such as to afford a margin of silver dollars in excess of silver certificates and treasury notes outstanding, such exchanges would be made.

Respectfully, yours,

J. G. CARLISLE, Secretary."

Thus, while President Cleveland was holding up the Treasury accumulation of silver as a scare-crow to frighten Congress and the people, the Secretary of the Treasury, nine days after President Cleveland transmitted his message to Congress, officially states that gold coin was recently offered for these despised "50-cent dollars," and the exchange could not be made because the Treasury did not contain any of this money available to supply the demands.

The Secretary also says that at that time, the department would not, and could not, exchange silver dollars for gold coin because it did not have them.

In the face of this statement of the Secretary, where is that awful avalanche of silver which so frightened the President, that he convened Congress in special session to save the country from being overwhelmed in disaster by it?

Here were holders of gold coin actually offering gold coin, that superior money, for silver.

One curious feature of this condition was, that, while the Secretary was paying out gold to the New York bankers for export, the average American citizen was offering to take silver in exchange for gold.

On the 10th of August, Mr. Wilson, of West Virginia, introduced House bill No. 1, providing for the repeal of the purchasing clause of the Sherman law. On the same day, a resolution was adopted limiting the debate on that measure to fourteen days.

Upon the appearance of this repeal bill in the House, the Chambers of Commerce, Boards of Trade, and various other commercial bodies flooded Congress with petitions praying for the repeal of that law.

The newspapers of the East kept up a terrific din urging Congress to prompt action.

Meanwhile, a great debate was going on in the House. On the 12th of August, Mr. Hendrix, a national banker, representing a Brooklyn district, delivered a speech in the House urging the repeal of the purchasing clause. He said:—

"Repeal the Sherman silver law, gentlemen; adjourn and go home; and let the country take care of the rest."

Further on, he predicted that a repeal of this law would compel England to make proposals for a monetary conference, whereupon the following colloquy took place between Mr. Hendrix and Mr. Bland:—

Mr. Hendrix: Let us try the experiment just once and see whether we cannot bring this proud old lady down from her perch. I predict to you that inside of three months—before this Congress meets again—if you repeal this Sherman law and adjourn, England will make proposals to this country to come into a monetary conference and see what can be done for the sake of her ward, India. The proposition is already said to have come through financial magnates. Their names are not given, and therefore I distrust the information, because when men are mentioned I like to know where I can find them.

Mr. BLAND: Will the gentleman allow me a question right there?

Mr. HENDRIX: Yes, sir.

Mr. BLAND: I understood the gentleman to say a moment ago that we were evoluting toward a gold standard.

Mr. HENDRIX: Yes, sir.

Mr. BLAND: And now you claim that England is evoluting toward silver. [Laughter.]

Such was the absurd inconsistency in which this national bank member of Congress involved himself. On the same day, M. D. Harter, of Ohio, also a national banker, with a view to show that there was an abundance of money in circulation, made the following statement:—

"Gentlemen talk a good deal about our circulation per capita. I have very little faith in this per capita claptrap. Let us talk a little about our per capita circulation. They tell us that we have got $24 of circulation per capita, but under our banking methods what have we got? First, the national banks have $27 per capita, as represented by deposits; the savings banks hold $27 per capita; for the trust companies and the private banks $18 is a very small estimate. Add these figures together and you will find what amount of circulation your banking methods give you. They give you $72 per capita. In other words, through this machinery of banking we have increased the currency of the country three times over. But that is not all. Look at the clearing house returns. They show that for the year ending with the 30th of June last, we had exchanges amounting to $1,000 per capita throughout this country."

In less than five minutes after this deliverance, he utterly overthrew his former assertions by the following:—

"Your boasted millionaires, your owners of banks, your men who employ thousands of operatives in their manufactories, are begging at the doors of the banks for accommodations as small as $100 and $200. And here at the capital of this great nation, with everything, according to the theory of the silver men, to make prosperity, if you go with a New York draft to a bank, a good bank—for there are none but good banks in Washington and not very many of any other kind in the United States—if you go to any of these banks with a draft on New York for $40, $50, or $100, you can scarcely get it cashed."

A perusal of the Congressional Record, containing this debate, will bear out the statement that every gold standard advocate who urged the repeal of the Sherman law, produced arguments in favor of repeal that ate each other up as fast as they issued from his mouth. Hon. Burke Cockran, that arrogant and much-vaunted orator, in the course of one of his usual frothy speeches, made the following statement, August 26th:—

"Mr. Speaker, I venture the assertion that we are not suffering to-day from a lack of money, but from a redundancy of money; and I think that proposition can be demonstrated to the satisfaction of any man who sits in this Hall. According to the statement of the Secretary of the Treasury the circulation to-day exceeds by some seventy millions the amount in circulation last year, but last year the volume of business was vastly greater than it is to-day. If a smaller amount of money be able to circulate a greater quantity of commodities, will anybody pretend that the quantity of money we have now is not sufficient for all the purposes of commerce?"

Fourteen days preceding this statement of Mr. Cockran, he had a check for $100 payable on a New York bank, and he could not get it cashed in Washington, because at that time the banks of the former city refused to pay the checks of their depositors.

Representative Bowers, of California, gives the following version of this fact, he said:—

"A curious circumstance happened to me yesterday. One of my constituents of California came to me with a $50 check on a New York national bank, drawn in Rhode Island, a few hours from here, and could not get it cashed at the banks in Washington. To-day, my friend, Colonel Cockran, many of you know him, came to me with a check for a hundred dollars, drawn on a New York bank, and he could not get it cashed in Washington. I sent it off for collection."

This statement of Mr. Bowers was made in the presence of Mr. Cockran, August 12, 1893, and yet, in view of this fact, the latter subsequently asserted that the country was suffering from a redundancy of money!

The mendacity of those members who spoke for repeal was shameless in the extreme.

Mr. Patterson, of Tennessee, strongly denounced silver in a speech made by him August 14th. He declared that the cause of the panic orginated from the fear of the people against the use of depreciated dollars.

At this identical period, the New York banks were offering a premium for the standard silver dollar.

The following debate took place between him and Mr. Williams:—

Mr. Williams, of Mississippi: If it be true that the masses who are scared by the causes which the gentleman states, but which they do not understand, and that the capitalist, who does understand this question, is scared for a different reason, why is it that the capitalists are to-day paying a premium for the silver dollar in New York City?

Mr. PATTERSON: Well, that, Mr. Speaker, is a business matter which I have not investigated. [Laughter.]

Mr. BYNUM: They are paying a premium for paper money, too.

Mr. PATTERSON: Yes, they are paying a premium, I understand, for other small currency. I cannot give the reason for that, unless it be to secure currency to pay wage-earners. The question is outside my line of thought and of my argument.

On the same day, Mr. Harter said that the silver dollar was worth only fifty-eight cents.

The following colloquy took place between him and Mr. Cox, of Tennessee:—

Mr. Cox: Will the gentleman from Ohio yield for an interruption?

Mr. HARTER: I yield with pleasure to my friend from Tennessee.

Mr. Cox: I have listened with a great deal of pleasure to the gentleman's argument. He has stated that the silver dollar is worth to-day fifty-four cents.

Mr. HARTER: Fifty-eight cents.

Mr. Cox: Well, fifty-eight cents. Now, the question is, do you know of any man in the United States who has silver dollars that he will sell at that price, fifty-eight cents?

Mr. HARTER: Certainly not, under present conditions. But I know every man who has a silver dollar——

Mr. Cox: One moment, please. Does not the 58-cent silver dollar buy just as much of the products of this country as any other dollar?

Mr. HARTER: To that I answer yes. But that is not

the point. That is the present condition under limited coinage, but you are proposing to change it. In further answer to my friend from Tennessee, whom I regard as an authority on his side of this subject, I say to him that while that is true to-day, the very morning that you have by your law established free coinage in this country, then it ceases to be true, and that every dollar in existence which is now held up to its full nominal value by our present law will sink to fifty-eight cents, the bullion value, as soon as your law becomes operative.

This is an example of the reckless statements put forth by these Cuckoo statement.

On August 21st, Mr. Cooper, of Indiana, who, by some mysterious process, had suddenly become an advocate of the gold standard national banking system, delivered a speech laudatory of credit. He said:—

"Some gentlemen may ask, Why not have more money and less credit? My answer to that is this with credit you would not need the money and you would not want it, and without credit it would not circulate, and you could not get it, however great the volume might be. Besides, the world is not moving in that direction. The time has come when 'a good name is rather to be chosen,' even in the commercial world, 'than great riches.' A good name will cause the transfer of more property to-day than all the camels of Job could have carried. A good name unlocks the vaults of the usurer, turns the wheels of industry, and sets the sails of commerce upon the seas. Cash is the law of the savage, confidence an inspiration and instrument of civilization."

At the time he made those remarks, the great national banks of New York City were discounting the checks of their depositors.

This distinguished (?) statesman, after his failure to return to Congress in 1894, gladly accepted the postmastership of a small city, in order to obtain some of that cash which he had denounced as "the law of the savage."

On August 14th, Mr. Boatner, who opposed the striking down of silver, severely arraigned the supporters of the repeal bill. He said:—

"I charge, sir, that the advocates of this measure, these thick-and-thin gold men of the Democratic party and of the Republican party who have been endeavoring ever since I have been in Congress to force this Government to an issue of cheap bonds, are responsible for the excitement which has created the destruction of public confidence, and has caused a run upon the banks and the withdrawal of large amounts of money from circulation. They are the men who have sown the wind, and we are now reaping the whirlwind. There is nothing in or about the Sherman law, there is no deduction that can be drawn from that law, which would justify anybody in making the assertion that the United States Government is not good for every obligation that it has put upon the market."

This charge of conspiracy on the part of the gold standard national banking element in the House was not denied by the supporters of that system.

On the 21st of August, Mr. Cox made the following attack upon Mr. Hendrix and the other national bank members of Congress. He said:—

"Mr. Hendrix, who sits just in front of me, delivered his defense of his position for this repeal. I charge here in his presence that nearly one year ago there was issued from the Bankers' Association at New York a circular to the rural banks all over this country, asking for a contribution to procure the repeal of the Sherman act. Does he or any man from New York City deny it? That was before the panic. True, a second circular followed, condemning the clerk of that association for issuing that circular, and probably discharged him; but have you retracted the purpose announced? I want a reply if I have done any one injustice.

"Did you tacitly agree or discuss the question in New York that you would not rediscount notes from the South unless we would vote for the unconditional repeal of the Sherman act? Did not one of your speakers in one of your bankers' meetings openly declare that you could and would control the finances of this Government?

"Did your papers not boast that you had in your city two hundred millions of gold hoarded in your vaults?

"If I do any man injustice, I pause for correction. Here is the fundamental error. Let this Government rule for the people. Let it rule its finances for the purpose of trade and commerce, and forever let it put its everlasting stamp of indignation and condemnation on legislation that legislates one man's property up and another's down. Give us a fair and equal fight for human happiness. [Applause.]"

At the time this debate was going on in the House, the banks of New York were refusing to pay checks drawn on deposits; and were issuing Clearing House certificates in lieu of money.

Exchange on New York banks ranged at from ten to fifty dollars on the thousand.

After quoting a New York bank circular, Mr. Hatch, of Missouri, made the following criticism on the national banks of that city.

On August 23d, he said:—

"Fifty dollars on a thousand dollars in exchange on New York. Why, sir, usually in the West New York exchange is at a small premium or at par. I received a few days ago a letter from the cashier of a bank in which I do my business at Hannibal, Mo. He informed me that he could not take New York exchange for anything less than $1 on the hundred dollars or $10 on the thousand dollars.

"I thought that enormous; but here it appears by this New York circular that there are other cities in the country that have not as much confidence in the New York banking system as the bankers in my own town. In some of these other cities they will not take exchange on New York at less than $50 on the $1,000.

"What have the banks of New York been doing to keep up confidence. Nobody ever lost confidence in the banks of New York until after they entered into that conspiracy in April last to produce a panic in this country—a money famine and a panic. But they lost confidence in each other.

"Let me tell my New York friends right now that, in my judgment, the most herculean task ever attempted in any legislative body on the face of God's green earth since the creation of Adam down to the present time will be to restore confidence between the New York bankers. They know each other too well. [Laughter.] And there is such a splendid minority of them that have embellished the pages of New York financial history in the last few years by moving across the line into Canada, that I suppose the next step would be to establish confidence between the bankers of New York on this side and those on the other side of the Canadian border.

"Mr. Speaker, I offered on yesterday evening to give my distinguished friend from New York [Mr. Fellows] part of my time, and I intended if he accepted it to make but one condition, because we all know him to be a splendid lawyer; but I wanted some legal ability to blaze the road along that way so as to point out in a clear manner the use of and the character of what is called 'clearing house certificates.'

"I ask the gentleman, or any other gentleman from New York when he gets the floor, to please tell us what a clearing house certificate is, and how it can be used as money without violating the laws of the United States? Do you pay any tax on it? What is it? The promise to pay of a class of men who will not take even their own promises to each other! And tell me another thing. Why is it every national bank in the city of New York to-day, and for the past thirty days, has been doing business in open and notorious violation of the law, absolutely refusing to pay its checks when presented at the counter? Why is that?"

This challenge of Mr. Hatch was not accepted by the able and brilliant Fellows.

The Missouri congressman truthfully portrayed the methods and character of the New York bankers in their systematic efforts to influence the legislation of Congress.

A member of that Congress bore testimony to the fact, that he had seventeen thousand dollars on deposit in a bank in New York City, and that he had presented a check for two hundred dollars at its counter for payment, and that he was refused his own money.

Matthew Marshal, the able financial editor of the New York Sun, exposed the conspiracy of the banks in aggravating the distress then prevalent.

On August 21, 1893, he said:—

"The question is, how much longer our banks can, without bringing on a catastrophe, continue in their course of increasing the volume of clearing house certificates and of denying to their depositors payment in lawful money of their checks. Thus far depositors have been very patient, and have good-naturedly submitted to the enforced scaling down of their dues; but they cannot be expected to submit to it forever. A bank that cannot or will not pay claims against it in the regular course of business is, by the decisions of our State courts, insolvent, and, if the Bankrupt Act of 1867 were now in force, a refusal by a bank for forty days to pay checks on demand would be a commission of bankruptcy."

The clique of nationl bank congressmen did not even attempt to repel these bitter accusations. They knew they were true in every particular.

During the panic now raging, a stock gambler of Wall street rushed into the Stock exchange, and excitedly announced that one of the greatest banks in the city had failed.

A tremendous fall of stocks immediately took place, and this knave bought in vast quantities of the securities injuriously affected by this false rumor.

It is said that this scheme netted this stock gambler the sum of $10,000,000.

On August 18, Hon. J. C. Sibley referred to the false reports spread abroad by these lawless speculators, and he instanced this recent case. He said:—

"Another reason for your panic has been chargeable directly to the action of your Wall street gamblers, who have circulated rumors by the wholesale. They permitted one of these gamblers to go into their chamber a few weeks ago and announce that one of the greatest banks in New York had failed. And how did that body punish him for putting in circulation this false report? They suspended him for a year; and it is said his profits through bear operations since this panic commenced have netted him in clear cash over $10,000,000. I think he can afford to stand the suspension."

Acts like that described by Congressman Sibley never failed to win the admiration of the stock gambling element.

Men who were able to engineer a comsummate piece of villainy like the above to a successful termination, were hailed as heroes by the smaller fry of Wall street.

The press of the city glowingly referred to such achievements as "master strokes of financial genius."

Mr. Sibley spoke of the great decline in the farm lands since 1873. He said:—

"We can only judge of the future by the past and

the present. Everything has declined since you demonetized silver, since you commenced hostile legislation against it. Pennsylvania farm lands to-day are not worth forty cents upon the dollar of what they were in 1873. Is not that correct?

"MR. HICKS: I am sorry to say it is the fact."

The gentleman upon whom Mr. Sibley called to verify his statement, was a Republican member of Congress, and a fanatical believer in the efficacy of a high protective tariff, and he made this admission long before the Wilson tariff bill became a law.

On August 25th, Representative Doolittle, of Washington State, exposed the means practiced by the bankers of the East in strangling the industries of the Pacific coast. He said:—

"There are many things I would be glad to say upon this subject, but my time is limited. A great deal has been said during this debate as to the cause or causes of the trouble that is now upon us. When I came to this city last January to witness the closing of the Fifty-second Congress, I left my home on the shores of Puget Sound, when, so far as confidence was concerned, everything was as placid as a May morning. There was not a man who had not the utmost confidence in the banks throughout that entire country. I know that during the latter days of that Congress an effort was made here to repeal this purchasing clause of the so-called Sherman law, and also to obtain an issue of gold-bearing bonds from the Government.

"I know that those attempts failed. Upon reaching my home early in April, I found that circulars were being received by every banking man and by people engaged in every business on the Pacific coast, from New York and other money centers of the country. I know that these circulars were full of statements foreboding financial disaster and ruin. They contained notice that credits should be shortened and that money should be withdrawn in many instances where it had been loaned to people in the West; and all this trouble was to result from the failure of the Fifty-second Congress in its last session to repeal the so-called Sherman Act. These people, interested selfishly in the repeal of the Sherman law and in their attempt to cause the issuance of gold-bearing bonds, were endeavoring to stampede business men all over the Western country into a support of their position.

"Now, Mr. Speaker, it is much easier for people to tear down credit and confidence than it is to establish that credit and confidence. The result of sending out these circulars over the West was that the confidence of people regarding financial conditions began to wane; they began to lose confidence in the banking and other financial institutions of their States and towns. This was the immediate cause, I know, generally over the Pacific coast of the failures that followed."

In the light of this accumulated evidence, who will deny that the murderous panic of 1893 was planned by the national banking money power to force a repeal of the purchasing clause?

The whole tenor of the arguments advanced by those who urged the repeal of the purchasing clause of the Sherman law was to restore "confidence," to prevent the exportation of gold to foreign countries, and to maintain the credit of the United States.

But the following declaration made by Mr. Hendrix, President of the First National Bank of New York City, otherwise known as "Fort Sherman," clearly shows what influence was brought to bear upon Congress to procure this legislation.

On August 28th, he said:—

"There are petitions from nearly thirteen thousand bankers in the hands of different members here which register the sentiment against the foolishness of our silver-supporting policy. The wave of popular opinion has reached this House. It betokens a revolution in the American mind. We are not to fool any longer with a depreciated and a rejected money metal, and try to bear alone a burden which civilized nations should share in common. The silver problem will, after our action, remain in the world, and on the world, but not on this country alone. We can take care of the forty cents of credit in our silver dollar. We can keep all of our large stock in free circulation on a parity with gold, and the banks will take care to keep in such position as to meet the demands for foreign exchanges."

The debate upon the repeal bill came to an end August 28th, and a vote was taken on the measure, and it was adopted by 239 yeas to 108 nays.

An analysis of this vote will prove that the Eastern Democrats and Republicans cast an almost solid vote for the bill. It is also evident that President Cleveland "worked in Congress" by means of the enormous influence of his patronage, for an inspection of the vote bears testimony to the fact, that scores of members of the House voted to repeal the purchasing clause who had been lifelong advocates of the free coinage of silver.

The unconditional repeal of that clause did not leave a single law upon the statute-books of the nation that would provide for the coinage of a single additional dollar of silver.

The national banking money power once more gained its point by wholly eliminating the further use of silver as money.

Immediately upon the repeal of the purchasing clause by the House, the New York bankers cabled the news to London.

The action of the House gave great satisfaction to

the money-lending classes of England, as the following extracts from the London press abundantly prove.

In speaking of the effect of the action of the House upon the price of silver, the London Times, on August 29th, said:—

"It is the expiring effort of the silver party. Silver, deprived of the support of the Sherman Act, will sink to a level too low to suit the bi-metallist notions of a proper ratio, or to facilitate the establishment of a double standard."

On the same day the Pall Mall Gazette editorially said:—

"When confidence and credit are restored by the repeal of the pernicious Sherman Act, the task of fiscal reform (single gold standard) in the United States will become easier."

The Daily News of the same date thus expressed its views:—

"The Daily News to-day expresses the opinion that the repeal of the Sherman Act will prove a serious blow to bi-metallists throughout the world, but a great victory for common sense and the single standard."

It appears, therefore, that the sole object of repealing the purchasing clause of the Sherman law was for the express purpose of depriving silver of its only support, thus lowering its value, and thereby furnishing reasons against its use as money.

Is it not singular, that every effort made by the associated banks of the United States against silver, met the hearty approval of the influential press of Great Britain?

CHAPTER XII.

SENATE VOTES FOR REPEAL.

"I believe in the people, in universal suffrage as fitted to secure the best results that human nature leaves possible. If corruption seems rolling over us like a flood, it is not the corruption of the humbler classes—it is millionaires, who steal banks, mills and railways; it is defaulters, who live in palaces and make away with millions; it is money kings, who buy up Congress; it is the demagogues and editors in purple and fine linen, who bid $50,000 for the presidency itself."—Wendell Phillips.

While this great debate was taking place in the House, the turmoil in the business circles throughout the United States was beyond the powers of description. Hundreds of great failures were occurring, including banks as well as other lines of business.

The colossal credit system, which had been built up by the national banking money power, fell with a crash that shook the business interests of the nation from one end to the other.

The juggernaut which the New York bankers had sent forth to trample down the business of the country in order to influence Congress, had got beyond the control of those lawless financiers who had assailed the credit of the nation, and who had destroyed the property rights of tens of thousands.

The concerted cry of "want of confidence" in the ability of the Government to redeem its obligations, returned, with ten-fold force, to assail the very national banks which had originated that false and delusive rumor.

Thousands of depositors immediately withdrew their money from the banks, aggravating the distress then prevalent.

That the rumors set afloat by the banks, attacking the credit of the Government, did not impair the confidence of the depositors in its financial ability is demonstrated to a certainty.

Greenbacks, treasury notes, silver, and silver certificates, were taken with avidity by the withdrawing depositors and hoarded. Gold was not demanded.

In a short time, the New York banks were unable to pay their depositors, and they, in common with the banks of Boston and Philadelphia, issued clearing house certificates to the amount of $63,000,000, which were used to pay their depositors in lieu of money.

This act of the associated banks of the East, in issuing these certificates, was a clear violation of the law which assessed a tax of ten per cent., upon State bank notes, and all other paper designed to circulate as money except national bank notes.

The very banking power, which had demanded and secured the passage of that law, was the first who violated its provisions.

Besides these lawless acts, the New York banks refused to cash the checks of their depositors, and charged a premium of three per cent. for paying out the money which they owed to the public.

In the meantime, the money brokers of New York were charging enormous rates of interest, and were selling money at a premium ranging from three to seven per cent.

The Washington Post is authority for the statement that one firm of money brokers in New York City made a profit of $600,000 by selling currency at a premium.

A financial writer of New York City stated that Russell Sage made a daily profit of twenty thousand dollars by loaning money at an enormous rate of interest during the panic.

As proof of the foregoing facts, a New York banking house issued the following circular letter August 18th:—

"The New York City bankers have $37,380,000 certificates outstanding. Boston has $11,100,000. Other bankers in the South and West perhaps have enough more out to make fifty millions of bank certificates. Adding these various amounts together, we find a possible increase of about one hundred millions since July 1 to replace the unknown amount of currency and gold drawn out of the banks and hoarded in vaults and other places since May last, "Where it resembled the one talent more than the ten talents."

"Currency commands three per cent. premium, and has sold as high as five per cent. Exchange on this city from many Western cities has recently ranged from five to fifty dollars per $1,000. Many Western people claim the degree of credit desired by Eastern bankers is shown by their willingness to pay depositors. Eastern banks appear to have no sympathy for Western methods in not issuing bank certificates. Many individuals have sold their checks on the street for funds to meet maturing obligations or make needed purchases. Credit seems to have been strained from here to the Pacific coast, and attacked on all sides and benefiting but few."

The Mercantile National Bank of New York City was the only bank that did not exact unlawful rates of interest.

Mr. St. John was at the head of this institution, and

he would not permit this bank to practice the extortion in vogue at the other banks.

When before the House Committee on Currency, in December, 1894, he testified as follows:—

MR. HAUGEN: What rate of interest did you charge during the panic a year ago?

MR. ST. JOHN: The Mercantile National Bank of New York never exacts more than 6 per cent. from its dealers, under the present administration of thirteen years. There was one instance during that panic of 1893 in which we did exact 8 per cent., I think. We had been badly abused, and might have exacted 20 per cent.

MR. HAUGEN: What was the current rate about?

MR. ST. JOHN: There was no current rate. Lenders got anything they chose to exact.

MR. HAUGEN: It was much higher than it is now?

MR. ST. JOHN: Yes; brokers paid on prime security three-fourths per cent. per day and 6 per cent. per annum; 276 per cent. per annum for some days.

MR. JOHNSON, of Indiana: Can you give us, in a succinct form, your explanation as to how there can be a remedy for the high price of money in the agricultural districts in crop-moving times?

MR. ST. JOHN: If there were a larger aggregate of money in the United States it could circulate over our vast territory without occasioning alarm. If I knew that the world believed that Louisville is absolutely prosperous, I would like to lend much of my money in Louisville. I would do so with the same certainty that I have mentioned as pertaining to New York. I merely take Louisville as the illustration, because you mention it.

The statements of President St. John shows the extent of the panic in New York City, and affords a view of the Shylock tactics practiced by the money lords of the East.

It has been asserted by competent authority, that while these banks were refusing to pay out the funds due their depositors, that this money was loaned out by them through brokers at the rates of interest stated by Mr. St. John, viz., 276 per centum.

Not only did the banks of New York City disobey the law by issuing clearing house certificates, but the great elevator owners and flour manufacturers of Minneapolis bought millions of bushels of wheat by paying for it in certificates similar to those of New York City.

The clearing house of Birmingham, Ala., issued certificates for sums as low as fifty cents.

The excuse tendered by the banks for not paying out money was, that the depositors were frightened by a "want of confidence," and that they, the banks, had not the money to pay claims against them.

It was during this time of scarcity of money, that the Hon. Bourke Cockran declared that the country was suffering from a redundancy of currency!

The unlawful acts of the New York banks became so notorious that, on the 22d of August, 1893, the following resolutions of inquiry were offered in the Senate by Mr. Peffer:—

"Resolved, That the Secretary of the Treasury be directed to inform the Senate—

"First, Whether, and in what respect, the national banks, or any of them, in the cities of Boston, New York, and Philadelphia are being now conducted in violation of law.

"Second, Whether said banks are paying depositors' checks promptly in lawful money.

"Third, Whether said banks, or any of them, are demanding rates of interest higher than those provided by law for the loan of money or in discounting notes and bills."

Immediately upon the appearance of this resolution, Senator McPherson, the national bank sugar trust speculator, moved its reference to the Finance Committee.

This was done for the purpose of smothering the resolution.

Senator Gorman apologized for the delinquent banks, and asserted that, if the Comptroller strictly enforced the law, many of these banks would be compelled to close their doors. He argued that the banks were the best judges of what should be done in the case.

In reply to the remarks of Senators McPherson and Gorman, Senator Hill said:—

"I am as anxious, sir, as the Senator from Maryland can possibly be to relieve the financial distress of this country. I will go with him as far as he will go in the effort to keep out partisanship in the disposition of the financial question. From the hour we first met in this body my efforts have been toward bringing about a proper solution of the question, and my efforts have been just as zealous, just as earnest, as have been the efforts of the Senator from Maryland. My position upon this great financial question has not been misunderstood. I spoke upon this subject last February when I thought I saw the danger coming to the country. I did not hear the eloquent voices of some other gentlemen aiding me in that contest.

"What is the precise question? Gentlemen do not understand one another upon the other side of it. I thought I heard an intimation that there had been something wrong somewhere. I judged that much from the suggestion of the Senator from Massachusetts. He disavowed any intention of saying that there had been any wrong anywhere. Then the Senator from Maryland steps forward and says, 'Yes; there has been a violation of the law, a conceded violation of the law, on the part of national banks, winked at by officials.'

That is the idea we get from his remarks. I do not know whether that is true or not. I think, whether it is true or not, it ought to be investigated.

"What do you want to refer to this committee? Is it a committee of investigation to investigate the acts of the Comptroller of the Currency?—No. For what purpose is the resolution to be referred? As I understand the Senator from Maryland, the only object of a reference to the committee is for the purpose of not acting upon it, for the purpose of suppressing it in the interest of the public welfare. That seems to be the idea. There has never been a cause so bad in the history of the country that its advocates have not always felt that they acted in the interest of the public welfare.

"The resolution is a simple one. What is it? It simply asks the Comptroller of the Currency to give us certain information in his possession as to what has been done in his office, or by the national banks of the country, so far as he understands what has been done. The details of the resolution I do not propose to give. What is the objection to it? Is it a proposition to try the Comptroller of the Currency? Is it a proposition to arraign the national banks for a violation of their duty?—No; it is a simple, ordinary and proper resolution; and I say courtesy to the distinguished Senator from Kansas entitles the resolution to be passed here and now. What reason can there be given against it?

"The Senator from Maryland says there are great times in the history of the country when we must rise above partisanship. I agree with him. What has that to do with this question? There are great times when we must be equal to the occasion. What has that to do with suppressing an ordinary resolution of inquiry? The resolution does not provide for the appointment of a committee to investigate anybody. The resolution does not provide for making charges against anybody.

"Are you afraid of the facts? This very debate will cause inquiry into what has been done. This debate in the Senate of the United States will direct attention to the question, and every person will be apt to inquire to-morrow morning what has been done by national banks, and what has been done by the Comptroller of the Currency, that the Senate of the United States dare not pass a simple, ordinary resolution of inquiry? What are you afraid of? Are we not trying to quiet the existing panic? Is the panic to be quieted by such proceedings as this? Are resolutions calling for information to be suppressed, put down, shelved, put into a committee and there pigeonholed? Can we not stand the light of day on this subject? Cannot the acts of our officials, whoever they may be—and I myself make no charges against them whatever—stand a simple inquiry?

"What will this committee do? The Senator from New Jersey says that the committee will look into the matter, and the fair inference from his remarks is that if they find anything wrong, they will not report the resolution, but if they find everything has been right, then they will report the resolution. Why can we not make that inquiry now? I appeal to the Senators around this Chamber that there is no reasonable, tenable objection that is presented why the resolution should not be passed. Why should not the distinguished Senator from Kansas be treated the same as every other member of this body? He has the same rights to offer a resolution and have it passed.

"How long is it since a resolution of inquiry has been referred to a committee before being allowed to pass? I have not heard it in the last year and a half that I have been here. Therefore, I say to you, it is not a question of patriotism. It is not a question as to what should be done in this great hour of distress. It is a simple, ordinary question of senatorial courtesy; and I have heard no reason yet presented why the resolution of the Senator from Kansas should not be passed. I do not agree with him in his peculiar notions of finance. I do not belong to his party. He has his own views upon these questions, but he has a right to have any proper, legitimate information spread upon the records of the Senate, and there can be no objection to it."

Senator Washburn expressed his fears that the passage of the resolution would close almost every bank in the country, and place it in the hands of a receiver. He said:—

"It seems to me if the resolution is passed and we receive the reply which is inevitable, that it will be notice to the Comptroller of the Currency to administer the law literally and technically; the result of which will be to close almost every bank in the country and place it in the hands of a receiver. That is a calamity which, it seems to me, we should look forward to with great hesitation. I do not believe it is the duty of patriotism, of party, or of good common sense to inject anything of that kind into the present deplorable condition."

The Senator who made the above statement was a supporter of the national banking system, and the remarks above quoted will exhibit the lawless character of those men, who attacked the credit of the United States, and who violated the laws of State and nation in almost every transaction in which they were engaged.

During the debate on the motion to refer to the Finance Committee, Senator Teller said:—

"The banks have another function, which is to transmit money from one bank to another. Commerce can scarcely be carried on unless that function is in active force. Business cannot be done between New Orleans and Chicago, New Orleans and New York, and all around, unless bills of exchange can be used. They are the agencies of commerce.

"Have these banks fulfilled that function? For more than six weeks the banks of the city of New York, and other cities which I might mention, have simply declined to pay drafts drawn on them by outside banks for the money that those banks have on deposit. Between a city that is entered by at least six railroad trains a day, and can be reached in twenty-four hours, and the city of New York, the rates of exchange have been $3 on the hundred; and between the city of New York and the city of Philadelphia there has been an absolute refusal on the part of the banks of Philadelphia to pay drafts on the city of New York in any kind of money.

"I have in my drawer here a letter from a Western banker, who tells me that through his bank he had a draft of $7,000 on a Philadelphia bank, which he sent to a bank in the city of New York, and the bank there returned it to him saying, 'We will present no drafts to the banks of Philadelphia, because they decline to pay.' Then, through other agencies, this banker sent his draft to Philadelphia for money admitted to belong to the drawer, and the banks of Philadelphia simply said: 'We cannot afford to pay this, and we will not pay it.'"

Senator Butler added the following testimony to that adduced by Mr. Teller. He said:—

"I would state one fact which comes within my own personal knowledge. I met a gentleman on a train last night, who informed me that, as President of a large manufacturing establishment in the South, he had deposited in one of the banks of the city of New York a large amount of money, and had telegraphed and written to that bank to send him $5,000 of currency with which to pay his laborers on Saturday night.

"Mr. Allison: A national bank?

"Mr. Butler: I am not prepared to say that it was a national bank—I do not know about that—but it was one of the banks of the city of New York. He said that that bank at first declined to do it, but finally sent him $5,000 in currency and charged him 1½ per cent. for sending him his own money. I said to this gentleman, 'You certainly did not pay it?' 'Why,' said he, 'I was obliged to pay it.' 'To pay 1½ per cent. for sending you your own money?' 'Yes, sir.' That is one instance. As has been stated by some Senator, I believe that a check on a man's own deposit has to be discounted at 3 per cent.

"I have heard a great deal about the want of confidence in the country, brought about by the Sherman Act. The Sherman Act has about as much to do with that want of confidence as a pebble in a mill pond has to do with stirring the waters. It is, unless we are all misinformed, a want of honesty—and we may as well speak plainly—and the sooner the country finds it out the better it will be for everybody."

These were but a few of the facts brought out by the debate on this resolution with reference to repeated violations of law, and of the mean oppressions practiced upon the people by those lawless national bankers, who had boasted that they would teach the people an "object lesson."

The resolution was finally referred to the Finance Committee, which subsequently reported it back in a modified form and it was passed.

On September 16th, the Deputy Comptroller made a report in reply thereto, in which he stated that the Comptroller had no official information that the national banks of New York, Boston, and Philadelphia were violating the law.

It will be noticed that the Comptroller himself did not reply to the resolution, and secondly, that the resolution did not call for official information. Furthermore, the sub-treasury in New York City was a member of the Clearing House Association, and, as such, was cognizant of the methods of the national banks composing that body.

During this time, the Senate was debating the question of repealing the purchasing clause of the Sherman law.

On August 25th, Senator Hill, of New York, strongly arraigned those men who brought on the panic. He said:—

"Some portion of the present panic may be traced to a concerted effort on the part of numerous monometallists to produce it, in order to further discredit silver as a part of the standard money of the country. That fact is apparent everywhere we turn. We observe it in their senseless arguments constantly used against free bi-metallic coinage and their ceaseless endeavors to confuse the present issue by characterizing it as a contest between monometallism and bi-metallism. They seemed to be delighted when the first ray of financial trouble appeared. They hailed the recent action of India with ill-concealed saisfaction. They talked against silver, morning, noon, and night.

They denounced, not simply the Sherman silver purchase bill, but the future use of silver as money. With ghoulish glee they welcomed every bank failure, especially in the silver States, little dreaming that such failures would soon occur at their own doors. They encouraged the hoarding of money, they inaugurated the policy of refusing loans to the people even upon the best of security; they circulated false petitions, passed absurd and alarming resolutions, predicted the direst disaster, attacked the credit of the Government, sought to exact a premium upon currency, and attempted in every way to spread distrust broadcast throughout the land.

"The best financial system in the world could not stand such an organized and vicious attack upon it. These disturbers—these promoters of the public peril—represent largely the creditor class, the men who desire to appreciate the gold dollar in order to subserve their own selfish interests, men who revel in hard times, men who drive harsh bargains with their fellow men in periods of financial distress, and men wholly unfamiliar with the true principles of monetary science.

"It is not strange that the present panic has been induced, intensified, and protracted by reason of these malign influences. Having contributed much to bring about the present exigency, these men are now utterly unable to control it. They have sown to the wind, and we are all now reaping the whirlwind together."

The courage of the New York Senator was grandly illustrated in this speech, in which he points out the unlimited greed of those so-called financiers, to whom nothing was sacred during their traitorous warfare against the nation and the people.

One of the singular incidents, occurring during the struggle for repeal, was that in which Senator Sherman became a conspicuous adviser of President Cleveland and Secretary Carlisle!

The strange anomaly of this lifelong Republican becoming a warm supporter of the financial policy of the administration is one of the wonders of American politics.

On October 17th, Senator Sherman made the following prediction of the astonishing benefits that would accrue from a repeal of the Sherman law. He said:—

"In the present condition of affairs there is no money to buy cotton and corn and wheat for foreign consumption. Break down the barrier now maintained by the Senate of the United States, check this viper called obstruction to the will of the majority, give the Senate free power and play, and in ten days from this time the skies will brighten, business will resume its ordinary course, and the clouds that lower upon our house will be in the deep bosom of the ocean buried."

Is it not remarkable that this man, who, for many

years, has enjoyed the reputation of being one of the greatest of American financiers, should influence Congress to enact the law of July 14, 1890, and then, within a period of three years, assert that a repeal thereof would brighten the skies, cause the resumption of business, and bury the clouds in the bosom of the ocean?

Under the rules of the Senate, the repeal measure could not be forced through that body as rapidly as the national banking power desired.

In this great debate upon the bill to repeal the purchasing cause of the Sherman law, those Senators in favor of that measure persistently urged as a reason for repeal that a "flood of silver" threatened the financial stability of the Government.

The absurdity of that line of argument is apparent, when reference is had to the gold and silver production of the United States.

From 1792, up to and inclusive of 1892, the value of gold produced in this country was $1,987,000,000, of silver only $1,146,869,000, excess of gold over silver, $841,000,000.

Senator Teller challenged the gold monometallists to point out where this "flood of silver" was stored up.

They feebly referred to India!

The New York Press indulged in a vicious tirade upon Senator Voorhees, Chairman of the Finance Committee, taking him to task for what it called a dereliction of duty in not forcing a vote upon the bill.

On August 26th, the New York Evening Post uttered the following implied threats because the Sherman law was not repealed. It said:—

"We hear a great many reports from Washington to the effect that the Senate is firm against any repeal of the Silver Purchase law. We advise the public to attach little importance to the state of mind which prevails at the present moment in the Senate or among the senators' constituents. The medicine of the silver crisis is still working and the pangs which it produces will be more acute as the time goes on. One calamity will come thundering after another until the only possible remedy is applied. Banks will fail, railroads will default, manufactories will close, workingmen will lose their situations, there will be a shortage of money for crop-moving, affairs will grow steadily worse, until the mind cure is effected. Senators may roar against capitalists till the crack of doom without opening the pocketbook of one of them. In fact, the louder they roar, the tighter will those pocketbooks be closed. Nor will the time ever again come when money can be obtained with the customary ease so long as that silver law stands unrepealed. Hence we repeat that the frame of mind that the Senate may be in at the present time is no index of what it may be two weeks hence. There is dynamite enough in the financial situation to burst the Senate and both political parties."

The Philadelphia Press of the same date said:—

"The New York banks for several days have been endeavoring to bring a home influence on United States Senators, to induce them to vote for the repeal of the July silver law.

"To this end correspondents of the New York banks in the West and South have been told that they need not expect to get money from New York until the purchasing clause was repealed, and the Southern and Western bankers have been strongly urged to write to their senators and insist that they work and vote for immediate repeal. This movement has given rise to the recent feeling in New York that the silver majority in the Senate could be overcome, as the influence of the banks of the metropolis, when concentrated on any object, is regarded as invincible. There is a feeling that the strain is not as great as it was, and improvement is hoped for. Some anxiety exists as to the action of savings bank depositors when the thirty and sixty day limit expires next month. The requirements of money for the crops will also be a potent factor, but no one is disposed to contemplate future conditions, especially if they are likely to be unpleasant."

These papers were the organs of the national banks, and they spoke the sentiment of that power.

On September 22d, the Daily Indicator, a financial paper of New York City, published the following:—

"There are ominous rumors in the street that New York will again put the screws on the Senate. Whether this is street talk or not remains to be seen; but the hardening of the rate of sterling exchange at the time of large merchandise exports and in the middle of our exporting season, looks as if gold exports would be made to influence the silver lunatics. There is no question but that the banks of New York are still withholding money from merchants, while possessing millions of idle cash, because of a tacit arrangement not to unloose it until the Senate votes for repeal. Now, if the gold exporting movement began, that would be another striking occurrence on which to impinge public thought, and on which popular argument could be based. There is one point lacking in any program of this kind. The public have learned that the influence of the silver bill on business has been overestimated. The predictions of those who have urged that everything depended on repeal have not been verified. Indeed, much that was said has been disproved by recent occurrences, and the feeling that the influence of the law was wildly exaggerated for political effect has spread at Washington and elsewhere. Exports of gold at this time might emphasize this feeling and, rightly or wrongly, it would be said that the gold went out at the behest of Wall street. Not an hour would be gained in the Senate for the repeal cause by any such movement."

These are but a few of the many thousand bold utterances of the subsidized press of the national banking money power, and they afford conclusive evidence that the panic of 1893 emanated from the concentrated money power of the East.

If the foregoing are not evidence of the power of the New York banks to destroy the business of the country, then no facts could ever be proven.

September 29th, the New York Tribune cautioned the bankers to refrain from giving publicity to their threats. It said:—

"The Tribune trusts that bankers of this city will permit a suggestion which is for their own as well as the public interest. Several of them are reported as having made particularly alarming statements regarding the disasters which, they venture to predict, will follow a failure of the Senate to pass the pending Silver Purchase repeal bill. Such statements are not likely to do any good whatever, but are eminently calculated to do much harm. It is not to be supposed that these influential bankers are deliberately trying to get up another panic, with all its distressing consequences.

"They might well remember, however, that the remarks they are reported as having made, might, in a certain contingency, prove extremely costly to the banks and to the business men of this city.

"It is not as if there were any important end to be gained by such alarming utterances. On the contrary, it is highly probable that the urgency of New York bankers may go far to prejudice the very cause they desire to aid, particularly with some members of the Senate from the West and South whose support of the repeal bill is essential. Senators of the United States ought to be far above mere prejudice against a measure, because any worthy body of citizens advocates it with peculiar zeal. That some Senators are not is the unfortunate fact. The idea that a measure is passionately desired by New York bankers, in the judgment of those who know the Senate best, is apt to damage that measure more than it will help it. If bankers of this city wish to do their utmost to assist the passage of the repeal bill, they may find it wise not to talk vehemently for publication.

"It is a less important fact that sound business men are not by any means agreed about the necessity of action on the silver question at this time."

The Tribune proceeds to warn the banks against expecting too much from the repeal of the Sherman law. It said:—

"There was such agreement some time ago, before the widespread disasters which it was hoped to aver had come. But it is not so clear now as it was then supposed to be that a single act of legislation would unlock countless hoards, and bring untold millions hither from England, and restore confidence and set all the mills at work. Whether all these things would have resulted at once is not the question. There have been many thousand failures. More than seven hundred banks have failed with liabilities amounting to more than $170,000,000. A considerable part of the manufacturing force of the whole country has stopped operations. In many ways the conditions have changed.

"One of the ablest bankers in this city, having charge of a very important bank, recently remarked that it was no longer clear to him that repeal of the silver act would accomplish what he had expected. Its anticipated effect, he said, would have been largely sentimental, but it was no longer possible to restore confidence entirely and instantly, as he had thought it might be restored some months ago. What this banker thinks many other sound business men are thinking.

It does not seem to them wise any longer to hold out the idea that all our fortunes in this great country must turn upon an event which is not certain to take place. The repeal bill is, as we believe, a wise and highly desirable measure. But it is hardly wise or desirable to stake the future of all business upon the action or inaction of the Senate of the United States."

In the meantime, the New York bankers were holding meetings, and formulating plans to compel the Senate to act with more haste.

A New York special to the Washington Post, September 17th, contained the following remarkable language:—

"New York, September 17th.

"In a group of bankers at the Union Club to-day, the sentiment was given voice that the delay in the passage of the repeal bill had reached a point that needed explanation. At the Manhattan Club, where the Democratic bankers principally gather, almost the same idea was expressed, but Senator Voorhees personally was held responsible. It was argued that the Democratic caucus had done all it could, but that the Indiana Senator had not lived up to the confidence reposed in him. The same assertion is made more bluntly in the open street, and at the Windsor Hotel; the banking men were talking this evening about the difficulty of understanding what Voorhees was trying to gain by what was considered his too-considerate treatment of the silver minority.

"Practically the same opinions are held by business men who have no banking interests.

"The feeling here is that unless in a day or two Voorhees performs without further delay what is considered his duty, of pressing for a vote, he must find himself under the necessity of explaining what are his concealed motives. 'Candidly,' said a banker of high standing to the Post correspondent, 'we did not expect repeal to have been accomplished by this time, but the celerity with which the House passed the bill gave us reason to believe like speed would follow in the Senate. We know the ways of Senators pretty well, and we can understand some of the motives that seem to actuate Senator Voorhees. But his refusal to come to New York and talk with us has suggested wrong motives, and his weak stand against the aggression of the silver Senators is more than we can fathom. What does it mean? I ask the question because we must know. We have a right to know. If we are not given satisfactory reasons for the delay, as we have not to this hour, we cannot be blamed for believing that there is something behind it all. What can be Senator Voorhees' personal interest in keeping back repeal? That's what we'd like to know; for his political interests are to our minds not enough to explain the strange delay.'

"This talk of other motives than politics behind the delay has gained currency among certain bankers, but is rejected as unbelievable by others."

From the language of these bankers, it will be seen that they regarded Congress as a mere servant of the money power, and that the Senator, or Representative, who would not completely subject himself to their beck and call was liable to incur their censure.

The Clearing House Association of New York City transmitted a circular to various members of Congress, in which was detailed a financial plan concocted by these financiers. It proposed that Congress enact a law providing that, whenever the clearing houses of New York City, Boston, Chicago, and other great cities, decide that the country is in a state of panic, these associations could deposit securities with the Government which should put up money for these great financial rings.

This is an example of the arrogant demands of the panic breeders, railway wreckers, trust organizers, stock, and grain gamblers.

That these men presumed that they owned the fee simple of the United States Government, is evident from an interview with a banker, published by a New York paper. In substance it is as follows:—

It was rumored that the President and the Secretary of the Treasury had a conference with reference to removing the ten per cent. tax on State bank notes. A reporter requested the opinion of Mr. Simmons, President of a great national bank of New York, upon the merits of the proposed measure. Mr. Simmons replied as follows. He said:—

"Well, I have not examined the proposition very closely, but do not think that I would like it. However, there need not be any solicitude, because the administration will not pass any financial legislation without consulting us; hence there need be no anxiety on the part of the public regarding the subject."

Another banker, on being interviewed by the reporter, stated that no financial bill would pass which did not meet the approval of the bankers.

After a long debate in the Senate, the repeal bill was passed October 30, 1893. It was sent back to the House for concurrence, as the Senate had added a few slight amendments to the House bill.

After a short debate the House concurred in the Senate amendments, and the bill became a law November 1, 1893.

The effects of the panic, which was created by the national banking money power to coerce Congress into repealing the purchasing clause of the Sherman law, are beyond the descriptive powers of language.

The New York World, of August, 1893, published a list of great railway companies whose bonds declined in value from ten to fifty-five per cent. These were gold bonds.

The decline of prices of agricultural products, since the repeal of the purchasing clause, was greater than ever before known.

On June 1, 1893, wheat sold for 83 cents per bushel.

On October 31st, it brought 69 cents, a decrease of fourteen cents. We quote New York prices.

The total loss on wheat to the farmers for the year 1893, was $70,000,000.

Cotton fell two and one-fourth cents per pound.

Other agricultural products fell at the same ratio.

It is safe to state that the loss on agricultural products, resulting from the repeal of the Sherman law in the United States and the closing down of the mints of India to the free coinage of silver, amounted to hundreds of millions of dollars.

And yet the passage of that Repeal Act was procured on the false pretense that prosperity would return to bless the people.

It was further stated that the repeal of the Sherman law was necessary to prevent the exportation of gold from the United States. This was another hypocritical plea to aid in the passage of the repeal, for, in a single year after that act was consummated, one hundred and twenty millions of dollars in gold were drawn out of the Treasury by that set of knaves who had urged repeal as a means to protect the gold reserve.

The number of failures for the year 1893 loomed up to the portentous figures of 15,242, with liabilities of $346,779,889.

The extent of suffering among the working classes cannot be estimated, all of which was the direct result of the conspiracy organized by the national banking money power, and which was executed by its minions throughout the length and breadth of this land.

The New York Tribune estimated the shrinkage of value of all kinds of property at ten billions of dollars during this panic, which it had urged the bankers to inflict upon the people as an "object-lesson."

Other competent writers estimate the shrinkage of values, in 1893 and 1894, at not less than twenty billions.

It was lamentable.

CHAPTER XIII.

EFFORTS OF ADMINISTRATION TO FORCE CARLISLE BILL THROUGH CONGRESS.

"When the laws undertake to add to these natural and just advantages artificial distinctions; to grant titles, gratuities, and exclusive privileges; to make the rich richer and the potent more powerful, the humble members of society, the farmers, mechanics, and laborers, who have neither the time nor the means to secure like favors to themselves, have a right to complain of the injustice of their Government."—Andrew Jackson.

During the struggle for the repeal of the purchasing clause of the Sherman law, several financial measures were introduced in Congress.

Among these proposed bills was Senate bill 453, to permit national banks to issue circulating notes up to the par value of the bonds deposited for the security of their circulating notes.

This bill proposed to donate to these banks an additional $25,000,000 of currency.

Senator Cockrell brought forward an amendment, by which the holders of United States bonds could deposit them with the Secretary of the Treasury, and receive therefore an amount of United States legal tender notes of the same nature as greenbacks, equal to the par value of the bonds so deposited.

This was applying the principle of bond security for these proposed notes.

The national banks immediately opposed this amendment, as they readily perceived that this amount of money would escape their control. There were many individual holders of these bonds who would have gladly availed themselves of the opportunity to obtain these notes by a deposit of bonds therefor.

The banks were powerful enough to defeat this amendment which would have set afloat many millions of legal tender currency.

The national banks and their allies, the stock gamblers, were so elated over their success in securing the repeal of the purchasing clause, that on December 5, 1894, they made an effort to force a bill through the House to permit railway corporations to form pools, or trusts, to maintain high rates of transportation.

This bill was in charge of Mr. Patterson, an advocate of the single gold standard. The measure was so skillfully drawn that it would have placed the entire country at the absolute mercy of the railways.

It was evident that the stock gamblers who attempted to railroad this bill through Congress, were actuated with the sole purpose of enhancing the value of railroad stocks and bonds, and thus dispose of them on a rising market. It was a stock gambling scheme, pure and simple.

Although the iniquity of this bill was thoroughly exposed by those who opposed it, the House passed it by a decisive vote. It failed to go through the Senate. During the great panic which was ravaging the country, more than seven hundred banks had failed with liabilities of $170,000,000. A great many of these failures were national banks, and, in many instances, they were precipitated by the conduct of the officers and directors squandering the money of depositors in speculation.

To remedy this evil, Mr. Cox, of Tennessee, introduced House bill 2,344, which read as follows:—

"That no national banking association shall make any loan to its president, its vice-president, its cashier, or any of its clerks, tellers, bookkeepers, agents, servants, or other persons in its employ until the proposition to make such a loan, stating the amount, terms, and security offered therefor, shall have been submitted in writing by the person desiring the same, to a meeting of the board of directors of such banking association, or of the executive committee of such board, if any, and accepted and approved by a majority of those present constituting a quorum."

The provisions of this bill would impose a most salutary check upon those officers and directors of national banks who endeavored to use the money of their depositors in stock gambling and grain speculations.

This bill had been before the House for some time, and Mr. Eckels, Comptroller of the Currency, opposed its passage in the following language:—

"It would be unwise to forbid an association to loan or to discount for its several directors, as they are usually selected from among the leading men of the various branches of business, for the reason that they possess information of great value in passing upon paper offered by those in some line of trade with themselves."

This remarkable language of the Comptroller, in a measure, corroborates the statement, that the officers and directors of national banks consisted chiefly of the great speculators, stock gamblers, railway magnates, organizers of trusts, and those who monopolize the various lines of business.

On October 16, 1893, this bill was called up by Mr. Cox, and immediately every national banker in Congress, as well as those stock gambling members, opposed its passage. Among those who vehemently attacked this measure were Mr. Lockwood, of New York, Mr. Cannon, a banker of Illinois, and Mr. Bingham, of Pennsylvania.

The following debate took place between Mr. Cox and Mr. Bingham:—

Mr. Bingham: Will the gentleman permit an inquiry?

Mr. Cox: With pleasure.

Mr. Bingham: What paragraph of this bill includes directors?

Mr. Cox: I think the original language of the bill included them, but they are now included by amendment.

Mr. Bingham: Now, I want to put this practical proposition to the gentleman——

Mr. Cox: That is right. That is the kind of question I like.

Mr. Bingham: I am a director of a bank——

Mr. Cox: So was I, until sent here.

Mr. Bingham: I do not say that I am personally; but I am simply putting my proposition in that way.

Mr. Cox: Well, I was a director of a bank.

Mr. Bingham: I am a director of a bank and I am also a stockbroker, doing a large stockbroking business. The market is an active market. At 1 or 2 o'clock in the day my customers come in and buy large amounts of stocks and sell large amounts of stocks. Between 2 and half-past 2 o'clock I have to take the securities that I have bought for my customers on a margin (the universal way of doing such business) and go to the banks and borrow $100,000, $200,000, $300,000, often larger amounts, for which I give the best gilt-edged collateral in the market. Now, how am I to do that business if I have to wait for a quorum. Three o'clock comes and if I have not placed my stock and secured my customers and covered my margins, what am I to do? I put that to the gentlemen as a business proposition.

Mr. DOOLITTLE: Stop stock gambling. [Laughter.]

Mr. BINGHAM: Oh, it is not stock gambling. I have described a very ordinary transaction in New York, or Philadelphia, or Chicago, or any of the other large cities where such transactions often cover millions of dollars.

Mr. Cox: I am aware of that. But what ought that man to do, that broker who wanted the money, and what ought the cashier to do in a good, solvent, well-regulated bank? When the broker comes and makes his application for a loan to meet the transactions of the day, they ought to get the executive board together; and I never saw a bank in my life, even in the rural districts, where you could not get an executive board of two members together.

Mr. BINGHAM: You cannot do it in the great cities.

Mr. Cox: Why not?

Mr. BINGHAM: Because the men are engaged in their regular vocations. A directorship in a bank is not a paying employment.

Mr. Cox: Is not banking a vocation?

Mr. BINGHAM: A director is paid no salary.

Mr. Cox: He gets his salary in the way of dividends and profits.

Mr. BINGHAM: That is the interest upon his money.

Mr. Cox: Can you tell me of any case where they could not get two members of the board together?

Mr. BINGHAM: I say they do not do it.

Mr. Cox: Oh, I know they do not do it; but could they not do it?

This extract from the Congressional Records bears out the charge, so often made, that the leading stock gamblers are officers and directors of national banks, and that they use their official position, as such officers, to obtain control of the bank funds to gamble in stocks.

Mr. Bingham is an example of that class of men who

represent Eastern constituencies in the halls of Congress.

We quote further from this interesting debate:—

Mr. Lockwood: Why do you want to legislate against these individual men?

Mr. Hall, of Missouri: I will answer it. For the very reason that it has a tendency to prevent these men from robbing the banks, the very thing the Comptroller of the Currency, not only this one but every other one, has tried to prevent.

Mr. Lockwood: Right there I want to correct you. The present Comptroller of the Currency has never sanctioned this bill. On the contrary, my information is that he disapproves of this bill. And I will say further, that he ought not to commend any such bill as this. Now, I beg to complete my statement without being interrupted. I say this further, that by the passage of this bill——

Mr. Cox: Will you yield to me for one moment?

Mr. Lockwood: Yes.

Mr. Cox: I gave you the floor yesterday.

Mr. Lockwood: Certainly.

Mr. Cox: Let me ask you this. You stated that your President and your cashier are members of your Finance Committee, or your Executive Committee: the name is not important.

Mr. Lockwood: Yes.

Mr. Cox: Now, then, the paper is submitted to them, as you stated to the House a moment ago.

Mr. Lockwood: Yes.

Mr. Cox: Do you mean that that paper is discounted without consultation with the directors? Now, tell me what objection there is to that Executive or Financial Committee reporting it back to the board of directors and making a record on their minutes?

Mr. Lockwood: My dear sir, what would be the use of, after it had been discounted, their reporting it back, when they will not have a chance, perhaps, to report it back to the board of directors for one or two months after the money has been borrowed? It would be of no benefit or information to the board of directors. Any member of the board of directors can look at the discount ledgers and see at any time what is going on and what discounts there are recorded in that book.

Mr. Cox: Do you mean to say that your directors do not meet in less than two or three months?

Mr. Lockwood: I state with great frankness that in many of these large banks, the board of directors do not meet more than once a month or two months, and there is no law requiring them to meet at any specific time, except twice each year.

Mr. Dunphy: But they are at the bank every day.

Mr. Lockwood: Furthermore, if this bill is passed, it will cause many of the most active, upright, and business-like men of the country to refuse to act either as officers or directors of national banks. All will concede that a national bank, to be successful, must have for its stockholders, directors, and officers, active, wide-awake business men. The stockholders select the directors, and the directors in turn select the officers of the bank, the most competent and trustworthy men they can find. All understand full well that the value of their stock and the success of the bank depends upon the confidence of the people in the judgment and wisdom shown in the selection of the officers and directors of the bank.

According to the opinion of Mr. Lockwood, thus publicly expressed in this debate, Comptroller Eckels was on very friendly terms with the national banks, for, assuming the word of this prominent supporter of the administration to be true, the Comptroller was opposed to any restriction that could be thrown in the way of those bank officials who did not hesitate to gamble in stocks and bonds with the money of depositors.

It was, however, the generally expressed opinion of the press, and of many public men, that had Comptroller Eckels exercised as much diligence in keeping the national banks within the letter and spirit of the law, as in attending their banquets, where he showered fulsome eulogies upon the national banking system, it would have conduced much to the public welfare. Following in the footsteps of all his predecessors in that office, Mr. Eckels has graduated from the Comptrollership of the Currency to the head of a great national bank.

Another inference to be drawn from Mr. Lockwood's statements is, that the most upright men in the business communities in which these banks are situated, would not consent to act as directors unless they had free access to the money of depositors. The bill was defeated.

On October 23, 1893, House bill No. 139, known as the Torrey Bill, was brought forward in the House. The purpose of this measure was the creation of a uniform system of bankruptcy throughout the United States.

The passage of this bill would be class legislation of the worst character, as, under its stringent provisions, any merchant who was unable to pay a debt within thirty days after it was due, could be forced into United States courts as a bankrupt. This was the darling scheme of the wholesale associations of the United States, and one at which they had labored unceasingly to force through Congress.

The power which was behind this bill, and which was urging its passage through Congress, was that gigantic trust—the wholesale dealers' associations of the United States.

The measure failed to pass, notwithstanding the prodigious efforts of the lobbyists to push it through that body.

During the month of February, 1894, a bill was introduced in the House to coin the seigniorage lying in the Treasury. This seigniorage was the gain between the bullion value and that of the coinage value of the silver, purchased under the Sherman law. It passed the House March 1, 1894, by a vote of 168 yeas to 129 nays. It then went to the Senate, where, on March 15th, it passed by a vote of 44 yeas to 31 nays. The bill was disapproved by President Cleveland, and the House failed to pass it over his veto by the necessary two-thirds vote.

During this time, gold coin was offered in exchange for silver dollars, and the action of President Cleveland in vetoing the bill is seemingly unaccountable.

The passage of this measure would have added $55,156,681 to the circulating medium of the country.

In October, 1894, the National Bankers' Association met at Baltimore. During this meeting Hon. J. C. Hendrix, of whom mention has been made in these pages, delivered a speech, in the course of which he thus sneeringly referred to Congress:—

"Men who never had a discount in their lives, and would not be entitled to one; whose highest occupation has been sitting on a barrel at a corner grocery, whittling a piece of wood; others who have followed the plow all day in the hot sun and tried to settle, by the rule of thumb, questions of political economy, over which men of scientific attainments have studied and grown gray—such men come or send their like to the halls of Congress, and they want to dictate the financial policy of the country.''

This sarcastic allusion to members of Congress was cheered to the echo by the hundreds of national bankers present during its delivery.

This cuckoo national bank member of Congress, who spoke so derisively of his fellow legislators, had been, prior to his election to that body, a citizen of Missouri, and from thence had migrated East. He was appointed postmaster of Brooklyn during the first administration of President Cleveland, and after his term of office had expired, became President of a national bank. He was elected to Congress, where his labors in behalf of banks were indefatigable.

It was during this bankers' convention that Charles C. Homer, President of a national bank of Baltimore, brought forward what is known as the Baltimore plan of banking, a scheme which met the approbation of the associated banks.

This plan proposed that all paper money should be issued through the medium of the national banks, and that the redemption of all such bank notes should be guaranteed by the Government.

In the meantime, the banking monopoly was forming plans to seize upon, and to appropriate to itself, the complete and absolute issue and control of the currency

These deeply-laid schemes did not coincide in every particular, but they all concurred in the principle that the banks should issue bank notes to circulate as money, and that the Government should burden itself with the responsibility of finally redeeming all such notes eventually in gold.

The banks of issue, however, were to be the sole beneficiaries of each and every system so proposed.

President Cleveland aligned himself in behalf of these demands of the banks.

This man who persistently exhibited the supposed dangers of a 'fiat money," and who wanted the "best money of the world" as a medium of exchange, was really a fiatist of the most extreme type.

He concentrated all his energies and influence to the end that the banks might grasp the fiat of the nation for their profit.

He was a national bank fiatist.

On December 3, 1894, Congress convened in general session, and President Cleveland transmitted his message to that body.

In the course of this document, he stated that the Secretary of the Treasury had prepared a bill providing for an elastic bank currency.

The President said:—

"Questions relating to our banks and currency are closely connected with the subject just referred to, and they also present some unsatisfactory features. Prominent among them are the lack of elasticity in our currency circulation, and its frequent concentration in financial centers when it is most needed in other parts of the country.

"The absolute divorcement of the Government from the business of banking is the ideal relationship of the Government to the circulation of the currency of the country.

"This condition cannot be immediately reached; but as a step in that direction and as a means of securing a more elastic currency and obviating other objections to the present arrangement of bank circulation, the Secretary of the Treasury presents, in his report, a scheme modifying present banking laws and providing for the issue of circulating notes by State banks, free from taxation under certain limitations.

"The Secretary explains his plan so plainly, and its advantages are developed by him with such remarkable clearness, that any effort on my part to present argument in its support would be superfluous. I shall therefore content myself with an unqualified endorsement of the Secretary's proposed changes in the law, and a brief and imperfect statement of their prominent features.

"It is proposed to repeal all laws providing for the deposit of United States bonds as security for circulation; to permit national banks to issue circulating notes not exceeding in amount 75 per cent. of their paid-up and unimpaired capital, provided they deposit with the Government, as a guarantee fund, in United States legal tender notes, including treasury notes of 1890, a sum equal in amount to 30 per cent. of the notes they desire to issue, this deposit to be maintained at all times, but whenever any bank retires any part of its circulation, a proportional part of its guarantee fund shall be returned to it; to permit the Secretary of the Treasury to prepare and keep on hand ready for issue in case an increase in circulation is desired, blank national bank notes for each bank having circulation, and to repeal the provisions of the present law imposing limitations and restrictions upon banks desiring to reduce or increase their circulation—thus permitting such increase or reduction within the limit of 75 per cent. of capital to be quickly made as emergencies arise."

This scheme outlined in the message of President Cleveland was one of the most remarkable plans of banking ever proposed by the wit of man. It aimed to drive out of circulation every greenback and treasury note, and to totally eliminate silver by an abundant supply of bank notes. Under the false and delusive cry of "The absolute divorcement of the Government from the business of banking," the President sought to throw the business of government into the hands of the banks.

These recommendations of the President demonstrated that he was as fanatical in his belief in the efficacy of a banking monopoly and aristocracy as John Sherman.

He gave official notice that the demands of the banking interest should be granted if he could be successful in swinging Congress into line with his policy.

In a speech of great ability, Hon. Henry W. Coffeen, of Wyoming, referred to these various schemes of banking as follows. He said:—

"PLANS TO AMEND PRESENT SYSTEM.

"One is to give more power to the banks by issuing to them a greater amount of currency without compensation—that is, by issuing to them not only 90 per cent. on their deposits of United States bonds at a charge of 1 per cent. per year, but to furnish them 100 per cent. or possibly 114 per cent. while the Government bonds stand at 14 per cent. premium, and release them also from paying even 1 per cent. tax or interest on this currency furnished thus to the banks, and, as in all of these bank plans, it provides for the issuance of more bonds payable in gold.

"OTHER BONDS FOR SECURITY.

"Another is to allow banks to deposit other than United States bonds for security, and yet make the Government liable for ultimate redemption of all the bank notes and issue gold bonds in place of the greenbacks.

"BALTIMORE PLAN.

"Another plan is to allow banks to have a national form of currency printed for them that may be issued and loaned out as notes of the banks based nominally on bank assets, but the Government to guarantee ultimate redemption. This is the Baltimore or bankers' own plan.

"CARLISLE PLAN.

"Another is to practically turn the entire responsibility of supplying currency over to both State and national banks under a sort of supervisory provision upon deposit of a 5 per cent. and 30 per cent. fund in legal tenders; but relieving the Government entirely from all responsibility of final redemption of circulating bank notes.

"ECKELS PLAN.

"Another is to take 50 per cent. of assets of the bank on which to determine amount of note issues allowed to the banks, and an additional amount may be allowed them under heavy Government charge or taxation as an emergency currency."

His summary of the results of these various systems that were urged on Congress is a masterpiece. He said:—

"WHAT THESE AND OTHER BANK PLANS INVOLVE.

"All of these plans involve the following:—

"1. The banks to control the volume of currency.

"2. The banks to secure all the profits on currency.

"3. The banks to be allowed to exercise the principle called elasticity, another name for sudden contraction or expansion, as their own profits may dictate, without public notice and without regard to the rights or needs of the people generally.

"4. The banks to protect one another as note holders (for they are the principal holders of bank notes under the deposit system of our country), while depositors are left completely unprotected.

"5. The banks to have to themselves and all creditor classes, all the benefits of a highly appreciated gold-standard money, possessing double the purchasing power that money should have in exchange for all other property, while the burden of maintaining the gold redemption for a time and the dishonor of an ultimate and certain breakdown will fall on the Government.

"6. The banks to have all and unrestricted opportunity for pooling their interests and to have all limitations that are disagreeable to them removed, under the pretense of removing obstructions to elasticity.

"7. The banks and money dealers to have the most absolute and fully legalized control over the prices and values of all property, all profits, all industries, all equities of contract, and through these channels they will have the most complete control over all political power and governmental administration that the world has ever seen in any age or clime.

"8. If there is anything else in sight that Congress can give them, they will, as humble conservators of financial integrity and wisdom and as saviors of the country in its time of need, accept that also."

This admirable analysis of the variously proposed schemes of the banks was made by one of the ablest members of Congress.

Mr. Coffeen was not only a practical banker but a very learned student of political economy.

The most important and distinguishing feature between the plans of banking enumerated in his summary and that of the Bank of England is most vital.

In all the plans put forward by the bank monopolists, the Government would be the sole redeemer of the bank notes that would be issued by them.

Under the charter of the Bank of England, the latter was compelled to redeem its own notes in gold. Reaping the profit, it bore the burden of redemption.

The national banking power of the United States, it will be seen, was far more voracious in its greed than that of England.

In pursuance to the recommendation of the President, the currency problem was taken up by the House at once, and on December 10, 1894, the Committee on Banking and Currency began a series of hearings upon this question.

Secretary Carlisle presented his plan to the committee, and he was followed by Comptroller Eckels.

A number of leading bankers also appeared before this committee and gave their views upon this subject.

During the hearings before the committee, Mr. St. John, President of the Mercantile National Bank of New York City, appeared before that body, and the following question was propounded to him by Mr. Cobb:—

"Are you opposed to the use of the greenbacks? If so, state why; and if you are not, state why not."

To which question Mr. St. John made the following reply:—

"I am opposed to asking any sacrifice of the people at large in order to provide profit to banks. I do not dare ask any such thing. I never did and I never will. I would not so sacrifice the popularity that the national banks of the United States have legitimately earned. The great popularity to which they are entitled is being sacrificed by well-meaning doctrinaires, outsiders, who know little about banking. Think of it, the United States issues $100,000,000 of bonds, on which interest is to be paid for ten years at 5 per cent. per annum. At the same time it is proposed that $346,000,000 greenbacks, a debt which does not bear interest, and therefore is saving (at 5 per cent. per annum) $17,300,000 a year to the people at large, shall be retired. More interest-bearing debt to issue to retire them. And as a feature of the proposal is that bank notes, yielding profit to banks as the first essential of their existence, shall supersede them! It is preposterous!"

Of all the financiers who appeared before this committee to give their views, Mr. St. John was the sole banker who opposed the retirement of the greenbacks, the issue of bonds, and an enlargement of the powers of the national banks.

By a vote of 9 to 8, the committee adopted the plan of Secretary Carlisle, and decided to report it to the House without any change, with a recommendation that four days be allowed for debate, and then a vote be taken on the bill.

The bill was reported to the House, December 17th, and a spirited debate at once sprung up regarding the merits of the Carlisle plan.

The main features of this plan of banking proposed that national and other banks could issue circulating notes up to seventy-five per cent. of their paid-up capital. These notes were to be secured by a guarantee fund, consisting of treasury notes, including notes issued under the act of July 14, 1890, equal to thirty per cent. of the circulating notes applied for by the banks. Thus, a bank by depositing $30,000 of greenbacks, or treasury notes, with the Secretary of the Treasury, would receive $100,000 in bank notes—a clear gratuity of $70,000 of loanable capital.

At this time, there were in circulation greenbacks and treasury notes to the amount of $498,287,283. The treasury notes and greenbacks were locked up in the vaults of the banks, and, therefore, by depositing this currency with the Treasury, as a guaranty fund, the banks would have been entitled to receive $1,660,-000,000, which could have been loaned out by them, netting them an annual income exceeding $100,000,000, being a profit of twenty per cent. upon the greenbacks and treasury notes so deposited by them.

This plan provided for a safety fund, whose maximum should be five per cent. upon the total amount of national bank notes so outstanding. This safety fund was to be raised by a small semi-annual tax upon the circulating notes of the banks.

The redemption of these notes would rest upon the Treasury of the United States.

One section of bill proposed to repeal section 9 of the act of July 12, 1882, renewing the charters of the national banks, which section prohibited those banks from surrendering more than $3,000,000 of their circulating notes per month.

This section of the act of 1882, which took away from the banks the absolute power of suddenly prostrating business by contracting the volume of money, was engrafted on that act by the energy and eloquence of Mr. Carlisle.

It was during the debate on this section of the Crapo resolution that he electrified the House and the country by that marvelous logic, which placed him in the forefront of those who antagonized the national banking power.

He now proposed to reverse his former position, by placing the great power of expanding and contracting the volume of money in the hands of the banks.

Who can tell what influence prompted Secretary Carlisle to burn all the bridges behind him in this remarkable change of front since 1882?

Such was the iniquitous scheme suggested by President Cleveland, put into the form of a bill by Secretary

Carlisle, and coached in the House of Representatives by Mr. Springer, of Illinois.

This measure was shrewdly designed to still the demand for free coinage of silver by the substitution of a bank currency therefor.

The Western and Southern members of Congress immediately perceived the intent and scope of this bill, while the advocates of the national banks asserted that the adoption of the Carlisle bill, or the Baltimore plan, would be the "death knell of silver."

The New York Evening Post, December 19th, said:—

"Whatever may be the fate of the Carlisle bill, the movement for currency reform through better banking methods will go on, and it will draw more and more of Mr. Bland's cohorts. Already the newspapers of the mining States have taken the alarm. Some of them say that either the Carlisle bill or the Baltimore plan, if adopted, will be the 'death knell of silver.' Yes, gentlemen, the death knell of silver, in the sense that you mean, is already sounded. It was sounded when the attention of the public was drawn to a cheaper and speedier way of supplying the public with the instruments of exchange needed to transact their daily business."

The opponents of national banks and the single standard of gold knew, as well as the New York Evening Post, that the Carlisle bill was intended to sound the "death knell of silver."

Therefore on December 19th, Mr. Bland proposed to substitute a bill providing for the free coinage of silver.

Those members of Congress, who were urging the passage of the Carlisle bill, saw that there was no possibility of its passage by the House, and, therefore, the bill was withdrawn and a substitute brought in by Mr. Springer. This proposed substitute more nearly followed the Baltimore plan.

The substitute measure also met the approbation of Mr. Carlisle. The most dangerous feature of this substitute also repealed the ninth section of the joint resolution of 1882, which took away from the national banks the power to contract their circulating notes in any sum exceeding $3,000,000 per month.

It must be borne in mind, that it was through the powerful logic and eloquence of Mr. Carlisle that the power of suddenly contracting and expanding the national bank currency was taken away from the banks in 1882.

Yet such was the apostasy of this man to his former principles, that he now stood forth boldly and he unreservedly advocated a system that would give banks of issue the unlimited power to contract and expand the volume of money at their own unrestrained will, and thus place all industry and all property at the complete mercy of those financiers, who had repeatedly attacked the government credit, brought on every panic, and violated the laws of the country.

Mr. Springer, who had introduced the Carlisle bill, and who also brought in this substitute, had served in the House of Representatives for twenty years, during which time he had signalized his public career as a sturdy and consistent advocate of the free coinage of silver, and had always opposed the aggressions of the national banking monopoly.

We now ascertain that his conversion to the Tory system of finance was as sudden as that of Saul of Tarsus when he renounced the Jewish faith to accept the doctrines of Christianity. There the parallel ends.

Mr. Springer became the accredited agent of the administration in its efforts to force this banking bill through Congress.

The Washington Evening Star of January 4, 1895, described his tactics in the following language. It said:—

"His plan of canvass is to have one man of each delegation sound the sentiment of his colleagues. If this canvass is not satisfactory, he will probably still further postpone a caucus, so as to give an opportunity for administration influence to be brought to bear upon those members, who are ascertained to be not set in their purposes as to the measure."

Mr. Springer's efforts to ascertain the views of the House on this bill were anything but encouraging, and hence the administration repeated those tactics which were so influential in securing the repeal of the purchasing clause of the Sherman law.

Again the seductive power of patronage was brought into requisition to such a degree as to anger many of the members of the House.

Moreover, the veto of the seigniorage bill was wonderfully effective in opening the eyes of those Representatives who had voted for the repeal of the purchasing clause, and they saw the pit which the administration had dug for them.

This attempt of the administration to influence the House aroused the latent manhood of its members, and this undemocratic policy of President Cleveland received some well deserved rebukes from those members of the House, who had once been reckoned among the staunchest admirers of the President.

On January 8, 1895, that noble tribune of Democracy, Hon. J. C. Sibley, boldly assailed the coercive measures of the administration for its attempts to push this bill through under whip and spur, and the speaker incidentally exposed the dastardly means by which the repeal of the purchasing clause was secured in August, 1893. Mr. Sibley said:—

"Have Americans become so spiritless that they have no rebuke for the imperiousness of a would-be autocrat? No answer to the attempted usurpation of legislative rights? Do men tell me that the power of the administration was not used to force the repeal of the Sherman bill? Why, Mr. Chairman, there are members of this House who told me with their own lips that they were against the repeal of this bill, and four days afterward they came forward and voted for it, and when a few months afterward I asked them why, they told me that their banks asked it and that they had been promised positions for constituents if they supported the repeal! Are the offices, are the positions of trust of the country to be bestowed upon those persons, and those persons only, who support the will of the Chief Magistrate?"

Mr. Coombs: The gentleman from Pennsylvania makes a broad assertion against the administration. Now, is he willing to give the names of any members in relation to that statement?

Mr. Sibley: I will say to the gentleman from New York that I went two or three days ago and asked a member for the privilege of making the statement to which I have just referred when the matter came up for consideration in the House, and he said, 'Mr. Sibley, it would place me in a very bad position with my constituents, and I am unwilling to do it.'

A Member: I should think it would.

Mr. Coombs: I ask you if you think it fair to make so broad a charge against the administration of helping to bribe a member of the House, without being willing to give the name? In all fairness it is only right, as you have made the statement, to give the name of the party.

Mr. Sibley: Mr. Chairman, on the question of fairness and honor, I shall leave each man to be the judge for himself. The gentleman from New York must permit me to exercise that privilege. I am attempting to express my own opinion and endeavoring to show the influences which have prompted certain action in this House, and I have no hesitancy in saying that if you take the golden padlock off the lips of the members of this body, two out of three men in this House, I believe, would corroborate my statement, at least as to the justice of it—

Mr. Coombs: But the gentleman makes a statement which gives a right to every member on this floor to ask that he shall name the man.

Mr. Sibley (continuing): That Executive influence shall not be used. Mr. Chairman, I am going to 'talk out' this time. I am not going to be silent any longer. I have had a padlock on my lips as long as I propose to wear it. Why, you remember when old Dionysius—

Mr. Outhwaite: What was it put the padlock on your lips? [Laughter.]

Mr. Sibley: Because, sir, I did not want to rebuke an administration that I hoped, before the close of the year 1894, would see the error of its ways and keep with the American people the pledges which had been made by the Democratic party. [Applause.]

Mr. Outhwaite: But what was it put the padlock on your lips?

Mr. Sibley. When Dionysius, the tyrant of Syracuse—

Mr. Outhwaite: Was it Dionysius that put the padlock on your lips?

Mr. Sibley: Mr. Chairman, if I had an hour's time with my friend from Ohio I would like to have it out with him. I want to tell him that I am not talking here for the benefit of men who would rather ride to hell in a handcart than to walk to heaven supported by the staff of honest industry, as it has been said. [Laughter.] I am not talking for the benefit of those people who place more value upon a bobtail flush than they do upon a contrite heart. [Laughter.]

Representatives Coombs and Outhwaite, who had interrupted the speech of Mr. Sibley, were two of the most prominent cuckoos of the House. The last named member was well taken care of by the administration, by receiving an appointment as a member on the Ordinance Board, at a salary of $8,000 per annum.

During the time the Springer bill was up for consideration before the House, an amendment was offered to section 4 in the following language:—

"Section 4. That from and after July 1, 1895, ten per cent. of the cash reserve required by law shall be kept in coin or coin certificates, and not less than one half of such coin or coin certificates shall be in gold coin or gold certificates, and that such cash reserve required by law shall be kept in coin or coin certificates in amounts increased by ten per cent. of the whole cash reserve required to be kept by law, on and after the first day of each quarter of the calendar year, until the whole cash reserve shall be in coin or coin certificates; and not less than one half of such cash reserve shall be at all times in gold coin or gold certificates."

The object of this amendment to the Springer bill sought to compel the banks to maintain a reserve of gold and silver coin, and thus bear the burden of redemption which had heretofore been borne by the Government. The proposed reserve of gold and silver coin was designed as a substitute to take the place of the lawful money reserve, required by law to be kept by the banks.

It was from the bank reserves of lawful money that these institutions furnished the greenbacks and treasury notes to raid the gold reserve.

On February 6, 1895, this amendment was sharply attacked by Mr. Hendrix, on the ground that it would create a new demand for gold, and therefore would start a fresh raid upon the Treasury. This statement of Mr. Hendrix was made after Mr. Springer had stated that the national banks, on the 2d of October, 1894, held gold coin to the amount of $175,000,000, and that besides this amount of gold coin, these banks held $185,000,000 in legal tender notes.

From the debate upon this amendment we quote as follows:—

Mr. Hendrix: Mr. Chairman, I rise to oppose this amendment, because it is impracticable and unintelligent. It seeks to defeat the very purpose for which this legislation is presented to the House. You propose to attempt to stop the raid upon the Treasury for gold, and you turn around and compel 4,000 national banks of this country to immediately start a fresh raid upon the Treasury for the purpose of getting gold to comply with this law. Now, the banks are already charged with hoarding too much gold. We are doing our best to try to undo the tendency which is abroad to hoard the precious metal. You pass this clause of the bill and it becomes mandatory where it is now simply a matter of commercial option. You would compel the banks to send to the nine sub-treasuries with their treasury notes, and to the one sub-treasury at San Francisco and the one at New York with their United States legal tender notes to get gold coin.

"I want to call the attention of the gentleman from

Massachusetts (Mr. Walker) to something that will impress him at once. You have already provided in section 4 of this bill that all silver certificates now outstanding shall, when received in the Treasury of the United States, be retired and canceled, and silver certificates in denominations less than $10 shall be issued in their stead. I will ask the gentleman how he expects a bank in the city of Boston, or in the city of Worcester, to say nothing of the banks in New York, to settle their balances at the clearing houses on the days of heavy exchanges when they are drawn upon, as they frequently are, for $4,000,000 or $5,000,000, in silver certificates, if they are of denominations of less than $10? Why, sir, we would all have to go to the clearing house in a coach and four in order to settle under the operation of this clause."

MR. LIVINGSTON: With all the other paper of larger denominations than $10, why should there be any difficulty?

MR. HENDRIX: But you propose by this bill to retire the other paper money.

MR. LIVINGSTON: Not at all.

MR. HENDRIX: That is the essence of the proposition. Instead of letting the banks hold on to the greenback certificates, which they have now, and keep them in their reserve, you are going to destroy the value of those certificates as reserve money, and compel the banks to substitute for them one of two things, silver or gold. Now, if you were a banker, which would you choose? Every banker in the country, when obliged to make the choice, will choose the one that is the more precious in his opinion.

MR. LIVINGSTON: The gentleman forgets that the same section provides for the national banks issuing nothing less than ten dollar notes.

MR. HENDRIX: That is all right, but national banks cannot keep national bank notes as a reserve. A national bank is not authorized to count national bank notes as reserve. The point is that you destroy the practicability of making settlements at the clearing houses. A man comes in and wants legal tender, and under this clause you will have to cart him out a lot of silver or gold. Then he has to get a vehicle to take it to the place where he is to pay his legal tender. If you are going to destroy the value of the gold certificates as a reserve and compel the banks to keep gold, you are simply imposing a great burden upon them and upon the public in the transaction of their business. It is impossible to settle the clearing house balances in that way. The clearing house in New York has provided for the difficulty by issuing gold clearing house certificates, based upon coin, placed in the vaults by the Clearing House Committee; but this bill would destroy the use of those certificates as a part of the reserve, and would compel the banks to keep their reserve in the two coins or in the Government certificates therefor. It is simply impracticable to carry out this plan in the ordinary transaction of the banking business. The banks now are showing too great a tendency to hoard up gold, and I do not want to see anything put in this bill that is going to sequestrate gold. I want it made so free that the great deposit in the United States of America of the yellow metal will not be in the banks, but by the reason of the operation of this law, will be transferred to the Treasury of the United States, so that the public statements of the Treasury will give notice to the whole world that we have lots of gold, that we are on a gold basis, and that we are going to remain there. [Applause.]

Mr. Walker: Mr. Chairman, in the first place, as to the clearing house certificates, they are exactly what the clearing house chooses to make them, as to form and substance.

Mr. Hendrix: Mr. Chairman, I am surprised that a gentleman who has stood upon this floor as the great commercial apostle, should make such a statement.

Mr. Walker: I want to state to the gentleman

that the clearing houses of New York and in other cities, can make the clearing house certificates just what they choose; therefore we need not bother about them. They are not within the law; they are outside of it, and their certificates are entirely within the control of the clearing houses.

"Now the banks have got $175,000,000 in gold to-day, and if gold goes to a premium the banks will get the premium on it, and the gentleman from New York knows, and everybody else knows, that that is why they are hoarding the gold. But if we compel them by law to hold the gold as a part of their reserve, we destroy the interest the bad bankers have in putting gold to a premium. Is not that so? [Cries of "Yes, yes," and laughter.]

"You have one silver man here, the gentleman from Montana (Mr. Hartman), offering an amendment to cut out half of the use of silver at the custom house, and you have had another man, an enemy of silver, though he thinks himself its friend, trying to prevent it from being used in denominations above $10. Now, I stand here as a true friend of silver. [Laughter.] The gentleman from New York (Mr. Hendrix) stands here as a banker.

"Mr. Chairman, the bankers, not one of them in the whole country, from Maine to Georgia, from the Atlantic to the Pacific, has offered a single suggestion in a practical bill to relieve the Treasury. They have all been for banks. They meet at Baltimore; they meet at Boston; they pass resolutions adopting proposed amendments to the law to increase their own profits, and they tell us on the floor of this House that it is none of their business what becomes of the Treasury of the United States. They have got $175,000,000 of gold. They will hold on to it as long as they can, and when it goes to a premium they will get the premium upon it. Now, I want a law to compel them to use that gold to redeem their own notes over their own counter, and thus relieve the United States Treasury, and also in that way take away any inducement they may have to put gold to a premium."

Mr. Hendrix: Will the gentleman permit an interruption?

Mr. Walker: I will yield for a question.

Mr. Hendrix: If you provide that the note redemption fund at the Treasury Department shall be kept in gold, will not that meet your desire to have the banks redeem their notes in gold?

Mr. Walker: Not at all, or only partially. [Laughter.] How much time have I remaining, Mr. Chairman?

The Chairman: The gentleman has one minute.

Mr. Bryan: Mr. Chairman, I ask unanimous consent that the gentleman be allowed to proceed for five minutes longer.

There was no objection.

Mr. Walker: Now, Mr. Chairman, I will ask the gentleman from New York to repeat his question.

Mr. Hendrix: My question is this: Would you not be satisfied with having the note redemption fund which the national banks are obliged to provide, kept in gold at the Treasury, where the banks are required by law to redeem?

Mr. Walker: Do you mean the 5 per cent. redemption fund?

Mr. Hendrix: The 5 per cent. redemption fund.

Mr. Walker: No, sir. I want to say to the gentleman and to the House and to the country that the people of the United States propose to keep all their dollars of equal value. The people of the United States have made a long step in advance in discovering that it is costing them millions upon millions for the United States Government to do this—redeeming of paper money at the United States Treasury, not maintaining the 5 per cent. redemption, but redemption in large blocks. Therefore they are upon the eve of making the banks do it at their own risk and at their own cost and over their own counters, thus relieving the people of the tax of twenty or thirty million dollars a year which they now pay for this service to banks, and that the banks themselves ought to do.

"Here in this section of this bill is the first step in that direction—nine tenths of 1 per cent. to be kept in both kinds of coin—four and a half tenths of 1 per cent. to be kept in gold coin. The banks now hold $175,000,000 in their vaults. When these bankers go to bed at night and say their prayers, they say, 'O Lord, we beseech Thee to keep gold from going to a premium tomorrow.' But they know if it does go to a premium they will make 2 or 3 or 4 per cent. profit on the gold in their vaults. When they get up in the morning they say —following the fashion of some prayers which we hear at the Speaker's desk and elsewhere, informing the Lord what has been done—'O Lord, we thank Thee that gold has not gone to a premium,' but it is no more than human for them to remember, as the night before, the profit if it should go to a premium. The question is, shall the bankers of this country protect every dollar of their own paper circulation at their own expense and their own risk and not compel the people to be taxed to do it for them at the United States Treasury?"

Mr. COOMBS: Will the gentleman allow me an inquiry?

Mr. WALKER: Yes, if it is short.

Mr. COOMBS: Does not the gentleman by this provision put it in the power of the banks and make it their duty to hoard gold, thereby holding a larger whip over the community than they otherwise would? I submit that this amendment would force the banks to become hoarders of gold, instead of leaving it in the channels of trade and in the hands of the people.

Mr. WALKER: Now, the gentleman is making an argument. If he wishes to do that, let him get his own five minutes. It is 'in the channels of trade' when it is in bank reserves, as the gentleman well knows.

"Mr. Chairman, I want to say another thing, which I regret to say. I have the very highest respect for banks and bankers. I remember the record of George Peabody, and of Corcoran of this city, and hundreds of other bankers. Noble men! Many men of this class have been the most generous, noble-hearted, public-spirited men outside of their business there ever have been in this world. But I remember also that never in any country, under any circumstances whatever, did the bankers ever improve the banking and currency laws or the financial conditions of their country except at the point of the financial bayonet, held by the Government of the country in which the banks were located, namely, by the force of law devised in parliament. We have got to adopt that policy in this country.

"Now, I challenge Henry W. Cannon of New York, I challenge Lyman B. Gage of Chicago, I challenge George E. Leighton of St. Louis—three as honorable men as live and as skilled in finance, men who in financial matters stand the peers, if not above, any other three men in this country—to draw a bill that will do what they are saying ought to be done, and lecturing us for not doing. Bankers are condemning members of Congress as clowns and fools because we do not accomplish what they want us to do; yet they themselves could not draw a bill which would do it that would get two votes in five in this House in this generation or the next. I say we ought not to heed here and now the protests of the bankers against their being brought into line with the banks of every first-class nation of the world." [Applause.]

These extracts, taken from the Congressional Record, exhibit several remarkable facts. They show that the national banks, while demanding that the United States should redeem all its obligations in gold, and issue bonds to maintain a gold reserve for that purpose, were utterly opposed to being compelled to maintain a gold reserve for the redemption of their notes.

The extreme selfishness of these financial institutions is exposed by Mr. Walker, a stanch friend of the national banking system, wherein he states that the redemption features of the national banking system had cost the people from $20,000,000 to $30,000,000 per annum. He shows that the cost of this system of redemption was thrown on the Government.

On February 7, 1895, Mr. Springer brought up a motion to engross the bill and pass it to a third reading. This was defeated by a vote of 162 nays to 135 yeas. He then moved to reconsider this vote, but, on motion of Mr. Hatch, it was laid upon the table by a vote of 135 yeas to 124 nays.

The defeat of the Springer bill was decisive.

Therefore this measure, which the gold standard fanatics openly boasted would be the "death knell" of silver, fell at the hands of the public executioner.

The grip of this Tory-Republican administration was loosened for all time to come.

CHAPTER XIV.

NATIONAL BANKS AND THE ADMINISTRATION COMBINE TO ISSUE BONDS IN TIME OF PEACE.

"Avoid the accumulation of debt, not only by shunning occasions of expense, but by vigorous exertions in time of peace to discharge the debts which unavoidable wars may have occasioned, not ungenerously throwing upon posterity the burdens which we ourselves ought to bear."—Washington.

Ever since the special session of Congress, beginning on the 7th of August, 1893, the national banks of New York City continuously bent all their energies toward depleting the gold reserve of the Treasury and forcing an issue of bonds.

Without the active co-operation of these associated banks, it would have been impossible for the gold speculators to have obtained the greenbacks and treasury notes to present to the Treasurer for obtaining the gold for exportation to Europe. As the national banks of New York City persevered in the policy of hoarding up all greenbacks and treasury notes, that found their way over their counters in the ordinary transactions of business, the means of exhausting the gold reserve were practically unlimited. In fact, more gold was actually shipped abroad than was needed in Europe. It was asserted by unquestioned authority, that these banks exported tens of millions of gold to Europe, and that it was returned without the packages containing it ever having been opened; and that this policy was carried on by the banks, with the avowed intention of compelling Congress to fund the greenbacks and treasury notes into bonds.

One of the reasons stated by the President in his message of August 8, 1893, was, that the purchasing clause of the Sherman law must be repealed, as the only remedy to check the exportation of gold. This was the sum and substance of all the arguments, advanced in both Houses of Congress, by those who urged the repeal of the Sherman law.

These reasons and arguments were the merest subterfuges of those public men who were determined, at all hazards, to manacle the American people to a single standard of gold, and to make all business pay toll at the counters of national banks.

As heretofore stated, the gold gamblers persevered in draining the Treasury of its gold during the time that the repeal bill was pending in Congress, a policy which was upheld by the subsidized press. Every withdrawal of gold was given prominence, in these journals, as a means of frightening the timid.

As shown by a report of the Comptroller of the Currency, the national banks of New York City, on the 2d of October, 1894, held gold coin to the amount of $175,000,000, in addition to legal tender notes or greenbacks to the amount of $185,000,000. On the 19th of December, of the same year, the bank holdings of legal tenders had decreased to $119,513,000.

These figures demonstrate that, while the banks held $175,000,000 in gold, they had used their legal tender notes, or greenbacks, in looting the gold reserve to obtain gold to buy these bonds.

In speaking of this course of the bankers in thus forcing an issue of bonds, the New York World editorially said:—

"The banks have no apparent use for gold.

"They have absolutely no obligations of any kind, near or remote, which are payable in gold.

"Nevertheless these banks are hoarding gold in large quantities, at a time when to do so is to subject the Government to heavy and needless expense.

"Thus the clearing house banks of New York alone, hold over $81,000,000 in gold for which they have no use."

In referring to the immense holdings of gold by the New York banks, the World further said:—

"If they should turn it into the Treasury and take greenbacks instead, they would be in every respect as well equipped as now to meet their obligations, while the Government would not have to issue another $100,000,000 of bonds, which it will cost the country $220,000,000 to pay, principal and interest.

"Are they seriously expecting gold to go to a premium?

"Or are they and the banks all over the country in a tacit "combine" to compel repeated bond issues for their speculative profit? These banks ought to answer these questions."

On the following day, the World, in speaking of the answers of the New York bankers to this accusation, editorially said:—

"Their replies are evasive, shifty, insincere.

"They have no obligations payable in gold.

"There is no possible reason for them to hoard gold, except that they expect a premium upon it, or that they wish to force the Government to borrow money which it does not need."

Although the World was an advocate of the gold standard, yet it did not hesitate to censure the banks of New York City for their traitorous attempts to cripple the United States. With renewed energy, the banks persevered in their attack upon the gold reserve, and from the 17th day of January, 1895, to February 13th, they drew gold out of the Treasury to the amount of $38,262,540. In a single day, January 25th, they drew out $7,156,046, although at that time these identical banks held a stock of gold exceeding $100,000,000.

The influential Journal of Commerce, charged that the New York banks, owing to their combined policy to cripple the Government, had purposely caused a needless and artificial scarcity of gold to the amount of $503,000,000.

On February 4, 1895, it editorially said:—

"WHY MUST WE BORROW?

"1. Because, while up to 1892 the banks supplied all gold required for export, since July 1, 1892, they have drawn for that purpose from the Treasury, two hundred and thirty millions.

"2. Because, within the same period, the banks have withheld gold from customs, payments which, under their former usage, would have given the Treasury a gold income amounting to two hundred and seventy-three millions.

"3. Because, within the last thirty-one months, the Treasury has suffered from this policy of the banks a direct and indirect artificial gold depletion of five hundred and three millions.

"Here, in a nutshell, is the explanation of the condition of the Treasury and of the causes compelling its virtually needless loans."

On the other hand, the New York Times, with its accustomed loyalty to the money power, urged these banks to coerce Congress to do their bidding. It said:—

"But we close, as we began, with the unqualified statement that Congress will not do this—that it will not do anything, unless it be forced to action by the overwhelming pressure of public opinion. It is sheer folly to rely on anything else. This force organized, directed, and concentrated upon Congress, as it was in the spring of 1891, when the free coinage bill was killed, as it was in 1893, when the repeal bill was enacted, will do the work. Nothing else will."

Since the repeal of the purchasing clause of the Sherman law up to this time, gold to the amount of $172,-000,000 was withdrawn from the Treasury, despite the fact that President Cleveland, in his message of August 8, 1893, gravely declared that the repeal of the purchasing clause of the Sherman law would stop the depletion of the gold reserve.

On the 17th day of January, 1894, the Secretary of the Treasury invited bids for the sale of bonds to strengthen the gold reserve. The amount offered was fifty millions for sale, and delivery was to be made February 3d.

At the time of this sale of bonds, the banks of New York City held many millions of gold, but, instead of using their holdings to pay for these bonds, they presented treasury notes, and drew out of the Treasury $20,211,000 in gold to take up these bonds.

Therefore, while these banks were demanding issues of bonds to maintain the public credit, they utilized this very issue as a means to further deplete the Treasury of its gold.

The Secretary claimed that, under the provisions of the Resumption Act, he had full authority to issue bonds for the redemption of the greenbacks. The gold reserve, thus expanded beyond the one hundred million dollar mark, was again attacked by these conspirators with the evident purpose of forcing gold to a premium, and to compel an additional issue of bonds.

The gold reserve again began to melt away, and, on

November 13, 1894, the Secretary of the Treasury advertised for bids for the sale of an additional $50,000,000 of 10-year 5 per cent. bonds. Four hundred and eighty-seven bids were received for these bonds so offered.

To pay for these new bonds, immense quantities of gold were again withdrawn from the Treasury. United States Senator Gray, a gold standard champion, admitted this fact in a speech in which he stated that, from December 1, 1894, to February 13, 1895, $80,785,000 was exchanged for treasury notes, of which only $36,852,389 was exported.

As a matter of fact, a large amount of this was hoarded for future purchases of bonds.

On December 5th, the reserve had been expanded to $111,142,021, and immediately this gold reserve, thus freshly built up by this second sale of bonds, was again attacked by the New York bankers, by exchanging greenbacks for gold at the sub-treasury in New York City.

In the beginning of February, 1895, the withdrawal of gold became greater than ever before known, and the banks openly avowed their intentions to force a third issue of bonds. Meanwhile, it was rumored in Wall street, that the Secretary of the Treasury had secretly negotiated a sale of bonds to Messrs. Belmont and Morgan.

In speaking of both of these facts, the New York Press, of February 7th, said:—

"GOLD TO BUY BONDS—WALL STREET READY TO ROB TREASURER PETER TO PAY PAUL.

"Fully $700,000 in gold coin was withdrawn from the sub-treasury yesterday. While this is not a large amount as compared with other days, it is significant and suggestive. It means nothing more or less than that the banks and trust companies in the city are preparing to take up a considerable portion of the prospective bond issue.

"But it is more than likely that the banks will get even with the Government after all. The quiet gold hoarding that is going on just now means that this money is to be used to buy the new bonds, and after they are once obtained, it will be a comparatively easy matter for the purchasers to replenish their vaults and safes, with practically the same coin again by means of legal tenders. In short, it is only another instance of Peter being robbed to pay Paul.

NO ISSUE AT PRESENT.

"Both Mr. Morgan and Mr. Belmont were at their offices yesterday, which gave color to the report that everything was "fixed" so far as the new issue is concerned. Mr. Belmont declined to be interviewed, and Mr. Morgan had only this to say for publication: 'I am satisfied that no announcement of a bond issue will be made until after a vote in the House on the Springer bill. I am also satisfied that President Cleveland and Secretary Carlisle are keenly alive to the situation."

On February 8, 1895, the Secretary of the Treasury negotiated a secret contract with two great banking houses of London, England, for the sale of $62,000,000 of 4 per cent. thirty-year bonds.

The text of the infamous contract is as follows:—

"CONTRACT.

"This agreement entered into, this 8th day of February, 1895, between the Secretary of the Treasury of the United States, of the first part, and Messrs. August Belmont & Co., of New York, on behalf of Messrs. N. M. Rothschild & Sons, of London, England, and themselves, and Messrs. J. P. Morgan & Co., of New York, on behalf of Messrs. J. S. Morgan & Co., of London, and themselves, parties of the second part.

"Witnesseth: Whereas it is provided by the Revised Statutes of the United States (section 3,700) that the Secretary of the Treasury may purchase coin with any of the bonds or notes of the United States authorized by law, at such rates and upon such terms as he may deem most advantageous to the public interests; and the Secretary of the Treasury now deems that an emergency exists in which the public interests require that, as hereinafter provided, coin shall be purchased with the bonds of the United States, of the description hereinafter mentioned, authorized to be issued under the act entitled 'An act to provide for the resumption of specie payments,' approved January 14, 1875, being bonds of the United States described in an act of Congress approved July 14, 1870, entitled 'An act to authorize the refunding of the national debt.'

"Now, therefore, the said parties of the second part hereby agree to sell and deliver to the United States 3,500,000 ounces of standard gold coin of the United States, at the rate of $17.80441 per ounce, payable in United States 4 per cent. thirty-year coupon or registered bonds, said bonds to be dated February 1, 1895, and payable at the pleasure of the United States after thirty years from date, issued under the acts of Congress of July 14, 1870, January 20, 1871, and January 14, 1875, bearing interest at the rate of 4 per cent. per annum, payable quarterly.

"First, Such purchase and sale of gold coin being made on the following conditions:—

"1. At least one half of all coin deliverable hereinunder shall be obtained in and shipped from Europe, but the shipments shall not be required to exceed 300,000 ounces per month, unless the parties of the second part shall consent thereto.

"2. All deliveries shall be made at any of the subtreasuries or at any other legal depository of the United States.

"3. All gold coins delivered, shall be received on the basis of 25.8 grains of standard gold per dollar, if within limit of tolerance.

"4. Bonds delivered under this contract are to be delivered free of accrued interest, which is to be assumed and paid by the parties of the second part at the time of their delivery to them.

"Second, Should the Secretary of the Treasury desire to offer or sell any bonds of the United States, on or before the 1st day of October, 1895, he shall first offer the same to the parties of the second part; but thereafter he shall be free from every such obligation to the parties of the second part.

"Third, The Secretary of the Treasury hereby reserves the right, within ten days from the date hereof, in case he shall receive authority from Congress therefor, to substitute any bonds of the United States, bearing 3 per cent. interest, of which the principal and interest shall be specifically payable in United States gold coin of the present weight and fineness for the bonds herein alluded to; such 3 per cent. bonds to be accepted by the parties of the second part at par, i. e., at $18.60465 per ounce of standard gold.

"Fourth, No bonds shall be delivered to the parties of the second part, or either of them, except in payment for coin from time to time received hereunder; whereupon the Secretary of the Treasury of the United States shall and will deliver the bonds as herein provided, at such places as shall be designated by the parties of the second part. Any expense of delivery out of the United States, shall be assumed and paid by the parties of the second part.

"Fifth, In consideration of the purchase of such coin, the parties of the second part, and their associates hereunder, assume and will bear all the expense and inevitable loss of bringing gold from Europe hereunder; and, as far as lies in their power, will exert all financial influence and will make all legitimate efforts to protect the Treasury of the United States against withdrawals of gold pending the complete performance of this contract.

"In witness whereof, the parties hereto have hereunto set their hands in five parts, this 8th day of February, 1895.

J. G. Carlisle,
Secretary of the Treasury.
August Belmont & Co.,

On behalf of Messrs. N. M. Rothschild & Son, London, and themselves.

J. P. Morgan & Co.,

On behalf of Messrs. J. S. Morgan & Co., London, and themselves.

Attest:

W. E. Curtis.

Francis Lynde Stetson."

If any citizen of the United States doubts that there is a great international gold and bond trust, seeking to bind the world to its golden chariot, let him read this notorious contract and be convinced of his error.

A construction of this contract discloses the following remarkable facts: First, that two American banking companies of New York City represented two great banking houses of London, England, and Secretary Carlisle presumably the United States. Second, the gold coin so purchased should be paid into the Treasury at the rate of 300,000 ounces per month, except these foreign firms should agree to make larger monthly payments. One half of this gold was to be obtained in Europe. Third, the Secretary of the Treasury bound himself not to offer or sell any bonds of the United States to any other parties, on or before the 1st day of October, 1895, without first offering all such bonds to this foreign syndicate. This placed the Government at the absolute mercy of alien bankers, and was a most cowardly surrender of the interests of the people to a foreign gold trust. Fourth, the Secretary of the Treasury reserved the right to substitute bonds specifically payable in United States gold coin, provided Congress should confer authority upon him to make such substitution. The purpose of this clause in the contract was, should Congress consent thereto, to issue bonds specifically payable in gold coin, and thus commit the country to an issue of gold bonds. Therefore, should the United States issue an obligation specifically payable in gold, this example would be followed by every creditor, and every mortgage, bond, note, or other security or evidence of debt, would become a gold obligation, and the nation and its citizens would be bound hand and foot, and delivered over to the tender mercies of the national banking money power and the international gold trust.

Is there an international gold trust? Clause five of paragraph four of this contract is an explicit acknowledgment on the part of the United States, that there is such an institution. That clause is as follows: "In consideration of the purchase of such coin, the parties of the second part, and their associates hereunder, assume and will bear all the expense and inevitable loss of bringing gold from Europe hereunder; and as far as lies in their power, will exert all financial influence, and will make all legitimate efforts to protect the Treasury of the United States against the withdrawals of gold, pending the complete performance of this contract."

Think of it! This great nation having resources far exceeding the whole of those of Europe, with a population of seventy millions of energetic people, ascertaining that its Secretary of the Treasury had bought the protection of a foreign bond syndicate!

Let them further ponder, that this syndicate considered itself so powerful, that it could protect the Treasury of the United States against the withdrawals of gold therefrom.

In speaking of this transaction, the New York Tribune asserted that this syndicate could control the money of the world. It said:—

"No plan that did not provide for getting gold from Europe, and that did not also provide a means to check shipments of gold to Europe, could give the Treasury one dollar of permanent relief. This undertaking to change the whole course of exchange, must necessarily be expensive, but the syndicate can do it, and the Treasury is accordingly benefited."

As a result thus far of President Cleveland's warfare upon silver, we find that this high public officer, who wanted the purchasing clause repealed to check the withdrawal of gold from the Treasury, made an unconditional surrender to the international gold trust. He sought to buy its protection.

The bonds so issued under this secret contract were sold at a premium of only four and one-half cents on the dollar. At that time, the same class of bonds having but twelve years to run, sold at a premium of ten and one-half cents. In the meantime, it was rumored that the administration had entered into a secret negotiation with this syndicate, and on the 8th of February, 1895, President Cleveland transmitted this contract to Congress, accompanied by a message, in which he requested permission of Congress to substitute a 3 per cent. gold bond in lieu of the bonds so sold to this syndicate. Immediately upon the appearance of this message in the House, Mr. Wilson, of West Virginia, reported a joint resolution authorizing the Secretary of the Treasury to issue gold bonds to the amount of

$65,116,275. At the same time, a similar bill was introduced in the Senate by Mr. Vilas, of Wisconsin.

During the debate on these measures, it was pointed out by the silver advocates that the 4 per cent. bonds sold to this syndicate were worth $1.19½, although they had been sold at $1.04½, netting the syndicate a profit of not less than $10,000,000 by this transaction. It was also charged that the administration had sold these bonds to the banking houses of Rothschild and Morgan at this low figure, with the express purpose of depreciating the national credit with a view of forcing an issue of gold bonds.

The attempt to force the Wilson resolution through the House failed by the decisive vote of 167 nays to 120 years.

The absurd pretense put forth by President Cleveland and his adherents, that the national credit must be strengthened by substituting the term gold, for that of coin in its obligations, was fully exposed by subsequent events.

Ten days after the issue of the original bonds, nearly thirty millions of them were sent to London to be sold by the syndicate. In twenty-two minutes after these bonds were placed on the market, the subscriptions for them amounted to ten times the sum total of the bonds.

To-day, these bonds that were thus disposed of by this nefarious contract to a foreign syndicate at $1.04½, are now worth $1.29½—being an advance of twenty-five cents on the dollar!

Again the bold attempt of President Cleveland to fasten the gold standard on the country ignominiously failed.

On February 7, 1895, one day previous to the communication of the bond contract, House bill 8,705 was brought forward in the House of Representatives. This measure proposed to authorize the Secretary of the Treasury to issue $500,000,000 of bonds to maintain a sufficient gold reserve, and to redeem and retire United States notes.

These repeated attempts of the administration, and its satellites in Congress, to burden the people with an enormous bonded indebtedness, is one of the most remarkable phenomena in all history. It seemed that the whole energy of President Cleveland was directed with an eye single to loading down the country with a vast perpetual debt, even though it would ruin the party which had honored him so frequently. He unscrupulously used the immense patronage of his office to force his measures through Congress, but beyond securing the repealing of the purchasing clause, he failed in every instance to coerce Congress into submission to his will. He likewise failed in this proposed bond measure, for, on a motion to engross the bill and pass it to a third reading, it was defeated by a vote of 162 nays to 135 yeas.

In a few months after the secret bond contract with the Morgan Rothschild syndicate, the attack upon the gold reserve began anew, as the bank of England bid $4.91 for gold, being equivalent to a premium of one per cent. on the dollar. Whenever the bank of England desired to increase its stock of gold, it raised the price at its counter, and this policy attracted gold from all over the world. The usual exchange value of a British sovereign in gold is $4.86, therefore, by raising the price to $4.91, it gave notice to all the world that it was offering a premium for gold.

In August, 1895, while the rate of exchange stood at $4.91, the New York bankers raided the reserve to obtain gold to ship to London for this premium. In that month, $15,000,000 was withdrawn from the Treasury and exported to that country. In the following month, the high rate of exchange still continued, and the gold gamblers of Wall street drew $16,000,000 out of the Treasury for exportation. This process still continued, and, in the meantime, the administration opened negotiations with the banking house of J. P. Morgan & Co., for the disposal of $200,000,000 of thirty-year 4 per cent. bonds at private sale.

This brazen attempt of the administration to again sell bonds at private sale to this syndicate, at a figure away below the market price, brought forth such a storm of indignation and protest that even President Cleveland quailed before it.

Therefore, on January 6, 1896, Secretary Carlisle issued a circular, inviting proposals for the sale of 4 per cent. thirty-year bonds. The bids received for this proposed series of bonds aggregated $568,259,850— more than five times the amount of the bonds offered.

The Morgan syndicate offered to take the whole issue at $1.1069. This bid was six per cent. higher than the syndicate would have paid at private sale, had it been consummated. It was a little over six per cent. more than the syndicate paid for the issue of the $62,000,000 of February 8, 1895. There were 780 bids at prices higher than that offered by the Morgan syndicate.

It will be borne in mind that this bid of the syndicate for these bonds, at an advance of six per cent. over that of the same Morgan-Rothschild syndicate for the issue of February 8, 1895, was for coin bonds of the same kind as this latter issue. The fact that this syndicate was willing to pay several million dollars more for the same class of bonds, as those negotiated under the secret contract of February 8th, is evidence that the objections of President Cleveland to coin bonds, rested upon the flimsiest pretense.

It must be remembered that this increased price was offered many months after Congress refused to authorize the Secretary of the Treasury to issue bonds specifically payable in gold coin, and that the Matthews resolution adopted by Congress, January 25, 1878, declaring that the bonds of the United States could be legally paid in standard silver dollars of 412½ grains, was unrepealed, and was in full force and effect as declaratory of the financial policy of the United States.

The continued efforts of President Cleveland to retire the greenbacks and treasury notes, and to issue bonds in lieu thereof, seemed to have taken possession of his mind with a zeal approaching that of mania.

His determined attitude on these public questions, exercised great influence upon the opinions of many Democratic members of Congress. Hence, many of the leaders of that party, who, prior to 1892, were the most consistent advocates of free coinage of silver, suddenly changed their positions upon these important questions, and did the bidding of President Cleveland, in his attempt to fasten a gold standard and a national banking system upon the people, with a zeal that was remarkable. Many of these Congressmen were defeated in the election of 1894, and President Cleveland manifested his fatherly care for his new-born protégés by appointing them to Federal offices; judgeships, postmasterships, and various other appointments, were handed around to these apostates to Jeffersonian principles, as a reward for their treachery to the people, and their fidelity to that man who had sought to disrupt that great and historic party, which had taken him from obscurity and elevated him to the highest positions in the gift of the people.

The total amount of bonds issued during his administration was $262,000,000.

In the meantime, Secretary Carlisle announced that he would redeem silver dollars in gold, should it become necessary to maintain the parity of the metals. The scheme of the national banking money power was now consummated, as far as it lay in the power of the Secretary, inasmuch as he evidenced a purpose to treat more than 500,000,000 standard silver dollars as mere credit money, redeemable in gold. This paved the way for a demand of the national banks, that the Government issue sufficient bonds to take up and retire this silver money from circulation.

While President Cleveland was "working in Congress" by means of his patronage, the money power was working through its various associations and through the press to train the people to accept the absurd principle, that the question of money did not fall within the province of laws and legislation, but that its solution rested solely with commerce—that is the banking power.

In a letter written by George S. Coe, President of the American Exchange National Bank, one of the most powerful in the country, to José F. De Navarro, the former exhibited his supreme contempt for the powers of Congress. The closing sentences of this letter, dated April 10, 1893, are as follows:—

"Commerce is larger than governments and will certainly prevail over them all. When once this conviction prevails, we shall all be surprised to see how easily natural laws will conquer local prejudice and legislation."

This writer who made his wealth and secured his fame out of the law-making power of the Government, now spurns that constitutional authority, as inferior to the unlimited greed of that class of which he is a shining light.

In a speech delivered before the Chicago Bankers' Club, April 7, 1895, William C. Cornwall, a leading banker of Buffalo, said:—

"On this silver question the American people are beginning to discard the old delusion that law can regulate the value of coin."

The New York Sun, April, 1895, said:—

"The issue is between gold and silver as the standard of currency, the value of each metal with respect to each other and to other commodities, being totally beyond the power of any financial legislator or convention to change."

This was the gist of the specious argument of the gold standard press and national banking power throughout the country.

The money power became so elated at its success in having silver stricken down, that it grew so bold as to threaten the political future of any public man who did not align himself with that interest. It was abject submission or political death.

In the speech of Banker Cornwall, April 7, 1895, from which we have quoted, he said:—

"The politician, high or low, who to-day turns from the straight course of sound money and the gold standard, stabs dead once for all every chance of political success, especially if he wants to be President."

This bold threat was greeted with the tumultuous cheers of the bankers before whom this speech was delivered. The gold standard press indorsed these sentiments of the money power.

During the remainder of the Cleveland administration, the President was wholly unable to carry any of his financial projects through Congress. He became a leader without a party. Even the Republicans, whose financial policies he had so strenuously endeavored to force upon the Democracy, seized upon every opportunity to severely denounce his management of public affairs, despite the fact that their notable leaders had warmly defended his course in repeatedly issuing bonds to maintain the "parity of the metals."

Outside of the clique of national bank presidents, trust magnates, stock speculators, bond syndicates, and sycophantic office holders, the President had no following worthy of the name of party.

The facts detailed in the foregoing pages exhibit the wonderful prescience and the consummate plans of the national banking money power, as follows:—

1. It secured the partial demonetization of government legal tender currency in 1862-3;
2. The payment of interest upon a vast bonded debt in coin, and, therefore, it obtained absolute control of the gold of the country;
3. The establishment of national banks to issue paper money, which could only be put into circulation by building up a creditor and a debtor class;
4. The control of the entire volume of money in the country, as a means of securing possession of the great railway properties, and to organize those mighty trusts which now monopolize all production and distribution;

5. The demonetization of silver as a means of holding the West and South in subjection to its will;

6. The consolidation of all great moneyed corporations, with the view of subjecting the productive energies of the nation to its domination;

7. It has joined hands with the money power of England in its efforts to control Federal legislation;

8. It had, time and again, used its immense power to thwart the will of the people as expressed through Congress;

9. It has asserted a superiority above all law and the Constitution, and has declared that its fiat is more powerful than the authority of this nation;

10. It has robbed the Government of its highest sovereign power—that of issuing and controlling the medium of exchange.

THE REMEDY.

1. The restoration to the Government of the power of issuing and coining money.

2. The permanent destruction of the national banking system.

3. The application of the principles of Jefferson to the administration of government.

"Oh, beware my fellow-citizens, of stock jobbers or banking associations who have an interest as distinct from that of the community, as that of drones from that of bees. Oh, beware, ye legislators, how you create a moneyed aristocracy, as dangerous to government as Pretorian bands in Rome, or Janissaries in Turkey. Let me repeat that I behold this country as the asylum of the afflicted, the sanctuary of the oppressed, on which the eyes of philanthropists are everywhere fixed with affection and anxiety. Moral feelings, common interests, and general principles unite as a band of brothers. Whatever appertains to the general welfare should emanate from the general Government. This is the spirit of our Constitution—this is the central axis upon which the Union must revolve, and any important deviation must make all return to chaos. If I am assailed for this interference I shall reply, Homo sum et nihil humani a me alienum puto."—Thomas Jefferson.

CHAPTER XV.

CAMPAIGN OF 1896.

"You shall not crucify mankind upon a cross of gold."—William J. Bryan.

"It is to the property of the citizen, not to the demand of the creditor of the State, that the original faith of society is pledged. The claim of the citizen is prior in time, paramount in title, and superior in equality."—Edmund Burke.

The course of President Cleveland, in his continued and energetic efforts to revolutionize the principles of the Democracy, and to commit that party to the espousal of the national banking money power was disastrous in the extreme.

As stated, the Congressional elections of 1894 went overwhelmingly in favor of the Republicans, and they carried the House of Representatives by a tremendous majority.

Notwithstanding this great reverse, he persevered in his financial policy to the last, and he boldly and unscrupulously prostituted the immense official patronage at his disposal, to force his views upon the millions of the rank and file of that party which he had practically disrupted. Strenuous efforts were put forth by the national banking, stock-gambling, gold standard, and office-holding element, to elect a sufficient number of delegates to the coming national convention, and thus dictate the platform, and align the party in compliance with the views of the administration.

While the administration and its satellites were bending their whole energies to accomplish this design, the associated banks, particularly of the East, as heretofore, laid their plans to manipulate the conventions of both the leading political parties.

In the early part of 1896, a large number of bankers met at the Murray Hotel in New York City, and after adopting a series of resolutions denouncing the free coinage of silver, announced their plan in the following language:—

"Resolved, That we urge upon the delegates to the national conventions of both of the political parties, the necessity of insisting on such action as will secure a plain and unequivocal declaration on the maintenance of the present gold standard."

On March 23d, the American Bankers' Association issued the following instructions to the bankers of the country:—

> The American Bankers' Association,
> 2 Wall Street and 90-94 Broadway,
> New York, March 23, 1896.

"To the Bankers of the United States:—

"At a meeting of the Executive Council of the American Bankers' Association, held in this city, on March 11, 1896, the following declaration was made by a unanimous vote:—

"The Executive Council of the American Bankers' Association, declare unequivocally in favor of the maintenance of the existing gold standard of value, and recommend to all bankers, and to the customers of all banks, the exercise of all their influence as citizens in their various states, to select delegates to the political conventions of both great parties who will declare unequivocally in favor of the maintenance of the existing gold standard of value.

"Your influence is earnestly requested to give practical effect to this action.

> Eugene H. Pullen, President.
> James R. Branch, Secretary.
> Joseph C. Hendrix,
> Chairman Executive Council."

Pursuant to these instructions, the associated banks actively began operations to secure a sufficient number of delegates who would embody the demands of the bankers in the platforms of both great political parties.

While the national bankers and their allied interests were thus actively engaged in manipulating the selection of delegates to the two great conventions, the Democratic rank and file were even more vigilant to checkmate these schemes, and they finally succeeded in defeating the machinations of this Hessian money power, which had hitherto thrown its strength to the party that gave them the greatest pecuniary benefits.

On the 16th of June, the Republican National Convention met in St. Louis to select its standard bearers.

Hon. C. W. Fairbanks, of Indiana, a very wealthy railroad lawyer, from which fact he received great consideration as a coming leader of his party, was chosen Temporary Chairman of the convention.

Hon. John M. Thurston, of Nebraska, was honored with the Permanent Chairmanship.

The significance of Mr. Thurston's selection to preside over this convention will be appreciated, from the fact, that he was the general legal counselor of the Union Pacific Railway Company—a corporation whose corrupt practices have done more to debauch Western courts and legislatures than any other agency in the land.

Suffice it to say that this great corporation, built by the munificence of Congress, gave birth to that gigantic scandal of the age, the Credit Mobilier, which caught in its meshes a Vice-President of the United States, and many distinguished Senators and Representatives of Congress.

A great number of the Western Republicans, led by Senator Teller, made a desperate struggle to obtain recognition for the free coinage of silver. They were overwhelmingly defeated and therefore withdrew from the convention.

The financial plank of the platform declared against the free coinage of silver, unless it could be secured by an international agreement with the leading commercial nations of the world, and, in case of failure to obtain such agreement, the existing gold standard should be maintained.

This expression in favor of an international agreement, was the merest subterfuge on the part of the gold standard element, to obtain the votes of those Republicans who favored free coinage.

H. H. Kohlsaat, of the Chicago Times-Herald, was influential in securing the adoption of the money plank. In speaking of the language of this plank, the correspondent of that paper, who was present during the St. Louis convention, used the following language with reference to the labors of Mr. Kohlsaat in securing its adoption. He said:—

"The qualifying words used by the committee, pledging the party to endeavor to promote an international agreement, are intended to strengthen the platform from the political point of view without in any way weakening it as a frank and fearless declaration for the gold standard. As it is and has been, the Republican policy to promote international bi-metallism, and as such bi-metallism is earnestly desired by almost every one in the country of both parties, nothing is lost and something is gained by giving the Western Republicans a ray of hope in the future."

On the 6th of June preceding, this man Kohlsaat,

who had written the Republican platform, made the following editorial reference to international bi-metallism. He said:—

"Any reference to an international agreement is shifty and futile. It deceives nobody because everybody knows, first, that there is not the slightest possibility of an international agreement at any ratio; and, second, that if such an agreement were formally entered into, no Government could be bound to abide by it a day longer than its own industrial and commercial interests would appear to warrant."

It will be seen that Mr. Kohlsaat, on the 6th of June, declared an international agreement as "shifty and futile."

On the 16th of June he embodied this "shifty and futile" scheme into the form of a solemn declaration of party principles!

It was evident that Major McKinley, of Ohio, was the prime favorite of the majority of the Republican delegates for the Presidential nomination.

The chief manager of Mr. McKinley's canvass for the nomination of President before the Republican Convention, was the noted Marcus A. Hanna, of Cleveland, Ohio. Mr. Hanna was a multi-millionaire, and he displayed a marked interest in securing the financial and political success of Major McKinley. It was due to the organization effected by Mr. Hanna, that the candidacy of Major McKinley received that impetus that carried him successfully to the first place on the ticket as the standard bearer of the Republican party.

In fact, Mr. Hanna became the Warwick of American politics.

Major McKinley first attained political prominence as a member of the national House of Representatives, to which he was first elected in 1876. He voted for the free coinage measure as originally introduced by Mr. Bland, and gave his support to the Bland-Allison Silver Coinage Act of 1878. When President Hayes vetoed this bill, Mr. McKinley gave his vote to pass the bill over the veto.

In 1878, he supported the Matthews Resolution, which declared that United States bonds were legally payable in standard silver dollars.

In 1890, he voted for the so-called Sherman Silver Purchasing Law.

In a speech at Toledo, Ohio, in 1891, he severely censured President Cleveland for his antagonism to the silver dollar, and stated that, "During all the years Mr. Cleveland was at the head of the Government, he was engaged in dishonoring silver."

Mr. McKinley's chief fame, however, grew out of his untiring advocacy of the benefits to be derived from a high protective tariff. The McKinley Tariff Act of 1890 has become history.

For Vice President, the convention selected Garrett A. Hobart, of New Jersey. Mr. Hobart had not been very prominent in politics until his nomination for this high office. He was a distinct representative of the corporate interests of the East, and it was said he was a director and stockholder in forty-five different corporations, such as railways, street railways, national banks, and the like. He was also an arbiter in that gigantic trust, known as the Joint Traffic Association, composed of thirty-three great railroads entering New York City. These railroads were mainly owned and operated by British capitalists.

The nomination of Mr. Hobart was supposedly designed with the view of attracting heavy contributions from the trusts, combines, and corporations of the East to aid in carrying the elections.

Meanwhile, the Western and Southern Democracy broke away entirely from the leading strings of the East, and gave unequivocal notice to that section that its dominating influence had ceased, and that an adjustment of the party was needed to plant it on the time-honored principles of Jefferson and Jackson.

The desperation of the administration element became greater than ever, which fact was abundantly evidenced by the high-handed methods of Don M. Dickinson in Michigan, who, with the aid of a host of federal officers, actually overrode the will of the Democracy in the selection of gold standard delegates.

His use of the federal patronage in that state, to overawe the free expression of the people, aroused the greatest indignation throughout the country.

In the state of Nebraska, the office-holding Cleveland element, led on by J. Sterling Morton, was extremely jealous of the wonderful popularity of that splendid young tribune of the people—William Jennings Bryan.

In the early part of July, the party leaders gathered at Chicago, where the convention was to be held, to make a choice of its standard-bearers.

When the convention was called to order, July 7th, the National Committee, a majority of whom were friendly to the money power and the single standard of gold, presented the name of Senator David B. Hill, of New York, as its choice for Temporary Chairman of the convention

This action was strictly in harmony with party usage, but the stern and determined men who made up the vast majority of the delegates thereto, knew that this was the initial step of the gold standard element to obtain control of the convention.

The free coinage element refused to acquiesce in the selection of the committee, and Senator John W. Daniel, of Virginia, was brought forward as the choice of those delegates who were utterly opposed to national banks and the gold standard.

Upon a roll call of the convention, the candidacy of. Senator Daniel was successful by a vote of 556 to 349 for the New York Senator.

Upon taking the chair, the Virginian Senator delivered one of the most eloquent and notable speeches ever heard in any body.

The seats of the regular delegation from Nebraska, headed by the eloquent Bryan, were contested by a contingent of federal office-holders. In the hearing of this contest before the National Committee, it did the bidding of the administration, and ousted the Bryan delegates and had seated the contestors.

This action of the Committee in unseating the regular delegates was carried before the convention on appeal, and its decision was reversed by a decisive majority, and the regulars were admitted to their seats.

This effort to nullify the will of the people of Nebraska, came to an ignominious end.

The Michigan gold standard delegates, headed by that shrewd manipulator, Don M. Dickinson, were unseated, and the contestees were admitted to a voice in the deliberations of this convention. The great struggle arose upon the report of the Committee on

Resolutions, which had brought forward declarations in favor of the free and unlimited coinage of silver, without waiting for the aid or consent of any other nation on earth. The ratio was fixed at 16 to 1.

Another plank of the platform criticised the Federal Supreme Court for its reversal of its late decision on the income tax law, one of the most just measures ever enacted by Congress.

Government by Federal Court injunction was severely denounced, on the ground that this system of jurisprudence was the means by which corporations wreaked their vengeance upon their striking employés.

Under this process of the courts, trial by jury was abrogated, and the Federal Judge had unlimited power to try, convict, and execute his unrestrained will upon helpless men.

Moreover, the Federal judiciary was the mainstay that upheld the aggressions of corporations upon the rights of the people. The great majority of the Federal judges were, prior to their appointment to these responsible positions, corporation lawyers, and had secured their positions through the influence of railways and trusts.

In a celebrated case in one of the Eastern states, the United States District Attorney instituted a suit against a great railway trust, with a view of having its organization declared illegal under the provisions of that absurd so-called Sherman Anti-Trust law. He presented his bill to eight different United States District and Circuit Judges.

Out of these eight supposed infallible organs of the law, the district attorney discovered that seven of these high functionaries held stock in the various railroads composing this gigantic trust.

Is it strange that the people had lost faith in the Federal judiciary?

A strong declaration was adopted, denouncing that Tory-Republican system of finance — the national banking system.

In the debate upon this report of the committee, Mr. Bryan had the closing speech, and his magical eloquence carried the convention by storm, and he easily became the most conspicuous figure in that body of great men.

Upon roll-call, the report of the committee was adopted by a decisive majority. As a concession, the administration element pleaded for an endorsement of President Cleveland, but it was voted down by a nearly two-thirds vote.

Thus, this gathering of distinguished leaders of Jeffersonian principles utterly repudiated the policy of President Cleveland, and vigorously rebuked his methods in attempting to handcuff the Democracy to the gold standard.

He, who was, in 1892, the chosen idol of that great historic party, was now given notice that it had no lot or part with him.

As a result of the deliberations of the convention, William J. Bryan was nominated for President, and Arthur Sewall, of Maine, for vice-president.

Mr. Bryan was a Democrat of the old school, and was a warm admirer of the principles and achievements of Jefferson and Jackson. He had served four years in the House of Representatives with distinguished ability, where he easily carried off the palm for eloquence. His speeches in behalf of tariff reform, the free coinage of silver, and those opposing the single standard of gold, the issue of bonds in time of peace, and the enlargement of national banking powers, were marvels of logic, argument, and noble oratory.

Mr. Sewall was a distinguished citizen of Maine, and had been a life-long advocate of the free coinage of silver.

The silver Republicans and the Populist party endorsed the candidacy of Mr. Bryan, and combined their patriotic efforts with those of the Democracy, to wrest the control of the country from the plutocracy of the East.

On September 2d, the Cleveland, or gold standard, national banking faction of the Democratic party, met at Indianapolis, ostensibly to place a Presidential ticket in the field. These bolters made no secret of their intentions to defeat the regular Democratic ticket at all hazards.

Foremost among these bolters was Ex-Governor Flower, of New York, who had served in Congress, and who had earned a fine political reputation for his admirable administration as the chief executive of New York. He, however, trained with the stock gamblers of Wall street, where he was recognized as one of the heaviest operators on the Stock Exchange, and where he had amassed a fortune of many millions in speculating in stocks and bonds. He was a firm believer in the gold standard and the national banking system.

In his speech before the Indianapolis convention—composed, as it was to a very large extent, of Federal office-holders, national bankers, money lenders, promoters of trusts, stock gamblers, and would-be aristocrats—Mr. Flower referred to the principles of Jefferson and Jackson, of which he asserted that the body which he addressed were the true representatives, and denounced the Chicago platform as a departure from the traditions of Democracy!

The Indianapolis platform declared in favor of the gold standard and the national banking money power.

Gen. John M. Palmer, of Illinois, was nominated for President; and General Buckner, of Kentucky, was chosen as his colleague on the ticket.

The nomination of General Palmer was made with a view of attracting votes from the soldier element of the North; that of General Buckner to obtain the support of the Ex-Confederate element in the South.

During the first part of this memorable campaign, the tide was flowing mightily in favor of the regular Democratic nominees, and the success of the ticket seemed certain.

It was then that the strategy of Chairman Mark Hanna, of the Republican National Committee, came to the rescue of McKinley, by calling into requisition, the moneyed assistance of the gigantic corporate interests of the nation.

The great railway corporations, controlled to a very large extent by British capital, organized their hundreds of thousands of employés into "sound money" clubs, who were plainly given to understand that further employment depended upon the success of the Republican candidates.

The loan and mortgage companies of the East, holding billions of dollars of mortgages on the farm lands of the West and South, notified their debtors, that, in the event of the success of Mr. Bryan, they would close in on them and sell them out; but that if McKinley was elected, these mortgages would be renewed.

The immensely wealthy life insurance companies flooded the country with millions of letters, urging their policy holders to support McKinley and Hobart, and these philanthropic corporations stated, in these documents, that they did not wish to be compelled to pay their policies in "cheap dollars." This scheme was very effective.

The saving banks, and building and loan associations were also guilty of this deception. Thousands of banks notified their multitudes of borrowers, that it was necessary to elect the Republican ticket in order to obtain a continuation of banking favors.

This species of coercion reached hundreds of thousands of business men, and it was in turn communicated to their employees.

Individual lenders carried out the same policy, and, in many cases, legal process was brought to bear against those debtors who refused to surrender up their manhood, at the behest of these minions of despotism.

Manufacturers fell in line at the command of Mark Hanna, and exhibited large orders for their manufactured products, calling the attention of their employees to a stipulation, common to these contracts, providing for their cancellation in case of the election of Bryan.

Millions of money were poured into the campaign fund to elect the Republican ticket.

In the meantime, the gold standard bolting Democratic newspapers and speakers, near the close of the campaign, openly advised their followers to vote for McKinley and Hobart, and thus secure the adoption of "sound money."

Such were the rascally, desperate, treacherous, and tyrannical schemes, hatched by the criminal minds at the head of the national banking money power to win this election as a means of perpetuating its reign.

As a necessary result of this campaign of fraud, lying, coercion, and intimidation, practiced upon the people, the Republican ticket was elected, receiving 271 electoral votes, to 176 for Bryan and Sewall.

One remarkable feature of this election was the enormous increase in the vote in the states of Iowa, Michigan, Wisconsin, Illinois, Indiana, Kentucky, Ohio, and West Virginia, all of which were carried for McKinley and practically assured his election.

Immediately upon the results of the election becoming known, the national banking money power made known its demands through the press.

On the day succeeding the election, Lyman J. Gage, President of the First National Bank of Chicago, came out in an interview published in one of the leading Chicago papers, in the course of which he stated that sufficient bonds should be issued to take up all the silver dollars in circulation, and the bullion composing them should be thrown upon the market and sold as "junk"; that the greenbacks and treasury notes should likewise be taken up by an issue of bonds and destroyed; that a billion of bonds payable in gold, and running for one hundred years, and exempted from taxation, should be issued as a basis for national bank currency.

This is an example of that mad greed that rejoiced in the election of McKinley.

The President-Elect was duly inaugurated.

His cabinet consisted of the following:—for Secretary of State, John Sherman; for Secretary of the Treasury, Lyman J. Gage, of Illinois; for Secretary of War, Russell A. Alger, of Michigan; for Secretary of the Navy, Ex-Governor Long, of Massachusetts; for Postmaster General, James A. Gary, of Maryland; for Secretary of Agriculture, James Wilson, of Iowa; for Attorney-General, Judge McKenna, of California. With possibly one exception, the members of this cabinet were noted for their enormous wealth.

The appointments of Mr. Alger to the Secretaryship of War excited considerable criticism, as he had never displayed any unusual talents as a public administrator. His brief war record was inglorious, as the military reports of General Sheridan, Merritt, and Custer, prove. The methods by which he obtained his great wealth, can be ascertained by a perusal of the Supreme Court Reports of Michigan. In a celebrated case before this court, in which Mr. Alger was a leading party, the opinion of this tribunal, as announced by Justice Sherwood, is a scathing arraignment of the business methods of the present Secretary of War.

The appointment of Mr. Sherman to the head of the State Department, was a clever piece of strategy to secure a vacancy in the United States Senate, to which Marcus A. Hanna was appointed. As United States Senator from Ohio, Mr. Hanna is recognized as all powerful with the administration.

Shortly after his induction into office, President McKinley called a special session of Congress, which reformed the tariff by the passage of what is known as the "Dingley Bill."

This tariff bill raised the duties on imports higher than ever before known, with the result that this measure has received the nickname of "Dingley's Deficit," by reason of the enormous falling off of revenues.

In the meantime, President McKinley had appointed Senator Wolcott, of Colorado, Ex-Vice President Stevenson, and General Paine, of Boston, as an international commission to proceed to Europe, and obtain the consent of the Powers to enter into a treaty to secure that "shifty and futile" experiment—internatonal bi-metallism.

While this commission was abroad, hobnobbing with foreign potentates, Secretary Gage incubated a scheme of banking which he laid before the special session of Congress, accompanied by a report in which he stated that his bill proposed "To commit the country more thoroughly to the gold standard."

Upon a knowledge of this scheme of banking reaching London, the Wolcott Commission found itself in a dilemma, for, while it was endeavoring to secure international recognition of silver, the administration had come squarely out for the gold standard. It was a dastardly stab in the back on the part of the administration.

The British press greeted the efforts of the Wolcott Commission with gibes and sneers, and pointed to the Gage banking bill as evidence that its mission was a fake.

In addition to the Gage banking scheme, various other plans of currency reform(?) were brought forward, all of which aimed at the elimination of the greenbacks and treasury notes from circulation, and the substitution of a bank currency in lieu thereof, the Government to be the guarantor and redeemer of these proposed bank notes. One of these schemes was concocted by a convention held at Indianapolis, composed of national bankers, gold Democrats, trust magnates, corporation lawyers, and men of that ilk. One Hugh H. Hanna, nephew of Mark Hanna, was the moving spirit who formed the plan that resulted in the calling of this self-constituted body of legislators.

As the Senate is strongly in favor of the free and unlimited coinage of silver, without waiting for the aid or consent of any other nation, it is now evident that none of these robber schemes of finance, can be passed by that body under the fraudulent and delusive cry of "currency reform." The upper House is now the safeguard of the nation.

In the latter part of 1897, after the passage of the Dingley Bill, heavy reductions of wages were made in the large cotton mills of the New England States, even the city where he of Dingley fame resides, did not escape from the general cut of rate of wages.

The same policy is being carried out in the iron manufacturing districts, and the railway corporations are engaged in the same process of restoring "prosperity."

On the 29th of January, 1898, the millionaire aristocracy of the East, gave a costly and gorgeous banquet in the most fashionable hotel of New York City. President McKinley was the guest of honor at this gathering of the plutocratic element of New York City, and entertained his hosts with one of his usual homilies, in which much was said about "prosperity," the "maintenance of the public faith," the "upholding of the nation's honor," and other stereotyped phrases.

He committed his administration to the maintenance of the gold standard and in favor of currency reform. By the latter phrase, he undoubtedly referred to some one of the various schemes of banking concocted by Secretary Gage, Hugh H. Hanna, Representative Fowler, and other would-be reformers of the currency.

The speech of President McKinley was highly gratifying to the Tory press of Great Britain.

On January 31, 1898, a leading gold standard paper of Chicago, published a cablegram from London, headed as follows:—

"American stocks advance." "McKinley's speech pleases British speculators and investors."

The article goes on to show that American railway stocks led the market, and that Spanish bonds rose in value.

On the same page of the journal, from which we have quoted, is a special dispatch from New Castle, Delaware, exhibiting an awful state of affairs among the working people of that city.

This article is headed as follows:—

"Dire want in New Castle, Delaware." "Six families found starving—six hundred idle iron workers."

This dispatch goes on to show that the families of six hundred idle iron workers were crying for food, and that fifty families had left the town in a single week to escape starvation.

Starvation for honest Americans, wealth for British stock gamblers and speculators.

This is an illustration of the effects of the policy of

President McKinley, who, during the campaign of 1896, struck an impressive attitude before the cheering multitudes, and told them that the only means of restoring prosperity were to "open up the mills."

In the meantime, trusts and other illegal combinations of capital continued to multiply with alarming rapidity, having for their object the absolute monopoly of production and distribution.

Foremost was that colossal railway trust, the Joint Traffic Association, with a capital of more than $2,000,000,000, and organized through the efforts of J. Pierpont Morgan, the American agent of British capitalists. To a very large extent, this association was formed out of the railways wrecked during the panic, and whose stocks were purchased by these foreign capitalists at a mere fraction of their former values.

To place before the reader the immense possibilities for oppression that is within the power of a combination like the Joint Traffic Association, the fact should be constantly kept before him, that single railways have been empowered, by unjust discriminations in freight charges between different localities, to blight the prosperity of towns, cities, and even whole sections of the country, and to build up more favored points on the ruins of the former; that these corporations have, by systems of secret rebates, bankrupted tens of thousands of enterprising citizens, while a few favored shippers have been enabled to create the most gigantic monopolies of any age, and to accumulate the wealth earned by the toil of millions. It is true that this railway trust was declared illegal by a late decision of the Federal Supreme Court by a vote of five to four of the Judges composing that tribunal. The decision was scarcely announced, ere the promoters of this combination publicly declared their intention to "move on Washington," and obtain the passage of a pooling law to avoid the effect of the ruling of the Court.

To give their avowed purpose the apparent sanction of public opinion, the managers of the railways composing this trust are now circulating petitions among their employes for their signatures, requesting Congress to enact a law to legalize trusts, and, as a consideration for these signatures so obtained, the railways agree not to oppose legislation demanded by their workingmen. This is coercion patterned after that of 1896.

At the present time, there are hundreds of trusts in full operation, and they have become so menacing to the rights of the people, that the public press is demanding prompt action against these combinations by the Federal Government.

In almost every instance, the promoters and managers of these trusts are closely identified with the national banking money power.

The national banks of New York City, Boston, and other commercial centers are combining their assets, now aggregating more than $4,000,000,000, under single managements.

Flushed with political success in 1896, the privileged money power and the trusts are reaching out to control the influential colleges and universities of the land—seats of learning whose precincts should be sacred to the dissemination of knowledge—but which are now sought to be made instrumentalities to uphold the tenets of an aggressive plutocracy.

In the early part of 1897, occurred the most notable instance of this attempted perversion of these centers of learning, in which it was sought to humiliate the learned and distinguished E. Benjamin Andrews, President of Brown University.

Be it remembered that this renowned institution was placed in the front rank of American colleges mainly through the ability of Professor Andrews.

The minions of corporate greed regarded this scholar and educator as a shining mark against which to direct their attacks, and incidentally to pattern this university after that of Oxford, England, which has always been the servile apologist of kingly tyranny.

This last mentioned institution was a school, which, for centuries, taught the infamous doctrine that kings rule by divine right, and that they can do no wrong.

To quote the language of Pope: "The divine right to govern wrong" was the special birthright of British kings according to the tenets of Oxford.

At the command of the dissolute Charles II., it had exiled its greatest ornament, John Locke; and had committed the sublime works of Milton to the flames, because this great man advocated the rights of conscience, the liberty of thought, and the enlightenment of the masses.

We aver that no right-minded American citizen is desirous that Brown University, or any other American school, should degenerate into a mere organ of a privileged class.

President Andrews was a distinguished advocate of the free and unlimited coinage of silver, and his works in behalf of that principle were regarded as among the ablest ever written. As an author, he dealt the gold monometallists some very hard blows, and it was determined to punish him for exercising the common rights of an American citizen.

President Andrews, in his official capacity, never sought to impress his financial views upon the students of the University.

During his absence in Europe, whence he had gone for a much needed rest, the son of John D. Rockefeller, the Standard Oil magnate, who is reputed to be the wealthiest man in America, graduated from the University.

By some means, it was caused to be rumored that Mr. Rockefeller, upon the graduation of his son, had proposed to bestow the munificent sum of $1,000,000 upon the University, but, owing to the free coinage views of the President thereof, he had abandoned his alleged beneficent purpose.

This was merely affording a pretext to depose President Andrews from the head of this great institution.

At the first meeting of the Board of Trustees of the college, while President Andrews was still absent in Europe, Hon. Joseph H. Walker, a Representative in Congress from the Third District in Massachusetts, introduced a resolution demanding the resignation of the President, on the ground that his advocacy of free coinage had resulted in a loss of $1,000,000 to the University!

The action of Congressman Walker was vigorously supported by a multi-millionaire cotton manufacturer of Rhode Island, who, in his remarks supporting the resolution, spoke indignantly of the conduct of President Andrews as undermining the morals of the students, by advocating "cheap dollars" and attacking the "public honor!"

This disreputable scheme, by which it was sought to humiliate Professor Andrews by deposing him from the Presidency, aroused a storm of criticism within the United States, and these distinguished defenders of the "public faith" drew back appalled, from the tempest of popular wrath.

This wealthy manufacturer, who displayed such anxiety to "Maintain the public faith untarnished," who would be judge, jury, and executioner of the absent President, manifested his great humanity by reducing the wages of his thousands of employes sixteen per cent.

The only hope of the producing classes is a rise in prices, and the prospects are that, owing to a general failure of European crops in 1897, the demand for American farm products will be so extensive as to greatly enhance the value of our exports of bread stuffs.

Should this desirable condition occur, it will be only temporary relief, and it will afford the national banking, gold standard money power, an opportunity to point to the imports of gold, sent here for the purchase of our surplus farm products, as an argument that the volume of money is ample for the needs of business, although the rise in prices sweeps away the argument that gold is a stable money.

The Presidential election of 1900 is destined to be the most important in our history, inasmuch as the national banking system will expire by limitation of law in 1904, hence, the corporations composing this system will bend every energy to secure a renewal of the law authorizing a continuation of this privileged class.

The coercive tactics of the money power, by which a victory was won in 1896, will not be a circumstance compared to the gigantic efforts that will be put forth to win a triumph in 1900.

It behooves every citizen of this great republic to verse himself in the principles of free government, to watch diligently the trend of public opinion, to scan the proceedings of legislative bodies, to familiarize himself with the character of the public men who aspire to be the legislators of the people, that he may cast his vote in a manner becoming an American freeman.

THE END

www.ingramcontent.com/pod-product-compliance
Lightning Source LLC
Chambersburg PA
CBHW051847300426
44117CB00006B/297